Public Relations Theory

Public Relations Theory

Application and Understanding

Edited by Brigitta R. Brunner

WILEY Blackwell

Registered Office(s)
John Wiley & Sons, Inc., 111 River Street, Hoboken, NJ 07030, USA

Editorial Office
101 Station Landing, Medford, MA 02155, USA

For details of our global editorial offices, customer services, and more information about Wiley products visit us at www.wiley.com.

Wiley also publishes its books in a variety of electronic formats and by print-on-demand. Some content that appears in standard print versions of this book may not be available in other formats.

Library of Congress Cataloging-in-Publication Data

Names: Brunner, Brigitta R., 1971– author.
Title: Public relations theory : application and understanding / Brigitta R. Brunner.
Description: First Edition. | Hoboken : Wiley-Blackwell, 2019. |
    Includes bibliographical references and index. |
Identifiers: LCCN 2018046344 (print) | LCCN 2018052947 (ebook) |
    ISBN 9781119373131 (Adobe PDF) | ISBN 9781119373148 (ePub) | ISBN 9781119373117 (hardback) |
    ISBN 9781119373155 (paperback)
Subjects: LCSH: Public relations. | BISAC: BUSINESS & ECONOMICS /
    Advertising & Promotion.
Classification: LCC HM1221 (ebook) | LCC HM1221 .B78 2019 (print) |
    DDC 659.2–dc23
LC record available at https://lccn.loc.gov/2018046344

Cover Design: Wiley
Cover Image: © Nik Merkulov/Shutterstock

Set in 10/12pt Warnock by SPi Global, Pondicherry, India
Printed in Singapore by C.O.S. Printers Pte Ltd

10 9 8 7 6 5 4 3 2 1

Contents

Notes on Contributors

Shelley Aylesworth-Spink is the Associate Dean of the School of Business at St. Lawrence College in Kingston, Canada. Her interests include the perception of pervasive global disease outbreaks in studying the interdisciplinary application of public relations, media studies, cultural studies, and science and technology studies fields. She was formerly Principal Lecturer in Public Relations at the University of Westminster, England, and Senior Lecturer in Public Relations at the University of West London, England. Her areas of professional practice for organizations in the health, higher education, and manufacturing sectors include communications strategy, crisis communications, media relations, and corporate communications.

Tor Bang is an Associate Professor at the Department of Communication and Culture at BI Norwegian Business School, located in Oslo. He serves as the Associate Dean for the school's bachelor program in communication management and teaches classes in communication management to master's students. Previously employed in Norway's maritime sector, Bang holds a social science MA from the University of Oslo, with a thesis on freedom of expression in digital media. His PhD from the University of Bergen was a dissertation on communicative strategies in the Norwegian labor movement during the 1930s.

Brigitta R. Brunner is a Professor at the Auburn University School of Communication & Journalism. She has been on faculty at AU since 2002 teaching PR classes at the undergraduate and graduate levels. She is editor of the *Journal of Public Interest Communications*. Her research interests include civic engagement, civic professionalism, diversity, and education. She has published two edited books, *Creating Citizens: Liberal Arts and Community & Civic Engagement in the Land-Grant Tradition* (2016) and *The Moral Compass of Public Relations* (2017), and numerous refereed journal articles.

Yi-Ru Regina Chen is Associate Professor of Public Relations at Hong Kong Baptist University. Her research areas include strategic communication, social media engagement and gamification, government affairs, and corporate social responsibility and creating shared values in greater China. She has published in the *Journal of Medical Internet Research, Journalism and Mass Communication Quarterly, Journal of Public Relations Research, Public Relations Review, International Journal of Strategic Communication, Journal of Communication Management*, and *Information, Communication & Society*. Chen is also the research fellow of the Behavioral Insights Research Center of the Institute for Public Relations (Gainesville, Florida).

Erica Ciszek is an Assistant Professor at the Stan Richards School of Advertising & Public Relations at the University of Texas at Austin. Her research explores the intersections of public relations, activism, and social change. Her work encompasses a triadic focus: (1) activism as public relations (conceptualizing social movement organizations as strategic communicators); (2) public relations as activism (conceptualizing public relations practitioners as organizational change agents); and (3) activism and strategic communication (considering how key stakeholders engage with communication materials aimed at them). Ciszek's research has been published in the top journals in the field, including the *Journal of Communication*, as well as advocacy journals such as the *Journal of Homosexuality*.

W. Timothy Coombs is the George T. and Gladys H. Abell Professor in Liberal Arts in Department of Communication at Texas A&M University and an honorary professor in the Department of Business Communication at Aarhus University. His primary areas of research are crisis communication and corporate social responsibility. He is the current editor for *Corporation Communication: An International Journal*. His research has appeared in *Management Communication Quarterly*, *Public Relations Review*, *Corporate Reputation Review*, *Journal of Public Relations Research*, *Journal of Communication Management*, *Business Horizons*, and the *Journal of Business Communication*.

Karen Freberg is an Associate Professor in Strategic Communications at the University of Louisville. Her research areas are in social media, public relations, and crisis communications. Freberg is author of the SAGE textbook *Social media for strategic communication: Creative strategies and research-based applications*.

Sherry J. Holladay is Professor of Communication at Texas A&M University in College Station, Texas. Her research interests include crisis communication, issues management, corporate social responsibility and irresponsibility, and activism. Her work has appeared in *Public Relations Review*, *Management Communication Quarterly*, *Journal of Communication Management*, *Journal of Public Relations Research*, and *International Journal of Strategic Communication*. She is co-editor of the *Handbook of crisis communication* and co-author of *It's not just PR: Public relations in society*, *Public relations strategies and applications: Managing influence*, and *Managing corporate social responsibility*.

Chun-Ju Flora Hung-Baesecke teaches at Massey University in Albany, New Zealand. For three years in a row (2015–2017), she was named an Arthur W. Page Legacy Scholar. She is the Vice Chair of the International Communication Association's Public Relations Division and the Secretary General for Overseas Affairs, Public Relations Society of China. Hung-Baesecke is on the advisory board of International Public Relations Research Conference and on the editorial boards of *Journal of Public Relations Research* and *International Journal of Strategic Communication*. Her research interests include organization–public relationships, corporate social responsibility, social media, employee communication, and stakeholder management.

Samsup Jo is a Professor in the Department of Public Relations & Advertising at the Sookmyung Women's University in South Korea. He earned a PhD in mass communication from the University of Florida in 2003. He served as president of Korean Academic Society of Public Relations from November 2014 to November 2015. His research interests include public relations, specifically the public relations function in society, public relations ethics, and organization–public relationship measurement. His articles have appeared in the *Journal of Public Relations Research*, *Public Relations Review*, and *Journal of Communication Management*.

Michael L. Kent is a Professor of Public Relations and Advertising at the University of New South Wales in Sydney Australia. Kent's public relations research has focused on dialogue, new technology, public relations theory, social media, and engagement. His theory of dialogic public relations is currently one of the most influential frameworks in the field. Kent is a Fulbright Scholar (Riga Latvia, 2006), and has lectured and taught internationally for more than two decades.

Spiro Kiousis is Executive Associate Dean for the College of Journalism and Communications at the University of Florida and is a Professor of Public Relations. His current research interests include political public relations, political communication, and digital communication. Specifically, this interdisciplinary research explores the interplay among political public relations efforts, news media content, and public opinion in traditional and interactive mass mediated contexts. Kiousis has had articles published in several leading journals, including *Communication Research*, *Journal of Communication*, the *Harvard International Journal of Press/Politics*, *Mass Communication & Society*, *Public Relations Review*, *Journalism and Mass Communication Quarterly*, *Journal of Public Relations Research*, and several others.

Dean Kruckeberg, APR, Fellow of the Public Relations Society of America (PRSA), is a Professor at the University of North Carolina at Charlotte. He is co-author of the books *Public relations and community: A reconstructed theory*; *This is PR*; and *Transparency, public relations, and the mass media*. He has been presented with the National Communication Association Lifetime Achievement Award for Contributions in Public Relations Education, the PRSA Atlas Award for Lifetime Achievement in International Public Relations, was PRSA national "Outstanding Educator," and was awarded the Jackson Jackson & Wagner Behavioral Research Prize and the Institute for Public Relations Pathfinder Award. He was co-chair of the Commission on Public Relations Education for 15 years.

Alexander V. Laskin is a Professor of Strategic Communication at Quinnipiac University, USA. He is an author of over 50 publications, focused primarily on investor relations, international communications, emerging media technologies, and evaluation. He has two books published in 2018: *Handbook of financial communication and investor relations* and *Social, mobile, and emerging media around the world: Communication case studies*. Laskin is a chair of the Financial Communications section of the Public Relations Society of America. He is also a Fulbright Specialist, Page Legacy Scholar, and Plank Fellow.

Minqin Ma is a PhD student of communication studies at Hong Kong Baptist University. Her research interest focuses specifically on corporate social responsibility communication from the employees' perspective and its contribution to crisis communication and corporate reputation. She presented the paper "The moderating effect of response and sources on the relationship between sadness and reputation" in 2017 to the Annual Conference of the International Association for Media and Communication Research. She is currently preparing her prospectus for confirming PhD candidature and working on a paper regarding the pro-environmental behavior of Chinese individuals.

Juan-Carlos Molleda is a tenured professor and the Edwin L. Artzt Dean of the School of Journalism and Communication at the University of Oregon. He is also a US Fulbright Senior Specialist. In addition to his outreach to the professional community, Molleda is a member of the Board of Trustees of the Institute for Public Relations, a Latin American liaison of the Public Relations Society of America's Certification in Education for Public Relations, and a member of The LAGRANT Foundation Board of Directors.

Dean Mundy is an Assistant Professor of Public Relations in the University of Oregon's School of Journalism and Communication, where he researches issues related to diversity and inclusion, as well as LGBTQ advocacy. He explores how public relations best practices can be used to help champion the needs of individuals from underrepresented and marginalized groups – both within organizations and in society more broadly. He received his PhD, MA, and BA from the University of North Carolina at Chapel Hill, and spent approximately 10 years in the corporate world before entering academia.

Barbara Myslik is a PhD student at the University of Florida in the public relations department where she is working on her dissertation under the guidance of Dr. Spiro Kiousis. Her research interests include agenda-building and agenda-setting theories, political messages, populism, and transnational comparisons of political public relations outcomes. Apart from working on her research, she teaches public relations research and principles of PR. To stay current on industry trends, she consults on local political campaigns, working with candidates on their media strategy, speeches, media appearances, forum and debate preparation, and other campaign elements.

Cindy Sing-Bik Ngai is an Assistant Professor and program leader for the MA in Bilingual Corporate Communication at the Hong Kong Polytechnic University. Her research interests include bilingual communication in the corporate context, leader communication, and new media communication. Ngai has published two research books, *New trends in corporate communication: Language, strategies and practices* (2012) and *Role of language and corporate communication in Greater China: From academic to practitioner perspectives* (2015). Her work has also appeared in international journals such as *Public Relations Review, Journal of Business and Technical Communication, International Journal of Business Communication*, and *Discourse and Communication*.

Geah Pressgrove is an Assistant Professor at the Reed College of Media at West Virginia University where she teaches introductory, skills, and advanced courses in strategic communications. Her published and in-progress research examines the ways in which key communications variables influence relationship quality, behavioral outcomes, and loyalty. She explores the organization–public relationship paradigm primarily in the nonprofit, corporate social responsibility, community, and political contexts. She has more than 15 years of professional agency and freelance experience working with diverse clients, including nonprofits, foundations, corporations, entertainment properties, municipal governments, political campaigns, and healthcare organizations.

Ana María Suárez-Monsalve is an Associate Professor at the University of Medellín, Colombia. She is a member of the communication studies research group GRECO (under Colciencias, a Colombian department for science, technology, and innovation); the Colombian Communication Research Association, ACICOM; the Latin American Communication Research Association, ALAIC; and the International Association for Media and Communication Research, IAMCR. She is also a member of the research team of the Latin American Communication Monitor, as well as such professional associations as the Public Relations Society of America and European Public Relations Education and Research Association. She has published more than 20 articles and chapters. Her work can be viewed in *Public Relations Review, Comunicación, Revista Internacional de Relaciones Públicas, Organicom, Anagramas Rumbos y Sentidos de la Comunicación*, and *Alaic*, among others. Her PhD is in Latin American Studies.

Elina Tachkova is a PhD student at the Department of Communication at Texas A&M University. Her area of concentration is organizational communication, and crisis communication in particular. Tachkova's research studies the effectiveness of different crisis response strategies on organizational reputation and stakeholder perceptions after a crisis. She is currently investigating the relationship between scandals and crises and the communicative implications it poses for both crisis communication research and practice. Additional research interests include further testing situational crisis communication theory (SCCT).

Maureen Taylor is a Professor at the University of Technology Sydney, Australia. Taylor's public relations research has focused on nation building and civil society, dialogue, engagement, and new technologies. In 2010, Taylor was honored by the Institute for Public Relations as a Pathfinder for an "original program of scholarly research that has made a significant contribution to the body of knowledge and practice of public relations." Taylor is a member of the Arthur S. Page Society and serves as editor in chief of *Public Relations Review*. In 2018, she was elected a Fellow in the International Communication Association.

Chiara Valentini is a Professor of Corporate Communication at Jyväskylä University, School of Business and Economics, Finland. Her research interests focus on public relations, corporate communication, crisis communication, public affairs, and social media. Her work has appeared in numerous international peer-reviewed journals, international handbooks, and volume contributions. She is the past chair of the Public Relations Division at the International Communication Association and serves as reviewer and editorial board member of several international journals.

Marina Vujnovic is an Associate Professor of Journalism in the Department of Communication at Monmouth University, New Jersey. A native of Croatia, Vujnovic came to United States in 2003 to pursue her graduate education in journalism and mass communication. She received her PhD at the University of Iowa in 2008. She is author of *Forging the Bubikopf nation: Journalism, gender and modernity in interwar Yugoslavia*, is co-author of *Participatory journalism: Guarding open gates at online newspapers*, and co-editor of *Globalizing cultures: Theories, paradigms, actions*. Vujnovic's research interests focus on international communication and the global flow of information; journalism studies; and explorations of the historical, political-economic, and cultural impact on media, class, gender, and ethnicity.

Richard D. Waters is an Associate Professor in the School of Management at the University of San Francisco where he teaches in the graduate business, public, and nonprofit administration programs. His research focuses on nonprofit communication, fundraising, and relationship management. He has published more than 75 peer-reviewed journal articles on public relations topics, and he currently serves on nine editorial review boards. He has served in leadership positions in the Public Relations Society of America and the Association for Education in Journalism and Mass Communication.

Ying Xiong is a PhD candidate in the School of Advertising and Public Relations at the University of Tennessee. Her research explores how public relations contributes to society and facilitates social movement engagement in activism. Xiong has earned master's degrees of arts from University of Oklahoma, USA, and Huazhong University of Science and Technology in China. Prior to returning to her PhD program, she worked in a public relations agency assisting Toyota's national public relations campaigns.

Acknowledgments

This book only exists because of the hard work and support of many people. Many thanks are owed to our amazing editorial team at Wiley, especially Haze Humbert and Kelley Baylis. Haze and Kelley believed in me and encouraged me every step of the way. I have the greatest praise and gratitude to these people and their colleagues for their patience and kindness. I also want to extend our appreciation to our reviewers whose suggestions helped shape this volume into what it is.

Brigitta thanks Troy and Kai Johnson for their encouragement; she also thanks the Auburn University College of Liberal Arts and School of Communication & Journalism for the support received while conceptualizing, writing, and editing this book.

1

What Is Theory?

Brigitta R. Brunner

Everyone uses theory, whether they realize it or not. Theory helps us to understand. It helps us to make sense of what is going on around us. Sometimes the meaning is clear. Sometimes it is not. Sometimes the meaning is shared, but sometimes it can be individual. Theory can identify patterns so we know what to expect. It can help us to figure out how to act. Theory can also draw our attention to what is important. It can help us to predict. In other words, theory helps us to better interpret what is going on in our world. A theorist begins her work with something abstract such as a thought or an idea about something she has experienced or seen. In essence, "any attempt to explain or represent an experience is a theory, an idea of how something happens" (Littlejohn, 1999, p. 2). In public relations, theorists, both practitioners and academics, will use words to help establish understanding about the abstract (Toth & Dozier, 2018). Noted public relations theorist James Grunig (2013) called this primary step in developing theory "semantic structuring" and reminds us that public relations uses language to build theories about our observations. "Good theory helps make sense of reality, either positive or explanatory theory or normative theory that helps improve reality; to understand how public relations is practiced, to improve its practice – for the organization, for publics, and for society" (Grunig, 2013, p. 2).

Defining the Concepts: What Is Theory?

Theory can be broadly defined as a description or explanation of an observed or experienced phenomenon (Gioia & Pitre, 1990). However, it is never the be-all, say-all on a subject. It is built upon observations, which then lead to hypotheses, concepts, models, and assumptions. Theories are then reevaluated and refined, meaning theories often change and evolve. The basic goals of theory are to explain, predict, and control (Infante, Rancer, & Womack, 1997). Theory gives people ways to see new and useful things (Littlejohn, 1999); it can also predict future outcomes and explain the reasons for the outcomes (Griffin, Ledbetter, & Sparks, 2015). Theories have four purposes (Infante et al., 1997): to describe or to answer questions such as what is happening; to explain or to answer questions such as how or why something happens; to predict or answer questions such as what will happen; and to control or answer questions such as how should something happen. Theories also have four functions – organizing experience, extending knowledge, guiding future research, and allowing scientists to anticipate events even if they cannot observe them (Infante et al., 1997). The following example might help you to better understand how theory is used in public relations work.

Public Relations Theory: Application and Understanding, First Edition. Edited by Brigitta R. Brunner.

Having a headache is a health condition to which most, if not all, people can relate. However, not everyone has experienced a migraine headache. Migraines are one of the most common health issues workers experience (Mitchell & Bates, 2011). In fact, nearly one in four US households includes someone with the condition (Migraine Research Foundation, 2018). It is estimated that $14.5 billion is lost annually by employers due to the missed work and lack of productivity migraines cause (Reuters Solutions for Excedrin, 2016). Unfortunately, research conducted by GlaxoSmithKline, parent company of the Excedrin brand, has found that many migraine sufferers believe people do not understand what a migraine is or how debilitating one can be (Bulik, 2017). In fact, 35% of respondents stated that they believe co-workers think they are faking when they say they have a migraine and 63% said they would push through their symptoms to stay at work (Bulik, 2017). Based on this research and insight, Excedrin executives saw an opportunity to foster understanding about migraines while boosting product sales.

In 2016, the Excedrin Migraine Experience was released (Kanski, 2016). Using virtual reality (VR), migraine sufferers could demonstrate to their friends and families what they experience during a migraine. Some symptoms from which they could select were auras, sensitivity to light, and floating spots (Kanski, 2016; Mosbergen, 2016). Overwhelmingly, the people who experienced the VR migraine were overcome by how disorienting the condition was (Mosbergen, 2016). Along with the VR experience, this stage of the campaign also had videos of people experiencing their friend's or family member's migraine, and television ads about the videos and the Excedrin brand (Kanski, 2016). The Excedrin Migraine Experience was well received and had close to 4 million views within three weeks, as well as about 400,000 interactions on social media (Kanski, 2016; Liffreing, 2017). As Amardeep Kahlon, US marketing director for respiratory and pain relief at GlaxoSmithKline, said, "People engaged with long content – a two-minute video – because it pulled on the emotional heartstrings … The campaign videos leveraged real sufferers and their partner with a visualization of their reactions. It makes [the viewer's] heart melt" (as quoted in Kanski, 2016, para. 8). Therefore, through this campaign, the Excedrin brand was able to build understanding and empathy for people who suffer from migraines from those who do not.

The campaign has since been expanded so that it has more reach. For example, the VR simulation can now be shared through an app and cardboard headset, allowing more people to experience it (Tode, 2017). In addition, there have been new components added through the Excedrin Works campaign. Some elements of Excedrin Works are a Migraine Conversations guide (Excedrin, 2017). The guide is meant to help people when discussing migraines in the workplace and shows a series of videos superimposing migraine symptoms on a person trying to make it through his workday (Bulik, 2017; Kanski, 2017). In addition, racing car driver Danica Patrick has been highlighted in videos talking about her experience with migraines in the hopes that, by sharing her story, others will too (Kanski, 2017). This campaign is based on building relationships and dialogue and has the goal of forming more meaningful relationships between those afflicted by migraines and the Excedrin brand (Kanski, 2017). "'If we can help foster and facilitate conversation, hopefully that makes the plight of the migraine sufferer much easier,' Scott Yacovino, senior brand manager for Excedrin and the US pain business at GlaxoSmithKline Consumer Health, said" (Bulik, 2017, para. 3). As we can see, this campaign was built on the foundation of research, but it also seems to have elements of theory at work within it. For example, it seems as if principles of dialogic theory and relationship management theory (two theories you will learn more about in this book) have been invoked, since the campaign makes use of conversation, dialogue, and relationship building.

How and Why Is Theory of Concern to Public Relations?

As the Excedrin example illustrates, public relations is an applied field; however, it needs theory to guide its practice. Theory helps practitioners become better practitioners because it helps them better understand publics, messaging, strategy, and tactics. "Executing effective public relations starts with knowing and understanding the public relations theory that helps define the practice" (Toth & Dozier, 2018, 71). Public relations is a difficult field to describe. In fact, if you asked a group of people to define the term, they would all likely have a different definition. The fact that public relations does not have a universal definition has meant that theory and practice have been influenced by many and have charted numerous routes (Toth & Dozier, 2018). For example, some theorists and practitioners believe the core existence of public relations is to be a management function. This perception of public relations is based on the work of Grunig and Hunt (1984), who stated that public relations is "the management of communication between an organization and its publics" (p. 6). Other practitioners and theorists have put more emphasis on the building and maintaining of relationships. These people are more likely to define public relations similar to Cutlip, Center, and Broom (2006), who defined the field as "the management function that establishes and maintains mutually beneficial relationships between an organization and the publics on whom its success or failure depends" (p. 6). This book will introduce you to many theories used in public relations so you better understand how theory informs public relations practice.

However, Ferguson (1984) cautioned, "Theory is not an explanation based on supposition or conjecture. It is a way to understand events and to predict future events based upon research findings supporting the theory" (p. 3). Theory should be important to public relations practitioners and academics alike. Without theory, we base our decisions on instinct. With theory, we are able to base decisions on empirical evidence (Ferguson, 1984). It's more than guesses. Theory lays the groundwork for data-driven decision-making.

Metaphors for Theory

Griffin et al. (2015) suggest some metaphors for theory – nets, lenses, and maps – because theory has different levels and can be used in many different situations. Theory is like a net because theories can be cast to capture what makes the world around us. The net can be all encompassing, much like a grand theory, or it can be small, and of fine mesh, similar to a specialized theory. Theory is like a lens because it can be used to focus on a certain aspect of public relations or it can push other items to the back; either way, theory highlights and shapes the perceptions one has about an idea. Finally, theory is like a map because it guides us through what are often unfamiliar territories as we expand or build new theories. Similarly, Toth and Dozier (2018) write about Nastasia and Rakow's (2010) categorization of theory as either map reading or map making. Theories that encompass the idea of map reading use reasoning, both deductive and inductive, to explain why things work as they do. To test whether or not a theory holds true, evidence needs to be gathered for map reading. Therefore, when theory is applied to new and different situations it becomes an even more useful map-reading theory. As an example, Toth and Dozier (2018) relate how in public relations we generally do not build relationships with the "general public," but rather prioritize strategic publics and build and maintain relationships with them. Theories categorized as map making help us to better understand new and up-and-coming actions and behaviors. For example, when practitioners and theorists work to determine how new and emerging media have affected public relations practice, they "construct a map that suggests how to use social media strategically and how to measure the impact of social media" (Toth & Dozier, 2018, p. 72). When a theory is classified as map making, it is a theory that helps us to ponder different significances and to develop new ways of analyzing and ultimately applying its concepts. Map-making theories remind us that theory changes and is adapted over time.

Grand Theories and Theories of Middle Range

According to McQuail (2010), there are several types of theories used within communication – social science (empirically based); normative (theories of how things such as media should work); working (normative theories applied to specific areas such as public relations), and common sense (based on inherent knowledge). Classifying a theory as either normative or positive is common in public relations. Scholars working with normative theory only have to demonstrate that "if an activity were to be conducted as the theory prescribes, it would be effective" (Grunig & Grunig, 1992, p. 291). Many normative theories build models, which are meant to improve practice if followed by practitioners (Grunig & Grunig, 1992). Normative theories of public relations (PR) have centered on relationship building, dialogue, and two-way communication (Archer & Harrigan, 2016), and therefore, dialogic theory would be an example of a normative public relations theory. In contrast to a normative theory, a positivist theory seeks to explain what is rather than what should be (Dozier & Broom, 2006). "Positive theories describe phenomena, events, or activities as they actually occur (Grunig & Grunig, 1992, p. 291). An example of a positive theory of public relations would be the public relations role theory. In addition, Grunig and Grunig (1992) say, "the evidence from research supports the conclusion that the four models [of public relations] provide a good positive theory: Public relations practitioners do indeed practice all of them" (p. 292).

Theory can also be broken down to the levels at which it operates. For example, some theories apply to intrapersonal levels of communication, others interpersonal (dyad), others to group communication, and still others to the organizational and mass levels. Public relations practitioners can work on all these levels and should be aware of how theory can guide their practice whether they are talking to one person or large groups.

A grand theory is an abstract way of thinking about concepts (Mills, 1959). Scientists believe there is one truth and that theory is like a mirror reflecting that truth. They are objective and believe that once a truth is found it will continue to be true in the future. Therefore, science has grand theories such as the theory of relativity. Mass communication and public relations don't operate in quite the same way. Although grand theories, all-encompassing and generalizable, do exist in the physical sciences, they do not seem possible for mass communication. For one reason, the social sciences, and mass communication in particular, are relatively new disciplines. Also, there is much intersubjectivity in these fields so agreements are at times difficult to come by. Theory resides on a continuum between objective and interpretive (Griffin et al., 2015). Therefore, theorists who are more interpretive believe theory is socially constructed, meaning it changes depending on context rather than having a universal meaning, as a theorist who works from the objective side of the spectrum believes. Mass communication has made attempts at finding a grand theory, but they have been disproven. For example, Schramm's (1971) magic bullet theory was an attempt at finding a grand theory for the discipline. Building on persuasion, the magic bullet theory claimed that if media messages hit their intended targets, a certain effect would follow. However, the theory did not account for individualism and instead assumed that all people would interpret messages in the same way. People did not. Therefore, the magic bullet theory was disproven as grand theory. Some people even thought of the excellence theory as a grand theory; however, that perspective has changed with the advent of more theories in public relations (Taylor & Kent, 2014).

Rather than being defined as grand theories, mass communication and public relations theories are theories of middle range. Middle-range theories make specific explanations rather than broad generalizable ones. Merton (1968) described middle-range theories as having a limited scope and explaining a limited range of concepts and phenomena rather than explaining phenomena on a broader level. This approach to theory also integrates empirical research. Theories of middle range describe what a theory can and cannot do. These theories focus on the measurable aspects of social reality rather than attempting to explain the entire social world. Communication fields have been encouraged to create theories of middle range because they were thought to be superior to grand theories as specific explanations rather than broad, generalizable ones (Craig, 1993). Similarly, Wehmeier (2009) suggests practitioners prefer general theories and theories of middle range. Some examples of middle-range theories you may have learned about in other classes include cultivation theory and uses and gratifications theory. In public relations, most of our theories fall into the category of middle-range theory, too.

Theory Building

As we have covered, there are different levels of theory as well as a continuum of theories' objectivity. Theory development is an ever growing and ever expanding process. Since public relations is a relatively new field, there is much room for growth in terms of theory. This section will cover how we build and expand upon theory.

Theory is built every day by both practitioners and academics as they follow what is happening within the field. They will look at the issues. They will address problems. They will examine the trends. All this work is done to better the field and to develop new solutions. Academics most commonly build theory through their research, which might include publishing refereed journal articles, delivering conference papers, or publishing books. Practitioners can also publish books and articles, but might have their work featured in trade journals rather than academic ones. Practitioners also share their knowledge and insight at conferences, and might also have blogs to further discuss their ideas. In fact, even the debates playing out on social media can help to build theory (Toth & Dozier, 2018). Theory building is a social experience; theorists bring their own experiences, worldviews, and presuppositions to the process (Botan & Hazleton, 1989).

Much theory in the communication discipline comes from a Western perspective (Littlejohn, 1999). Theory from the United States tends to focus on communication from an objective perspective based in quantitative methods. European scholars are more likely to use historical, critical, and cultural approaches to theory. In addition, European theory is also quite frequently influenced by Marxism (Littlejohn, 1999). Theory with an Eastern perspective is more likely to focus on Confucian principles (Kim, 2003). Another well-established region for public relations scholarship is Australia and New Zealand (Botan & Hazleton, 2006). Emerging areas of theoretical influence are South America and Asia (Botan & Hazleton, 2006). One trend in public relations is the weakening of American dominance when it comes to theory due to the internationalization of the field. This occurrence is helping to bring new ideas, perspectives, and cultural insights to the field (Botan & Hazleton, 2006). As public relations continues to expand globally, it seems fitting that its theory will be influenced and reshaped by theorists from around the world. "In a field where creativity is a desirable characteristic, a broad knowledge of theories and methods will lead to the recognition of multiple, alternative solutions for practical as well as theoretical problems" (Hazleton & Botan, 1989, p. 7).

Theory is not set in stone; it represents what we know at this moment in time (Botan, 1989). Kaplan (1964) suggests that theory grows by extension or intension. Kuhn (1970) says a third way to grow theory exists: scientific revolution. When theories develop by extension, they grow to include more concepts; when they develop by intension, further refinement is based on a deeper understanding of the original concepts; and in scientific revolution, previously accepted theories are rejected in favor of new ones (Infante et al., 1997). Extension uses current understandings to reach out and understand a new area (Botan, 1989). When we use theory developed before social media came on to the scene to try and understand how and why using social media in certain ways is successful in public relations, we are expanding theory via extension. Intension is similar to using a microscope; it is when theory is used to more closely examine our current understanding in order to bring about new thoughts (Botan, 1989). When a theorist uses critical theory to more closely examine the diversity of the field of public relations, she is using intension to advance theory. Scientific revolutions can lead to an entirely new approach to a field, including new practices (Botan, 1989). Scientific revolutions can lead to defensiveness, as the theorists whose ideas have been overturned protect their contributions and fight to keep them relevant (Littlejohn, 1999). However, while theories are rarely rejected, they are frequently revised (Grunig, 1992). In order to build and expand public relations theory, alternative theories addressing the same issues need to be compared (Botan & Hazleton, 1989). Public relations needs not only to keep developing new theories, but also to critique all existing theories in order to grow as a field; without those struggles, the field will be stagnant (Botan & Hazleton, 2006). Botan and Hazleton (2006) suggest areas still in need of theory and scholarship include the role of gender in the field; fundraising/social responsibility; and financial/investor relations.

In order to grow and develop new theories, a four-step process of testing is followed (Infante et al., 1997). First, a hypothesis is developed. Then the theorist decides how best to test the hypothesis. The appropriate research is then conducted to test the hypothesis. Finally, the theorist interprets the observations. While a theory cannot be proven, a theory can be falsified, meaning there are enough counterexamples to reject the theory. During theory testing, a theorist wants to be sure the theory is both reliable (replicable) and valid (with the ability to measure what the theory states it measures). There are many evaluative criteria used to determine a theory's worth. While scholars debate what criteria are necessary to evaluate and compare a theory, here are some suggestions. Shaw and Costanzo (1970) say there are three necessary criteria for a good theory. The necessary criteria are logical consistency, meaning the theory does not have any contradictory parts; consistency with accepted facts; and testability or, in other words, the potential for the theory to be disproven. Shaw and Costanzo (1970) also say there are desirable, but not necessary, criteria for theory evaluation. These additional criteria are simplicity, parsimony, consistency with related theory, interpretability, usefulness, and being pleasing to the mind.

Social scientists also "agree on four criteria a theory must meet to be good – relative simplicity, testability, practical utility, and quantifiable research" (Griffin et al., 2015, p. 25). Therefore, a good objective theory will do the following six things: predict future events; explain an event or human behavior; be simplistic/no more complex than it needs to be; be testable (meaning it is possible to have hypotheses); have practical utility or usefulness; and use quantitative means and research to compare differences (Griffin et al., 2015). By using such criteria, researchers can compare and contrast theories and determine where the strengths and weaknesses of each lie.

However, not all theory is scientific or objective. Some is interpretive. Interpretive theory also has standards. A good interpretive theory brings light to values, meaning it identifies the underlying ideology of the theory (Griffin et al., 2015). Some examples might be ethical perspective, equality, and freedom. Interpretive theory gives new insight into people and their actions and behaviors typically based on small, unique groups or individuals. Interpretive theory is also aesthetically appealing, meaning it is more creative and less likely to follow a standard format. Interpretive theory has the support of communities of scholars. It also is meant to generate change and/or to transform society by reexamining the accepted wisdom of a culture. Lastly, interpretive theory uses qualitative research to support its assertions.

Public Relations Theory

Grunig (1989) stated "one can think of many theories that apply … but it is more difficult to think of a public relations theory … that has not been borrowed from another" (p. 18, cited in Ledingham, 2003). Similarly, Ferguson (1984) suggests that a theory of PR is a unicorn, a mythical beast, and notes some critics have questioned whether or not PR is worthy of theory. It seems today that these criticisms can be laid to rest as public relations does have theory and it is applicable to its practice. Because public relations as an academic field is relatively young, it is important to recognize how far the field has come and how much research has been done in order to advance our understanding of the practice and the theory that guides it (Toth & Dozier, 2018).

While the roots of public relations are in journalism, its theory has developed with the interjection of humanistic and social science approaches (Botan & Hazleton, 1989). In the 1950s and 1960s, public relations and its theory were closely tied to mass communication and focused on the effectiveness of media relations and campaigns (Grunig, Grunig, & Dozier, 2006). However, researchers found that media effects had more influence on what people thought about than how they behaved or how they formed attitudes, thereby lessening their importance to public relations (Grunig et al., 2006). Around that time, theorists began thinking about public relations differently and noting its ties to two-way communication and management (Grunig et al., 2006). Soon public relations theorists, most notably J. E. Grunig, G. M. Broom, and D. M. Dozier, began investigating public relations from a management and communication perspective by looking at concepts such as symmetrical communication and roles (Grunig et al., 2006). There was a theoretical shift from PR concentrating on managing communication to emphasizing negotiating relationships (Kent & Taylor, 2002).

Much like scientists, public relations practitioners and academics would like to have a set of proven and true theories (Grunig, 1992). It would be comforting to know that using a certain strategy would guarantee the desired results. Unfortunately, that is not how public relations works. The possibility of laws of public relations existing would likely lead to much debate because of the diversity of perspectives and worldviews held by theorists (Botan & Hazleton, 1989). "A domain of scientific or scholarly inquiry, such as public relations, is held together not so much by agreement on theories as by agreement on the problems that theories used in the domain should solve" (Grunig, 1992, p. 7). Meaning that while academics and practitioners may not agree on the best theory or approach to an issue, they can agree that theory is needed to better understand certain aspects of public relations such as strategy, media relations, ethics, or crisis communication. Academics and practitioners will try to explain these areas in different ways because we have different perspectives, worldviews, and ideas (Grunig, 1992). Developing theory and practice together helps each to inform the other (Strömbäck & Kiousis, 2013). After all, the only way to find how valid a theory truly is is to apply and test it through research and in various contexts. Also, it's OK that not all theories will work in all situations. Building theory is about new ideas, even ideas that are uncomfortable to some (Botan, 1989).

Most Utilized Theories in Public Relations

Meadows and Meadows (2014) conducted research to follow the development of public relations theory since 1975. To complete their work, they randomly selected articles published in the *Journal of Public Relations Research* and *Public Relations Review*. Eighty-seven theories and one model were found in this sample, with the most frequently utilized theories being agenda setting, the situational theory of publics, critical theory/critical discourse analysis, and framing theory. Similarly, Pasadeos, Berger, and Renfro (2010) examined the citations of public relations articles published between 2000 and 2005. Their work found that excellence theory was the most cited theory in public relations. Relationship management theory was the second most cited theory. In the following paragraphs, I will detail these two public relations theories to give readers a better understanding of them since they are so fundamental to public relations theory.

The excellence theory is probably the most influential work in the establishment of public relations theory (Botan & Hazleton, 2006). Excellence theory is a general theory of public relations that brings together ideas about and practices of communication within organizations (Grunig, 1992). The theory is about excellence and effectiveness in public relations. Excellence theory is an attempt at creating a general theory of the field, by bringing together middle-level theories to answer questions and solve problems of concern to academics and practitioners (Grunig et al., 2006). The excellence study gave us a benchmark for theory in the field through its use of research and logic (Grunig et al., 2006). It benchmarks important success factors across different types of organizations, which adds to its theoretical value (Grunig et al., 2006). Excellence theory provides a way to evaluate PR departments, is a means to explain the value of PR, shows how to gain the most value from PR efforts, and offers an avenue for teaching public relations (Grunig et al., 2006). In essence, excellence theory helps to establish the value of public relations at the organizational level.

Excellence theory has five propositions common to organizations with excellent public relations. These propositions are a participative culture, symmetrical internal communication, organic structures, equal opportunities for all employees, and higher job satisfaction (Grunig et al., 2006). CEOs who had excellent PR departments valued communication twice as much as those with less excellent departments and also believed PR should function as described in excellence theory (Grunig et al., 2006).

Overlap exists between excellence theory and relationship management theory, because they both examine organization–public relationships (Coombs & Holladay, 2015). However, it was Ferguson's (1984) conference paper that moved the field toward the idea that public relations is about relationships and relationship management. Ledingham (2001) suggested that by refocusing the field on relationships, public relations was able to move past its historic ties to journalism and embed itself within management.

Ledingham (2003) proposed a theory of relationship management, stating, "Relationship Management is ethical and efficient management of an organization–stakeholder relationship, focused over time, on common interests and shared goals in support of mutual understanding and mutual benefit" (p. 190). The theory recognizes that for a relationship to continue in the long term, the goals and objectives of the organization and its publics must be similar. If the organization and publics have different interests, the relationship will not last. In addition, if one party finds the relationship gives it benefits, but the other does not, the relationship will dissolve (Ledingham, 2003). For example, if a foreign company is operating on US soil, there are benefits to both that country and the United States. For example, the foreign country may benefit from this relationship by having access to a skilled labor force or to natural resources. The United States derives benefits from the arrangement because jobs have been created and perhaps the foreign company pays into the local tax base, making that area more prosperous. At this point, both countries have similar and compatible goals and objectives. They have a positive and beneficial relationship. However, if the United States were to impose new tariffs on the products being manufactured by the foreign corporation, the relationship might no longer be beneficial to the foreign company. It might restructure its production worldwide and decide to close its US factory, which would also be harmful to the workers and local economy. The relationship would be over because it would no longer be beneficial to the parties involved.

By taking a relationship management approach to public relations, the role of the field is clarified, understanding is built, and the way public relations contributes to achieving organizational goals is explained (Ledingham, 2003). In other words, relationship management theory helps public relations practitioners become a part of the dominant coalition and helps practitioners explain what public relations is (and what it is not) so that others understand how and why public relations is a strategic part of any organization.

Conclusion

In order to grow, PR needs to face not only its past but also its complex present. Shifts signal opportunities for further theory development (Kent & Taylor, 2002). They should be viewed as exciting. New theories and theory building should be persuasive and move people toward changing their ideological viewpoints (Gioia & Pitre, 1990). There needs to be a diversity of theories and perspectives for public relations to grow (Botan & Hazleton, 2006).

The rest of this book is designed to give you a more in-depth look at the practice of public relations and how theory fits within it. Each chapter will focus on an area of public relations practice such as strategy, ethics, and community. In addition, each chapter will define terms, explain the importance of each topic to public relations, detail theories of importance, and give examples of when and how theory can be applied. Finally, the chapters include short case studies to help you better understand the links between theory and good practice. You may notice some chapters detail the same theory as others. This choice was made to show you how the same theory could be applied in different contexts. You may also notice that some theories are strictly used in the domain of public relations, with others coming from communication or other fields. Again, the decision to include this range of theories was made to more fully demonstrate the breadth of public relations and the work of its practitioners. With this design, students, such as you, will not only learn how functions of public relations can be served by the application of multiple theories, but you will also learn how theories can be implemented within different professional settings. Ultimately, this book should help you to better answer the questions of what theory's place is within the practice of public relations.

References

Archer, C., & Harrigan, P. (2016). Show me the money: How bloggers as stakeholders are challenging theories of relationship building in public relations. *Media International Australia*, *160*, 67–77.

Botan, C. H. (1989). Theory development in public relations. In C. H. Botan & V. Hazleton, Jr. (Eds.), *Public relations theory* (pp. 99–110). Hillsdale, NJ: Lawrence Erlbaum.

Botan, C. (2006). Grand strategy, strategy, and tactics in public relations. In C. H. Botan & V. Hazleton (Eds.), *Public relations theory II* (pp. 223–248). Hillsdale, NJ: Lawrence Erlbaum.

Botan, C. H., & Hazleton, V. (Eds.) (1989). *Public relations theory*. Hillsdale, NJ: Lawrence Erlbaum.

Botan, C. H., & Hazleton, V. (2006). *Public relations theory II*. Hillsdale, NJ: Lawrence Erlbaum.

Bulik, B. S. (2017, September 4). *Empathy at work: GlaxoSmithKline extends Excedrin Migraine campaign to include sufferers on the job*. Retrieved from https://www.fiercepharma.com/marketing/empathy-at-work-gsk-extends-excedrin-migraine-campaign-to-include-sufferers-job

Coombs, W. T. & Holladay, S. J. (2015). Public relations' "Relationship Identity" in research: Enlightenment or illusion. *Public Relations Review, 41*, 689–695.

Craig, R. T. (1993). Why are there so many communication theories? *Journal of Communication, 43*, 26–33.

Cutlip, S. M., Center, A. H., & Broom, G. H. (2006). *Effective public relations* (9th ed.). Upper Saddle River, NJ: Prentice Hall.

Dozier, D. M., & Broom, G. M. (2006). The centrality of practitioner roles to public relations theory. In C. H. Botan & V. Hazleton (Eds.), *Public relations theory II* (pp. 137–170). Hillsdale, NJ: Lawrence Erlbaum.

Excedrin. (2017). *Excedrin® discussion guide for migraines in the workplace*. Retrieved from https://www.excedrin.com/migraines/prevention-tips/migraines-at-work-discussion-guide/

Ferguson, M. A. (1984, August). *Building theory in public relations: Interorganizational relationships as a public relations paradigm*. Paper presented to the Public Relations Division, Association for Education in Journalism and Mass Communication Annual Convention, Gainesville, Florida.

Gioia, D. A., & Pitre, E. (1990). Multiparadigm perspectives on theory building. *Academy of Management Review, 15*, 584–602.

Griffin, E., Ledbetter, A., & Sparks, G. (2015). *A first look at communication theory* (9th ed.). New York: McGraw Hill Education.

Grunig, J. E. (1989). Symmetrical presuppositions as a framework for public relations theory. In C. H. Botan & V. Hazleton (Eds.), *Public relations theory* (pp. 17–44). Hillsdale, NJ: Lawrence Erlbaum.

Grunig, J. E. (Ed.) (1992). *Excellence in public relations and communication management*. Hillsdale, NJ: Lawrence Erlbaum.

Grunig, J. E. (2013). Furnishing the edifice: Ongoing research on public relations as a strategic management function. In K. Sriramesh, A. Zerfass, & J.-N. Kim (Eds), *Public relations and communication management: Current trends and emerging topics* (pp. 1–26). New York: Routledge.

Grunig, J. E., & Grunig, L. A. (1992). Models of public relations and communications. In J. E. Grunig (Ed.), *Excellence in public relations and communication management* (pp. 285–326). Hillsdale, NJ: Lawrence Erlbaum.

Grunig, J. E., Grunig, L. A., & Dozier, D. M. (2006). The excellence theory. In C. H. Botan & V. Hazleton (Eds.), *Public relations theory II* (pp. 1–20). Hillsdale, NJ: Lawrence Erlbaum.

Grunig, J. E., & Hunt, T. (1984). *Managing public relations*. New York: Holt, Rinehart, and Winston.

Hazleton, V. (2006). Toward a theory of public relations competence. In C. H. Botan & V. Hazleton (Eds.), *Public relations theory II* (pp. 199–222). Hillsdale, NJ: Lawrence Erlbaum.

Hazleton, V., & Botan, C. H. (1989). The role of theory in public relations. In C. H. Botan & V. Hazleton (Eds.), *Public relations theory* (pp. 3–16). Hillsdale, NJ: Lawrence Erlbaum.

Infante, D. A., Rancer, A. S., & Womack, D. F. (1997). *Building communication theory* (3rd ed.). Prospect Heights, IL: Waveland Press.

Kanski, A. (2016, October 26). How Excedrin brought VR to drug marketing with The Migraine Experience. *MM&M*. Retrieved from https://www.mmm-online.com/campaigns/how-excedrin-brought-vr-to-drug-marketing-with-the-migraine-experience/article/568012/

Kanski, A. (2017, December 28). Excedrin's survival guide for a headache at work. *PRWeek*. Retrieved from https://www.prweek.com/article/1453113/excedrins-survival-guide-headache-work

Kaplan, A. (1964). *The conduct of inquiry: Methodology for behavioral science*. San Francisco: Chandler.

Kent, M. L., & Taylor, M. (2002). Toward a dialogic theory of public relations. *Public Relations Review, 28*, 21–37.

Kim, Y. (2003). Professionalism and diversification: The evolution of public relations in South Korea. In K. Sriramesh & D. Verčič (Eds.), *The global public relations handbook: Theory, research, and practice* (pp. 106–120). Mahwah, NJ: Lawrence Erlbaum.

Kuhn, T. S. (1970). *The structure of scientific revolutions*. Chicago: University of Chicago Press.

Ledingham, J. A (2001). Government–community relationships: Extending the relational theory of public relations. *Public Relations Review, 27*, 285–295.

Ledingham, J. A. (2003). Explicating relationship management as a general theory of public relations. *Journal of Public Relations Research, 15*, 181–198.

Liffreing, I. (2017, September 6). Excedrin is using virtual reality to show what having migraines are like. *Digiday UK*. Retrieved from https://digiday.com/marketing/excedrin-using-virtual-reality-show-migraines-like/

Littlejohn, S. W. (1999) *Theories of human communication*. Belmont, CA: Wadsworth.

McQuail, D. (2010). *McQuail's mass communication theory* (6th ed.). Los Angeles: Sage.

Meadows, C., & Meadows, C. W., III. (2014). The history of academic research in public relations: Tracking research trends over nearly four decades. *Public Relations Review, 40*, 871–873. doi:10.1016/j.pubrev.2014.06.005

Merton, R. K. (1968). *Social theory and social construction*. New York: Free Press.

Migraine Research Foundation. (2018). *Migraine facts*. Retrieved from http://migraineresearch foundation.org/about-migraine/migraine-facts/

Mills, C. W. (1959). *The sociological imagination*. Oxford: Oxford University Press.

Mitchell, R. J., & Bates, P. (2011). Measuring health-related productivity loss. *Population Health Management, 14*, 93–98.

Mosbergen, D. (2016, April 8). Emotional video shows people experiencing migraines for the first time – in virtual reality. *HuffPost*. Retrieved from https://m.huffpost.com/us/entry/us_57075b60e4b0c4e26a225176

Nastasia, D. I., & Rakow, L. F. (2010). What is theory? Puzzles and maps as metaphors in communication theory. *Triple C, 8*, 1–17.

Pasadeos, Y., Berger, B, & Renfro, R. B. (2010). Public relations as a maturing discipline: An update on research networks. *Journal of Public Relations Research, 22*, 136–158.

Reuters Solutions for Excedrin (2016). *Employees hide headaches, migraines from supervisors*. Retrieved from https://www.reuters.com/brandfeatures/excedrin/employees-hide-headaches-migraines-from-supervisors

Schramm, W. (1971). The nature of communication between humans. In W. Schramm & D. F. Roberts (Eds.), *The process and effects of mass communication* (pp. 3–516). Urbana, IL: University of Illinois Press.

Shaw, M. E., & Costanzo, P. R. (1970). *Theories of social psychology*. New York: McGraw-Hill.

Strömbäck, J., & Kiousis, S. (2013). Political public relations: Old practice, new theory-building. *Public Relations Journal, 7*, 1–11.

Taylor, M., & Kent, M. L. (2014). Dialogic engagement: Clarifying foundational concepts. *Journal of Public Relations Research, 26*, 384–398.

Tode, C. (2017, October 16). How Excedrin's standalone VR experience evolved into a viral video. *Mobile Marketer*. Retrieved from https://www.mobilemarketer.com/news/how-excedrins-standalone-vr-experience-evolved-into-a-viral-video/507086/

Toth, E. L., & Dozier, D. M. (2018, April). Theory: The ever-evolving foundation for why we do what we do. In Commission for Public Relations Education, *Fast forward: Foundations + future state. Educators + practitioners* (pp. 71–77). New York: Commission for Public Relations Education.

Wehmeier, S. (2009). Out of the fog and into the future: Directions of public relations theory building, research, and practice. *Canadian Journal of Communication, 34*, 265–282.

2

Strategy

Ana María Suárez-Monsalve and Juan-Carlos Molleda

In the city of Medellín, Colombia, in 1994, the METRO transportation system was inaugurated and constituted as the Mass Transportation Enterprise of the Aburrá Valley (a.k.a. Metro de Medellín, or Metro hereafter). Medellín is the second most important city of Colombia in terms of economics and politics. With close to 3 million inhabitants, it is the capital city of the department of Antioquia and is in the center of the Aburrá Valley. The valley is made up of 10 neighboring municipalities, which together have a population of 5 million inhabitants. The Metro joins the Metropolitan Area as a north–south axis and the center of the Metrocables (cable cars) and the Tranvía trams in the Integrated Transport System of the Aburrá Valley, SITVA.

At a time of high violence in the city and in the wake of the ravages of the war against drug trafficker Pablo Escobar Gaviria (killed on December 2, 1993), the company set out to create a new culture among the inhabitants of the Aburrá Valley. Leaders of the Metro came together and working in tandem built trust and relationships with people living in the neighborhoods near the Metro stations and lines. This outreach was aimed at generating a sense of belonging and cultivating an attitude of care and preservation for the transportation system.

The company says the Metro culture is the result of the social, educational, and cultural management model built, consolidated, and delivered by company leaders with the citizens of the city. This has been adopted in all the areas where the SITVA operates and the company offers it as a model that can be adopted by other institutions "whose purpose is the construction of a new civic culture, coexistence in harmony, good behavior, solidarity, respect of basic rules for the use of public goods, respect for oneself and for the other, among other aspects" (Metro de Medellín, 2018).

On February 14, 2018, Metro de Medellín suffered one of its worst crises in 24 years as a result of an electric shock caused by atmospheric effects in the Aburrá Valley. With the paralysis of the integrated transportation system, accompanied by torrential rains over a period of eight hours, the city collapsed. It happened when many people were out buying gifts and celebrating Valentine's Day. Celebrating Valentine's Day has spread to some Latin American countries through the transmission and influence of international marketing strategies. The transportation crisis affected more than 200,000 Metro users. However, instead of people reacting with outrage and complaints, the situation generated a surge of support and appreciation for the transportation system. Metro transformed the Valentines's Day crisis into an opportunity for people to express their attachment to the mass transit system because of the strategic relationships and culture it had cultivated with them over the years. What would most likely be a difficult situation for any transportation system, instead became a day on which people demonstrated their love for the Metro.

Public Relations Theory: Application and Understanding, First Edition. Edited by Brigitta R. Brunner.
© 2019 John Wiley & Sons, Inc. Published 2019 by John Wiley & Sons, Inc.

Social media was the most effective platform for people to publicly display their appreciation. Using Twitter and Facebook, users commented about how this crisis situation demonstrated the importance of the system of mass transportation in a city that had previously had three environmental crises due to poor air quality. The company's leaders created the hashtags #MiMetroMeMueve (my Metro moves me) and #AmoMiMetro (I love my Metro) and thousands of messages of support were posted during the crisis. The strategy of "Metro Culture" certainly proved successful.

Defining the Concepts: What Is Strategy?

The word strategy includes a sense of cunning and calculation (Alonso, 2001). Strategy contains communicative factors identified in signs, symbols, interpretation of behaviors, and messages, in addition to the deconstruction of the word and action. From oriental culture, strategy is conceived of as the adequate use of resources, initiative, and a clear and deep vision of the social, economic, political, and cultural situation. These areas are mediated by meanings that are shared to define a purpose and establish multiple relationships.

In the Western perspective, the term strategy comes from the Greek *strategia* and its original meaning referred to the direction of troops. At that time, its meaning was associated with leadership and leadership skills (Alonso, 2001). We often hear the word strategy used in conjunction with the term public relations, but strategy is not an easy concept to understand. In fact, it is difficult to define. So difficult that Lukaszewski (2001) says that strategy is one of the most mysterious aspects of public relations. Some people think about strategy as being the thoughts and logic behind an idea for a campaign (Robert, 1997). In contrast, Drucker (1954) says that strategy is about an organization's future positions and focuses on what should be done rather than how things should be done. Steyn (2007) states that strategy gives focus and direction to an organization's communication activities. Others such as Werder and Holtzhausen (2009) suggest that strategy is about messaging, and Ki and Hon (2007) say it is about relationship building. Mintzberg (1994) sees strategy as a set of consistent behaviors shown by organizations. While there is no single, clear definition of the term, we do know it is an important part of public relations and would benefit from more scholarly work (Steyn, 2003, 2007).

A central aspect of strategy is its anticipative nature, which involves the ability to calculate the possible circumstances surrounding a situation, a decision, or a project to be carried out. In the 1960s, the strategic point of view was introduced into economic and administrative sciences by Woodward (1965) with his contribution to the theory of contingency applied to organizations. Woodward's theory recognizes that organizations exist because of their relationships with their individual internal and external environments (such as organizational culture and climate, political and economic contexts, or crisis situations inside or outside organizations), which forces them to adapt to constant changes.

An organization's internal and external environment can affect the decisions leaders make about strategy (Kim, 2016). Understanding how the environment can affect strategy and strategic decisions is important for professionals. For example, the behaviors and attitudes of key publics toward an issue, product, or service can have an effect on an organization's strategy. Therefore, professionals need to constantly scan the environment to inform themselves and so they can alert organizational leaders to any changes they foresee. As the environment changes, so will the organization's decisions about strategy. Moreover, professionals need to be adaptable and willing to make adjustments and modifications to their strategic ideas (Shimizu, 2017). However, despite the changes in their organization's internal and external environments, professionals are still expected to meet strategic goals. To enhance effectiveness, Tan and Tan

(2005) suggest professionals should not only be aware of their environments, but also evaluate, research, and use the opportunities presented by their environmental surroundings to their advantage. Awareness can help professionals when it comes to anticipating how organization–public relationships might change and how publics might react to messages.

While forecasting and considering the future and probabilities, strategists must also remember that the circumstances of the environment can affect their work (Mintzberg & Waters, 1983). The decisions made to take advantage of or deal with unexpected circumstances are those that put to the test the ability of a professional to read the environment, know his or her own capabilities, and direct actions to address the situation.

In this chapter, strategy can be defined as the reasoning behind why an organization believes it can reach its goals and objectives and why the approach proposed is the best one possible. However, in order for a strategy to work, professionals must constantly read the environment and be clear about the variables that could affect their work; they must consider the difference between strategic intentions and the strategic results.

How and Why Is Strategy of Concern to Public Relations?

Ways to Think about Strategy

Alberto Pena (2001) proposed eight dimensions of strategy: anticipation, decision, method, position, frame of reference, perspective, discourse, and relationship with the environment. Strategy as anticipation refers to considering the future and its probabilities. Organizations define their vision, mission, and objectives to look toward the future, and they therefore employ strategy. The dimension of *decision* will be addressed in the next section from a public relations perspective.

Strategy as a method focuses on how to achieve the purpose of a public relations campaign or activity. That is, once it is clear what to do, it is a priority to determine the necessary steps to achieve it. Therefore, strategy as a method considers the sequence of actions to achieve the desired results.

Strategy as a position and as an advantage refers to the permanent desire to maintain a privileged situation so that a professional's interests, clients, employers, and/or causes are promoted. This aspect of strategy requires professionals to know their own organizations and client well, both their strengths and weaknesses. Without this understanding, professionals would have difficulty in determining what positioning generates advantage. This model of strategic position has two currents (Pena, 2001), one that refers to achieving a favorable location, with a static understanding of position, and a second with a more projective emphasis, which points out the right way to go to about achieving a position of advantage.

Strategy as a frame of reference refers to the ability of a professional to frame collective behavior. In managerial terms, it refers to the collective understanding of the purposes and actions taken by an organization. When this understanding is in writing, it delineates the minimum and maximum actions, both individual and group, needed to generate coherence and move a strategic idea from concept to reality.

The framework of a strategy must be known, learned, and shared by the entire group of people who contribute to its execution and fulfillment. Having a shared framework allows integration, unity, and coherence, while also reducing unforeseen events.

Strategy as perspective and vision highlights the necessity of having a clear idea about what one aspires to be, to obtain, or to gain. These qualities help professionals to define the focus of their efforts, so that the decisions they make guide the way and identify the appropriate position for the organization, its people, and its products. Perspective and vision help professionals to solidify their purpose while moving beyond identifying goals to achieving them.

Strategy as discourse and logical action draws attention to how all strategy relies on prediction. Pena (2001), using the work of Ricoeur (2008), stated that discourse is the way in which human beings say what they do. Professionals need to understand that strategy is in itself a discourse of action. When a strategy is stated in a logical manner and explains what will be done, why it will be done, what will motivate publics to act in desired ways and with what means and for what purpose, it moves beyond intuition because meaning is articulated.

Strategy as a realm of the environment reminds practitioners of the anticipative sense needed to gauge the environment. Strategies are, therefore, planned, anticipatory, and projective. However, the professional needs to scan the environment to determine how best to develop relationships with the different publics that will be affected by a strategy.

Developing and Writing Strategies

The use of the strategy in economic and business areas has diverse antecedents, but experts agree with Peter Drucker's introduction to his book *The practice of management* (1954). The concept of strategic decision makes explicit the relationship of business policies to the setting of objectives, the definition of real and possible actions, the optimization of factors, and the forecast of micro and macro economic environments (Levitt, 1960; Chandler, 1962; Ansoff, 1965)

Communication strategies are developed from the same concept of strategic decision, specified in a planned communication with intention, objectives, and duly justified actions. These strategic decisions in communication are based on research and on a permanent evaluation of the actions that involve the organization with its stakeholders. A contemporary approach to public relations is strategic, and most practitioners see themselves as strategic communicators (Smith, 2013).

Strategic management, and its application in strategic communication, requires the development of four phases. Different public relations authors have written about the application of these phases, summarized in acronyms that complement each other. Smith (2013) summarized these contributions in RACE (research, action, communication, evaluation), introduced by Marston (1963); ROPE (research, objectives, programming, evaluation), presented by Hendrix and Hayes (2009); and RAISE (research, adaptation, implementation strategy, evaluation) (Kendall, 1997). Other authors, such as Kelly (2001) and Crifasi (2000), each introduce a fifth step in ROPES (research, objectives, strategy, program, evaluation stewardship) and ROSIE (research, objectives, strategy, implementation, evaluation), respectively.

The strategic management process refers to the methods by which strategies are derived and consists of different phases or steps. These phases are interactive and do not necessarily always occur in the order presented below.

Phase 1: Research and Environmental Analysis

The first phase in which all these authors and their models coincide is in the research and analysis stage. With the investigation, the documentation begins to enable knowledge and understanding of the situation that requires strategic decisions. This first phase R. D. Smith (2013) calls formative research and he suggests distributing it in three steps: analyzing the situation, analyzing the organization, and analyzing the publics.

The information required for this phase can be obtained by applying primary research using new and original information generated by quantitative and qualitative means. Also, some authors such as Wilcox, Cameron, and Reber (2015) suggest taking secondary research into account: techniques from archival research in an organization's files to reference books, computer databases, online searches, and digital analytics of websites and social media platforms.

According to Narayanan and Fahey (1987), environmental analysis consists of four analytical stages: scanning to detect warning signals; monitoring to gather and interpret sufficient data on trends to discern patterns; forecasting future directions of changes; and assessing current and future changes with regard to their implications for the organization.

Although an organization cannot directly influence forces in the societal environment, it can collect information on stakeholders, events, and issues that are occurring, feed that information into the strategic management process, and anticipate issues and trends which will help it buffer threats and take advantage of opportunities. Environmental analysis can therefore be seen as the linking pin between the organization and the stakeholder environment (Carroll, 1996).

Phase 2: Strategic Thinking and Strategic Decisions

In the second phase, there is a concentration on reflexive and analytical thinking, which leads to identifying possible scenarios and anticipating results. Costa (2001) identified this as an anticipatory thought that establishes a frame of reference on which to build a discourse and a logic of action. This phase specifies the strategic thinking and strategic decisions supported by analytical and determined consideration of measurable and controllable actions that impact the previous environmental analysis.

Clear statements express the principles, the value of the decisions, and the perceptions of the determinants and scopes that are required for the strategy to be successful. Strategic decisions in communication necessarily involve the proper construction of messages that will determine trust and credibility. In this phase, then, the discourse that contains the philosophical principles of the organization and its position in relation to the actions to be carried out is defined.

With strategic decisions, communication principles must first be defined. These principles will require the professional to develop a philosophical and ethical position that also supports the values of the organization. Once the professional has established these principles and values, objectives and messaging can be written to elicit a public response. It is necessary for the professional to write each tactical and promotional piece so that it reflects the shared meaning of the communication principles and so that it will guide the strategy. An example can be taken from the case discussed and recommended for reading later in this chapter: the public relations and communication strategy for the multisectoral Strategic Plans of the North and South of the Aburrá Valley (Suárez, 2009a; and to complement the same case, Suárez, 2009b). The guiding communication principles which produced a successful strategy were the following:

- Transparency in communication processes guarantees the natural reflection of the actions that are developed.
- Coherence is the management of communication so that what is said is also done.
- Cohesion is the integration of all parties to achieve the proposed objectives.
- Trust is the most essential value for relationships to be established between the representatives of organizations and their publics so that members of the publics become involved.

After defining the communication principles, the professional must identify target publics and determine how to involve them in the process so that the strategy is successful. The common characteristics of the members of each public might be considered to develop a consistent and unifying message. By doing so, even latent publics could become active ones when they identify with the messaging.

This stage also indicates the establishment and the prioritization of goals. Often a politically charged process, goal formulation involves the personal values, perceptions, attitudes, and power of the managers and owners involved in the strategic management process. Although economic or financial goals usually dominate the goal formulation process, it is becoming increasingly clear that economic and social goals are not necessarily at odds with each other – rather, they can be reconciled so that the organization's as well as the stakeholders' best interests are simultaneously served. Typical areas in which social goals might be set include affirmative action, consumer product safety, occupational safety, corporate philanthropy, and environmental protection (Chrisman & Carroll, 1984).

Mintzberg (1994) and Robert (1997) maintain that strategic thinking is not the same as strategic planning. Strategic thinking is the process used by the organization's management to set direction and articulate their vision, that is, to think through the qualitative aspects of the business (the opinions, judgments, even feelings of stakeholders) and the environment it faces.

According to Andrews (1987), four major determinants of the strategy formulation decision are the identification and appraisal of strengths and weaknesses (what can be done); opportunities and threats in the environment (what might be done); personal values and aspirations of management (what they want to do); and acknowledged obligations to society (what ought to be done).

Strategic thinking reviews and questions the direction of the business, producing a profile that can be used to determine which areas will receive more or less emphasis – it is both introspective and externally focused (Robert, 1997). Strategic decisions produce a framework for the strategic and operational plans and attempt to determine what the organization should look like, that is, the strategy. Strategic thinking is problem-solving in unstructured situations, being able to recognize changing situations. Most important, it involves selecting the right problems to solve (Digman, 1990).

Phase 3: Strategic Actions Plan
In this phase, decisions become actions. These actions are communicative and interactive and are organized according to the logic already defined. They are formulated in communication plans, programs, and projects that impact the relationships of the actors and groups involved in the situation for intervention, and contain objectives, tactics, resources, and control.

The strategic objectives spell out actions that are accompanied by responsible compliance times and, in turn, satisfactory response actions for the development of the entire strategy. The form, style, and channels identified for presenting that message to the groups involved in the situation are part of this phase because they operationalize the appropriate treatment during implementation. Therefore, the content of strategic planning is explained in relation to the type or types of public, the background of that relationship, and the future perspective involving them.

For Smith (2013), the selection of tactics in a communication strategy is grouped into four categories: face-to-face communication, organizational media (controlled media), news media (uncontrolled media), and advertising and promotional media (another form of controlled media). For Wilcox et al. (2015), it is necessary to determine in detail the time, the sequence, and the budget, in order to correctly allocate the resources as progress is made in the logic of strategic action indicated.

The third phase, then, focuses on the planning of the strategic decisions in alignment with the message and logic raised in the previous phases, and the operability of controllable tactics and techniques, but with an awareness of any need to adapt unforeseen circumstances to the defined plan, so that the achievement of the strategic objectives is on target.

The different takes on strategic planning summarized in the acronyms RACE (Marston, 1963), ROPE (Hendrix & Hayes, 2009), RAISE (Kendall, 1997), ROPES (Kelly, 2001), and ROSIE

(Crifasi, 2000) differ in the denomination of the second and third phases in the formulation of communication strategies; however, in the end, their contributions are focused on indicating that it is necessary to make explicit the actions, procedures, and those responsible through a program that indicates the times of implementation of the tactics, administers the resources, and allows control and the necessary adjustments during its application.

Strategic planning is not a means to create strategy, but rather to operationalize strategies already created by other means (Wheeler & Sillanpää, 1997). It is therefore no substitute for strategic thinking, but formalizes and operationalizes the strategy process. The chosen strategy is created for each division or business; the result is a strategic, long-range master plan which integrates the activities of the organization and specifies the timetable for the completion of each stage. Strategic planning puts the strategy into practice (Robert, 1997), helping to choose how to get there.

In the implementation phase, the strategy is turned into reality by means of more detailed and shorter-term plans and schedules at progressively lower operating levels (Digman, 1990). Operational planning allocates tasks to specific existing facilities to achieve particular objectives in each planning period. Operational or action plans incorporate a number of elements (Pearce & Robinson, 1997):

- specific functional tactics (actions/activities), to be undertaken in the next week, month, or quarter;
- key routine, but unique, activities identified and undertaken by each function, such as marketing or corporate communication or human resources, that help to build a sustainable competitive advantage;
- one or more specific, immediate (short-term) objectives or targets for each tactic to be identified as outcomes;
- a clear time frame for completion;
- accountability, by identifying persons responsible for each action in the plan.

In the control phase, management seeks to ensure that the organization stays on track and achieves its goals and strategies.

Phase 4: Strategic Evaluation

In the processes of strategic planning, evaluation is the last phase. However, strategic evaluation must be constant, overarching, and dynamic. The evaluation is nourished by the enunciation of strategic objectives because they determine the changes; that is, what actions and results will indicate the success of the decisions made. Also, the process of tactical operation, the implementation of the programs, and executions of actions are important for evaluation. Therefore, this phase spans formulation and strategic operation, requires consistency over time, and facilitates the balance of the entire process.

The evaluation is carried out at different times in the strategic approach to relationships and communicative actions, and provides indicators, decisions, and actions to meet the different needs outlined in those plans, projects, and campaigns. As background, Grunig and Hunt (1984), Pavlik (1999), and Dozier (1984) have contributed important considerations on formative and evaluative or summative evaluations. Some Ibero-American authors have also contributed to the construction of this topic, such as Castillo and Álvarez (2015) and Massoni (2013).

Castillo and Álvarez (2015) proposed a comprehensive measurement and evaluation model structured in three phases: strategic, tactical, and operational. In the strategic evaluation phase, measurement activities are concentrated on those that determine the organizational management model, the selection and definition of organizational objectives, and specifically, the definition of strategic communication objectives. In a second phase, the tactic focuses on variables of interest to be evaluated in accordance with the outcome objectives. It also includes the determination of the dimensions and indicators to be measured of the variables and observable and verifiable items. In the operative phase, the model specializes in establishing measurement levels and techniques, as well as the analysis and interpretation of results and the elaboration of indexes. This phase ends with the design of the reports and their presentation, which will feed new strategic decisions.

With the advance of this millennium, new forms of measurement have arrived to inform these perspectives of communication auditing, and one has been developed by Almansa and Castillo (2005), who proposed models, techniques, and variables for measuring image exposure, reputation, and messages on digital media.

In Argentina, Sandra Massoni (2013) designed a strategy model based on communication as a cultural device. She is one of the Latin American scholars who has developed a methodology applied to the Global South. In this model, strategy is conceived as a multidimensional process that constitutes the direction of sociocultural changes. The basic characteristics of this model are the following:

1) It identifies a priority problem and the communication process that will generate a cognitive transformation in the understanding of the institutional objectives and the context.
2) It is a framework of coordinated participation among the actors involved in the problem.
3) It promotes medium- and long-term changes, planned by knowledge and process objectives.
4) It allows the management of innovations by tracing product goals, actions, programs, projects, and strategies.
5) It fosters self-assessment processes by stages and at different levels of management, so results and corrective actions can be adjusted based on the complexity of the issue.

Example: Strategic Plans of the North and South of the Aburrá Valley in Medellín, Colombia

To exemplify what is meant by strategy building, we can examine the communication and public relations strategy implemented by the multisectoral alliance called Strategic Plans of the North and South of the Aburrá Valley, in Medellín, Colombia. In this example, the target publics who were recipients of the public communication strategy used by the multisectoral alliance were classified into three main levels:

• Level 1: Residents of the area: at this level, the inhabitants of the area comprised of families, the elderly, adults, young people, and children were brought together, with communication products for broad dissemination and messages of an informative and persuasive nature to achieve a favorable attitude toward the general activities of the alliance.
• Level 2: Strategic actors: this level included community artistic, environmental, civic, and political organizations, citizen representatives, administrators and officials, municipal planning councils, entrepreneurs from each municipality and the various sectors of the economy, and mass media. These publics were necessary in order to influence others and help garner favorable attitudes about the activities of the alliance.
• Level 3: At this level, people and institutions responsible for administrative and regulatory decisions of the 10 municipalities of the Aburrá Valley (such as the Metropolitan Board) were integrated to ensure the execution and continuity of the projects. This public was important because of its impact upon guidelines and conventions.

Once priority publics are identified, and the components of the strategy are specified and grand tactics that integrate actions to achieve strategies are employed. In the case of the public relations strategy for the Strategic Plans of the North and South of the Aburrá Valley, in Colombia, the tactical components were visual identity, public information, discussion and conciliation processes, and lobbying.

In the visual identity component, the visual element reflecting the alliance was developed. This logo was used in all promotional pieces such as print and digital, stationery and graphic products, book dividers, posters, and billboards. The design and development of this visual identity allowed professionals to use these communication products in all the phases of the process because there was a coherent visual strategy at work.

The public information component included information management. Information meant for mass media and alternative media was disseminated at strategic intervals so the public was aware of the alliance's work and progress. Information was also shared with the public through newsletters, websites, and audiovisual products, further allowing the professionals to release information in planned and strategic ways.

The third tactical component was the hosting of events, workshops, forums, and meetings to foster two-way communication. All constituents were invited to join these planned events and were encouraged to listen and also to express their opinions. The exchange of information in such a personalized and direct manner helped to build relationships among constituents, and also made it easier for people to meet in the future.

Finally, lobbying, defined here as strategic relations and communication actions to influence legislative or executive decisions, focused on the action of influence in the municipal and metropolitan representation bodies, the formulation of interinstitutional documents resulting from the deliberations, and the sharing of these initiatives with citizens.

Digital communication, the immediacy of information, and mobile devices demand a strategic perspective that adapts to a complex, diverse, and connected world. Capabilities for strategic analysis and action must be constantly developed and updated.

How, When, and Why Is Theory Applied to Strategy?

In the modern world, strategies determine decisions, the optimization of resources, and the commitment of publics such as community members, clients, interest groups, and members of the organization. In today's world, globalization, technological hyperconnectivity, and transnationalism mean people are even more connected and strategies have a greater reach.

In a public relations strategy, there is a plurality of voices, publics, communication spheres, and influences. However, to be successful, a strategy must have a message that is integrated, united, and presented in a coherent manner without the space or medium being used for interfering with its purpose (Pena, 2001).

When a public relations strategy is defined, one of the first acts of agreement between the work team is the definition of the goals to be achieved as a result of this strategic action. To be truly strategic, it is necessary to consider a series of variables that mark the context of the communicative action, much as a theory would.

For a responsible professional, one priority is to establish the values or principles that will guide the strategic action. Of course, the tactics that will be employed will also have to fit within this orientation. No communication product or event exists by itself; instead, each item has a distinct purpose and is expected to have an effect on the behavior of the target audiences. Theory can be used to help guide strategies and attain desired results.

Examples of Theory Used with Strategy

The NO Strategy

On October 2, 2016, the president of Colombia, Juan Manuel Santos, asked the voting public to endorse the peace agreement signed with the Revolutionary Armed Forces of Colombia (FARC) in Havana, Cuba in September 2016, after four years of negotiation. The FARC was established as an insurgent movement against the government and the political and economic elites of Colombia in 1964 (Botero, 2017, p. 370). It demanded agrarian reforms and land rights for peasants. The armed confrontations lasted five decades and affected more than six million victims, including more than 600,000 deaths, in addition to many kidnappings and attacks across the country (Semana, 2014).

The Colombian government announced a plebiscite for citizens to vote Yes or No to the final agreement to end the conflict with the guerrilla group, planned in the midst of a polarized environment in this South American country. Campaigns in favor and against the peace agreement took place. The campaign to motivate voters to support the peace agreement brought together an alliance of political parties and movements that were also supportive of Santos's government. In public declarations, a representative of the Colombia Yes to Peace foundation, Mauricio Vega, agreed that this organization would focus its messaging on requesting the pardon of Rodrigo Londoño (a top FARC leader) after the signing of the final peace agreement. This foundation would also reinforce the campaign for Yes with overwhelming support from the international community for the peace process (M. Vega, quoted in *El Tiempo*, September 28, 2016). To position this message, Colombia Yes for Peace used traditional mass media such as radio and television, as well as town halls and meetings where community members in the different regions of the country had direct contact with the leaders of the various political groups. "Our strategy will focus on radio and television commercials, and on Sunday we will receive the results in an event to which the President of the Republic and the heads of all political parties, among others, are invited" (M. Vega, quoted in *El Tiempo*, September 28, 2016).

However, there were also people who did not support the rush to Yes for the peace agreement. The movement promoting the No was led by former president (2002–2010) Álvaro Uribe Vélez and his followers. Uribe Vélez led an opposition movement against the Santos administration, and therefore did everything possible for the peace agreement to fail. In an interview offered to the newspaper *La República*, the director of the campaign in support of No in the plebiscite for peace explained the strategic thinking behind the campaign and how it was developed in consultation with Colombian citizens.

The Campaign for No concentrated its strategic messaging on motivating citizens to demonstrate their disdain for the signing of the peace agreement. The campaign organizers motivated this outrage by bringing up sensitive issues such as impunity, eligibility, and tax reform. They then worked to reach segments of the publics via specific mass and social media and used framing theory, in an unethical way, to convey a message of indignation by playing up sensitive issues. Using social media, the Campaign for No had an even broader reach. Due to the expansive power of social media, the movement for No and its supporters multiplied the power and influence of their messages, regardless of the truth of the information they delivered. According to the testimony of Juan Carlos Vélez, director of the movement for No, this strategy can be summarized as follows:

> We discovered the viral power of social networks. For example, in a visit to Apartadó, Antioquia, a councilman passed me an image of Santos and "Timochenko" [leader of the FARC] with a message about why the guerrillas would be given money if the country was

in the pot [bankrupt]. I published it on my Facebook and last Saturday had 130,000 shares with a reach of six million people.

We made an initial stage of reactivating the entire structure of the Democratic Center in the regions by distributing leaflets in the cities. Some strategists from Panama and Brazil told us that the strategy was to stop explaining the agreement to focus the message on the outrage. In broadcasters of medium and high strata we rely on non-impunity, eligibility and tax reform, while in low-income stations we focus on subsidies. Regarding the segment in each region we use their respective accents. On the coast we sing the message that we were going to become Venezuela. And here he did not win without paying a peso. In eight municipalities of Cauca we passed radio propaganda on Saturday night focused on victims. (J. C. Vélez, quoted in *El Colombiano*, October 6, 2016, in translation)

The referendum results were very close and the strategy using framing theory unethically won in the polls by a small margin (0.43%). The message of outrage, strategically framed in specifically targeted mass media and especially in social media, garnered the desired effect of tipping the vote toward the option of No. President Santos did not need to call for a plebiscite, he did it as an expression of democratic participation. The results were a total surprise for the national and international community because it was defeated by a manipulative campaign led by a populist movement with a conservative orientation or center-right perspective. However, we can not say whether the results are good or bad for Colombia. The fact is that the peace agreement was signed. The future may change the direction of this historical moment because in the second round of the presidential election of June 17, 2018, the candidate of the Democratic Center won and may challenge aspects of the agreement.

Although the margin of difference between the No (50.21%) and the Yes (49.78%) was minimal (53,894 votes) (Registraduría Nacional de Colombia, 2016), this strategy became a political phenomenon for three reasons.

First, the results of this referendum vote did not support the peace accords signed a few days earlier by the Colombian government and FARC. Second, the statements of the director of the Campaign for No, who explained in an interview with the newspaper *La República* the details of the strategy, were scandalous. It was only three days after the elections and the director implied his manipulation of information, misrepresented the content of the peace agreement, and used social media to help false information about sensitive issues compete with value judgments. The political Democratic Center disavowed the head of the Campaign for No and he was forced to resign, but not before retracting his statements, which put sponsors, business-people, and political leaders in a compromising situation (Sarmiento, 2017; El Colombiano, 2016). Third, more than half of voters, 62.56%, abstained from voting in the referendum. Only 37.4% of Colombians eligible to vote went to the polls to affirm or withhold their approval of the peace agreement meant to end an internal conflict of more than 50 years. This example is a cautionary tale about how strategy and theory can be used by unethical professionals to manipulate the public.

The Green Tunnel Strategy

Members of a community group in the municipality of Envigado in the Metropolitan Area of the Aburrá Valley, in Colombia, became quite active when they learned of the imminent felling of more than two hundred trees along an environmental boulevard in an urban area. The trees were to be removed in order to build a bus system of medium capacity called Metroplús. Spontaneously, the young people of the community who opposed the decision of the mayor of Envigado to remove the trees, designed communication messages for different publics through social media and called for direct and public action, such as stakeholder meetings, on the boulevard surrounded by the trees.

The communication strategy used to mobilize members of the public focused on ensuring the civil rights of the citizens of the community, generating enthusiasm for citizen participation, and gathering favorable public opinion behind the idea that people had the right to a city with an environmental heritage. In a few months, what had been spontaneous tactics consolidated to form a public relations strategy for environmental concerns that even reached the neighboring municipalities.

Using agenda-setting theory, the organizers of this movement managed their messages in the news media through meetings with leaders of environmental movements, media tours with experts, researchers, and academics from the leading universities of the city, meetings with representatives of the municipal government, and social networks such as Facebook and Twitter to disseminate information, issue calls for marches, and gather feedback from stakeholders.

The media's coverage of the messages of the organizers gave the campaign third-party endorsement. The legitimacy of the message was further enhanced by international events such as the Colombia Moda fashion week and cultural shows, which allowed it to become part of the national agenda. In this way, municipal governments were informed of citizen dissatisfaction with unilateral decisions that ignored the importance of a road infrastructure designed to create a corridor of trees. This green tunnel was meant to keep citizens and the environment healthy. The unilateral decision by the local government to fell the trees threatened the right of citizens to a healthy environment and the protection of an environmental resource, which bordered the municipalities. In the end, the local government and the Metro and Metroplús transportation companies had to agree to a design review of their plans, as well as to holding meetings with citizens so they could have a say in the proposals and voice any concerns or disagreements. In addition, there was a legal ruling which called for a review of the environmental authorizations for logging. The tactics and messaging used in this campaign targeted emotions as well as the importance of the preservation of the trees as part of the cultural assets of the inhabitants of the Envigado municipality, which built solidarity with the citizens of Medellín.

Thanks to the precautionary measure taken and the popular action provoked by the Colectivo Túnel Verde with the help of the legal clinic of the University of Medellín, a legal ruling to stop the construction of the Metroplús line pending further consultation with the community came out in favor of the social movement, but above all in favor of the citizenry. The efforts of volunteers to collect more than twenty thousand physical signatures, as well as the resolve, desires, donations, and other resources of volunteers and members of the Green Tunnel Collective demonstrate how strategy and theory can help a reactive and spontaneous response become an example of a campaign based in consistency and coherence which helped to build citizen–government relations while defending citizens' rights to an environmentally green and healthy city.

The Rural Strategy of Carmen de Viboral

In the Department of Antioquia, in Colombia, the government of the municipality of El Carmen de Viboral states that the development of the territory takes place with community participation. The municipality's belief in the "common benefit" helps create conditions of equity in both the urban and the rural areas of the territory. The local government uses tools such as a multidimensional approach to frame development and generate trust in communities, which allows a dynamic environment for inhabitants. The framework of the community is built around developing, training, acquiring, and sharing values that put peaceful coexistence in the forefront of decisions (El Carmen de Viboral, 2016). To foster these ideals, the 2016–2019 municipal development plan has six strategic goals:

- El Carmen de Viboral, territory of life and peace;
- citizen security and well-being;
- building identity through the social;
- infrastructure for equity;
- agricultural and environmental sustainability;
- modern institutionalization, a government for people.

The projects undertaken by each government office follow these strategic guidelines. The third line, "building identity through the social," has been instrumental in strengthening the culture of the area because it acts as the axis of the social dynamics of the municipality. In other words, the strategic approach taken by the municipality is grounded in relationship management theory. Factors such as trust, satisfaction, and commitment are developed communally, through effective access to basic community needs such as health, education, sports and recreation, housing, and employment.

In order to build better relationships with the youth of the area, the municipal administration of Carmen de Viboral has been reaching out to teens. Government officials want to build two-way communication between themselves and the local youth to gain an understanding of teens' personal health decisions and behaviors, as well as family life. It is hoped that with this understanding, municipal officials can help young people to become advocates for their health and educational concerns. By building trust with these constituents, the government officials want to challenge and encourage teens to exercise their right to be heard, to be present in participatory processes, to engage in citizenship, and become the main actors in the human and social development of their local municipalities.

In the first semester of 2016, an unusual event occurred in one of the schools of the municipality. Two high school students were found consuming psychoactive substances inside the educational buildings. To address the situation, a meeting was held between the Ministry of Health, the Ministry of Education, and the directors of educational institutions, in order to find solutions to mitigate and put an end to the problem. While investigating the occurrence, it was discovered that mental health prevention actions and information had not been distributed or implemented in either of the two municipal institutions since 2011. With this knowledge, a strategic public relations campaign was designed to increase the knowledge of adolescent students about the effects of drug use. Both parents and educators were brought together to raise awareness about drug use among local teens. By bringing these constituents together, trust was enhanced and relationships were forged.

The primary strategy of the program used relationship management theory as well as dialogue theory. Activities for teens to enjoy after school were developed. Tactics such as workshops and conferences were employed to foster discussion and communication among the key publics. Based on these conversations, several outreach programs were developed. The most successful of these activities was a theater contest. Teens were challenged to develop plays and skits to reinforce the lessons they learned about abuse of drugs and psychotropic substances. These performances were evaluated by a panel of experts from the municipality's Institute of Culture. Through dialogue and relationship building, not only did government and educational leaders see a change in the attitudes and behaviors displayed by young people about using drugs, but it also led to opening more discussion about other important topics affecting adolescents, such as parents, other family members, teachers, and others in the community struggling with addiction.

Major Topics/Questions Needing to Be Addressed by Public Relations Theorists Working in Strategy

Strategy is a word that has become common. However, is understanding of strategy as common among professionals? In today's world there is immediacy of information, hyperconnectivity, and increasingly active audiences, and these generate critical situations deserving of strategic treatment. But how to be strategic in the face of a postmodern world that implies immediate reactions, attention to the constant evolution of the market, and adaptation to changes in traditional values and habits is a critical question yet to answered.

In the academy, the processes to develop strategies are taught, and the phases and actions that contribute to making decisions and carrying out strategic actions are presented. However, in professional life, multiple political, economic, and cultural experiences test the mastery of these phases and the strategic capacity that must be applied with less time and with great financial and social consequences. Another question that needs to be addressed is how academics can better prepare professionals to face strategic decisions in an economically unstable reality, within the context of a society with constant and diverse social conflicts.

Strategy can also be used for the good of society. For example, there is now an urgent need to develop policies and resources to guide the sustainability of the planet and its resources. Public relations should take a leading role in this endeavor. Therefore academics and professionals should work together to create public relations strategies which can be used to create political, economic, and cultural strategies for a sustainable planet. Such an alliance among the educational sector, the governmental and legislative sector, and the industrial, economic, and financial sector must also consider diversity and intercultural sensitivities. Such strategic decisions will require relationships between society and special interest groups. Researchers, teachers, professionals and students will become indispensable actors in a strategic public relations alliance for sustainability.

Suggested Case to Explore to Demonstrate Theory at Work with Strategy

"Alliances based on communication strategies," published in *Anagramas* (Suárez, 2009a), and "Building multi-sector partnerships for progress with strategic, participatory communication: A case study from Colombia" (Molleda, Martínez, & Suárez, 2008) are two articles that will help you to better understand how theory and strategy go hand-in-hand. By examining the public relations and communication strategy used by the multisectoral alliance called Strategic Plans of the North and the South of the Aburrá Valley, in Colombia, discussed earlier, you will have a better understanding of how communication links to culture.

In addition to public relations and communication strategy, this campaign also included an advertising component that was also positively acknowledged. All the tactical elements, including advertisements, helped to build awareness and identity through the use of consistent image and design components. The publication of information in mass media about the advances of the alliance highlighted both information about the alliance's effort, and also the strategy behind releasing information at key moments in the process. In addition, all the communicative acts encouraged understanding and enhanced trust. The evaluation of the public relations and communication strategy employed by the alliance gives the reader insight into assessment. One aspect of the campaign that needed improvement was the communication of results. Since the project involved diverse public and allied institutions, informative coverage in the community was in high demand, but it was not accomplished. Overall the campaign was a highly representative process, which made the delivery of information costly; however, broad participation was achieved because people were knowledgeable about the project and they were willing to combine their resources to build relationships.

Discussion Questions

1 What are the characteristics of strategic thinking?

2 What steps are included in strategic planning in public relations?

3 How important is Alberto Pena's "shared framework" for the success of strategic planning?

4 Can you reduce the number of phases of strategic planning in public relations? How would it be done?

5 What skills do you recognize as a professional for acquiring strategic competence?

Suggested Readings

Some Theorists and Publications Frequently Cited in Latin America

Castillo, A., & Álvarez, A. (2015). *Evaluación en comunicación estratégica*. Madrid: McGraw-Hill.

Massoni, S. (2013). *Metodologías de la comunicación estratégica: Del inventario al encuentro sociocultural*. Rosario, Argentina: Homo Sapiens.

Pascuali, A. (2011). *La comunicación mundo: Releer un mundo transfigurado por las comunicaciones*. Manganeses de la Lampreana, Spain: Comunicación Social.

Pérez, R. (2001). *Estrategias de comunicación*. Barcelona: Ariel.

Preciado, A. (2012) *Comunicación directiva: Influencia del estilo de dirección en la comunicación interna de las organizaciones*. Medellín, Colombia: Universidad Pontifica Bolivariana.

Preciado, A., Guzmán, H., & Losada, J. C. (2013). *Usos y prácticas de comunicación estratégica en las organizaciones*. Chía, Colombia: Ecoe.

Rebeil Corella, M. A. (2006). *Comunicación estratégica en las organizaciones*. Huixquilucan de Degollado, Mexico: Trillas.

Ricoeur, P. (2008). *From text to action*. New York: Continuum.

Tironi, E., & Cavallo, A. (2008). *Comunicación estratégica: Vivir en un mundo de señales*. Santiago, Chile: Taurus.

Some Theorists and Publications Frequently Cited in the United States

Austin, E. W., & Pinkleton, B. E. (2006). *Strategic public relations management: Planning and managing effective communication programs* (2nd ed.). Mahwah, NJ: Lawrence Erlbaum.

Berlo, D. (1960). *The process of communication: An introduction to theory and practice*. San Francisco: Rinehart.

Galvis, C., & Suárez, A. M. (2008). *Comunicación pública, organizacional y ciudadana: Comunicación e identidad*. Medellín, Colombia: Sello, Universidad de Medellin.

Grunig, J. E., & Hunt, T. (1984). *Managing public relations*. New York: Holt, Rinehart, and Winston.

Johnston, D. D. (1994). *The art and science of persuasion*. Boston: McGraw-Hill.

Parkinson, M., & Ekachai, D. G. (2005). *International and intercultural public relations: A campaign case approach*. Boston: Allyn and Bacon.

Smith, R. (2013). *Strategic planning for public relations* (4th ed.). New York: Routledge.

Watson, T., & Noble, P. (2007). *Evaluating public relations: A systematic approach* (7th ed.). Newbury Park, CA: Sage.

Wilson, L. (2000). *Strategic program planning for effective public relations campaigns* (3rd ed.). Dubuque, IA: Kendall-Hunt.

References

Almansa, A., & Castillo, A. (2005). Relaciones públicas y tecnología de la comunicación: Análisis de los sitios de prensa virtuales. *Organicom*, 2(3), 132–149.

Alonso, M. (2001). 2500 años de estrategia: El paradigma militar. In R. Pérez, *Estrategias de comunicación*. Barcelona: Ariel.

Andrews, K. R. (1987). *The concept of corporate strategy* (3rd ed.). Homewood, IL: Richard D. Irwin.

Ansoff, I. (1965). *Corporate strategy*. New York: McGraw-Hill.

Botero, S. (2017). El plebiscito y los desafíos políticos de consolidar la paz negociada en Colombia. *Revista de Ciencia Política*, 37(2), 369–388.

Carroll, A. B. (1996). *Business and society: Ethics and stakeholder management* (3rd ed.). Cincinnati, OH: South-Western College.

Castillo, A., & Álvarez, A. (2015). *Evaluación en comunicación estratégica*. Madrid: McGraw-Hill.

Chandler, A. D., Jr. (1962). *Strategy and structure: Chapters in the history of the industrial enterprise*. Cambridge, MA: MIT Press.

Chrisman, J. J., & Carroll, A. B. (1984). Corporate responsibility: Reconciling economic and social goals. *Sloan Management Review* (Winter), 59–65.

Costa, P.-O. (2001). Estrategias de comunicación: El esquema director. In R. Pérez, *Estrategias de comunicación*. Barcelona: Ariel.

Crifasi, S. C. (2000). Everything´s coming up ROSIE. *Public Relations Tactics*, 7(9).

Digman, L. A. (1990). *Strategic management* (2nd ed.). Homewood, IL: BPI/Irwin.

Dozier, D. (1984). Program evaluation and the roles of practitioners. *Public Relations Review*, 10(2), 13–21.

Drucker, P. (1954). *The practice of management*. New York: Harper and Row.

El Carmen de Viboral. (2016). *Plan de desarrollo municipal, 2016–2019*. Retrieved from https://issuu.com/diegomontoyadmproducciones/docs/plan_de_desarrollo_municipal

El Colombiano (2016, October 6). "Estábamos buscando que la gente saliera a votar verraca": Juan C. Vélez. *La República*. Retrieved from the website of *El Colombiano*: www.elcolombiano.com/colombia/acuerdos-de-gobierno-y-farc/entrevista-a-juan-carlos-velez-sobre-la-estrategia-de-la-campana-del-no-en-el-plebiscito-CE5116400

El Tiempo (2016, September 28). *Campañas por el "Sí" y el "No" entran en la recta final*. Retrieved from the website of *El Tiempo*: https://www.eltiempo.com/politica/proceso-de-paz/plebiscito-por-la-paz-campanas-por-el-si-y-el-no-entran-en-la-recta-final-28392

Grunig, J. E., & Hunt, T. (1984). *Managing public relations*. New York: Holt, Rinehart, and Winston.

Hendrix, J., & Hayes, D. C. (2009). *Public relations cases* (8th ed.). Belmont, CA: Wadsworth.

Kelly, K. S. (2001). Stewardship: The fifth step in the public relations process. In R. I. Heath & G. M. Vasquez (Eds.), *Handbook of public relations* (pp. 279–290). Thousand Oaks, CA: Sage.

Kendall, R. (1997). *Public relations campaign strategies: Planning for implementation* (2nd ed.). New York: Addison-Wesley.

Ki, E., & Hon, L. C. (2007), Testing the linkages among the organization–public relationship and attitude and behavioral intention. *Journal of Public Relations Research, 19*(1), 1–23.

Kim, S. (2016). Strategic predisposition in communication management: Understanding organizational propensity towards bridging strategy. *Journal of Communication Management, 20*(3), 232–254.

Levitt, T. (1960). Marketing myopia. *Harvard Business Review, 38*(4), 45–56.

Lukaszewski, J. E. (2001). How to develop the mind of a strategist. *IABC Communication World, 18*(3), 13–15.

Marston, J. E. (1963). *The nature of public relations.* New York: McGraw-Hill.

Massoni, S. (2013). *Metodologías de la comunicación estratégica: Del inventario al encuentro sociocultural.* Rosario, Argentina: Homo Sapiens.

Metro de Medellín. (2018). *Cultura metro.* Retrieved from the website of Empresa Metro de Medellín: https://www.Metrodemedellin.gov.co/cultura-Metro

Mintzberg, H. (1994). *The rise and fall of strategic planning.* New York: Simon and Schuster.

Mintzberg, H., & Waters, J. (1983). The mind of the strategist(s). In S. Sivastra (Ed.), *The executive mind.* San Francisco: Jossey-Bass.

Molleda, J. C., Martínez, B., Jr., & Suárez, A. M. (2008). Building multi–sector partnerships for progress with strategic, participatory communication: A case study from Colombia. *Revista Anagramas, Rumbos y Sentidos de la Comunicación, 6*(12), 107–128. Retrieved from https://revistas.udem.edu.co/index.php/anagramas/issue/view/83

Narayanan, V. K., & Fahey, L. (1987). Environmental analysis for strategy formulation. In W. R. King & D. I. Cleland (Eds.), *Strategic planning and management handbook.* New York: Van Nostrand Reinhold.

Pavlik, J. (1999). *La investigación en relaciones públicas.* Barcelona: Gestión 2000.

Pearce, J. A., II, & Robinson, R. A. (1997). *Strategic management: Formulation, implementation, and control.* New York: McGraw-Hill.

Pena, A. (2001). Las dimensiones de la estrategia. In R. Pérez, *Estrategias de comunicación.* Barcelona: Ariel.

Pérez, R. (2001). *Estrategias de comunicación.* Barcelona: Ariel.

Ramírez, J. (2016, October 4). El No ha sido la campaña más barata y más efectiva de la historia. *Asuntos Legales.* Retrieved from https://www.asuntoslegales.com.co/actualidad/el-no-ha-sido-la-campana-mas-barata-y-mas-efectiva-de-la-historia-2427891

Registraduría Nacional de Colombia. (2016). *Boletín plebiscito octubre 2, 2016.* Consulted February 2, 2018, at https://elecciones.registraduria.gov.co/pre_plebis_2016/99PL/DPLZZZZZZZZZZZZZZZZZZ_L1.htm

Ricoeur, P. (2008). *From text to action.* New York: Continuum, 2008.

Robert, M. (1997). *Strategy pure and simple II* (rev. ed.). New York: McGraw-Hill.

Sarmiento, D. J. (2017, June 4). Centro democrático reitera que desautoriza las declaraciones de Juan Carlos Vélez sobre la campaña del NO. *La República.* Retrieved from https://www.larepublica.co/economia/centro-democratico-reitera-que-desautoriza-las-declaraciones-de-juan-carlos-velez-sobre-la-campana-del-no-2516911

Semana. (2014). *Seis millones de víctimas deja el conflicto en Colombia.* Retrieved from the website of *Semana*: https://www.semana.com/nacion/articulo/murio-hector-ulloa-don-chinche-uno-de-los-personajes-mas-queridos-de-la-television/585957

Shimizu, K. (2017). Senders bias: How can top managers' communication improve or not improve strategy implementation? *International Journal of Business Communication, 54,* 52–59.

Smith, R. D. (2013). *Strategic planning for public relations* (4th. ed.). New York: Routledge.

Steyn, B. (2003). From strategy to corporate communication strategy: A conceptualization. *Journal of Communication Management, 8*(2), 168–183.

Steyn, B. (2007). Contribution of public relations to organizational strategy. In E. L. Toth (Ed.), *The future of excellence in public relations and communication management: Challenges for the next generation* (pp. 137–172). Mahwah, NJ: Lawrence Erlbaum.

Suárez, A. M. (2009a). Alliances based on communication strategies. *Revista Anagramas, Rumbos y Sentidos de la Comunicación, 7*(14), 93–104. Retrieved from https://revistas.udem.edu.co/index.php/anagramas/issue/view/49

Suárez, A. M. (2009b). Estrategias basadas en comunicación. In *Comunicación pública, organizacional y ciudadana: Comunicación e Identidad.* Medellín, Colombia: Sello, Universidad de Medellin.

Tan, J., & Tan, D. (2005). Environment–strategy co-evolution and co-alignment: A staged model of Chinese SOEs under transition. *Strategic Management Journal, 26*(2), 141–157.

Werder, K. P., & Holtzhausen, D. (2009). An analysis of the influence of public relations department leadership style on public relations strategy use and effectiveness. *Journal of Public Relations Research, 2*(4), 404–427.

Wheeler, D., & Sillanpää, M. (1997). *The stakeholder corporation.* London: Pitman.

Wilcox, D. L., Cameron, G. T., & Reber, B. H. (2015). *Public relations: Strategies and tactics* (11th ed.). New York: Pearson.

Woodward, J. (1965). *Industrial organization: Theory and practice.* Oxford: Oxford University Press.

3

Crisis Communication, Risk Communication, and Issues Management

W. Timothy Coombs, Sherry J. Holladay, and Elina Tachkova

Public relations includes specialties that deal with crisis communication, risk communication, and issues management. Though separate areas, there are strong connections between these three specialties (Coombs, 2015). Risk is the key component of crisis preparation and mitigation, because a crisis is often the manifestation of a risk. Moreover, crisis events often require the use of risk communication. Proactive issues management can be driven by attempts to manage risks and avoid crises because issues emerge from risk. Effective crisis communication can help to avoid the need for issues management, while failed issues management can trigger a crisis. Because of the close connections between these three specialties, this chapter addresses all three.

Defining the Concepts: What Are Crisis Communication, Risk Communication, and Issues Management?

A critical element of theory is conceptual clarity. Chaffee (1991) emphasized the need for what he called concept explication. Part of concept explication is creating a conceptual definition that explains what a concept (or variable) means. Conceptual definitions can be created by identifying the essential elements or dimensions of a concept. Crisis communication and risk communication are concepts with a variety of definitions. Therefore, the conceptual definitions provided in this chapter will rely upon essential elements rather than specific definitions of the concepts.

Crisis and Communication

"Crisis" is an extremely broad term related to disruptions of some kind. For this chapter, we are focusing on organizational crises rather than disasters. Organizational crises refer to situations that affect the relationship between an organization and its stakeholders. An organizational crisis has three essential elements: (1) it involves the perceived violation of stakeholder expectations; (2) the perceived violation threatens to disrupt operations and/or seriously damage reputational assets; and (3) the perceived violations may pose a danger to stakeholders.

Crises are driven by the stakeholder perceptions of the situation. If stakeholders believe there is a problem with the organization, managers must consider that there is a crisis. Ignoring stakeholder concerns may further damage the organization–stakeholder relationship and other vital organizational outcomes (Coombs, 2015).

Public Relations Theory: Application and Understanding, First Edition. Edited by Brigitta R. Brunner.

A crisis will harm an organization in some way, but the extent of that harm is largely dependent on the crisis management efforts. Historically, crisis management was developed to address potential disruptions to operations, what can be termed operational crises. An industrial accident is an example of an operational crisis. Crisis management efforts can prevent an industrial accident from disrupting operations or limit the extent and duration of the disruption. Operational crises tend to be event based (e.g. accidents and product recalls) and pose some threat to the safety and security of stakeholders, such as employees, community members, and customers. The primary concern during an operational crisis is the safety and security of the stakeholders placed at risk by the crisis – the crisis victims (Coombs, 2015).

A crisis will harm organizational reputation in some manner. The crisis response can limit the amount and duration of damage inflicted on the organizational reputation. Reputational crises are situations where the dominant concern is the reputational harm created by the crisis (Sohn & Lariscy, 2014). Advertisements that offend segments of stakeholders, or firms irresponsibly sourcing raw materials are examples of reputational crises. While operational crises inflict reputational damage, the focus of the crisis response will be on the safety threat created by the operational crisis. Reputation crises allow for a more selfish response as managers can focus on protecting the organization's reputation from the dangers presented by the crisis. Moreover, reputational crises often are removed from specific events, and thus reflect the perceptual nature of crises. Managers must recognize a crisis is emerging and acknowledge the situation is a crisis – validate the perceptions of the stakeholders. Rather than being triggered by events, reputational crises frequently arise from revelations by management. For example, an explosion at a manufacturing facility is an event that most people will perceive as a crisis. In contrast, when some customers are offended by an advertisement, managers must realize that the concern constitutes a crisis (Coombs, 2014). The distinction between operational and reputational crises has implications for the application of various crisis communication theories.

Risk Communication

Risk communication has evolved from a simple, linear transmission model that focuses on understanding the technical aspects of risk to an interactive model that emphasizes the social understanding of risk (Heath & O'Hair, 2009; Lundgren & McMakin, 1998; Palenchar, 2005; Tansey & Rayner, 2009). Risk communication seeks to improve communication between risk bearers (those who might suffer the consequences from the risk) and those creating the risks. The essential elements of risk communication are (1) an interactive communication process that (2) seeks to increase awareness and response to a risk, (3) seeks to build tolerance for a risk, and (4) is premised on understanding and acknowledging perceptions of risk.

Risk communication should include some element of interactivity even if it is limited to gathering information about the affected stakeholders (risk bearers) prior to communicating with them. Ideally, the risk communication is more of a dialogue between the risk bearers and risk creators (Heath & O'Hair, 2009; Palenchar, 2005). Awareness remains a key goal in many crisis risk situations, coupled with a desire for risk bearers to take action based on this new information. For instance, firms want to make customers aware of a harmful product and to return or discontinue use of the product (Freberg, 2012). Government agencies want citizens to be aware of a flu outbreak and to take precautions against it. Another goal is to increase the risk tolerance of risk bearers. Chemical companies have abandoned seeking support for or acceptance of the risks they create because tolerance is a much more realistic outcome (Heath & O'Hair, 2009). Finally, risk communication should begin from the perspective of the risk bearer. Risk communicators must understand how risk bearers perceive the risk and why they hold those perceptions. The focus on the risk bearer assumes an active perceiver and is rooted in cultural theory and the work of Mary Douglas (Tansey & Rayner, 2009).

Issues Management

An issue is a point of contention between two or more parties. Issues management began as a systematic and effective means for business to influence public policy decisions (Chase, 1984). It has since evolved into to a broader set of communicative interventions designed to influence decisions. The essential elements of issues management are (1) a systematic set of communication interventions, (2) designed to influence decision-making, (3) predicated on issue identification and analysis, and (4) requires balancing the interests of organizations and stakeholders to facilitate mutually beneficial relationships. Issues management is a complex process that involves a variety of communicative interventions designed to influence people in various ways. The discussion of the catalytic model (also called the issue catalyst model) will illustrate this point.

The primary purpose of issues management is to influence decisions. Decisions can include policy decisions made by political actors and organizational decisions made by managers. At its core, issues management is about exercising influence. Issues management was intended to be proactive. A proactive approach requires managers to scan the environment in order to identify potential and existing issues that could affect the organization. Once an issue is identified, managers analyze the issue to determine if action is needed, and if so, what types of communicative actions to take. Issue identification and analysis guide the strategic focus of the issue management efforts. Finally, organizations cannot abuse their power positions to win issue battles without consideration for the effects on their relationships with other stakeholders. Heath and Palenchar (2009) caution that issues management efforts should "increase satisfaction between parties and foster mutual benefits" (p. 14). Abusing power in the issues management process can ferment long-term damage to relationships.

How and Why Are Crises, Risk Communication, and Issues Management of Concern to Public Relations?

Public relations should not be applied to every problem or concern in an organization. Public relations is frequently linked to building and maintaining favorable relationships with stakeholders (e.g. Ledingham, 2003). Relationships are more a means to an end rather than an end in themselves. This view is evident in the research that links relationships to other organizational outcomes such as reputation. Ultimately, a key purpose of public relations is to facilitate the achievement of the larger organizational objectives (Heath & Coombs, 2006). Crisis communication, risk communication, and issues management have applications to relationship management and achieving organizational objectives.

Crises create threats to reputations, purchase intentions, share price, and stakeholder relationships. Crisis communication is a form of strategic communication used to lessen the damage a crisis inflicts on an organization and to rebuild the organizational reputation and stakeholder relationships (Coombs & Holladay, 2015b). The crisis response strategies can serve to lessen the damage from a crisis and to repair the damage from a crisis. Crisis communication, as a form of public relations, helps to achieve key organizational objectives as well as to maintain relationships.

Risk communication is mandated by law in some industries. Moreover, there are situations where risk communication is essential to relationship management and achieving organizational objectives. Many societal problems are centered on risk. In turn, these societal problems create tensions between organizations and stakeholders. For example, if stakeholders are angered by a risk created by an organization and take actions against the organization, the resistance can damage relationships and reduce the ability to achieve organizational objectives. Risk communication provides a mechanism for reducing the uncertainty related to these problems. Risk communication is one of the ways by which public relations helps to create a fully functioning society (Heath, 2006).

Issues management is a means for influencing the organization's operating environment and organizational operations. Organizations can employ issues management to create more favorable operating environments that make it easier to achieve organizational objectives. Issues management allows managers to use various communicative strategies in attempts to influence governmental decision-making. Issues management can shape the operating environment by preventing restrictive government actions such as new regulations and by encouraging government actions beneficial for the organization such as deregulation (Crable & Vibbert, 1985). Heath (2005) warns organizations that abusing their position of power in issues management can damage relationships with stakeholders, and ultimately these actions come back to harm the organization.

Stakeholders also can use issues management to change organizational behaviors they deem to be irresponsible. By exposing irresponsible behaviors through various communication channels, stakeholders can leverage an organization into changing behaviors. Issues management can create a threat to the organizational–stakeholder relations and threaten organizational objectives, thereby pressuring an organization to change its behaviors. Consider how the Greenpeace Detox campaign changed the chemical use behaviors of most major apparel manufacturers by exposing how dangerous and irresponsible many of the chemicals in the supply chain were to society (Coombs, 2014). Issues management can be an agent of change for stakeholders.

Crisis communication, risk communication, and issues management are all variants of strategic communication. Each of the three utilize communication strategically (the how) to manage stakeholder relationships and achieve organizational objectives (the why).

How, When, and Why Is Theory Applied to Crisis Communication, Risk Communication, and Issues Management?

These three strategic communication functions typically are applied in either a proactive or a reactive fashion. Crisis communication, risk communication, and issues management can be used to anticipate or react to situations. Moreover, the three strategic communications functions are interlocking. Risk can create crises or be the reason issues management is necessary. Crises can raise awareness of a risk and give birth to an issue. Issues all have some level of risk and issues management efforts can span crises (Coombs, 2015; Jaques, 2017). This section separates the three to clarify the explanations with the realization that crisis communication, risk communication, and issues management are often inseparable.

Proactive Actions

Part of crisis communication is mitigation and preparation, and this phase is termed the pre-crisis phase. Crisis communication can be used before a crisis (when) to prepare organizations and stakeholders for when a crisis does occur (why). The how of precrisis communication involves a number of communication activities. Inside the organization, managers must create crisis communication plans and train crisis management teams. Managers must scan regularly for crisis risks and monitor any actions taken to mitigate those risks. Outside the organizations, stakeholders must be trained in how to prepare for a crisis. For instance, community members may need to learn how to shelter-in-place. The precrisis focus on risk illustrates how crisis and risk communication can overlap. Mitigation prevents a crisis from occurring and harming stakeholders and/or organizational assets. It facilitates both relationship management and organizational objective achievement.

Organizations have a need to educate people about emerging health, safety, and environmental risks. Chemical manufactures are mandated by law to engage in risk communication about their chemicals with the community. Government agencies frequently warn citizens about emerging health or safety threats. The risk communication involves creating awareness of the risk, educating people about the risk, and trying to persuade people to take action to limit their exposure to the risk. Risk communication seeks to keep people informed about risks and ways to protect themselves from the risk. This promotes public safety. Risk communication also may attempt to reduce the stakeholder outrage created by a risk.

Managers can create an issue that will work to their advantage. The catalytic model is devoted to the idea of creating rather than reacting to an issue (Crable & Vibbert, 1985). Managers can push for regulatory or legislative changes that will give their organization a competitive advantage. The various communication strategies identified in the catalytic model can be used to facilitate the creation of an issue, awareness of the issue, and support for the issue, and build pressure for a favorable policy decision. In a similar way, stakeholders can engage in issues management to define an organization's behavior as an issue of irresponsibility. Communication strategies can be used to define the behavior as irresponsible, create awareness of the irresponsible behavior, and pressure the organization to change the behavior. Returning to the Detox campaign, Greenpeace defined the use of a certain toxic chemical as irresponsible, used social media and in-store protests to make customers aware that H&M, a global retailer based in Sweden, was using the toxic chemical in its clothes, and eventually forced H&M to remove the chemical from its clothes – H&M detoxed (Coombs, 2014). This case illustrates how risk can be used to create an issue that threatens to become a reputational crisis (Coombs & Holladay, 2015a).

Reactive Actions

Mitigation is never 100%. Hence, organizations often need to respond to actual crises. Crises can be events or perceptions of a situation as problematic. When a crisis occurs, managers must act to protect both stakeholders and the organization from the ill-effects of the crisis. When a crisis creates a threat to public health and safety, the first task for crisis managers is to supply instructing and adjusting information to stakeholders. Instructing information helps people to protect themselves physically from a crisis, while adjusting information helps people to cope psychologically with a crisis.

Once instructing and adjusting information is provided, crisis managers can add reputation management strategies. Typical reputation management strategies in an operations crisis include an apology, compensation, and bolstering. An apology is when the organization accepts responsibility for a crisis and asks for forgiveness. Compensation is when stakeholders are offered money, goods, or services above reimbursements for costs incurred by the crisis. For example, covering medical costs would be part of adjusting information, while giving the victims an additional $5,000 would be compensation. Bolstering reminds stakeholders of past good works by the organization or praises those who have helped during the crisis.

Stakeholders expect organizations to address the concerns of victims. This expectation means the failure to provide instructing and adjusting information will intensify a crisis.

Showing concern can lessen anger toward an organization, while omitting instructing and adjusting information can increase anger. Anger motivates stakeholders to engage in negative behaviors toward the organization and erodes the organizational reputation. Instructing and adjusting information can limit the damage a crisis inflicts on the organization and its stakeholders. Apology, compensation, and bolstering communication strategies try to offset some of the negativity created by the crisis by adding positive organizational actions to the situation. Research supports the idea that adjusting information, apology, compensation, and bolstering can all benefit an organization during a crisis by limiting reputational damage, protecting purchase intentions, and reducing anger (Coombs, 2007; Ma & Zhan, 2016). Successful crisis communication can reduce the perceived risk associated with the organization and lessen the likelihood of the crisis spawning an issue. However, if stakeholders see a need for the government to regulate organizational behavior as a means of preventing similar crises in the future, stakeholders may initiate issue management to address perceived risks posed by organizational operations.

Risk managers may face situations where stakeholders are outraged by the risk. Although outrage often is caused by people overestimating the risk, the outrage exists and can be challenging to manage. Simply reporting the "correct estimation" of the risk, as determined by science experts, will not end outrage. Risk estimates by stakeholders are driven by perceptions, not by analytics. If people are worried about a risk, simply telling them the risk is low does not constitute effective risk communication. When people are outraged or concerned about a risk, managers must engage in a dialogue to identify and to validate those concerns. Through dialogue, risk managers seek to create tolerance of the risk by stakeholders and to build trust. If stakeholders tolerate the risk, they are less likely to oppose the organization. However, it is unlikely these stakeholders will support the organization. Tolerance simply creates quiescence. Stakeholder quiescence can aid achievement of organization objectives, while opposition can hinder those same efforts. For instance, if community members continually protest a manufacturing facility, the managers of the facility will find it more difficult, and perhaps even impossible, to achieve its desired outcomes. The reactive use of risk communication tries to limit the negative effect that risk can have on achieving organizational goals.

Issues management involves multiple actors seeking a variety of outcomes (Crable & Vibbert, 1985). It probably is more common for managers to be *reacting* to issues being managed by others than to be creating their own issues. An essential part of issues management is scanning for issues. When managers locate an emerging issue or encounter a prominent issue through scanning, their issues management effort is considered reactive. Once identified, various communication strategies can be used to prevent the issue from becoming policy or to change the nature of the final policy decision (Jones & Chase, 1979). The communication strategies for issues management include redefining the issue, questioning the legitimacy of an issue, and promoting an alternative policy solution option to the issue (Crable & Vibbert, 1985; Jones & Chase, 1979).

Examples of Theory Used during Times of Crisis, Times of Risk Management, and Times of Issues Management

We have selected three theories each to illustrate important aspects of crisis communication, risk communication, and issues management. We chose these theories based upon their frequent utilization and applicability to public relations-related problems.

Crisis Communication Theory

Image repair/restoration theory (IRT) draws from the rhetorical tradition to identify a list of crisis response strategies that can be used to categorize and critique crisis responses. IRT assumes that people perceive a wrongdoing and that the organization is responsible for the wrongdoing. Moreover, IRT assumes communication is goal-directed and reputation management is a common goal in communication (Benoit, 1995). IRT identifies five categories of crisis responses (image repair strategies): (1) denial, claims the organization has no responsibility for the crisis; (2) evading responsibility, seeks to reduce perceived responsibility for a crisis; (3) reducing offensiveness, attempts to improve perceptions of the organization; (4) corrective action, restores the situation to its precrisis state and/or seeks to prevent a repeat of the crisis; and (5) mortification, seeks forgiveness by accepting responsibility for the crisis and expressing sympathy to victims (Benoit, 1995). IRT is used to analyze the organization's reactive response to accusations of wrongdoing. Additional data are collected to indicate the success or failure of the crisis communication. The critic then interprets the results by connecting the choices of crisis response strategies to the outcomes of the crisis communication effort. The dominant research method for IRT is qualitative case study.

Situational crisis communication theory (SCCT) is cognitive-based, derived from attribution theory, and centers on crisis responsibility (Coombs, 1995; Coombs & Holladay, 2002). People naturally make attributions for negative events. They create explanations for their occurrence (Weiner, 1995). Crisis responsibility refers to the amount of responsibility for the crisis that stakeholders assign to the organization experiencing the crisis. SCCT is premised on the finding that as attributions of crisis responsibility increase, so too does the damage a crisis inflicts on an organization. That damage can be to the organizational reputation and purchase intentions (Coombs, 2007). SCCT posits that the crisis response should match the communicative demands of the crisis situation. Moreover, SCCT argues that reputation management should occur only after managers have conveyed instructing information (told people how to protect themselves physically from a crisis) and adjusting information (helped people to cope psychologically with a crisis). SCCT recommends providing instructing and adjusting information any time a crisis creates victims or potential victims. Reputation management strategies, such as compensation and apology, should be added when crisis responsibility is high. Crisis responsibility will be high when crises are viewed as preventable or the organization has a history of crises and/or a negative prior reputation (Coombs, 2007).

SCCT is prescriptive in its recommendations. A crisis communication effort can be evaluated by identifying the key elements of the crisis situation, the crisis response, and the outcomes of the crisis communication effort. Ideally, the proper or improper application of SCCT's recommendations can explain the success or failure of the crisis communication effort. SCCT relies heavily upon quantitative experiments and quasi-experiments to test its assumptions and recommendations (Ma & Zhan, 2016).

Stealing thunder emphasizes the timing of a crisis response. A number of studies consistently have shown that when an organization is the first to disclose the existence of a crisis, the crisis inflicts less harm on the organization (Arpan & Pompper, 2003; Claeys, 2017; Claeys & Cauberghe, 2012). For instance, less reputational damage is experienced by an organization when the organization itself discloses its own crisis compared to when the news media disclose the same crisis information (Claeys & Cauberghe, 2012). Stealing thunder does have some boundaries. It is not always possible for an organization to steal thunder, managers are hesitant to steal thunder (Claeys & Opgenhaffen, 2016), and stealing thunder is more effective for product harm crises than for moral violation crises (Beldad, Hegner, & van Laar, 2017). Overall, research consistently supports the benefits of stealing thunder for crisis communication.

Issues Management Theory

Drawing upon the work of Taylor, Vasquez and Doorley (2003), we have identified systems, rhetorical, and engagement as the three theories to feature from issues management. The systems approach emphasizes environmental scanning and the systematic nature of issues management. Managers limit surprises by using issues management to locate threats and opportunities in the environment. Issues management offers a structured approach to using communication tactics to influence decisions. The Jones and Chase model captures the systems approach to issues management with its five steps: (1) identification of issues through environmental scanning, (2) prioritization of issues in terms of salience to the organization, (3) selection of a response strategy, (4) creation and implementation of the response, and (5) evaluation of the issues management effort (Jones & Chase, 1979).

The rhetorical approach to issues management focuses on meaning management with an emphasis on defining the issue. The catalytic model represents the rhetorical approach and outlines the life cycle of an issue that is composed of five stages or statuses: (1) potential, an issue is recognized, (2) imminent, support for the issue builds, (3) current, widespread recognition of the issue develops, (4) critical, pressure to make a decision about the issue builds, and (5) dormant, the issue is considered resolved for a time. Four communicative strategies are used in attempts to move an issue through its life cycle. Definition is used to create the issue. Legitimacy is used to build a base of support for the issue. Polarization seeks to force people to choose a side in the issue conflict. Identification is used to persuade people to support a particular course of action for resolving the issue (Crable & Vibbert, 1985). The issue definition strategy is critical because issue managers seek to define an issue in a way that favors their course of action for resolving the issue (Coombs, 1992).

The engagement approach to issues management centers on relationship building. Issues management is seen as an opportunity to build organization–public relations rather than a simple contest between opposing sides of an issue. "An engagement approach posits that it is the convergence of organizational interests with public interests that provides both parties with the greatest opportunity for issue resolution through communication" (Taylor et al., 2003, p. 261). The engagement approach seeks mutual benefit, an outcome that is lacking in the systems and rhetorical approaches.

Risk Communication Theory

According to the social amplification of risk framework, cultural beliefs and worldviews determine how people experience and interpret risks (Kasperson et al., 1988). In other words, this framework proposes that how social institutions and individuals perceive risk will affect its impact upon society and the responses of management institutions (Kasperson & Kasperson, 1996).

The amplification process starts with either a physical event, such as an industrial accident, or the recognition of an unfavorable effect, such as global warming. Amplification is the intensification or attenuation of the risk and can be influenced by individual and social stations. The individual stations of amplification are people themselves and the filters they use to interpret the risk and make sense of it. Social stations of amplification include governments, the news media, and voluntary organizations (Renn et al., 1992).

The amplification process for individuals could be divided into the following steps: passing through attention filters; decoding of signals; drawing inferences; comparing the decoded messages with other messages; evaluating messages; forming specific beliefs;

rationalizing their beliefs; and forming a propensity to take corresponding actions (Renn et al, 1992). Characteristic for the risk interpretation of individual stations of amplification is that if the message is perceived to be consistent with the person's values or previous beliefs, the perception of risk is intensified. On the other hand, if the components of the decoded message contradict the values and beliefs of the receiver, the message is ignored or attenuated.

When people perceive and interpret risk as social stations of amplification, they do so according to the rules of their home organization, public institution, or social group (Renn et al., 1992). These rules often are determined by professional standards and rules pertaining to the specific position of the receiver of the information.

According to the framework, the social amplification of risk will evoke behavioral responses from individuals. These behavioral responses can lead to secondary impacts such as impact on business sales, political and social pressure, changes in education, etc. Furthermore, secondary impacts can, in turn, produce third-order impacts when perceived by other individuals or social groups. These impacts may have a "ripple" effect to other parties, which can spread outward, first to the directly affected victims, then touching the next level of those affected (e.g. a company or an organization), and, in extreme cases, can even reach to other social arenas that face similar risks (Kasperson et al., 1988). The second- and third-order impacts can trigger (by means of risk amplification) or hinder (by means of risk attenuation) positive changes for risk reduction.

The theory of risk perception is a broad theory based in the work of Slovic, Fischhoff, and Lichtenstein (1982). It is driven by a need to understand what people consider to be risky. This theory holds that risk is a function of how people perceive or assess the risk rather than the scientific determination of risk. Sandman (2003) refers to the scientific assessment of risk as "hazard" and the personal perceptual aspect as "outrage." These concepts lead to his widely cited formula: Risk = Hazard + Outrage. The perceptual nature of risk can lead people to be apathetic about risks that are serious and to be overly concerned about risks that are relatively minor. As a result, risk communication sometimes seeks to increase concern when a risk is underestimated and to decrease concern when a risk is overestimated (Covello & Sandman, 2001). The key point is that risk is a subjective judgment that must be central to any hazard management efforts.

Risk perception is complex and multidimensional, but not unknowable. Research in this area has sought to identify the factors that influence risk perception and develop an understanding of and an ability to anticipate perceived risk. Slovic et al. (1982) posit that "perceived risk is quantifiable and predictable" (p. 85). A long list of variables that affect perceived risk have been identified. Because there is not enough space in this chapter to discuss all variables that can facilitate outrage, we have identified a few to illustrate the point. People are more likely to view something as risky if it is unfamiliar to them and affects children. A strange, new foodborne illness that can harm children should be viewed as riskier than a well-known foodborne illness that poses little risk to children. Refer to Covello and Sandman (2001) for a more complete list of the outrage factors. Risk communication should be built upon understanding the risk perceptions of stakeholders. This knowledge provides the starting point for dialogues and partnerships between those creating the risk and those who must bear the risk (Palenchar, 2005; Slovic et al., 1982).

The extended parallel process model (EPPM) is used in risk communication research to guide message design and account for successes and failures in risk communication efforts (Witte, 1992). EPPM, grounded in work on fear appeals and message processing (Witte & Allen, 2000), assumes subjective understandings of risks and responses. Risk messages can be viewed as fear appeals designed to alert people to threats and prompt them to engage in recommended actions. When exposed to risk messages, people first appraise the threat (i.e. risk) to determine how and if it applies to them. Greater perceived vulnerability to the threat arouses fear, which leads to appraisals of the recommended response to the threat. Appraisals of the recommended actions trigger fear control processes and danger control responses.

Risk messages that elicit danger control responses create a protection motivation that leads to adaptive changes. These messages should be the most effective in promoting attitude change and gaining compliance with recommended actions. In contrast, messages that generate fear without providing efficacy lead people to focus on managing their fears rather than changing their behaviors to avoid or manage risks. Defensive motivations manifest through psychological protections such as denial, avoidance, and message distortion.

Thus, two categories of factors determine people's responses to threat: (1) susceptibility, and (2) efficacy. Perceived susceptibility to the threat (relevance of the threat, similar to likelihood or probability) and perceived severity of the threat (significance of the threat, similar to impact or severity of consequences) are appraised. Second, efficacy is evaluated in terms of perceived response efficacy (the effectiveness of the recommended actions in avoiding the risk) and perceived self-efficacy (the belief in one's ability to perform the recommended actions). The challenge is to develop risk messages that optimally address these two factors by activating danger control responses that lead to self-protective changes and avoiding fear control responses that prompt dysfunctional cognitive coping responses rather than beneficial actions. When perceptions of threat exceed perceptions of efficacy, fear control processes are triggered to the detriment of danger control processes.

When a risk or threat is perceived as both severe and relevant (high susceptibility and severity), and people believe the recommended behavior will be effective in addressing the threat and they are able to perform the behavior (high response efficacy and self-efficacy), people are more likely to experience danger control processes that prompt the recommended behaviors. Messages in which perceptions of efficacy are stronger than perceived threat will be more likely to evoke the desired behaviors.

If a risk or threat is perceived as irrelevant or minor (low susceptibility and severity), people are unlikely to respond to the message. They will not appraise response efficacy or engage in the desired protective behaviors. Additionally, if the perceived threat is high (high susceptibility and severity), and the recommended behavioral response is perceived to be ineffective in addressing the threat (low response efficacy), or if people believe they would be unsuccessful in enacting the behaviors to avoid the risk (low self-efficacy), people are unlikely to follow recommendations in risk messages. In this case, people focus on managing their fear rather than managing the danger.

Summary of Public Relations Theories Used in Crisis/Risk/Issues Management

Table 3.1 provides a summary of the nine theories we have presented in this chapter. Their primary purposes are categorized as either (1) descriptive and explanatory, or (2) prescriptive and predictive. The descriptive and explanatory theories concentrate on detailing how something is done and providing understanding of the topic. The prescriptive and predictive theories provide guidelines for professional communicators and predict specific outcomes for public relations interventions. Table 3.1 also indicates the core contribution each theory makes to public relations thinking.

Table 3.1 Review of crisis management, issues management, and risk communication theories

Area	Theory	Primary purpose of the theory	Core contribution
Crisis management	Image repair/ restoration theory	Descriptive and explanatory	Articulates thorough list of possible crisis response options.
	Situational crisis communication theory	Prescriptive and predictive	Uses of situational factors to predict crisis response effectiveness.
	Stealing thunder	Prescriptive and predictive	Initial disclosure of the crisis benefits the organization in crisis.
Issues management	Systems theory	Descriptive and explanatory	Details the issues management process.
	Catalytic	Descriptive and explanatory	Explains the critical communicative strategies in the issues management process.
	Engagement	Descriptive and explanatory	Focuses attention on relationship management.
Risk communication	Social amplification of risk	Prescriptive and predictive	Shows how others influence perceptions of risk.
	Risk perception	Prescriptive and predictive	Details list of factors that influence perceptions of outrage.
	Extended parallel process model	Prescriptive and predictive	Shows how susceptibility and efficacy evaluations shape responses to threats.

Major Topics/Questions Needing to Be Addressed by Public Relations Theorists Working in Crisis Communication, Risk Communication, and Issues Management

In crisis communication, a primary concern for theorists is the need to clarify what is meant by crisis within the context of a particular theory or line of research. Most crisis communication research in public relations understandably is related to organizational crises such as industrial accidents or product harm. Research into disasters and public health crises may also be conducted within the general category of public relations. However, organizational crises, natural disasters, and public health crises reflect very different crisis domains, with varying communication demands and constraints. Serious problems arise when theory and research fail to explicate unique considerations within the crisis domains. Unfortunately, some research inappropriately generalizes across contexts and integrates research findings from the different domains as if they were equivalent. This is a sloppy, imprecise practice that leads to conceptual and methodological confusion over myriad concerns such as message construction and effects.

Another issue that warrants consideration is our understanding of adjusting and instructing information in crisis responses. What are the parameters of these two response options? How do these response options mesh with risk communication? Though we consider adjusting and instructing information to be fundamental components of any crisis response, our understanding of these is quite limited (Holladay, 2009).

In the area of risk communication, public relations theorists need to continue to identify how relevant risk-related work from other disciplines, such as health communication and technical communication, can aid risk message construction and dissemination. For example, research has just begun to explore the potential value of EPPM to the practice. Similarly, research on the social amplification of risk in social media is in its infancy. Because the framework emphasizes the importance of the social construction of risk across stations, social media research in public relations is a logical arena for exploring how access to others' ideas and responses influences individual interpretations and behaviors in response to risk messages.

After intense interest in the 1980s and 1990s, issues management has faded to the fringes of public relations research and theory. The lack of attention to issues management seems surprising in light of increasing environmental complexity stemming from access to information, the influence of social media, and the development of advanced technology that simplifies environmental scanning. The purpose of issues management and the need for organizations to influence the environments in which they operate probably have not changed. Has the arena for issues management changed? Perhaps public relations theorists need to consider how social media may have altered the nature of the issues management process and to what the extent issues management has evolved from its original conceptualizations. Has social media empowered stakeholders in ways that reduce the importance of an organization's issues management? Are new theories of issues management processes needed? Have communication imperatives traditionally associated with issues management been absorbed into other public relations practices? Of the three areas, issues management is the one with the greatest theoretical deficit.

Suggested Cases to Explore to Demonstrate Theory at Work with Crisis Communication, Risk Communication, and Issues Management

In February of 2014, General Motors (GM) began recalling vehicles for faulty ignition switches. The failure of the switches had caused accidents by turning off while a vehicle was in use. The problem had been occurring for about 10 years and had been linked to over 120 deaths and over 270 injuries. The recall and related costs are in the billions of dollars (Bomey, 2017). In September of 2015, Volkswagen (VW) began recalling diesel vehicles because the computer system in the vehicles could deceive emission testing devices. The recall and related costs are over 20 billion dollars for VW (Schwartz & Bryan, 2017). Both automobile manufacturers faced crises related to faulty vehicles. In both cases, management was responsible for the crisis and knew about it before the crises broke in the news. Interestingly, VW has fared far worse from the crisis than GM even though the GM crisis involved deaths and injuries while VW was only a devious computer. By worse we mean that VW suffered greater and more prolonged reputational damage than GM.

One way to understand the odd reputational disparity in the outcomes of the cases is to examine the crisis communication by the leadership at GM and VW. VW tried to dance around responsibility for the crisis. Michael Horn, CEO of Volkswagen Group of America, claimed the emission deception was a result of a few rogue engineers at VW (Puzzanghera & Hirsch, 2015). Stakeholders were very skeptical that upper management were unaware of a problem that had existed for years. New GM CEO Mary Barra took a different approach. Barra accepted responsibility for the crisis and pledged to install new procedures to help prevent a repeat of a problem lingering internally at GM for years without action being taken. Stakeholders prefer managers to take responsibility when the organization is the reason for the situation that created the crisis (Coombs, 2007). The two cases highlight the value of effective crisis communication for firms. GM's more appropriate response did seem to reduce the amount and length of its reputational damage compared to VW's inappropriate response. Moreover, the cases raise issues about risk and issues management as well. There are concerns about how the two firms managed risk and risk communication, along with the potential need for new legislation to address these risks.

Some additional cases to consider are the following. For crisis: Coombs (2004) on the explosion at the West Pharmaceutical plant in 2003; Cowden and Sellnow (2002) on the response of North West Airlines to the 1998 pilots' strike; Fortunato (2008) on the Duke University lacrosse scandal; Sisco, Collins, and Zoch (2010) on Red Cross crisis response. For risk communication: Bakir (2005) on Greenpeace and Shell; Barnett and Breakwell (2003) on the October 1995 oral contraceptive pill scare; Witte (1991) on AIDS prevention. For issues management: Bostdorff and Vibbert (1994) on issues advocacy; Veil and Kent (2008) on inoculation and Tylenol's advertising.

Discussion Questions

Crisis

1 When stakeholder expectations for organizational behavior are not met, one of the conditions for a crisis is established. Why do some violations of expectations lead to crises and others do not? Are some stakeholder groups more likely to perceive that their expectations for organizational behavior are not being met? Why might the expectations of some stakeholder groups be perceived as more important than the expectations of other stakeholder groups?

2 This chapter focused on crisis communication with external stakeholders. How might crisis communication with internal stakeholders (employees) need to differ from crisis communication with external stakeholders? How might crisis communication with internal stakeholders about operational crises differ from crisis communication about reputational crises?

Risk

3 In what situations might risk messages need to be adapted to different stakeholder groups? How could the need for adaptation be identified? How could a range of different message contents be created without appearing to be inconsistent?

4 Identify examples of risk messages you have seen. For example, think about risk messages on products, in restaurants, and at transportation facilities like airports and train stations. What commonalities are evident in these messages? Are these messages examples of an organization's proactive or reactive actions? What recommendations do you have for making the content of risk messages easy to understand?

5 How scary should risk messages be to prompt appropriate action but avoid exaggerating a threat? What might happen when risk messages fail to provide response efficacy information? How do people develop self-efficacy? Is it the organization's responsibility to help people develop self-efficacy?

Issues Management

6 How does the issues management process differ from conflict between an organization and a stakeholder group? Are there areas of overlap between conflict management and issues management?

7 Identify recent examples where you have seen the issues management process at work. To prompt your thinking, consider cases that have generated controversy and received considerable media attention, such as conflicts between consumers and organizations over how personal data is handled in online environments or ongoing conflicts between groups holding different positions on how the right to free speech should be guaranteed in online and offline environments. How could the catalytic model be applied to understand how the conflict unfolded through the communication efforts of opposing groups? Can you identify the specific communication strategies used by opposing groups?

Suggested Readings

Crisis

Arendt, C., LaFleche, M., & Limperopulos, M. A. (2017). A qualitative meta-analysis of apologia, image repair, and crisis communication: Implications for theory and practice. *Public Relations Review, 43*(3), 517–526.

Coombs, W. T. (2015). *Ongoing crisis communication: Planning, managing, and responding* (4th ed.). Thousand Oaks, CA: Sage.

Frandsen, F., & Johansen, W. (2017). *Organizational crisis communication*. Thousand Oaks, CA: Sage.

Risk

Mase, A. S., Cho, H., & Prokopy, L. S. (2015). Enhancing the social amplification of risk framework (SARF) by exploring trust, the availability heuristic, and agricultural advisors' belief in climate change. *Journal of Environmental Psychology, 41*, 166–176.

Palenchar, M. J. (2009). Historical trends of risk and crisis communication. In R. L. Heath & H. D. O'Hair (Eds.), *Handbook of risk and crisis communication* (pp. 31–52). New York: Taylor & Francis.

Witte, K. (1995). Generating effective risk messages: How scary should your risk communication be? *Annals of the International Communication Association, 18*(1), 229–254.

Issues Management

Heath, R. L., & Palenchar, M. J. (2009). *Strategic issues management: Organizations and public policy challenges* (2nd ed.). Thousand Oaks, CA: Sage.

Strauss, N., & Jonkman, J. (2017). The benefit of issue management: Anticipating crisis in the digital age. *Journal of Communication Management, 21*(1), 34–50.

References

Arpan, L. M., & Pompper, D. (2003). Stormy weather: Testing "stealing thunder" as a crisis communication strategy to improve communication flow between organizations and journalists. *Public Relations Review, 29*, 291–308.

Bakir, V. (2005). Greenpeace v. Shell: Media exploitation and the social amplification of risk framework (SARF). *Journal of Risk Research, 8*(7–8), 679–691.

Barnett, J., & Breakwell, G. M. (2003). The social amplification of risk and the hazard sequence: The October 1995 oral contraceptive pill scare. *Health, Risk & Society, 5*(3), 301–313.

Beldad, A. D., Hegner, S. M., & van Laar, E. (2017). Proactive crisis communication when precrisis reputation is rotten? The moderating roles of precrisis reputation and crisis type in the relationship between communication timing and trust and purchase intention. In M. Stieler (Ed.), *Creating marketing magic and innovative future marketing trends* (pp. 679–684). New York: Springer.

Benoit, W. L. (1995). *Accounts, excuses, and apologies: A theory of image restoration.* Albany: State University of New York Press.

Bomey, N. (2017, January 18). GM pays $1M SEC fine over ignition-switch scandal. *USA Today.* Retrievedfromhttps://www.usatoday.com/story/money/cars/2017/01/18/general-motors-securities-and-exchange-commission-sec-ignition-switch/96717570/

Bostdorff, D. M., & Vibbert, S. L. (1994). Values advocacy: Enhancing organizational images, deflecting public criticism, and grounding future arguments. *Public Relations Review, 20*(2), 141–158.

Chaffee, S. H. (1991). *Communication concepts.* Thousand Oaks, CA: Sage.

Chase, W. H. (1984). *Issue management: Origins of the future.* Stamford, CT: Issue Action.

Claeys, A. S. (2017). Better safe than sorry: Why organizations in crisis should never hesitate to steal thunder. *Business Horizons, 60*(3), 305–311.

Claeys, A. S., & Cauberghe, V. (2012). Crisis response and crisis timing strategies: Two sides of the same coin. *Public Relations Review, 38*, 83–88.

Claeys, A. S., & Opgenhaffen, M. (2016). Why practitioners do (not) apply crisis communication theory in practice. *Journal of Public Relations Research, 28*(5–6), 232–247.

Coombs, W. T. (1992). The failure of the task force on food assistance: A case study of the role of legitimacy in issue management. *Journal of Public Relations Research, 4*(2), 101–122.

Coombs, W. T. (1995). Choosing the right words: The development of guidelines for the selection of the "appropriate" crisis response strategies. *Management Communication Quarterly, 8*, 447–476.

Coombs, W. T. (2004). West Pharmaceutical's explosion: Structuring crisis discourse knowledge. *Public Relations Review, 30*(4), 467–473.

Coombs, W. T. (2007). Attribution theory as a guide for post-crisis communication research. *Public Relations Review, 33*, 135–139.

Coombs, W.T. (2014). State of crisis communication: Evidence and the bleeding edge. *Research Journal of the Institute for Public Relations, 1*(1). Retrieved from http://www.instituteforpr.org/wp-content/uploads/CoombsFinalWES.pdf

Coombs, W. T. (2015). *Ongoing crisis communication: Planning, managing, and responding* (4th ed.). Thousand Oaks, CA: Sage.

Coombs, W. T., & Holladay, S. J. (2002). Helping crisis managers protect reputational assets: Initial tests of the situational crisis communication theory. *Management Communication Quarterly, 16*, 165–186.

Coombs, T., & Holladay, S. (2015a). CSR as crisis risk: Expanding how we conceptualize the relationship. *Corporate Communications, 20*(2), 144–162.

Coombs, W. T., & Holladay, S. J. (2015b). Strategic intent and crisis communication: The emergence of a field. In D. Holtzhausen & A. Zerfass (Eds.), *The Routledge handbook of strategic communication* (pp. 497–507). New York: Routledge.

Covello, V., & Sandman, P. M. (2001). Risk communication: Evolution and revolution. In A. B. Wolbarst (Ed.), *Solutions for an Environment in Peril* (pp. 164–178). Baltimore: Johns Hopkins University Press.

Cowden, K., & Sellnow, T. L. (2002). Issues advertising as crisis communication: Northwest Airlines' use of image restoration strategies during the 1998 pilot's strike. *Journal of Business Communication, 39*(2), 193–219.

Crable, R. E., & Vibbert, S. L. (1985). Managing issues and influencing public policy. *Public Relations Review, 11*(2), 3–16.

Fortunato, J. A. (2008). Restoring a reputation: The Duke University lacrosse scandal. *Public Relations Review, 34*(2), 116–123.

Freberg, K. (2012). Intention to comply with crisis messages communicated via social media. *Public Relations Review, 38*(3), 416–421.

Heath, R. L. (2005). Issues management. In R. L. Heath (Ed.), *Encyclopedia of public relations* (Vol. 1, pp. 460–463). Thousand Oaks, CA: Sage.

Heath, R. L. (2006). Onward into more fog: Thoughts on public relations' research directions. *Journal of Public Relations Research, 18*(2), 93–114.

Heath, R. L., & Coombs, W. T. (2006). *Today's public relations: An introduction.* Thousand Oaks, CA: Sage.

Heath, R.L., & O'Hair, H. D. (2009). The significance of crisis and risk communication. In R. L. Heath & H. D. O'Hair (Eds.), *Handbook of risk and crisis communication* (pp. 5–30). New York: Taylor & Francis.

Heath, R. L., & Palenchar, M. J. (2009). *Strategic issues management: Organizations and public policy challenges* (2nd ed.). Thousand Oaks, CA: Sage.

Holladay, S. J. (2009). Crisis communication strategies in the media coverage of chemical accidents. *Journal of Public Relations Research, 21*(2), 208–217.

Jaques, T. (2017). *Crisis proofing: How to save your company from disaster.* Victoria, Australia: Oxford University Press.

Jones, B. L., & Chase, W. H. (1979). Managing public policy issues. *Public Relations Review, 5*(2), 3–23.

Kasperson, R. E., & Kasperson, J. X. (1996). The social amplification and attenuation of risk. *Annals of the American Academy of Political and Social Science, 545*(1), 95–105.

Kasperson, R. E., Renn, O., Slovic, P., Brown, H. S., Emel, J., Goble, R., … Ratick, S. (1988). The social amplification of risk: A conceptual framework. *Risk analysis, 8*(2), 177–187.

Ledingham, J. A. (2003). Explicating relationship management as a general theory of public relations. *Journal of Public Relations Research, 15*(2), 181–198.

Lundgren, R., & McMakin, A. (1998). *Risk communication: A handbook for communicating environmental, safety, and health risk* (2nd ed.). Columbus, OH: Battelle Press.

Ma, L., & Zhan, M. (2016). Effects of attributed responsibility and response strategies on organizational reputation: A meta-analysis of situational crisis communication theory research. *Journal of Public Relations Research, 28*(2), 102–119.

Palenchar, M. J. (2005). Risk communication. In R. L. Heath (Ed.), *Encyclopedia of public relations* (Vol. 2, pp. 752–755). Thousand Oaks, CA: Sage.

Puzzanghera, J., & Hirsch, J. (2015, October 8). VW exec blames "a couple" of rogue engineers for emissions scandal. *Los Angeles Times.* Retrieved from http://www.latimes.com/business/autos/la-fi-hy-vw-hearing-20151009-story.html

Renn, O., Burns, W. J., Kasperson, J. X., Kasperson, R. E., & Slovic, P. (1992). The social amplification of risk: Theoretical foundations and empirical applications. *Journal of Social Issues, 48*(4), 137–160.

Sandman, P. (2003). Four kinds of risk communication. *The Synergist, 8*, 26–27.

Sisco, H. F., Collins, E. L., & Zoch, L. M. (2010). Through the looking glass: A decade of Red Cross crisis response and situational crisis communication theory. *Public Relations Review, 36*(1), 21–27.

Slovic, P., Fischhoff, B., & Lichtenstein, S. (1982). Why study risk perception? *Risk Analysis, 2*(2), 83–93.

Sohn, Y. J., & Lariscy, R. W. (2014). Understanding reputational crisis: Definition, properties, and consequences. *Journal of Public Relations Research, 26*(1), 23–43.

Schwartz, J. & Bryan, V. (2017, September 29). *VW's Dieselgate bill hits $30 bln after another charge.* Retrieved from https://www.reuters.com/article/legal-uk-volkswagen-emissions/vws-dieselgate-bill-hits-30-bln-after-another-charge-idUSKCN1C4271

Tansey, J., & Rayner, S. (2009). Cultural theory and risk. In R. L. Heath and H. D. O'Hair (Eds.), *Handbook of risk and crisis communication* (pp. 53–79). New York: Taylor & Francis.

Taylor, M., Vasquez, G. M., & Doorley, J. (2003). Merck and AIDS activists: Engagement as a framework for extending issues management. *Public Relations Review, 29*(3), 257–270.

Veil, S. R., & Kent, M. L. (2008). Issues management and inoculation: Tylenol's responsible dosing advertising. *Public Relations Review, 34*(4), 399–402.

Weiner, B. (1995). *Judgments of responsibility: A foundation for a theory of social conduct.* New York: Guilford Press.

Witte, K. (1991). The role of threat and efficacy in AIDS prevention. *International Quarterly of Community Health Education, 12*(3), 225–249.

Witte, K. (1992). Putting the fear back into fear appeals: The extended parallel process model. *Communications Monographs, 59*(4), 329–349.

Witte, K., & Allen, M. (2000). A meta-analysis of fear appeals: Implications for effective public health campaigns. *Health Education & Behavior, 27*(5), 591–615.

4

Diversity
Dean Mundy

Perform a quick search on any major corporate website, and it is easy to see that "diversity" is "important." Diversity initiatives – or more appropriately diversity and inclusion (D&I) initiatives – have become central to organizational business models. Increasingly, companies hire chief diversity officers, publish D&I reports, and dedicate significant resources to enhance and promote their D&I efforts. The Thomson-Reuters D&I index launched in 2016 reflects these trends. The index researches the D&I programs of more than 5,000 companies globally, ranking the top hundred, and outlining the major trends among board leadership (Thomson Reuters, 2016). But what do we mean by "diversity"?

Defining the Concepts: What Is Diversity?

A single, all-encompassing definition of diversity is difficult to pinpoint. Even the *Oxford English Dictionary*'s lead definition is obscure: "The condition or quality of being diverse." At perhaps the most fundamental level, diversity highlights individual difference (or as the *OED* adds in its secondary definition, "a point of unlikeness ... distinction"). Markers of diversity are those factors that make us unique and shape our individual worldview. These dimensions of difference vary depending on who you ask, or the context in which they are being addressed. Certainly, when most of us think about diversity we initially consider demographic diversity – factors such as age, sex, gender identity, race, ethnicity, sexual orientation. Diversity extends beyond observable/identifiable characteristics, however, and addresses the variety of perspectives that result from individual belief systems, experiences, cultural backgrounds, and socioeconomic status. Perhaps more important than understanding the many individual factors of difference that diversity comprises, though, is the mandate of not just noting difference, but understanding it and valuing it.

Understanding the value of various perspectives that result from individual difference is what has made diversity so important to organizations. The standard narrative we often hear – and see on corporate websites – emphasizes the business case for diversity (Uysal, 2013). The argument, which research has supported, is that by being exposed to diverse perspectives in the decision-making process, a company is able to produce more creative thought, act more nimbly, develop products and services that better address stakeholder needs, and thus become more competitive and profitable (e.g. Badgett, Durso, Kastanis, & Mallory, 2013; Herring, 2009; Noland, Moran, & Kotschwar, 2016). The business case for diversity moves beyond a legal/equity-based rationale and builds buy-in for diversity initiatives by emphasizing that in order

Public Relations Theory: Application and Understanding, First Edition. Edited by Brigitta R. Brunner.
© 2019 John Wiley & Sons, Inc. Published 2019 by John Wiley & Sons, Inc.

to truly serve its stakeholders – to anticipate the needs and expectations of its stakeholders – an organization must reflect the range of diversity reflected among its stakeholders. As the Apple Corporation – known for its successful D&I programs – explains in the banner of its inclusion & diversity website section,

> The most innovative company must also be the most diverse. At Apple, we take a holistic view of diversity … A view that includes the varied perspectives of our employees as well as app developers, suppliers, and anyone who aspires to a future in tech. Because we know new ideas come from diverse ways of seeing things … We want Apple to be a reflection of the world around us. (Apple, 2017)

While there is much demonstrated merit in the business case for diversity, however, there are also substantial risks in using it as the sole basis for valuing diversity. First, as Hon and Brunner (2000) explained, what organizations mean by diversity has become vague. "Diversity has become a catchall phrase for a complex set of issues having to do with gender, racial, and other forms of discrimination; multiculturalism; and the social and legal responsibility the business community has to manage diversity proactively" (p. 311). Perhaps the greater challenge is that the business case for diversity risks reducing diversity to a commodity rather than positioning it as a true organizational value. Accordingly, there is a growing call for reclaiming "diversity" as a fundamental value of difference, regardless of its contributions to an organization's financial bottom line. In this regard, this approach to diversity focuses on cultural (and multicultural) inclusion – the importance of creating an inclusive culture that respects and values difference, and then communicating those values accordingly.

How and Why Is Diversity of Concern to Public Relations?

The fundamental role of public relations is to foster and manage relationships (Ferguson, 1984). The public relations function therefore has a heightened responsibility to understand and engage the factors of diversity specific to the communities where we live and serve. Consequently, public relations has a unique opportunity to take the lead in fostering true multicultural inclusion. It starts internally by helping create a diverse discipline, and then extends to our external audiences. Simply put, public relations has a crucial diversity-focused communication mandate. As the PR Coalition – a coalition of more than 20 communication-focused professional organizations – concluded in 2005, "public relations and communications professionals have an important role to play in seeing that there is a sustained focus on diversity in American life" (p. 11).

Accordingly, since the turn of the twenty-first century there has been an increased focus on diversity in public relations, in terms of how to become a more diverse discipline, as well as how to engage diverse audiences and publics. Recent studies investigating diversity within the discipline, for example, have highlighted two core themes consistent during the last 10 to 15 years. First, while public relations has been female-dominated generally, the executive and management levels are still largely limited to males, and pay inequity between male and female practitioners persists (Dozier, Sha, & Shen, 2013). Second, racial and ethnic minorities remain widely underrepresented across public relations, and they particularly lack access to leadership opportunities (Appelbaum, Walton, & Southerland, 2015; Ford & Brown, 2015; Jiang, Ford, Long, & Ballard, 2016). To address these remaining gaps, additional research has explored best practices in engaging diverse audiences and crafting effective D&I programs. First, D&I must start with leadership – management must be diverse, it must take an active role in D&I

programs, and it must be held accountable. Second, organizations must develop support structures to support diverse groups – in terms of networking spaces, paths to management, employee training, and forums that drive discussion.

Although research in terms of how public relations practitioners embed diversity values in their external communication practices is limited, a 2015 study showed that beyond communicating diversity values on organizational websites (i.e. D&I sections), and emphasizing the importance of diversity in employee recruitment literature, practitioners indicated that conveying diversity values was "not applicable" to their daily job (Mundy, 2015). At its core, though, practitioners have argued that organizations must first tell key publics "why" diversity is important (to that organization), and then show those publics "how" diversity is reflected and valued. Apple, for example, in addition to highlighting diversity's business case, profiles visibly diverse employees who, rather than discuss the value of diversity itself or their experience as diverse employees, simply explain what they do on the job at the corporation.

All this is to say that diversity is important to daily organizational life, and public relations practitioners have a central mandate to help foster an inclusive environment and then convey an organization's diversity values. And that mandate continues to grow. Our publics are changing and increasingly tuned in to messages of diversity and inclusion. A 2016 study co-sponsored by the Institute for PR and Weber Shandwick explored generational perspectives on diversity and found that close to half of millennials (47%) consider D&I an important factor in their job search, compared to approximately a third of baby boomers and Generation X-ers who feel the same (Kochhar, 2016). Accordingly, while the business case remains a central tool to build organizational support for D&I, public relations has a heightened responsibility to help us move to the next generation of D&I communication – emphasizing not just that we care for diverse publics, but showing how we foster inclusion itself.

How, When, and Why Is Theory Applied to Diversity?

There are direct parallels between the importance of engaging theory and engaging diversity. The goal of theory is to provide a framework – a set of principles – through which to explore and understand a concept or phenomenon. Similarly, diversity is about understanding the unique factors that contribute to the individual perspective that shapes our own framework – our own set of principles and guidance through which we understand the world. Therefore, theory provides a uniquely effective tool for understanding topics related to diversity. As I half-jokingly tell my students, and as was told to me, "Theory is like your underwear. It is not always visible – nor should it be – but without it you lose an important source of guidance." Such is our own guiding lens, created by our diverse experiences and backgrounds.

In terms of investigating issues of diversity, theory helps explain a variety of things, such as how identity, difference, acceptance, and culture are communicated, negotiated, and understood; how factors of diversity inform what we "know" to be true about the world; how difference leads to group differentiation, social identities, and prejudice; and how competing dimensions of power influence those dynamics. The theories that have been developed to help explain these types of phenomena originate from a variety of disciplines, including cultural studies, gender and queer studies, mass communication, social psychology, and sociology. The following examples certainly do not provide an exhaustive list, but reflect the various theoretical applications in exploring diversity.

Perhaps one of the most applicable theories in explaining the unique perspectives that individual difference creates is feminist standpoint theory. Traditionally attributed to Hartsock (1987), the theory argues that those who are more (most) marginalized in society have a unique – and arguably more powerful – perspective on society and reality than those who are least marginalized. The theory historically has been applied to the experience of women, but its application provides lessons for understanding marginalized identities more broadly. For those of us who are more visual learners, Dr. Patricia Parker, organizational communication scholar at the University of North Carolina at Chapel Hill, offers the visual tool of viewing society (and its corresponding power structures) as a bull's-eye. The center of the bull's-eye reflects the space occupied by the most dominant coalition (traditionally the heterosexual, older, white male). As you move away from the center, groups occupy less and less power, with those who are most marginalized (least powerful), occupying the outermost ring. (And there are intriguing discussions to be had regarding who falls where on the spectrum.) Accordingly, feminist standpoint theory posits that even though those standing on those outermost rings have the least power, they have a better perspective of the whole – on reality – than those who reside at the middle. It makes sense. Those who are in the center have a very specific, limited gaze compared to that of those who stand farther out. As will be discussed in the next section, such principles certainly offer specific guidance to communication planning.

When it comes to understanding the dynamics of power and how those dynamics contribute to potential prejudice, several theories are particularly instructive. First, social identity theory (SIT) (Turner, Brown, & Tajfel, 1979; Tajfel, 1982) posits the ways in which prejudice develops between groups. The premise argues that everyone seeks a positive sense of self – a positive identity. Accordingly, we tend to seek those things that contribute to a positive sense of self-worth – those spaces and groups through which our values and beliefs are reinforced and confirmed as valid and true. As we begin associating with those groups, however, we begin making comparisons between our social identity and that of others who belong to a group holding a different worldview. As a result, we start developing concrete ideas regarding in-groups (the groups with which we associate) versus out-groups (those groups that hold a different worldview). Consequently, the in-group versus out-group dynamics can lead to prejudice, where we make judgments about "those who are not like us," whether or not those judgments are accurate.

SIT's application helps investigate major issues related to complex issues of prejudice, particularly in regard to issues of race and ethnicity. Perhaps the easiest way to understand SIT, though, is through the bandwagon effect. For example, a sports team begins doing well. Suddenly, sales of its merchandise increase, and more people proudly display it (regardless of how long they have been fans). The impetus is to reinforce one's positive sense of self as a fan of a successful team, and then to convey to others that you belong to a specific group that is part of the current dominant coalition. Rival teams, and their supporters, by consequence are out-groups. Conversely, when a team is no longer as successful, fans might disassociate themselves.

Prejudice also can be understood through the concept of symbolic annihilation (Gerbner & Gross, 1976), which focuses on the invisibility of minorities as a powerful message in itself – particularly through the lens of the media. As Tuchman, Daniels, & Benét (1978) argued, mass media symbolically annihilate specific groups in one (or more) of three ways: by simply omitting their presence; by trivializing their importance or potential contributions; or by condemning them. While the work of Tuchman et al. focused on women's media representation, its application to other diverse groups is instructive. Scholars have found, for example, that historically media have framed racial and ethnic minorities as criminals and threats, and the LGBTQ (lesbian, gay, bisexual, transgender, queer or questioning) community as self-loathing. As Larry Gross (2001) explained, through the eyes of the media it has taken the lesbian and gay community decades to "ascend from pariah status of criminal, sinner, and pervert, to the respectable categories of voting bloc and market niche" (p. xvi). Beyond traditional media, Gross added that representation in advertising provided an important milestone for the gay community.

He explained, "to be ignored by advertising is a powerful form of symbolic annihilation, but to be represented in the commercial universe is an important milestone on the road to full citizenship in the republic of consumerism" (p. 233).

Additional theories have addressed how we can confront potential prejudice and break down boundaries to understanding diversity. First, the contact hypothesis (Allport, 1954) and parasocial contact hypothesis (Schiappa, Gregg, & Hewes, 2005, 2006) posit that the more substantive, interpersonal contact individuals from different (often competing) groups have with each other, the less likely they are to hold prejudicial views of each other. While the original contact hypothesis tests interpersonal, physical interaction, the parasocial contact hypothesis argues that the same effect can occur through online dialog. A recent real-world story, dubbed "hummus diplomacy" provides a good example. A restaurant in Israel ran a promotion offering a 50% discount on every meal shared among Arabs and Jews. As the restaurant owner explained via Facebook, "Are you afraid of Arabs? Are you afraid of Jews? For us there are no Arabs, but also no Jews. We have human beings! And real excellent Arab hummus! And great Jewish falafel!" (Cheslow, 2015). When explaining why the promotion was important, reflective of the contact hypothesis, the owner continued, "If you eat a good hummus, you will feel love from the person who made it ... You don't want to stab him."

Applying queer theory offers a more complex, fluid way to break down barriers to diversity. The theory developed partly in reaction to social constructionism, which constructs and studies society based on the shared experiences and perspectives of certain identity groups. The challenge is that such an approach, while useful in providing effective ways to study societal phenomena, risks categorizing identity in a way that normalizes/standardizes particular types of behavior, which in turn limits our ways of understanding. As McDonald (2015) explained, "at the heart of every identity category such as 'woman' or 'gay' are norms about what it means to be and act like a member of this category. As such, queer theorists construct and deconstruct identity categories by conceptualizing identities as multiple, fluid, unstable, changeable, and constantly evolving" (p. 319). He added that, consequently, queer theory is purposefully poststructuralist and anticategorical. The theory challenges us to begin our explorations without preconceived notions of groups, or group characteristics – removing our normative expectations regarding how individuals should act. While social identity theory reveals the prejudice caused by the in-group versus out-group dynamics based on constructed social identities, queer theory asks us to break down those identity categories in order to "capture the ways in which people experience privilege and disadvantage in relation to difference" (p. 322).

Examples of Theories Used with Diversity

Several theories help guide and inform investigations of diversity in public relations (Table 4.1 summarizes examples of diversity-related theory). Again, while this list is not exhaustive, the following five theoretical approaches demonstrate the various ways in which public relations principles and practice can be explored. In the prior section, for example, we walked through standpoint theory. Several public relations scholars have highlighted the powerful potential it has when applied to a public relations context (Pompper, 2007; Rakow & Nastasia, 2009; Vardeman-Winter, 2011; Kennedy, 2016). Often, we discuss how public relations initiatives conducted internationally by a US firm often come up short because they are planned and executed from a "dominant Western" perspective. They fail to account for the perspective of the communities they are trying to reach. Feminist standpoint theory challenges us to reapproach the planning process by evaluating our standpoint and trying instead to look from

Table 4.1 Examples of diversity-related theory

Theory name	Short description
Standpoint theory	Those most marginalized have a better perspective than those least marginalized.
Social identity theory	Our social associations can lead to "in-group vs. out-group," "us vs. them" dynamics and prejudice.
Contact hypothesis	The more one-on-one contact we have with those not like us, the less likely it is that we will hold prejudicial views of them.
Symbolic annihilation	Invisibility in media of certain markers of diversity is a powerful statement itself regarding place in society.
Queer theory	We must move beyond normative expectations of identity and approach identity instead as fluid and unstable.
Theory of communicative action	Ideal speech situation: everyone must be at the table, have an equitable voice, and speak in a way that leads to rational consensus.
Relationship management	Successful organization–public relationships depend on creating mutuality.
Circuit of culture	How meaning is constructed is situational, and is related to factors of difference and power.
Fully functioning society	Public relations has a responsibility to serve as a steward (advocate) for diverse perspectives.
Multicultural theory	Public relations must better integrate the impact of a multicultural perspective in core theory.

the perspective (and accordingly, the needs and expectations) of those with different experiences, backgrounds, and expectations – a different standpoint.

Public relations scholars also have advocated for Habermas's theory of communicative action (Habermas, 1984, 1987) as instructive for public relations (e.g. Burkhart, 2007; Roper, 2005). Habermas argued that truly ethical communication that produces substantive action can only be achieved by pursuing an ideal speech situation. Part of this situation requires that everyone affected should have a place at the table, and everyone's voice should be heard equitably. In the process, ethical communication itself depends on rational discourse, which depends on participants communicating in way that conveys intelligibility, truth, trustworthiness, and legitimacy. The goal is for participants – by creating a rational discourse based on communication conveying these four qualities – to reach an ethical, rational consensus regarding the way forward. Accordingly, if public relations is rooted in fostering and managing relationships with diverse publics, and charged with embracing the diverse communities and diverse perspectives an organization serves, then Habermas's framework provides intriguing guidance. As Burkhart (2007) explained, it could provide a model for consensus oriented public relations (COPR), a planning tool for public relations practitioners. A COPR model, he argued, provides a way "to evaluate the success of public relations activities not only in a summative sense (at the end of a public relations campaign) but also in a formative way (this means: step by step)" (p. 252). Similar to standpoint theory's potential, it offers a way to ensure that diverse perspectives – beyond the dominant coalition – are being considered in the planning and execution process.

Moreover, Habermas's focus on pursuing a rational discourse that leads to consensus parallels the core principles of the public relations-specific relationship management theory. The central premise posits that public relations should focus fundamentally on relationships, and "Effectively managing organizational–public relationships around common interests and shared goals, over time, results in mutual understanding and benefit for interacting organizations and publics" (Ledingham, 2003, p. 190). The goal is to pursue communication that creates mutuality between organizations and publics. As Ledingham explained, "mutuality is a cornerstone on which long-term organization–public relationships are constructed" (p. 191). Achieving "mutuality" in organization–public relationships depends on mutual understanding, benefit, trust, control, satisfaction, and commitment. One of the main reasons this theory is important to public relations is because it shifts the focus away from an organization-specific perspective, and argues for a better incorporation of the public perspective.

Heath (2006) also focuses on the central importance of relationships to public relations, but has emphasized the potential of the fully functioning society theory (FFST). He argued, if we accept the premise that "society consists of multiple collectivities, people living and working in groups with varying degrees of agreement, permeability, trust, power, and interdependence," then FFST positions the public relations role as "a steward of multiple ... interests in harmony and collaboration" (pp. 96–97). This approach positions the focus of public relations on how to be a champion (advocate) for the diversity of perspective and lived experience while identifying those spaces through which meaning is contested and ultimately constructed.

Accordingly, it is this construction of meaning – particularly related to issues of difference and power – which Curtin and Gaither (2005) echoed should help drive the public relations process. To that end, they applied du Gay et al.'s (1997) circuit of culture theoretical framework. The circuit posits that there are five moments in society where meaning is constructed: regulation, production, consumption, identity, and representation. Accordingly, the circuit emphasizes the role of difference and power, and argues that how these five moments are defined is situational and contested. Public relations has a mandate, then, to explore those specific and fluctuating situational factors that should direct our communication planning. As the authors explained, "Within the circuit, public relations is redefined as a culturally relativist practice that does not privilege Western, corporate models over the rich varieties of practice that exist in other regions of the world and in other applied arenas" (p. 106).

Finally, there has been a growing focus on how best to develop a theory focused on intercultural or multicultural public relations, and how to better address intersectionalities of identity (Hofstede, 2001; Hofstede, Hofstede, & Minkov, 2010; Sha, 2006; Sha, Tindall, & Sha, 2012; Vardeman-Winter & Tindall, 2010). To that end, some public relations scholars (e.g. Kang & Mastin, 2008) have relied on Hofstede's (2001) work, which argues that workplace values (and in turn communication values) are influenced by specific cultural dimensions which are unique to different national and societal contexts: power distance (power structure and level of acceptance regarding that structure); individualism (versus collectivism); masculinity versus femininity; uncertainty avoidance (the degree of discomfort with ambiguity); a focus on the long term versus short term; and the tendency toward indulgence versus restraint.

That said, an increasing number of scholars have called for development of theory specific to public relations to better incorporate a multicultural focus. Sha (2006) suggested, for example, extending the situational theory of publics, arguing that in segmenting publics, it is important to consider how cultural identity affects problem recognition, level of involvement, information processing, and information seeking. She explained, "Because culture influences the way a person sees the world, if schema is conceptualized as worldview, an individual's cultural identity logically may affect the manner in which that person views different situations and the problems found in those situations" (p. 60). Vardeman-Winter and Tindall (2010) added that we must move beyond exploring the impact that explicit silos of diversity have on the public relations practitioner or practice, and better explore how the intersections of those identities influence perspective.

Major Topics/Questions Needing to Be Addressed by Public Relations Theorists Working in Diversity

While the focus of public relations on diversity has increased during the last decade, diversity is a relatively nascent area of research, and its theoretical application remains underdeveloped. Admittedly, much of the work in this area has been limited to exploring the diversity reflected within the public relations discipline itself. As the first part of this chapter outlined, we are a largely female-dominated field, though women are underrepresented disproportionately at senior levels. Racial and ethnic minorities remain underrepresented at all levels in public relations.

While work is needed to address those persistent challenges, new topics related to diversity and inclusion are emerging that public relations must address. First, we must complicate how we identify, approach, and respond to publics. The communities in which we live and serve are becoming more diverse. To be seen as a legitimate member of these communities, therefore, we must complicate how we define and understand "publics." As Sha's (2006) study argued, adding multicultural dimensions in studies researching publics brings important nuances that should inform public relations practice.

Along the way, there also are new dimensions of diversity that need addressing. Some of these dimensions include age (old and young), ability (mental and physical), access (economic and physical), sexual identity (sexual orientation, gender identity, and the fluidity of identity), religion (and the nonreligious), and veteran status. The argument here is not that these are "new" dimensions – that our society suddenly has older people, younger people, or gay people. Rather, the argument is to move beyond the classic three dimensions of diversity – gender, race, and ethnicity – and incorporate in our exploration the perspectives of these additional groups whose perspectives have largely been unexplored. Accordingly, one of the biggest needs, as evidenced by the call in Vardeman-Winter and Tindall (2010), is the importance of working at the intersections. Certainly the experiences of a transgender woman of color who lives in a rural area differs from a white lesbian who lives in a major city. The experience of a black woman in the classroom differs from that of a gay white man. As queer theory adds, there is value in exploring these intersections, and the potential fluidity of those intersections. The lessons, moreover, are invaluable to public relations in the process of forging substantive relationships. As one of my own research participants argued when asked how he reached diverse publics, he said never to assume you know how they identify. Rather, to focus the public relations process around learning, and to have the courage to ask the questions to which you don't know the answer but think you should. Otherwise, a communication campaign will seem insincere and fall flat.

Finally, and perhaps most importantly, public relations should play a direct role in seeing that we help organizations move from the business-case narrative and help shape an inclusive environment that substantively values diversity, regardless of what it means for the financial bottom line. Internally, organizations can recruit diverse employees, but how are they treated once on the job? For example, if an organization touts that they have been able to recruit a higher percentage of female employees, does it also mean that those women are being paid the same as their male peers?

Externally, organizations have several D&I communication mandates, which public relations research and theoretical development must address. First, organizations must explore how to ethically, sincerely, convey their diversity and inclusion values to external audiences. There is real risk in misrepresenting how diverse an organization actually is – in conveying a picture of how they want to be rather than who they actually are. At the same time, it is important that an organization does reflect diversity in its communication practices in order to demonstrate a commitment to an inclusive workplace. Once again, the Apple Corporation provides an effective example. The company shows that much work needs to be done to hire more females and underrepresented minorities. It also shows, however, that while it will take time they are moving in the right direction. Moreover, the company shows that they pursued, and recently reached, pay equity.

The second external public relations challenge specific to D&I reflects the mandates of relationship management theory. If we are to take seriously the central role of public relations in developing relationships based on mutual understanding, benefit, trust, control, satisfaction, and commitment between our organizations and publics, then along the way we must explore and address specific factors of diversity among our publics. Building trust, for example, requires that our publics know we understand their specific needs and lens – the unique experiences that are central to their everyday lives. Moreover, an organization must consider if it is sincerely demonstrating commitment to a community's diversity – not just during a campaign, but over the long term.

The third, related public relations challenge is to explore when, and how, to publicly respond to potentially divisive issues related to D&I that affect our communities. And given an increasingly contentious political climate, this challenge is becoming even more crucial to organizational reputation and relationship management. For example, during the 2008 California Proposition 8 campaign – the campaign for a statewide ban on marriage equality – Google and Apple not only made public statements in opposition, they also donated money to fight the initiative. The companies felt it was important to convey clearly to their publics where they stood on this publicly contested issue. More recently, companies have made very explicit statements and public moves regarding "bathroom bills," such as North Carolina's House Bill 2, which prevents transgender people from using restrooms that correspond with their gender identity. Consequently, organizations across North Carolina have had to make business decisions and public statements regarding their stance on the bill. Externally, companies with business in North Carolina have had to do the same. The National Collegiate Athletic Association (NCAA), for example, has removed all competitions in all sports from the state until the bill is repealed. Public relations therefore must be in tune with these diversity issues, and help guide ethical, organizational action. Accordingly, theory helps provide guidance – the framework – through which to tease out and address the issues themselves.

Suggested Cases to Explore to Demonstrate Theory at Work with Diversity

There are several cases that help explain how theory can be applied to understanding diversity in public relations. Let's revisit the NCAA example. As the NCAA explains in its statement regarding North Carolina's House Bill 2, "Based on the NCAA's commitment to fairness and inclusion, the Association will relocate all … championship events." The statement then adds that the NCAA "must promote an inclusive atmosphere for all college athletes, coaches, administrators and fans. Current North Carolina state laws make it challenging to guarantee that host communities can help deliver on that commitment" (Emmert, 2016). There are several theoretical approaches possible in studying the NCAA's statement. Certainly the premise of relationship management theory – specifically its focus on building trust and demonstrating commitment – applies. Another possible application is the fully functioning society theory, which – as Heath explained – positions public relations as a steward of multiple interests and perspectives in harmony. Finally, an argument could be made that the NCAA's move is a powerful form of symbolic annihilation. As Tuchman et al. argued, absence in the media makes a powerful statement. And while the concept is applied typically to underrepresented communities being ignored or ridiculed by the media, in this case the NCAA is making a powerful statement by moving heavily televised events from the state because of an issue related to an underrepresented minority. The organization understands the powerful, symbolic message that is sent during the actual broadcast, when the audience is reminded why a certain event has been moved to the new location.

Curtin and Gaither's (2007) explication of smallpox eradication through the lens of the circuit of culture is also instructive. The authors walk through how the World Health Organization, by removing its Western-focused lens and truly understanding culturally specific factors related to production, consumption, regulation, identity, and representation, was able to switch course and eradicate smallpox. Simply put, it realized that a "one-size-fits-all" campaign, planned from the European perspective, was not going to be effective. Instead, it was able to customize and craft a campaign that addressed a specific culture's context.

Finally, regardless of where one stands on the issue of immigration, the immigration bans in early 2017 offer areas for exploration. First, in terms of understanding the language and parameters of the ban itself, exploration would be instructive through the lens of standpoint theory, social identity theory, or the contact hypothesis. In terms of application specific to public relations, certainly this is an example of the political overlapping into organizational management, where organizations are compelled to provide a statement regarding their stance. It would be interesting, for example, to see if companies reaffirm their commitment to diversity through the use of the business case narrative, or echo the NCAA's focus on the fundamental importance of inclusiveness.

Discussion Questions

1   In a way, social identity theory and the contact hypothesis stand on opposite sides of the same challenges regarding in-groups vs. out-groups. What are the principles of each, and how do they differ?

2   Provide an example of how the bull's-eye image in standpoint theory can be applied to a current real-world situation.

3   What is the circuit of culture's main focus? How is meaning negotiated in the circuit?

4   Habermas argued that substantive, ethical action can only come from rational discourse, as reflected through an ideal speech situation. What does he mean?

5   What are some of emerging topics related to diversity in public relations that need further exploration and theoretical development?

Suggested Readings

Commission on Public Relations Education. (2017). Diversity. In *Fast forward: Foundations and future state. Educators and Practitioners. Report on undergraduate education* (pp. 139–148). Retrieved from http://www.commissionpred.org/commission-reports/fast-forward-foundations-future-state-educators-practitioners/

Curtin, P. A., & Gaither, T. K. (2005). Privileging identity, difference, and power: The circuit of culture as a basis for public relations theory. *Journal of Public Relations Research, 17*(2), 91–115.

Ford, R., & Brown, C. (2015). *State of the PR industry: Defining and delivering on the promise of diversity.* Survey designed and conducted by the National Black Public Relations Society. Retrieved from https://www.instituteforpr.org/wp-content/uploads/NBPRS-State-of-the-PR-Industry-White-Paper.pdf

McDonald, J. (2015). Organizational communication meets queer theory: Theorizing relations of "difference" differently. *Communication Theory, 25,* 310–329.

PR Coalition. (2005). *Focus on diversity: Lowering the barriers, raising the bar.* Retrieved from https://instituteforpr.org/wp-content/uploads/Focus_Diversity_2005.pdf

References

Allport, G. W. (1954). *The nature of prejudice.* Cambridge, MA: Perseus Books

Appelbaum, L., Walton, F., & Southerland, E. (2015). *An examination of factors affecting the success of underrepresented groups in the public relations profession.* Report, City College of New York.

Apple (2017). *Inclusion and diversity.* Retrieved from Apple website: http://www.apple.com/diversity/

Badgett, M. V. L., Durso, L. E., Kastanis, A., & Mallory, C. (2013, May). *The business impact of LGBT-supportive workplace policies.* Study by Williams Institute, University of California at Los Angeles. Retrieved from http://williamsinstitute.law.ucla.edu/research/workplace/business-impact-of-lgbt-policies-may-2013/

Burkhart, R. (2007). On Jurgen Habermas and public relations. *Public Relations Review, 33*(3), 249–262.

Cheslow, D. (2015, October 23). *Hummus diplomacy: Israeli café discounts meals shared by Jews and Arabs.* Retrieved from website of National Public Radio: http://www.npr.org/sections/thesalt/2015/10/23/450905869/israeli-cafe-offers-discounts-for-jews-and-arabs-to-share-a-meal

Curtin, P. A., & Gaither, T. K. (2005). Privileging identity, difference, and power: The circuit of culture as a basis for public relations theory. *Journal of Public Relations Research, 17*(2), 91–115.

Curtin, P., & Gaither, T. K. (2007). *International public relations: Negotiating culture, identity, and power.* Thousand Oaks: Sage.

Dozier, D. M., Sha, B.-L., & Shen, H. (2013). Why women earn less than men: The cost of gender discrimination in US public relations. *Public Relations Journal, 7*(1), 1–21.

du Gay, P., Hall, S., Janes, L., Mackay, H., & Negus, K. (1997). *Doing cultural studies: The story of the Sony Walkman.* London: Sage.

Emmert, M. (2016. September 12). *NCAA to relocate championships from North Carolina for 2016–17.* Retrieved from website of National Collegiate Athletic Association: http://www.ncaa.org/about/resources/media-center/news/ncaa-relocate-championships-north-carolina-2016-17

Ferguson, M. A. (1984). *Building theory in public relations: Interorganizational relationships as a public relations paradigm.* Paper presented at the Association for Education in Journalism and Mass Communication conference, Gainesville, Florida.

Ford, R., & Brown, C. (2015). *State of the PR industry: Defining and delivering on the promise of diversity.* Survey designed and conducted by the National Black Public Relations Society. Retrieved from http://www.instituteforpr.org/wp-content/uploads/NBPRS-State-of-the-PR-Industry-White-Paper.pdf

Gerbner, G., & Gross, L. (1976). Living with television: The violence profile. *Journal of Communication, 26*(2), 173–199.

Gross, L. (2001). *Up from invisibility*. New York: Columbia University Press.

Habermas, J. (1984). *The theory of communicative action. Volume 1: Reason and the rationalization of society*. Boston: Beacon Press.

Habermas, J. (1987). *The theory of communicative action. Volume 2: Lifeworld and system: A critique of functionalist reason*. Boston: Beacon Press.

Hartsock, N. (1987). The feminist standpoint: Developing the ground for a specifically feminist historical materialism. In S. Harding (Ed.), *Feminism and methodology* (pp. 157–180). Milton Keynes, UK: Open University Press.

Heath, R. L. (2006). Onward into more fog: Thoughts on public relations' research directions. *Journal of Public Relations Research, 18*(2), 93–114.

Herring, C. (2009). Does diversity pay? Race, gender, and the business case for diversity. *American Sociological Review, 74*(2), 208–224.

Hofstede, G. (2001). *Culture's consequences: Comparing values, behaviors, institutions, and organizations across nations* (2nd ed.). Thousand Oaks CA: Sage.

Hofstede, G., Hofstede, G. J., & Minkov, M. (2010). *Cultures and organizations: Software of the mind* (rev. 3rd ed.). New York: McGraw-Hill.

Hon, L., & Brunner, B. (2000). Diversity issues and public relations. *Journal of Public Relations Research, 12*(4), 309–340.

Jiang, H., Ford., R., Long., P. A. C., & Ballard, D. (2016). *Diversity and inclusion: A summary of the current status and practices of Arthur W. Page Society members*. Retrieved from http://plankcenter.ua.edu/wp-content/uploads/2016/07/DI-FINAL.pdf

Kang, D. S., & Mastin, T. (2008). How cultural difference affects international tourism public relations websites: A comparative analysis using Hofstede's cultural dimensions. *Public Relations Review, 34*(1), 54–56.

Kennedy, A. (2016). Landscapes of care: Feminist approaches in global public relations. *Journal of Media Ethics, 31*(4), 215–230.

Kochhar, S. (2016, December 4). *Nearly half of American millennials say a diverse and inclusive workplace is an important factor in a job search*. Retrieved from Institute for Public Relations website: http://www.instituteforpr.org/nearly-half-american-millennials-say-diverse-inclusive-workplace-important-factor-job-search/

Ledingham, J. A. (2003). Explicating relationship management as a general theory of public relations. *Journal of Public Relations Research, 15*(2), 181–198.

McDonald, J. (2015). Organizational communication meets queer theory: Theorizing relations of "difference" differently. *Communication Theory, 25*, 310–329.

Mundy, D. E. (2015). From principle to policy to practice? Evaluating diversity as a driver of multicultural stakeholder engagement. *PR Journal, 9*(1). Retrieved from http://www.prsa.org/Intelligence/PRJournal/Vol9/No1/

Noland, M., Moran, T., & Kotschwar, B. (2016*). Is gender diversity profitable? Evidence from a global survey*. Working Paper 16-3, Peterson Institute for International Economics. Retrieved from https://piie.com/publications/working-papers/gender-diversity-profitable-evidence-global-survey

Pompper, D. (2007). The gender-ethnicity construct in public relations organizations: Using feminist standpoint theory to discover Latinas realities. *Howard Journal of Communication, 18*(4), 291–311.

PR Coalition (2005, May). *Focus on diversity: Lowering the barriers, raising the bar*. Retrieved from https://instituteforpr.org/wp-content/uploads/Focus_Diversity_2005.pdf

Rakow, L. F., & Nastasia, D. I. (2009). On feminist theory of public relations: An example from Dorothy E. Smith. In O. Ihlen, B. Van Ruler, & M. Fredriksson (Eds.), *Public relations and social theory* (pp. 252–277). New York: Routledge.

Roper, J. (2005). Symmetrical communication: Excellent public relations or a strategy for hegemony? *Journal of Public Relations Research, 17*(1), 69–86.

Schiappa, E., Gregg, P. B., & Hewes, D. E. (2005). The parasocial contact hypothesis. *Communication Monographs, 72*(1), 92–115.

Schiappa, E., Gregg, P. B., & Hewes, D. E. (2006). Can one TV show make a difference? "Will & Grace" and the parasocial contact hypothesis. *Journal of Homosexuality, 51*(4), 15–37.

Sha, B.-L. (2006). Cultural identity in the segmentation of publics: An emerging theory. *Journal of Public Relations Research, 18*, 45–65.

Sha, B.-L., Tindall, N. T. J., & Sha, T.-L. (2012). Identity ad culture: Implications for public relations. In K. Sriramesh & D. Verčič (Eds.), *Culture and public relations: Links and implications* (pp. 67–90). New York: Routledge.

Tajfel, H. (1982). *Social identity and intergroup relations.* Cambridge: Cambridge University Press.

Thomson Reuters. (2016, September 26). *Thomson Reuters launches D&I index – reveals top 100 most diverse & inclusive organizations globally.* Press release. Retrieved from https://www.thomsonreuters.com/en/press-releases/2016/september/thomson-reuters-launches-di-index-reveals-top-100-most-diverse-inclusive-organizations-globally.html

Tuchman, G., Daniels, A.-K., & Benét, J. (Eds.). (1978). *Hearth and home: Images of women in the mass media.* New York: Oxford University Press.

Turner, J., Brown, R., & Tajfel, H. (1979). Social comparison and group interest in ingroup favouritism. *European Journal of Social Psychology, 9*(2), 187–204.

Uysal, N. (2013). Shifting the paradigm: Diversity communication on corporate web sites. *Public Relations Journal, 7*(2), 8–36.

Vardeman-Winter, J. (2011). Confronting Whiteness in public relations campaigns and research with women. *Journal of Public Relations Research, 23*(4), 412–441.

Vardeman-Winter, J., & Tindall, NTJ (2010). Toward an intersectionality theory of public relations. In R. L. Heath (Ed.), *The Sage handbook of public relations* (pp. 223–235). Thousand Oaks, CA: Sage.

5

Ethics

Tor Bang

It is not difficult to come by examples of questionable ethical practice and behavior in the broad fields of public relations and strategic communications. When sharing such aspects, and insight, with peers, students, and society, authors must keep in mind that they should be balanced, fair, and objective.

It should be said that ethical practice is the norm within the public relations industry. Such practice does not get headlines – as little as good parenting, well-run municipalities, and caring for one another do. Bad practice does.

Actors in the field of public relations operate with a list of concepts, as dichotomous adjectives – *good* and *bad, ethical* and *unethical, moral* and *immoral* – describing and assessing community practice, adjectives which correspond with a community's cultural, ideological, or economic standards that touch upon public relations and strategic communication. They color relationships between individuals, and within and between organizations, parliaments, nongovernmental organizations (NGOs), and nations.

Adjectives are rarely objective descriptions; they are stereotypes, intentionally put there in order to label and categorize practices. Labels are qualitative and often not empirically reliable, however fit to qualify standards and practices. Bystanders' assessments of end results may turn out to be surprisingly simple. Well-qualified commentators and peers may settle for the simple dichotomies of *ethical* or *unethical, good* or *bad*.

After the first part of this chapter, which documents narratives on practices deemed unethical or ethical, there will be a section on ethical theory, and of norms and codes in the field of public relations. The chapter includes a discussion on two incidents in which unethical practices of major industries have been revealed, and ends with a short discussion on the codes of ethics developed by the Global Alliance for Public Relations and Communications Management.

Defining the Concepts: What Are Ethics and Ethical Practice?

At their core, ethics are our understanding of right and wrong. They are the rules one uses to solve problems when morals and/or values are uncertain (J. Grunig, 2000). Our understanding of ethics and public relations has been, and is still being researched by many scholars (for more information, see Bowen, 2007; Holtzhausen & Zerfass, 2012; Fawkes, 2012); however, there is still a need to further research this area of our practice, as many of the examples detailed in this chapter demonstrate.

Public Relations Theory: Application and Understanding, First Edition. Edited by Brigitta R. Brunner.
© 2019 John Wiley & Sons, Inc. Published 2019 by John Wiley & Sons, Inc.

Practitioners in the fields of public relations may study ethics to get an overview of relevant theories. Learning outcomes from studying ethics are not always measurable. The long-term objective is to make students and practitioners aware of, and empower them with an accrued body of knowledge, enabling them to assess ethical situations.

Students engaging in ethical discourse should strive to develop attitudes that are ethical. They should be able to assess a public relations situation, or *Kairos* – an optimal communicative moment, on a continuum scale with *ethical* and *unethical* at either end. Few such situations are ethical or unethical on a dichotomous scale. Quite often, there are ethical elements in public relations practice that at first glance may have seemed unethical, and vice versa.

Ethical Practice as Industry Standard

Most industries develop a set of ethical codes, imperatives for members and owners. Codes form common ground for what can be perceived as acceptable conduct. Codes should not be confused with *minimum standards*, as they usually express visions that member organizations are expected to live up to.

Responsible conduct by organizations includes assuming ethical responsibility not only for one's own actions, but for those of peers, colleagues, and competitors in the public relations community. An organization may be affected by disloyalty or ethical misconduct by one of its employees. That may affect competitors, bringing the industry into discredit. The notion that certain public relations conduct is perceived to be in a morally gray area could embarrass competitors and peers.

Conversely, the industry as a whole gains when practitioners earn and deserve praise. A favorable reputation is usually accrued slowly. It may, however, easily be ruined by misconduct. If the public perception is that there are rotten apples in an industry, the industry's legitimacy may be tarnished. Social trust, an industry cornerstone, may well be compromised. This may be the consequence if the free exchange of opinions and ideas is suppressed, or when communicators consciously attempt to mislead stakeholders or the general public.

How and Why Are Ethics and Ethical Practice of Concern to Public Relations?

Unethical and Ethical Practices on the Global Stage

Some nations have skeletons in their closets. They thus provide examples of the low hanging fruits of questionable public relations. Despite its close association with Germany and the overwhelming welcome the Austrians gave Nazi troops in March of 1938, Austria declared itself a victim of Nazism, a position supported by the Soviet Union, one of its postwar occupiers. A high and disproportionate number of Austrians played vital roles in the realization of Hitler's expansionist politics, as well as in the extermination of European Jewry. The global community long turned a blind eye to embarrassing parts of the country's history. Victim theory, *Opferthese* (Hammerstein, 2008), was a fundamental part of Austria's postwar history.

All that changed in 1986, when Austrians elected the former Waffen-SS officer Kurt Waldheim as its president. Waldheim had risen to the rank of *Oberleutnant*, lieutenant, stationed in Yugoslavia and Greece during World War II. Despite Waldheim denying any knowledge of Nazi atrocities, it was documented by NGOs that, while in Greece, he had been stationed in the outskirts of the city of Thessaloniki during 1943 when the city's 54,000 Jews were deported to Auschwitz concentration camp. The British newspaper *The Guardian* wrote in its obituary on Waldheim:

> Waldheim's offence was to lie, and when exposed for lying, to persist – even as the truth about his war service emerged piecemeal. First, he said he was not there, and then that he was there but had never known what was going on. Finally, he said he could not understand what all the fuss was about. The contrast with his German presidential contemporary, Richard von Weizsäcker, who took full responsibility and apologised for his own wartime service as a military intelligence officer, could not have been greater. (van der Vat, 2007)

During Waldheim's tenure as president, the country's global reputation was damaged. Austria became an international pariah. President Waldheim and his wife were officially declared persona non grata in the United States and several other countries, an unprecedented humiliation for a head of state of a presumed friendly nation (van der Vat, 2007). Austria has also earned a reputation for being a haven for extreme right-wing politics and politicians. A common joke about Austria was: "Question: Who is the world's best spin doctor? Answer: Austria: It has managed to convince the world that Hitler was German, and that Beethoven was Austrian."

There are many examples of poor judgment, and practices that are perceived as being of a poor ethical standard. This author's birth nation and home, Norway, demonstrates stubborn insensitivity to global protests against its whaling industry, which damages the nation's reputation and embarrasses many Norwegians. Some Spanish cities and regions have a love for bullfights – regarded by many to be a shocking ordeal – and this is highly controversial. World protests against animal suffering in religious rituals, such as throwing live goats from church towers in Zamora, made local authorities outlaw such practices, as did the highly influential region of Catalonia with its bullfights. Mexico's de facto, even if undeclared, war between drug cartels and the country's military forces is a disastrous blow to the nation's reputation. When Copenhagen's zoo found that it had too little space for its many giraffes, local preschool students were invited to witness the slaughtering of Marius, an adolescent bull. The well-documented mutilation of Marius, with wide-eyed kids as bystanders, witnessing the bloody spectacle, was a public relations disaster, not only for Copenhagen Zoo, but for the city, and the country.

On the other hand, many corporations are well aware that they have a lot to lose. A textbook example of ethical behavior, albeit back in 1982, happened shortly after the "Tylenol murders." The pharmaceutical giant Johnson & Johnson's flagship brand of paracetamol, Tylenol, enjoyed a US market share of circa 35%. In several drug stores in the Chicago metropolitan area, containers of Tylenol were tampered with and contaminated with cyanide, a poisonous, lethal chemical. Seven people died after taking contaminated Tylenol. Within a few days, 31 million bottles of Tylenol were pulled from shelves in all markets. After its return to shelves, Tylenol's market share dropped to 7%. Despite a huge financial loss, Tylenol, as well as Johnson & Johnson, seemed to consolidate their already rock-solid reputation. The incident seems to have changed the consumer product industry. On-the-shelf medical containers are now marketed in tamper-free, sealed containers. The owner company, as well as the brand, came out of the crisis relatively well. Tylenol has never regained its former market position, losing shelf space to competitors. However, the Johnson & Johnson corporate reputation seems to be intact.

In politics, the current German chancellor, Angela Merkel, has an exceptionally good image in her party, in her country, in Europe, and on the world stage. Lovingly nicknamed *Mutti*, Mummy, Merkel has been affably parodied on *Saturday Night Live*, by Kate McKinnon, and by Tracey Ullmann. The Merkel brand strength is usually perceived as the Merkel *personal image*, not party *strategy* or tactic.

Travel Industry Incidents

In the corporate world, amateur footage in 2017 shows Dr. David Dao screaming and bleeding while being dragged off a United Airlines flight at Chicago's O'Hare Airport. The flight, United's last one to Louisville, Kentucky that night, had been overbooked. The crew had not succeeded in persuading customers to voluntarily trade their seats for flight coupons, to make room for airline crew needed for service at Louisville the following morning. Flight management subsequently called airport police, who commanded Dr. Dao to leave. Refusing to do so, Dr. Dao was forcibly removed from the plane. The CEO of United Airlines, Oscar Munoz, issued a statement commending the flight crew, and labeling Dr. Dao *belligerent* and *disruptive*.

Some of Dr. Dao's fellow passengers documented crew and a United manager unsuccessfully negotiating with Dr. Dao, threatening him, and finally calling for airport security officers, who then forcibly removed him. Dr. Dao suffered injuries to his head and mouth when an officer threw him against an armrest.

Even prior to takeoff, smartphone videos went viral in social media. One of the videos was shared 87,000 times and viewed 7.6 million times within 24 hours of the incident. It was reported that the family origins of 69-year-old Dr. Dao were Chinese/Vietnamese, and some videos were spread to, shared, and viewed by millions in Chinese networks, stirring up questions about how United would treat passengers on their routes from China to the United States.

The United Express Flight 3411 incident opened floodgates for disgruntled airline passengers. Hundreds of incidents were uploaded on YouTube and shared on Facebook to document cabin crews' poor behavior. Websites like TripAdvisor enable passengers to subjectively *tell* their stories about airline employees misrepresenting their company. Video images objectively *show*, so publics may interpret images for themselves.

Talk-show hosts had field days, with dozens of spoofs on the United slogan "Fly the friendly skies." One news media cartoonist suggested that United passengers, for a mere $50, could "purchase an upgrade to not be beaten unconscious in an overbooking re-accommodation situation" (Beeler, 2017). CEO Munoz added insult to injury in releasing the following statement: "This is an upsetting event to us all at United. I apologize for having to re-accommodate these customers" (McCann, 2017). Myriads of new connotations of *re-accommodate* emerged.

Mr. Munoz was soon forced to apologize. Dr. Dao was paid off with an undisclosed amount. United stock did not seem to suffer; however, influential investors like Warren Buffett criticized United, as did politicians, calling it *horrible*.

The United Express Flight 3411 incident not only embarrassed the flight crew in question, but the airline, the airport security staff, and the industry. Among the obvious and relevant questions asked were:

- Are routines pertaining to airlines' overbooking flights good enough?
- Do flight coupons suffice as incentives for passengers to give up their seats?
- Do they think that offering coupons that do not cost the airlines a penny will iron out any problem?

More critical questions may be lurking in the public's mind, questioning the aviation industry's policies toward the travelling public, its relations with paying customers, and its *raison d'être*:

- Do airlines care about their customers?
- Where is their moral responsibility?
- Are the perspectives of airline chief executive officers and chief financial officers just based on the next quarterly report, so that they may claim their bonuses?

- Would this have happened to a Caucasian, middle-aged person?
- Is there racism, or at least, an insensitivity to minority issues?

While crew aboard one of his cruise ships was trying to put out an engine room fire and thousands of passengers endured another day on the *Carnival Triumph* with no power, little water, and very little food, the owner of Carnival Cruise Lines, Micky Arison, attended a professional basketball game in which his Miami Heat team played the Portland Trail Blazers: "Boss of Carnival cruise ship adds insult to misery by going to basketball game as 4,000 suffer aboard 'stinking stricken ship' with urine-soaked carpets and sewage in cabins" (Durante, Malm, & Boyle, 2013). Cruise travelers, active in social media, reminded Mr. Arison of the Carnival-owned *Costa Concordia* disaster the previous year; 32 people lost their lives when the ship's captain, in an apparent attempt to impress a female companion, sailed too close to the shores of the Tuscan island of Giglio, ran aground and sank. Media coverage was overwhelming. Negative publicity could hardly get worse, with more than 426,000 Google hits on the *Costa Concordia* disaster.

The Carnival group's board of directors wrote in their quarterly report on February 28, 2013: "Management believes the ultimate outcome of these claims and lawsuits will not have a material adverse impact on our consolidated financial statements." Micky Arison was quoted by *The Guardian* saying that "it will take up to three years to recover the company's reputation and profitability [after the *Costa Concordia* shipwreck]" (Porritt & Jones 2013). As of 2019, seven years after the shipwreck, Costa cruises were still suffering, with travel professionals announcing huge discounts on all Costa Cruises.

Spin Doctors

Public relations and communications industries are commonly accused of serving special interest groups, effectively the rich and the powerful. It is argued that influential elites may buy professional services to a much greater degree than private citizens. That is, of course, correct, although not much different than in other sectors of society. Corporate and personal wealth, and political influence, are commodities that are unevenly distributed in society. In what may be efforts to defuse criticism, the public relations communities in Europe often equate and compare their industry with legal counsel, which by all norms is a legitimate industry in the private and public spheres.

It is also claimed that public relations practitioners, more specifically in the sector of public affairs, operate as spin doctors. Spin doctors present one-sided news on organizations and individuals to the public, and are sometimes accused of concealing facts and inconvenient truths. The impression of the public relations professional as a cynical, overpaid employee with credibility issues sticks in the public mind. Politicians are often accused of recruiting spin doctors to explain away dubious behavior or oversell good stories.

Spin doctors usually operate tactically, not strategically, as witnessed in press conferences and news media. The daily White House press briefing in the United States, to mention one such platform, is a forum for giving praise, stretching observations, and explaining how policies and tweets should be interpreted. Former press secretary Sean Spicer, and his successor (from September 2017) Sarah Huckabee Sanders, have often circumvented reporters' questions to present presidential views favorably. Counsellor to the US president, Kellyanne Conway, coined the term *alternative facts*. In an effort to defend Sean Spicer's statement about attendance numbers at President Trump's inauguration, she used the term to describe demonstrable falsehood (NBC News, 2017).

How, When and Why Is Theory Applied to Ethical Practice?

Literary Review and Theoretical Underpinning

Leeper (1996) argues that while increasing attention is being paid by people in public relations to ethical theory, the predominant ethical perspective in the field is situational, not normative. The reasons for that, he claims, could be the loss of the societal grounds for moral objectivity: tradition, religion, and universal reason. However, a situational perspective fails to provide a common and universal ethical code of conduct in the field of public relations:

> The problem with the situational approach is that "from a logical viewpoint, any fact can be used to justify any action, and any principle is moral. The only constraint is that an individual must be able to live with an action-at least for the short term." After acknowledging this subjectivist perspective and the problems inherent in it, Pratt [1991, p. 146] suggests that public relations needs to develop ongoing, dialogical, two-way symmetrical public relations. (Leeper, 1996, p. 134; internal quote from Ryan & Martinson, 1984, p. 27)

Leeper claims that a two-way symmetrical public relations model, as argued by Grunig and Hunt (1984), is consistent with coorientation theory (McLeod & Chaffee, 1973), which "suggests methods for measuring the degree of mutual orientation of individuals, groups or organizations toward an object, or the consensus among them about an object – for example, a value system such as ethics" (Leeper, 1996, p. 134). He argues that terms and phrases used to describe two-way symmetric, as well as coorientation models, include "theories of communication rather than theories of persuasion"; "mutual understanding"; "dialogue [rather] than a monologue"; and "both management and publics will change somewhat." Leeper, as well as Grunig and Hunt (1984) and L. A. Grunig, Grunig, & Dozier (2002), lean on Habermas (1990), whose "approach is dialogical, two-way symmetrical, and cooriented" (Leeper, 1996, p. 134).

This chapter builds on Leeper's tradition of analyzing and seeing ethics as situational. It furthermore accepts and acknowledges two-way symmetric and coorientation approaches as preferred methods for ethical strategic communication, and thus ethical public relations.

Freedom of Expression

A fundamental prerequisite for exchange of opinions, for truth, for strategic communication, and for practicing public relations, is freedom of expression. The global body of the United Nations, and its Universal Declaration of Human Rights of 1948 establishes and protects freedom of expression. The UN can, however, do little about regimes and nations that do not adhere to the declaration. It might also lack credibility since states in the UN Human Rights Council, which oversees such issues, include Saudi Arabia, Cuba, Qatar, China, and the Democratic Republic of the Congo (as of 2019), none of which can be said to be torches of freedom and human rights.

Most nations in Western Europe have signed the European Convention on Human Rights (dating from 1950), which protects freedom of expression both legally and politically. The US First Amendment defining freedoms under the constitution and adopted in 1791 has inspired legislators all over the world, and, in many ways, still serves as an inspirational national *credo*. Freedom of expression is written into the constitutions of most Western democracies, such as that of the author's native Norway (adopted in 1814).

John Stuart Mill remarked that *freedom of the press* is a prerequisite for truth, and truth is a prerequisite for democracy. He argued that "If all mankind minus one, were of one opinion, and only one person were of the contrary opinion, mankind would be no more justified in silencing that one person, than he, if he had the power, would be justified in silencing mankind" (Mill, 1859, p. 33).

While free speech's legal and political base largely remains unchallenged in Western democracy, there are some areas where legislatures and judicial systems target controversial expressions, in efforts to achieve the greatest possible good for as many people as possible, in accordance with teleological ethics. One such controversy occurred in 2005–2006, after the Danish daily newspaper *Jyllands-Posten* had published cartoons of images of Muhammad, the prophet and founder of Islam. Some politicians and diplomats panicked and to some extent apologized for freedom of expression in Europe. In 2015, the world was shaken by attacks on *Charlie Hebdo*, a Paris-based satirical weekly. Political reactions were then more mature than in 2006: leaders from most European nations marched side by side in Paris, demonstrating that freedom of expression was an unquestionable right. Racist speech or slur is a criminal risk zone in many jurisdictions, while criticism of religion is a cornerstone of the idea of free speech. The dividing line between racial slur and legitimate criticism was questioned in the 2005–2006 and 2015 cases.

Some jurisdictions ban certain advertising, i.e. targeting minors during certain hours. The marketing of hand weapons, illegal drugs, and alcohol and tobacco products is generally outlawed, and usually not considered to be a case of limiting freedom of expression.

Legislators may regulate the media and other industries structurally, in terms of financial and organizational laws, but, in Western society, rarely media content. Russian privately owned media are expected to support the incumbent regime; if not, they may be shut down. One-party states, such as China, Cuba, North Korea, and many developing countries, give few or no publishing opportunities to oppositional views.

In societies with weak civil sectors, members of minorities may find themselves at risk of political suppression, and subjected to social control and cultural biases. Sàmi people in Northern Scandinavia, descendants of African slaves in the Americas, members of LGBTQ communities, religious minorities, and millions of women share a history and experience regarding lack of freedom of speech. Cheryl Glenn (2004) has written on unspoken and unheard voices, especially on minority and gender issues, and about the role and uncertainty of living at other people's mercy.

Examples of Theory Used to Ensure Ethical Practice

Normative Ethical Theory

Teleology, derived from the Greek terms *telos* alludes to *end* or *consequence*, and *logos*, in this context, to the study of *words* or *communication*. The term is therefore used to describe *usefulness of actions* toward the happiness the public relations procedures will create. Here, the outcome, or consequence of the action or the communication practice, will be the most important perspective when judging whether or not the relevant conduct is ethically acceptable. For a summary of this and other theories used in ethics, see Table 5.1.

The moral philosophy of John Stuart Mill is based on the principle that humans should strive for happiness as an outcome when planning a certain practice. Mill ranks happiness that is a consequence of actions in the categories *high* and *low*, on a continuum, not a dichotomous scale. A high level of intelligence, mental happiness, and health are examples of high-grade

Table 5.1 Summary of theories used in ethics

Theory	Summary
Teleology	The Greek term *telos* alludes to *end* or *consequence*, and *logos* to the study of *words* or *communication*. Teleology is used to describe the *usefulness of actions* toward the happiness the public relations procedures will create. The consequence of the action or the communication practice is the most important perspective when judging whether relevant conduct is ethically acceptable or not.
Deontology	Greek for *duty*, *deontos* points to the human duty to respect the rights of others and to treat others according to those rights. Supporters of deontological ethics assess conduct according to the conduct itself, not according to the happiness that is the outcome of the conduct.
The Other	Although not a theory per se, the Other, a concept coined by the moral philosopher Emmanuel Levinas, is an ethical imperative, with roots in teleological, as well as deontological thinking: Witnessing suffering and pain in the face of the Other, it is my duty as a human to help alleviate the pain of the Other.
Truth	The term and concept of truth is multifaceted. The following idea was expressed by Aristotle: To say of what is that it is not, or of what is not that it is, is false, while to say of what is that it is, and of what is not that it is not, is true.
Post-truth	A term related to, or denoting circumstances in which objective facts are less influential in shaping public opinion than appeals to emotion and personal belief.
Advocacy	Advocacy is to serve a client's and/or an employer's interests by acting as responsible advocates and by providing a voice in the marketplace of ideas, facts, and viewpoints to aid informed public debate

happiness. For low-grade happiness, Mill adds ignorance, stupidity, selfishness, laziness, and physical pleasure. Mill's moral philosophy, *utilitarianism*, usually ranks friendship, loyalty, and justice high in the high end category.

Mill also remarks that the birthright to free expression is a prerequisite for truth, and truth is a prerequisite for democracy. Mill's grounds of freedom of expression are arguments for liberal Western democracy. The US First Amendment (1791) precedes Mill (1806–1873); it is a document developed to realize the spirit of the Age of Enlightenment.

Deontology, from *deontos*, Greek for *duty*, points to the human duty to respect the rights of others and to treat others according to those rights. Supporters of deontological ethics assess conduct according to the conduct itself, not according to the happiness that is the outcome of the conduct. Attitudes and perceptions about what is ethical, and what is unethical, therefore vary with community standards.

Levinas's Ethical Imperative

Emmanuel Levinas discusses ethical issues of encounters between the "I" and the "Other" (Levinas, 1969). Such encounters place a burden of ethical conduct on the "I," who cannot escape an assumed responsibility for the Other. A responsible person, or institution, cannot act indifferently when encountering the Other, or the Others. Levinas did not merely discuss live or physical encounters. His philosophy is applicable in the abstract; in mediated and virtual settings. Images of suffering brought to us by mass media or online might define such encounters with the Other. Levinas's moral philosophy places a universal moral responsibility on humans that they cannot outrun. The "I" *cannot not* assume responsibility for the suffering and must do as much as possible to alleviate it.

A logical consequence of adapting Levinas's moral philosophy is that it is ethically indefensible to inflict any form of suffering. The infliction may be symbolic, like a picture uploaded in a media channel, a taunt in a text message, or an intimate video posted on social media channels.

Levinas's ethical imperatives for people in modern society are indeed extensive. Victims of natural disasters and hunger, the unemployed and poor are no longer faceless masses. Their images show up on billions of screens globally. From time to time, the world mobilizes when disaster strikes. Then again, the magnitude of knowledge of world suffering may overwhelm private citizens and leave them indifferent.

Levinas was a twentieth-century European, of Lithuanian Jewish origins and naturalized French. He was captured by the Nazis and his Lithuanian family was murdered in the Holocaust, an unspoken brutality and human degradation for which there are no words. Members of ethnic, sexual, and religious minorities may be perceived as representing a deviation from an imaginary social norm. As such, minorities may be subjected to notions of powerlessness, being in someone else's power, having their very existence subjected to the approval of the majority.

Levinas's philosophy is often discussed in contemporary Europe, for instance on migration issues. Despite its recent past, Europe demonstrates a general lack of pity for Asian and African migrants, thousands of whom drown in the Mediterranean before reaching hostile European shores. Contrary to the generosity shown during the post–World War II period, when Europeans opened their homes to unfortunate relatives trapped on the *wrong* side of new borders, there is a notion that Europe is full; *don't come here.*

Norms related to *the Other* can be interpreted as expressions of a universal, self-centered meta-norm: "Do not do unto others what you do not want them to do unto you." The norm is applicable to almost any imaginable situation where people must decide whether to do something that may have consequences for others. We can also imagine a proactive meta-norm with a more assertive imperative: "Do unto others as you would have them do unto you."

While the focal point of Islam, Judaism, and Christianity is on the individual, as member of a community, the philosophical foundation of Buddhism, Confucianism, teaches that *communities* rank above *individuals.* Collective views are prominent in other Eastern religions, such as Shintoism and Hinduism. It must be said that the essence of meta-norms will be recognized as a central ethical principle for a large number of people, almost regardless of religious or value justification.

Truth as an Ethical Requirement

Most people know media content or expressions to be true or false, accurate or inaccurate. It is important to know what "truth" is, to be able to detect deviation from truth. Ethical behavior and ethical expressions depend on truth as a prerequisite, meaning that public relations practitioners and strategists must have access to truthful information in order to make good choices. It is therefore important to be able to separate *true* from *false.*

The definition by Aristotle (b. 340 BCE) of falsehood and truth is objective: "To say of what is that it is not, or of what is not that it is, is false, while to say of what is that it is, and of what is not that it is not, is true" (*Metaphysics* 1011b25). If you claim that white snow is not white, you lie. Claiming that grass is green will, in many instances, be true. Separating truths from lies can be readily appreciated in trivial contexts, as in the color example. To think, that is, to hold something to be true, must sometimes be accepted. Laws and legal systems also take into account the qualifying element of expressing something in good faith.

However, there must be an ethical imperative that practitioners within the field of strategic communication and public relations must seek truth by checking facts and arguments presented as facts, checking sources, and comprehending research. If not, the consequences of non-truth or false claims can be passed on to others.

Post-truth?

In her essay "Covering politics in a 'post-truth' America," Glasser (2016) discusses new aspects of *truth* in contemporary discourse and uses the modern term "post-truth."

The distinguished Oxford Dictionaries chose the adjective "post-truth" as the 2016 word of the year. Remarking on this, cultural commentator Neil Midgley wrote that the term, although not new, got its spin during the campaigns leading up to the 2016 British referendum on continued membership of the European Union and in the 2016 American election campaign. Oxford Dictionaries (2016) defines the term *post-truth* as "related to or denoting circumstances in which objective facts are less influential in shaping public opinion than appeals to emotion and personal belief." What publics like to hear, or wish to be true, is more important to public opinion formation than opinion formation based on objective, observable reality. Before the June 2016 vote on Britain's continued membership of the European Union, rumor had it, and management of the *Leave* campaign stated, that a Brexit would release 350 million pounds each week, funds that could be channeled into the National Health Service, the British underfinanced public health system. If *Remain* won, it was said in the same breath, poor migrants from Central and Eastern Europe would flood the island kingdom in hordes of biblical proportions. Both claims were at best half-truths. They were, however, effective in the sense that they may have mobilized voter segments that were uncomfortable with abstract arguments on European values and shared culture, and historical references.

Donald Trump's campaign was, according to the *New York Times*, *Washington Post*, and a majority of the community of analysts and observers, a near endless series of post-truth claims. Voters flocked around emotional slogans like "Make America great again," or "Lock her up," aimed at Trump's opponent, Hillary Clinton, and "Build that wall." Trump supporter and CNN commentator Jeffrey Lord said fact-checking is just another "out of touch, elitist media-type thing," i.e. elements of and qualities of media presentations in discourse alien to common people.

Major Topics/Questions Needing to Be Addressed by Public Relations Theorists Working with Ethics and Ethical Practice

Industry Associations' Codes of Ethics

In this last section of this chapter, the need for a a global code of ethics will be discussed as a topic needing to be further addressed by public relations theorists working with ethics and ethical practice.

Codes of ethical conduct are usually general, developed by and for public relations consultants and their clients. Industry associations usually take on the task of developing ethical guidelines for use within professional communities in order to establish common grounds. Guidelines are usually a set of self-imposed restrictions that members are expected to adhere to. Working in public relations requires neither certification nor authorization. It attracts candidates from a wide variety of backgrounds: academics from advertising and the humanities, journalism and law, to mention some. Given the industry's diversity, the aim is to establish sets of broad ground rules for its members.

In Western Europe and North America, ethical guidelines for public relations focus on abstract key attitudes to meet client and community standards embedded in industry practice: they usually include codes of integrity and confidentiality, as well as requiring practitioners to possess relevant, adequate aptitudes and skills. Industry associations pledge to raise awareness in their membership about such issues.

The Global Alliance (GA) for Public Relations and Communication Management, a confederation of major public relations and communication management associations and institutions, represents 160,000 practitioners and academics around the world. In the preamble to its section on codes of ethics, GA stated that ethical awareness and ethical thinking are at the very core of its mission to raise professional standards (Global Alliance PR, 2016). Practitioners must possess, acknowledge, and adhere to those standards:

- mastery of a particular intellectual skill through education and training;
- acceptance of duties to a broader society than merely one's clients/employers;
- objectivity;
- high standards of conduct and performance.

GA values are, in the words of the association on its website, "the fundamental value and dignity of the individual free exercise of human rights, especially freedom of speech, assembly, media, essential to the practice of good public relations." Hence, its goal is to work for "better communication, understanding, and cooperation among diverse individuals, groups, and institutions of society," principles that could be written into the United Nations or the European human rights declarations. The GA key values are concretized into members obliging to conduct themselves professionally, with integrity, truth, accuracy, fairness, and responsibility with client publics, as well as with an informed society.

The following from the GA website in 2016 provides further elaboration of the organization's perception and practice of ethics in meeting clients, clients' clients, and society:

- *Advocacy*: to serve client and employer interests by acting as responsible advocates and by providing a voice in the marketplace of ideas, facts, and viewpoints to aid informed public debate.
- *Honesty*: to adhere to the highest standards of accuracy and truth in advancing the interests of clients and employers ...
- *Integrity*: ... to conduct business with integrity and observe the principles and spirit of the Code in such a way that [our] reputation and that of [our] employer and the public relations profession in general is protected.
- *Expertise*: ... to encourage members to acquire and responsibly use specialized knowledge and experience to build understanding and client/employer credibility. Furthermore, ... actively promote and advance the profession through continued professional development, research, and education.
- Loyalty: ... to insist that members are faithful to those they represent, while honoring their obligations to serve the interests of society and support the right of free expression.

The values do not essentially differ from ethical codes of other groups of professionals, such as lawyers, auditors, teachers, and journalists. Local PR ethics codes often stress that "integrity" also means that public relations practitioners should under no circumstances solicit third parties for personal and private advantage.

Many of the provisions have roots in Mill's ethics of consequence. A staff member should be able to identify different scenarios that may arise as a consequence of the action planned. Relevant and foreseeable consequences should be taken into consideration when developing public relations strategies for clients.

The GA code went on to specify concrete skills and mindsets:

- Acknowledge that there is an obligation to protect and enhance the profession.
- Keep informed and educated about practices in the profession that ensure ethical conduct.
- Actively pursue personal professional development.
- Accurately define what public relations activities can and cannot accomplish.
- Counsel its individual members in proper ethical decision-making generally and on a case-specific basis.
- Require that individual members observe the ethical recommendations and behavioral requirements of the code.

Individuals, organizations, NGOs, or corporations that solicit and buy services from public relations practitioners should be able to take it for granted that providers of such services are aware of ethical standards to optimally serve the customer. In the practical world, clients must be able to trust that public relations practitioners, like other businesses, have their customers' best interests at heart. Practitioners must not invoice for services not rendered or overbill clients. Professional ethics must be understood in light of the society in which they are exercised and the moral and ethical codes and values that form the norms of that particular society.

A major concern in all economic and organizational activities is the reciprocal requirement of confidence, a requirement crucial to all provider/customer relations to varying degrees, inspired by the universal, self-centered meta-norm. Someone who buys a ticket to see a movie expects the theatre staff to do their best to deliver the appropriate product. A butcher should be able to look his customer in the eye after the meat that he sold has been consumed. A person who consults a doctor must be able to trust that the doctor wants to do her best. Similar requirements apply to the field of public relations. A client should never have to doubt that the provider has the relevant ethical awareness.

The burden of professional responsibility needed to establish and maintain this confidence lies with the supplier. In a value chain, the supplier must establish a good working environment and secure mutual trust throughout the relationship. It may be too big a task for an unexperienced customer to get an overview of the number and competencies of public relations market actors, let alone to assess representatives' academic and professional excellence. Even the most diligent customer will probably not check diplomas, transcripts, and references from previous employers.

Client/professional initial trust is therefore based on assumptions: The client must be willing to bear the risk by handing over all or part of their communication and public relations activities to people they assume will handle them well. The assumptions may be founded on their own or others' experiences and the capacity the customer thinks they have to comprehend and understand the qualities of the public relations practitioners after only a short, maybe superficial encounter.

Nevertheless, customers may have exaggerated expectations of the results the provider can produce. Even the best public relations strategy plan has its limitations.

Suggested Case to Explore to Demonstrate Theory at Work with Ethics and Ethical Practice

The Case of Volkswagen 2015

When a research team at the University of West Virginia tested emissions from two random Volkswagen (VW) diesel cars in 2015, results showed that emissions were far higher than in

Volkswagen's laboratory tests, reports of which were used in the auto manufacturer's marketing strategies. The university researchers worked on behalf of the ICCT, the International Council on Clean Transportation, which had conducted similar tests in Europe and in some US states.

The US Environmental Protection Agency revealed after laboratory tests that Volkswagen had installed software designed to cheat testing programs in its diesel cars. The software was designed to recognize steering wheel and pedal movements typical for test situations, thus reducing emissions of environmentally harmful substances during tests. In normal use, the software feature would be turned off.

The actual emissions were up to 40 times higher than allowed for nitrogen oxide gas. The program was installed in EA 189 diesel engines, developed for use in small to medium-sized cars such as Polo, Golf (Rabbit or Caribe in North America), and Passat.

One of the world's largest car manufacturers, the Volkswagen Aktiengesellschaft group also owns the automobile manufacturers Audi, Skoda, and Seat, luxury brands Bentley, Bugatti, Porsche, and Lamborghini, and truck manufacturers MAN and Scania. It had installed 11 million software programs in passenger cars and vans marketed and sold globally. The group is one of the world's largest, with about 600,000 employees.

What Happened after the Revelations?

A couple of days after the news struck, the company's CEO, Martin Winterkorn, issued a statement in which he promised to give the matter the highest priority. He was then let go by the Volkswagen board of directors. The attorney general in Braunschweig (Germany) initiated criminal investigations against the company. It was revealed that a senior employee had tried to blow the whistle on the software fraud in 2011, without management listening, let alone taking action.

What was later coined the *VW Abgas-Skandal* (exhaust gas scandal) had enormous ripple effects:

- *Financial*: VW's board immediately put aside 6.5 billion euros to meet costs for recalling and adjusting cars, and for future fines and expected compensation claims. Some independent analysts suggested that costs could reach as high as 60 billion euros, a sum not verified, nor has VW revealed an estimated total cost.
- *Industrial*: Although no other car manufacturers were immediately involved, the scandal cast a shadow over an entire industry. Opinion polls taken after the scandal gave no clear answers on the extent to which it had hurt the VW Group. An online survey conducted in September 2015 by Prophet, a management consultancy firm, showed that most Germans, 65% of the respondents, believed that the "scandal had been exaggerated and that VW still built excellent cars." Furthermore, nine out of ten of the respondents in the sample, 91%, believed that other carmakers also manipulated omission tests, and "that VW was just the first to be found out" (Löhr, 2015). Thus, it might seem that the German public held the entire car industry responsible for something that only VW had done. Another survey, conducted by AutoPacific, showed that 64% of US car owners in the sample no longer trusted Volkswagen, and that a mere 25% held positive views of the company (PR Newswire, 2015).
- *Political*: On both sides of the Atlantic, the scandal triggered a political and public outcry and a demand for political action. An emerging issue was whether politicians should impose stricter requirements, even banning diesel cars in urban areas. In her speech to the pre-election party congress of the Christian Democratic Union in August 2017, German chancellor Angela Merkel commanded VW to restore its reputation. She added that "large parts of the

automotive industry have gambled away their credibility," before adding: "Ehrlichkeit gehört zur sozialen Marktwirtschaft," "Honesty is a part of the social market economy" (Automobilwoche, 2017; and for updates on the scandal, see Autobild, 2018). The reputation of Germany, Europe's economic and political locomotive, was at stake.

Discussion Questions

1 What is the relevance of the popular idea and concepts of ethics and morals in today's society?

2 What are the reasons why ethics is so often linked to religious beliefs and philosophy?

3 Given that truth is an ethical imperative, should there still be room for alternative norms in ethical communication?

4 Are there instances in which truth may not be the answer?

5 Leonardo Di Caprio is said to be planning a movie on the automobile diesel scandal, discussed in this chapter. What topics for teleological and deontological discussions for the Volkswagen and similar industrial frauds would you, as a writer and director, consider for such a docudrama?

Suggested Readings

Arnett, R.C., Deluliis, S. M, & Corr, M. *Corporate communication crisis leadership: Advocacy and ethics*. New York: Business Expert Press.

Cheney, G., May, S., & D. Munshi, D. (Eds.). (2011). *The handbook of communication ethics*. New York: Routledge.

Cooper, M. (2018). Decentering judgment: Toward a postmodern communication ethic. In J. M. Sloop & J. P. McDaniel (Eds.), *Judgment calls: Rhetoric, politics, and indeterminacy*. New York: Routledge.

Parsons, P. (2016): *Ethics in public relations: A guide to best practice*. London: Kogan Page.

Seib, P. M., & Fitzpatrick, K. (1995). *Public relations ethics*. Fort Worth, TX: Harcourt Brace College.

References

Autobild. (2018). Alle Infos zum Abgasskandal [All the information about the exhaust gas scandal]. Retrieved from http://www.autobild.de/artikel/vw-abgasskandal-aktuelle-news-und-updates-6077591.html

Automobilwoche. (2017, August 12). *Abgas-Skandal: Kanzlerin Merkel kritisiert Autoindustrie scharf*. Retrieved from https://www.automobilwoche.de/article/20170812/AGENTURMELDUNGEN/308129984/abgas-skandal-kanzlerin-merkel-kritisiert-autoindustrie-scharf

Beeler, N. (2017, April 11). Purchase an upgrade to not be beaten unconscious. *Columbus Dispatch*.

Bowen, S. A. (2007). The extent of ethics. In E. L. Toth (Ed.), *The future of excellence in public relations and communication management* (pp. 275–297). Mahwah, NJ: Lawrence Erlbaum.

Durante, T., Malm, S., & Boyle, L. (2013, February 13). Boss of Carnival cruise ship … *MailOnline*. Retrieved from https://www.dailymail.co.uk/news/article-2277914/Carnival-Triumph-CEO-Micky-Arison-takes-basketball-game-thousands-suffer.html

Fawkes, J. (2012). Saints and sinners: Competing identities in public relations ethics. *Public Relations Review*, 38(5), 865–872.

Glasser, S. B. (2016, December 2). *Covering politics in a "post-truth" America*. Brookings Essay. Retrieved from https://www.brookings.edu/essay/covering-politics-in-a-post-truth-america/

Glenn, C. (2004). *Unspoken: A rhetoric of silence*. Carbondale: Southern Illinois University Press.

Global Alliance PR. (2016). *Code of ethics*. Lugano, Switzerland: Global Alliance for Public Relations and Communications Management.

Grunig, J. E. (2000). Collectivism, collaboration, and societal corporatism as core professional values in public relations. *Journal of Public Relations Research*, 12(1), 23–48.

Grunig, J. E., & Hunt, T. (1984). *Managing public relations*. New York: Holt, Rinehart and Winston.

Grunig, L. A., Grunig, J. E., & Dozier, D. M. (2002). *Excellent public relations and effective organizations*. Mahwah, NJ: Lawrence Erlbaum.

Habermas, J. (1990). Discourse ethics: Notes on a program of philosophical justification. In J. Habermas, *Moral consciousness and communicative action* (C. Lenhardt & S. W. Nicholsen, Trans.). Cambridge, MA: MIT Press.

Hammerstein, K. (2008). Schuldige Opfer? Der Nazionalsozialismus in den Gründungsmythen der DDR, Österreichs und der Bundesrepublik Deutschland. In R. Fritz, C. Sachse, & E. Wolfrum (Eds.), *Nationen und ihre Selbstbilder: Postdiktatorische Gesellschaften in Europa*. Göttingen: Wallstein.

Holtzhausen, D., & Zerfass, A. (2012). Strategic communication: Opportunities and challenges of the research area. In D. Holtzhausen & A. Zerfass (Eds.), *The Routledge handbook of strategic communication* (pp. 3–17). New York: Routledge.

Leeper, R. V. (1996). Moral objectivity, Jurgen Habermas's discourse ethics, and public relations. *Public Relations Review*, 22(2), 133–150.

Levinas, E. (1969). *Totality and infinity: An essay on exteriority*. Dordrecht, The Netherlands: Kluwer.

Löhr, J. (2015, October 20). Two-thirds of Germans still trust Volkswagen after emissions scandal. *The Guardian*. Retrieved from https://www.theguardian.com/business/2015/oct/20/two-thirds-of-germans-still-trust-volkswagen-after-emissions-scandal

McCann, E. (2017, April 14). United's apologies: A timeline. *New York Times*.

McLeod, J., & Chaffee, S. (1973). Interpersonal approaches to communication research. *American Behavioral Scientist* (2017, March), 469–499.

Mill, J. S. (1859). *On liberty*. London: John W. Parker and Son.

NBC News. (2017, January 22). Kellyanne Conway: Press Secretary Sean Spicer gave "alternative facts." Retrieved from https://www.youtube.com/watch?v=VSrEEDQgFc8

Oxford Dictionaries. (2016). *Word of the year*. Oxford University Press. Retrieved from https://en.oxforddictionaries.com/word-of-the-year/word-of-the-year-2016

Porritt, L., & Jones, R. (2013, September 24). Carnival group anticipates three-year recovery after Concordia disaster. *The Guardian*.

Pratt, C. B. (1991). PRSA members' perceptions of public relations ethics. *Public Relations Review*, 17(2), 145–159.

PR Newswire. (2015, October 1). Volkswagen's reputation takes big hit with vehicle owners. Retrieved from https://www.prnewswire.com/news-releases/volkswagens-reputation-takes-big-hit-with-vehicle-owners-autopacific-predicts-tough-road-ahead-for-the-brand-300152504.html

Ryan, M., & Martinson, D. L. (1984). Ethical values, the flow of journalistic information and public relations persons. *Journalism & Mass Communication Quarterly, 61*(1), 27–34.

van der Vat, D. (2007, June 15). Kurt Waldheim. *The Guardian.* Retrieved from https://www.theguardian.com/news/2007/jun/15/guardianobituaries.austria

6

Dialogue and Organization–Public Relationships

Maureen Taylor, Michael L. Kent, and Ying Xiong

Certain words often mean one thing in everyday usage that they do not mean to professional communicators or scholars. Dialogue is just such a word, used informally every day by people to mean talk or conversation: "Ethiopia plans to release some imprisoned politicians in bid for national dialogue," a *Washington Post* headline reads (February 12, 2018). Or, as a *New York Times* headline suggests: "France condemns killings in Cameroon, urges dialogue" (February 3, 2018). The subject matter of such stories is often about politicians talking *to* voters or other politicians, rather than *with* others.

So, what is dialogue exactly? The concept of dialogue can be traced back to Martin Buber's book *I and Thou* (1958). Buber considered dialogue something that could occur in interpersonal interactions and believed that the persons involved in a dialogue should recognize the other's innate value. Thirty years later, Ron Pearson's dissertation (1989b) made the concept of dialogue relevant to public relations. Pearson regarded dialogue as a respectful and more ethical communication approach superior to other existing public relations approaches of the day. With the advent of the internet, Kent and Taylor (1998) first discussed dialogue through the co-creational perspective, as a way to improve organization–public (note, read the dash as "to") communication, and described dialogue as "any negotiated exchange of ideas and opinions" (p. 325). The mistake many have made is putting the emphasis on the exchange of ideas such as takes place in the mass media, rather than on the idea of negotiated exchange. Kent and Taylor also redefined the concept of dialogue against the backdrop of the internet era and identified five principles used through the World Wide Web, and then conceptualized five features of dialogic communication (Kent & Taylor, 1998, 2002).

In the past 20 years, scholars have applied the principles and features of dialogue to different contexts, such as charities, corporate social responsibility (CSR) communication, museums, nongovernmental organizations, pharmaceutical companies, social media, university recruiting, and dozens of other areas (e.g. Briones, Kuch, Liu, & Jin, 2011; Gordon & Berhow, 2009; Kent & Taylor, 2016; McAllister, 2012; McAllister-Spooner & Kent, 2009; Saffer, Sommerfeldt, & Taylor, 2013). Although public relations professionals understand a lot more about dialogue now than two decades ago, many questions still remain. We hope that this chapter explains dialogue in public relations and helps you see its value for your future career.

The chapter will explore dialogue and public relations through six areas. The first section explores the concept of dialogue, the origin of dialogue, the features of dialogic communication, the life cycle of dialogue, and the misconceptions about dialogue in public relations. The second section provides a discussion about how dialogue relates to organization–public relationships. The third section reviews how and why dialogue and relationships are such a concern for

Public Relations Theory: Application and Understanding, First Edition. Edited by Brigitta R. Brunner.
© 2019 John Wiley & Sons, Inc. Published 2019 by John Wiley & Sons, Inc.

public relations practitioners. The fourth section outlines how, when, and why dialogue is applied to relationships. The fifth section provides examples of how dialogue builds organization–public relationships. And the sixth section discusses the next steps to be taken by public relations theorists working in dialogue and organization–public relationships.

Defining the Concepts: What Is Dialogue?

In this section, the concept of dialogue will be discussed. As noted previously, the word dialogue has been applied in various ways in everyday life, and multiple ways in social science. So, before we begin, we need to understand the concept of dialogue in public relations.

The Origin of Dialogue

The word "dialogue" derives from the Greek word *dialogos* – where "dia" means "through" and "across" and "logos" means "word" and "meaning" (Cissna & Anderson, 1998). Martin Buber is regarded as one of the intellectual parents of modern dialogue. Writing in 1923, Buber described the concept of the *I-Thou* and *I-It* (Buber, 1958). "I-Thou" refers to a human's attitude to other persons, while the "I-It" reflects a human's attitude toward objects. "I-Thou" is a relationship with the characteristics of openness, directness, mutuality, and presence, while the "I-It" relation is a form of monologue, which is prevalent in daily life. One of the suggestions from Buber is to treat others as "thou," rather than "it," in ethical interpersonal relationships. (Table 6.1 presents a list of significant dialogic authors from Buber through to Anne Lane in current times.)

Going beyond interpersonal relationships, dialogue is also considered as an ethical framework in public relations and communication. Taylor and Kent (2014) wrote: "dialogue, as an established theory of ethics, says that organizations should engage with stakeholders and publics to make things happen, to help make better decisions, to keep citizens informed, and to strengthen organizations and society" (pp. 387–388). The implication here is that dialogue should be an imperative for organizations, and they should engage in dialogue when they communicate with publics.

Dialogue is a complex concept with multiple dimensions. Recently, Kent and Lane (2017) used a plant metaphor of a "rhizome" to describe the concept of dialogue: "Dialogue is not the one-off message of the tree, but the longevity of the rhizomatous relationships developed, their strength and endurance, their connection to other parts of a network through hidden bonds" (p. 573). By using the rhizomatous metaphor, Kent and Lane emphasized several features of rhizomatous dialogue, such as the multiple entry points, the enduring process, and the interactive, organic, and random rhizomatous exchanges among dialogic participants.

Kent and Lane argued that dialogue was essentially a long-term and relational process. They urged organizations to not simply treat employees, stakeholders, and publics as interchangeable parts, privileging the organization's needs over all others, but to learn and grow from their interactions with their publics. Organizations should take a longer-term view about their role in their environment.

Features of Dialogic Communication

What makes some communication dialogic and other communication not dialogic? The answer is: the orientation to others. Dialogic communication encompasses five features: mutuality, propinquity, empathy, risk, and commitment, as described by Kent and Taylor (2002, pp. 25–29), that together create an orientation to others.

Table 6.1 A summary of dialogic authors

Name and date of main works	Background	Main contributions to dialogue theory
Martin Buber (1923)	Jewish philosopher, born and raised in Vienna, eventually settled in Jerusalem. Renowned scholar of Midrash and Rabbinic literature.	Text: *I and Thou*. Focuses on dialogue as part of an interpersonal communication exchange. Deeply rooted ontology, experience, and Kantian ethics.
Carl Rogers (1957)	American, Columbia University trained psychologist; prolific scholar; master clinician.	Created person-centered psychology. Key concepts: "Unconditional positive regard for the other," genuineness, spontaneity, and face-to-face interactions.
Paulo Freire (1970)	Brazilian educator, an advocate for the poor and oppressed.	Text: *Pedagogy of the oppressed*. Developed a "critical pedagogy"; worked with migrant workers and the oppressed.
R. D. Laing (1961)	Scottish psychiatrist and scholar.	Text: *Self and others*. People make sense of the world in relations to others.
Hans-Georg Gadamer (1975)	German hermeneutic, dialogue scholar.	Text: *Truth and method*. Advocated for exploring biases; language was part of the art of finding truth.
Mikhail Bakhtin (1975)	Russian scholar, literary critic, semiotician, and linguistic philosopher.	Text: *The dialogic imagination*. Contextual and co-created meaning. Meaning is not limited to face-to-face communication. Dialogue is hermeneutic.
Jürgen Habermas (1981)	German sociologist and philosopher in the tradition of critical theory and pragmatism.	Text: *The theory of communicative action*. Critical theory, pragmatism; communicative rationality; public sphere.
Nel Noddings (1984)	American born feminist, philosopher, and educator.	Text: *Caring: A feminine approach to ethics and moral education*. Known for educational philosophy, theory, and "an ethic of care."
Kenneth Cissna and Robert Anderson (1980s and 1990s)	American interpersonal communication scholars.	Text: *Theorizing about dialogic moments: The Buber-Rogers position and postmodern themes*. Authored several dialogic texts and readers, responsible for substantial theoretical contributions to dialogic theory.
Barnett Pearce and Kimberly Pearce (2000)	American interpersonal communication scholars, community dialogue consultants.	Coordinated management of meaning; dialogic virtuosity; Cupertino Community Project; public dialogue consortium.
Ron Pearson (1990s)	Canadian ethicist; public relations scholar.	Text: *A theory of public relations ethics* (doctoral dissertation). Process-based approach to organizational dialogue and public relations.
Michael L. Kent and Maureen Taylor (1998/2002)	American public relations scholars.	Text: "Toward a dialogic theory of public relations." Dialogic model of web communication; outlined five features of dialogic communication.
Petra Theunissen (2012)	New Zealand public relations scholar.	Dialogic critic. Proposed a dialogic persuasion model "Per-Di" based on ideas from quantum physics.
Anne Lane (2015)	Australian public relations scholar.	Worked to make dialogue more practical; focus on engagement and implications of mandated dialogue.

First, *mutuality*. Mutuality is characterized by an "inclusion or collaborative orientation" and a "spirit of mutual equality." Collaboration and spirit of mutual equality are the two features of mutuality.

Second, *propinquity*, or "nearness." Dialogic propinquity means that publics are consulted in matters that influence them, and for publics, it means that they are willing and able to articulate their demands to organizations. Propinquity is created by three features of dialogic relationships: immediacy of presence, temporal flow, and engagement.

Third, *empathy*. Empathy refers to the atmosphere of support and trust that must exist if dialogue is to succeed. Supportiveness, communal orientation and confirmation are the three main features of empathy.

Fourth, *risk*. Risk means parties who engage in dialogue take relational risks. Vulnerability, unanticipated consequences, and recognition of strange otherness are characterized as the feature of risk.

Fifth, *commitment*. Commitment describes three characteristics of dialogic encounters: "genuineness" and authenticity, "commitment to the conversation," and a "commitment to interpretation."

Another key feature of dialogue that ties all of the five features together is the concept of *trust*. Without a willingness to engage and trust one another, dialogue is not possible. Trust, of course, also needs to be built. Organizations need to take steps as they engage their stakeholders to build relationships and foster trust through engagement and interaction (cf. Lane & Kent, 2018)

Each of the five dialogic features is about building and maintaining the relationship. *The five dialogic features are all necessary.* Indeed, the five dialogic features are the floor or lowest level of the bar that needs to be met before dialogue can be genuine. People who engage in dialogue spend time in close proximity (*propinquity*). Just asking employees, stakeholders, publics, or customers what they think, or for their ideas, is not dialogue. Spending time in meetings talking, building relationships is. Similarly, *mutuality* is necessary. When one party in an interaction tries to gather information about the other, or exploit what they know or believe, there is no dialogue taking place. Ultimately, sharing information with others and self-disclosing is a *risk*, and thus, risk and trust go hand-in-hand as dialogue is built. Part of the importance of building relationships through dialogue is for both parties to *empathize* or understand the other. Dialogue is not about persuasion but trust and coorientation or understanding. Finally, commitment emerges from the iterative communication. Dialogue is not about the episodic exploitation of others, but about building long-term relationships with others.

Life Cycle of Dialogue

Dialogue is an interaction and there are stages in its life cycle as interactants engage and disengage. Here, we discuss how a dialogue starts, how dialogue is achieved, and we explain how and whether dialogue has an ending point.

How a Dialogue Begins

When does a dialogue begin? Who should be the initiator of a new dialogic relationship? A dialogue begins with the awareness of others and willingness to turn to the other person (Cissna & Anderson, 1998). As Buber wrote, "the basic movement of the life of dialogue is the turning toward the other" (1965, p. 25). What Buber meant is that there is both an emotional and a physical "turning" toward another. Turning toward another occurs through a psychological orientation toward the other as well as a physical moving toward the other. Dialogue is not an individualistic process. Dialogic partners need to recognize the value of others and move together (Kent & Taylor, 2016; Taylor & Kent, 2014).

Empathy is another underlying precondition for professionals to apply dialogic communication. Empathy refers to "the ability to put yourself into the shoes of another person" (Kent & Taylor, 2016, p. 65). It is hard to achieve dialogue without the humanistic exchange of empathy (Kelleher, 2009). Public relations practitioners and their organizations need to be empathetic to the needs, attitudes, and behaviors of their stakeholders. Organizations must not view publics, especially activist publics, as obstacles or challenges. Instead, practitioners need to "walk in their shoes" to better understand how the organization can meet their needs. Remember, activists are actually trying to help organizations meet societal expectations, and change from within is always better than forced regulation or laws.

Achieving Dialogue

Dialogue is not an easy process to undertake. In fact, it can be slow, painful, and long. How do communication professionals ensure the success of the dialogic process? First, genuineness and authenticity are the key elements for a successful dialogue (Cissna & Anderson, 1998). Genuineness and authenticity are part of dialogic commitment, and mean being honest and forthright. Dialogue should not be undertaken in an attempt to manipulate.

The partners in a dialogue should not be concealing their true thoughts, nor pretending to listen to each other (Cissna & Anderson, 1998). In the social media era, many organizations have created social media accounts and regularly post messages to followers, consumers, and others. Some scholars have considered these online interactions as proof of dialogue (Adams & McCorkindale, 2013; Rybalko & Seltzer, 2010). However, online interactions are not sufficient proof of dialogue because most organizations do not apply genuine and authentic replies when they interact with their social media followers. Organizations often ignore uncomfortable questions and criticisms from followers in social media and use social media as a marketing tool. These organizational behaviors reveal an unwillingness or inability to enact dialogue (Taylor & Kent, 2014). More importantly, however, social media is a public forum and dialogue is an interpersonal activity. As a tool, social media cannot mimic real communication interactions. The public face of social media is not suitable for dialogic exchanges. But, as Kent and Taylor (1998) suggested, social media and the internet can be used to facilitate genuine *dialogic exchanges rather than dialogue.*

Second, no partner in a dialogic interaction should seek to manipulate or control the process of dialogue. In other words, one participant should not try to direct the outcome of the dialogue. Trying to direct outcomes reflects a functional approach to public relations and is antithetical to a dialogic orientation. When practitioners believe that they can "manage" organization–public relationships, they are not talking about enacting true dialogue. The word "manage" is not a dialogic concept.

Third, dialogue should emphasize the process of reciprocity, mutuality, and negotiation. Dialogic reciprocity is both an experiential state and a relational expectation. As Buber (1958) suggests:

> The tree is no impression, no play of my imagination, no value depending on my mood; but it is bodied over against me and has to do with me, as I with it – only in a different way.
>   Let no attempt be made to sap the strength from the meaning of the relation: relation is mutual. (p. 8)

> Between you and it [lived experience] there is mutual giving: you say *Thou* to it and give yourself to it, it says *Thou* to you and gives itself to you. (p. 33)

Thus, a dialogic encounter is a physical encounter with another human being in which both people are forced to negotiate shared meanings.

Reflecting Buber's idea of "I-Thou," which emphasizes the importance of mutuality in dialogue, communication scholars have repeatedly stressed the mutual and reciprocal relationship between dialogic partners. In a dialogic approach to public relations, the rules of dialogue are not determined just by organizations, but rather the rules are also influenced by publics. Organizations and publics need to negotiate meanings together to achieve a healthy dialogic relationship. The interactants (organizations and publics) involved in dialogue need to have the willingness to reach a mutually satisfying outcome with the process of open and negotiated discussion (Kent & Taylor, 1998).

Fourth, during the process of dialogic communication, trust is required for a genuine dialogic relationship. Trust means that dialogic interlocutors are not afraid that they might lose their jobs, offend others, or simply be used. Trust is not a free ticket to behave badly or inappropriately. Dialogue is a civil process and anyone entering into it with the intention of bullying others or dominating the conversation is actually not in a dialogue that engenders trust. "Dialogue is only possible when people spend time together interacting, understanding the rules of interaction, trusting the other person/people involved in an interaction" (Taylor & Kent, 2014, p. 390). Without trust, there is no potential for dialogue or dialogic communication.

Does Dialogue Have an End Point?

How long does dialogue last? Imagine that an organization cares about its publics and replicates every dialogic step, as we suggest in this chapter. Is there ever a terminus or finishing point for the organization to stop using dialogue? The answer is both yes and no. The possibility does exist for fleeting dialogic encounters between people. From time to time we meet someone who so enthralls us (and the feeling is mutual) that a conversation of trust and caring can emerge. But dialogue is also fleeting, and no one can live in the dialogic moment all the time.

That said, dialogue also takes time to grow and strengthen. Since dialogue should not be enacted for manipulative purposes, the power of the relationships that emerge, and networks or ties (Kent & Lane, 2017) that are built are long-lived. Ideally dialogue is seen as an ongoing process, not a one-off encounter or communication tactic.

The development and the effectiveness of dialogue cannot be achieved overnight. Looking at the effectiveness of dialogue should have a long-term or "Long Now" orientation (Kent, 2011, 2013) where the experiential present matters, but so too does the expectation of a long-lived encounter. Through long-term interactions, dialogic partners can establish rhizomatous relationships, which have hidden bonds, and profound and lasting networks (Kent & Lane, 2017).

Misconceptions about Dialogue

In public relations research, there are a lot of misunderstandings and misconceptions about how to apply dialogue in different contexts. The term dialogue is often used to describe any kind of two-way communication between an organization and its publics. However, as the discussion has suggested, a dialogic encounter involves a lot more than simply a two-way exchange of ideas and information.

Two-way communication is not enough for dialogue. Dialogue is not equivalent to two-way communication. Two-way communication is necessary for dialogue to occur, but it is not sufficient. Rather, it is the orientation to listening, learning, and agreeing to disagree that keeps the relationship moving forward.

Not all conversations should be dialogic. In many communication interactions, there is no need for dialogue. For instance, purchasing groceries, asking directions, or polite conversations do not involve dialogue. These informational interactions – indeed, most of our encounters in life – are just interactions. Kindness and empathy matter, of course, but the bar for these conversations is much lower than for dialogue. Additionally, dialogue is mutual and relational. Although we may develop a relationship or friendship with our local mechanic or hair stylist, that exchange is largely based on goods and services, not mutual understanding. As mentioned earlier, it is hypothetically possible to slip into an *I-Thou* dialogic encounter anywhere, but the *I-Thou* experience is rare. You have to work on it.

There is also the issue of monologues (one-way information) that pretend to be dialogue. In some scenarios, people speak with each other without really listening to others. Buber (1965) referred to this type of exchange as "monologue disguised as dialogue" (p. 22). Indeed, "hearing" without actually "listening," and talking without actually disclosing anything or saying anything has been a recognized problem for centuries (Macnamara, 2013).

Online interactions do not equal dialogue. Online organization–public interactions, such as posting messages on Twitter or Facebook, are not real dialogue (Smith, 2010). "Providing feedback to customers on a social media site, or posts on Twitter or Facebook are not examples of dialogue (just as rhetoric is the artful use of language, but not all language is rhetoric)" (Taylor & Kent, 2014, p. 390). Make no mistake, repeated online communication interactions can create two-way communication between people and between people and organizations. However, mediated communication is not the same as the face-to-face communication rooted in trust and involving personal and intellectual risk that Buber suggested was a requisite for dialogue. The value of high quality online communication is that it allows for people to exchange ideas, make arguments, and negotiate meaning. Social media lack a number of important dialogic qualities, including propinquity, commitment, mutuality, trust, and unconditional positive regard for others, that Kent and Taylor (2002) argued are necessary for true dialogue to occur.

How Dialogue Relates to Organization–Public Relationships

Organization–public relationships (OPRs) are the *raison d'être* for so much of public relations communication. Dialogue is just one of many theoretical frameworks that help us to understand OPRs. Dialogue relates to organization–public relationships because public relations professionals act as the conscience of organizations and guide their ethical decisions. A dialogic orientation places ethics at the center of both the relationship and the communication.

Dialogue as an Ethical Decision-Making Guide for Organizations

The public relations industry has long been criticized as architects of public opinions. Public relations professionals have been accused of using manipulation to pursue the economic self-interest of firms at the expense of the public interest (Holtzhausen & Voto, 2002; Hutton, 1999). Dialogue might be one way to counter negative stereotypes of public relations practice because it flips the equation that was once tipped in favor of the firm to an equation where mutual understanding is the key outcome of public relations.

According to Pearson (1989a), dialogue is a condition for ethical conduct. However, as noted, one cannot perpetually exist in a dialogic state, so dialogue also provides a model for how to behave, for how to treat stakeholders and public ethically. Dialogue offers an ethical framework for thinking about how to engage with others and enact long-term relationships (Theunissen & Wan Noordin, 2012).

Why Are Dialogic Relationships a Concern in Public Relations?

For more than one hundred years, public relations has sought to become a valued organizational function. Practitioners have gained influence with members of an organization's dominant coalition by helping to manage crisis, public affairs, lobbying, and other practices. Our focus has been on meeting the needs of internal stakeholders, managers, and other senior organizational members, rather than on building relationships that are as robust with our external publics. Dialogue shifts that focus somewhat by suggesting that our relationships should be centered on long-term, productive engagement with all relevant stakeholders and publics. We will be providing a discussion about how and why dialogue in public relations may be the best way to improve both the effectiveness of the practice as well as its reputation.

What Is Unique about Dialogue?

What makes dialogue unique is its capacity to serve both organizational and public interests. The co-creational turn in public relations has made dialogue a timely and valued framework for public relations (Botan & Taylor, 2004). Yet, many public relations practitioners lack the skill set needed to implement dialogue in their practice. From a practical standpoint, most professionals have never been trained in dialogue, thus making it difficult to take a dialogic orientation or apply dialogue in organizational settings. Instead, many instances of "disguised dialogue," "monologues," or, "DINO: dialogue in name only" (Kent & Theunissen, 2016) have emerged as organizations seek to give the impression that they are listening to public concerns.

Some public relations practitioners go through the motions to act dialogically online, yet offline still cling to the functional perspective of public relations that treats "publics and communication as tools or means to achieve organizational ends" (Botan & Taylor, p. 651). Lane and Bartlett (2016) remind us that "public relations practitioners do not understand what dialogue is. Despite being asked to focus on dialogue in their work, the examples the practitioners provided consistently did not actually involve … mutuality, propinquity, empathy, risk, and commitment" (p. 4087). Dialogue offers a unique perspective on organization–public relationships, but only if organizational communicators actually understand dialogue.

Within the academic study of public relations, "dialogic communication is an ethical practice approach that aims to improve community relationships and organization–public relationships and allow organizations to realize their social responsibilities" (Huang & Yang, 2015, p. 376). It is time for a change of the public relations paradigm (cf. Kuhn, 1970). For two decades or more, the functional paradigm dominated teaching and research in public relations (e.g. excellence theory, OPR, contingency theory) and has been widely applied to public relations (Taylor & Kent, 2014). However, to move public relations forward and so that it becomes a more ethical and transparent practice, public relations practitioners need to treat the public as partners in a meaning-making process (Botan & Taylor, 2004). Young public relations practitioners (like the readers of this book) need to be prepared for the current paradigm in public relations and have an open mind to embracing the potential other "paradigm shifts" down the road.

Moreover, many studies of dialogic public relations just take dialogue at face value, "claiming dialogue is occurring when in actuality none exists, more research is needed that clearly explains the difference between genuine dialogue and self-serving dialogue, or 'dialogue in name only'" (Kent & Theunissen, 2016; Paquette, Sommerfeldt, & Kent, 2015, p. 32). Academics need to be able to distinguish genuine dialogue from two-way interaction that is being called dialogue.

How to Apply Dialogue and Relational Concerns in Public Relations

One misunderstanding about dialogue is treating it as a panacea for all organizational opportunities and problems. Indeed, conversations and interactions happen every day and everywhere. But most are not dialogic. An "abusive use of dialogue" has existed in public relations for years (Toledano, 2017). One approach that might be more fruitful is for communicators to think about taking a "dialogic approach," or creating the "potential for dialogue" (Kent & Taylor, 1998), rather than simply calling two-way exchanges "dialogic".

Dialogue can be used by organizations as an approach of authentic relationship building with publics. In authentic dialogue, organizations give up the control over organization–public communication and form a profound "change-oriented outlook" (L'Etang, 2006, p. 25). Furthermore, as Theunissen (2014) argued, dialogue has the power to assist organizations and publics to co-construct corporate identity.

In the public relations industry, there is a consensus that social media are a way to engage in dialogue with the public. Making decisions about what is acceptable and what is not should not be the sole decision of the organization (Theunissen & Wan Noordin, 2012). To strive for dialogic communication in a social media platform, organizations need to revisit the core values of dialogue, emphasizing the importance of treating others with positive regard and empathy (Kent & Taylor, 2002, p. 25). Social media platforms are the tools, channel, and medium for organizations to practice public relations (Kent, 2014). But how to use the tools in a dialogic communication is another question. Posting messages on social media is not dialogic (Taylor & Kent, 2014). For the majority of organizations, social media are just another media channel to disseminate organization–related messages based on one-way and sender-to-receiver assumptions (Kent & Taylor, 2016).

A dialogic orientation can underpin ethical codes in organizations. "Dialogue reflects a central principle of Kantian deontological ethics, that respect and empathy for the other is paramount" (Paquette et al., 2015, p. 32). Professionals need to first get over the fear that organizational interests are at risk because of the unpredictability of external publics (Toledano, 2017). Professionals also need to acknowledge the interconnectedness of organizations and publics, and seek training in how to facilitate dialogue, and how to shape ethical leadership (Taylor & Kent, 2014).

How, When, and Why Is Dialogue Applied to Relationships?

Kurt Lewin, a founding father of social psychology, observed: "There's nothing so practical as a good theory." Dialogic theory is often defined as a *normative* theory that offers an idealistic and unreasonable view on best practice in the field, in opposition to a *positive* theory that describes how something is actually done. We disagree with this narrow characterization. Dialogic theory, indeed all good theories, should consist of both normative and positive precepts. Dialogue is normative because it is an idealistic approach to ethical public relations. Dialogic theory motivates us to think about the other, engage ethically, and look for co-created meaning. But, dialogic theory is also positive in that it represents what is already happening in many public relations contexts. It is a positive theory or, as Lewin would call it, practical, because it provides actual guidelines for how to engage in effective organization–public communication. Many scholars who have been cited, notably Kent, Lane, Pearson, Taylor, Theunissen, Toledano, and others, have outlined ways for dialogic theory to be used. The idea that dialogue is impractical is fiction. Next, we will introduce three scenarios for applying dialogic theory to relationship building.

Employing a Dialogic Approach to Website Design

In the Web 1.0 era, before the growth of social media, the majority of internet users were consumers of online content (Cormode & Krishnamurthy, 2008). In the mid to late 1990s, when the internet was just becoming available to the general public and organizations as a communication tool, Kent and Taylor identified five dialogic web principles that they argued could be used for building relationships through the World Wide Web. The five principles described the ways that websites should be designed in order to facilitate relationship building. Although the principles seem more mundane today, to people who have grown up with flash websites and interactive social media, in 1998 Kent and Taylor's principles were some of the first "how to" suggestions for public relations professionals who were responsible for website design and content creation. The principles included:

Principle 1: The dialogic loop. The dialogic feedback loop allows publics to communicate with organizations and help build mutually beneficial relationships.

Principle 2: Usefulness of information. Organizations are encouraged to respond to stakeholder questions and concerns and provide an assortment of information to website visitors as a means of building relational trust and commitment.

Principle 3: Generation of return visits. Ultimately, if people do not return, a relationship cannot be built. Designing websites that would engender return traffic and thereby create the foundation for long-lasting relationships is no easy task.

Principle 4: Intuitiveness/Ease of interface. Sites should be dynamic enough to encourage all potential publics to explore them, information rich enough to meet the needs of very diverse publics, and interactive enough to allow users to pursue further informational issues and dialogic relationships.

Principle 5: The rule of conservation of visitors. Websites should contain features that make them attractive such as updated information, changing issues, special forums, new commentaries, online question-and-answer sessions, and online experts to answer questions for interested visitors (Kent & Taylor, 1998, pp. 326–331).

Kent and Taylor's five principles have been examined on hundreds of websites (universities, nonprofit organizations, charity organizations, corporations, etc.) and the foundational principle, the dialogic loop, is often lacking. Although a number of scholars (cf. Briones et al., 2011; Gordon & Berhow, 2009; McAllister, 2012; McAllister-Spooner & Kent, 2009) have examined how to foster and maintain online relationships with individuals and publics, however, when the focus of communication remains fixed on an economic exchange model rather than a relational model, dialogue suffers (Kent & Taylor, 2016).

Websites are still relevant communication tools even in a social media age. Therefore, public relations practitioners should review organizational webpages to ensure that design features reflect dialogic principles. Consumer product companies, banks, telecommunications, and online marketplaces will be more valuable to visitors if the sites follow the dialogic principles and orientations.

Applying Dialogic Theory to Social Media Fostered OPRs

As the World Wide Web evolved, Web 2.0 allowed for more interactive features in mediated communication. Web 2.0 allowed organizations to develop platforms specifically for people who wanted to engage with organizations. Facebook, Twitter, YouTube, and other platforms allowed organizations to be more engaged with publics. Internet users also had new tools to create social networking profiles and personal blogs. Online users have shifted from content consumers to acting as both content producers and consumers (Cormode & Krishnamurthy, 2008).

However, most social media interactions still are not dialogic; rather, most social media function as just another type of asymmetrical communication, dissemination, or propaganda tool. Information is still just sent from organizations to followers via new platforms (Taylor & Kent, 2014). For many organizations, the basic motivation is to use social media as marketing tools, to increase sales, to increase profit, with little regard for the long-term health of the organization's relationships with its stakeholders, publics, and customers. The underlying assumption of most social media interactions is that the public is a passive entity to be acted on, persuaded, or motivated/convinced to act, rather than stakeholders and publics being treated as active, thoughtful, decision-making partners.

Kent (2013) identified several solutions for reconstructing online organization–public relationships in mediated spaces. These suggestions reflect a dialogic orientation to online relationships:

1) When we construct social spaces for individuals and publics, we should talk about what stakeholders and publics want to talk about. Serving the interests of our stakeholders actually serves our own interests.
2) Social media need to be genuinely social. When all that public relations and communication professionals can think to use social media for is social marketing, we have missed our calling as ethical communicators.
3) Public spaces and collective decision-making need to be revived. The best decisions are challenged and are made through consultation with outsiders and experts.
4) Taking the time to become more widely informed and acting as organizational counsels rather than corporate Tweeters should be a priority.
5) The focus of communication professionals needs to be on the long term and not the short term. The principles of the Long Now provide a guideline: serving the long view, fostering responsibility, rewarding patience, minding mythic depth, allying with competition, taking no sides, and leveraging longevity. (pp. 342–344)

This approach would make social media relationships more rewarding and move social media platforms closer to dialogic rather than economic relationships.

Applying Dialogic Theory to CSR Activities

Another way to apply dialogic communication to public relations is through specific contexts. Corporate social responsibility is a common public relations strategy (Taylor, 2012). CSR is premised on the idea that an organization's behaviors should contribute to society (Bhattacharya & Sen, 2004). When a firm donates money, employees' time, or products or services to help others, this is CSR. Other types of CSR initiatives include community based programs, scholarships, and corporate support of nonprofit and social cause groups.

Social media can help firms better understand how they can give back to communities. Public relations practitioners can "listen" to what members of the public identify as problems or opportunities and then respond. In order to use social media in CSR more effectively, and enact dialogic social media, a number of requirements must first be met. Kent and Taylor (2014) suggested three ways to incorporate dialogic theory in CSR: engagement of stakeholders, recognition of the value of others, and empathy with stakeholders and stake seekers.

Kent and Taylor (2016) offered *Homo dialogicus* as a model to rethink CSR and social media. Corporations need to actually engage individuals and interact with them on a one-to-one basis. Genuine dialogue is not a public activity but an interpersonal or group activity. Although most social media are used as one-way tools, they do not have to be (cf. Duhé, 2012). As people participate in discussions and as questions emerge, ad hoc discussion spaces (outside of Facebook) can be created where topics of interest can be genuinely explored in smaller groups, and with stakeholders and publics who have a real interest in particular substantive issues. These small discussion groups could be guided by dialogic principles and all participants could be made aware of dialogic discussion rules that would empower the participants (cf. Pearce & Pearce, 2000a; Pearson, 1989a; Taylor & Kent, 2014) and facilitate dialogue. In the Homo dialogicus model, public relations communicators move from being functional "sender to receiver" content creators, treating people as ends rather than means, to co-creational communicators who have an interest in genuine relationships with others and care about their stakeholders and publics. Dialogue becomes possible.

The second dialogic issue is to recognize the value of others. Being dialogic means caring about others and having "unconditional positive regard" (Rogers, 1992, p. 828) for the other. A dialogic organization needs to be more reflective and ask itself difficult questions about honesty, trust, and risk. Through CSR, corporations seek to become better community members and better corporate citizens. That relational process begins with the dialogic concepts of trust and risk.

In keeping with the Homo dialogicus metaphor, scholars and professionals should remember that dialogic theory comes from interpersonal communication theories. Dialogic partners respect and trust one another. For organizations to build dialogic relationships, they should stop keeping secrets. Although some organizations might argue that too much organizational transparency creates risk – what happens if stakeholders, stake seekers, and publics do not like what an organization has to say? Dialogic communicators and organizations need to be honest and committed to getting their house in order and sharing or resolving the organizational secrets that they are afraid or ashamed to reveal publicly. Is it better to tell the truth and "steal the thunder" from a media investigation or wait for the inevitable release of embarrassing information? Research says it is best to be straightforward and honest (Arpan & Pompper, 2003).

The third dialogic issue in CSR is empathy. Empathy refers to the ability to put yourself into the shoes of another person. Currently, the narrow focus we see among corporations, focused almost exclusively on return on investment, does little to immediately impact people's lives. Dialogic communicators are open to other people's ideas and opinions, and value what they have to say. Communicators need to be trained to be dialogic. Having dialogically trained professionals would allow communicators to build relationships and trust, and more effectively interact with stakeholders and publics. CSR is about giving back to one's community and doing what is ethical and morally right. More than that, both CSR and dialogue are ethical orientations toward others. For this to happen, organizational leaders need to be trained in dialogue, better informed about actual stakeholders and publics, willing to listen to the actual voices of stakeholders and publics, and be willing to be changed.

Integrating Theory and Practice: Steps to Building Organization–Public Relationships

Pearson (1989a) identified the steps to building dialogic relationships. The steps to facilitating dialogic relationships don't have to be sequential and there are no doubt dozens of other steps beyond what we recommend here. Our goal in this section is to identify steps that organizations can enact to create the foundation for dialogue. We suggest that organizations start with the easier steps and then move toward higher level steps as they are ready.

One step is for organizations to use their social media sites for listening rather than as one-way marketing, advertising, or messaging tools. The goals should be to engage individuals and publics in organizational decision-making and issues management. Indeed, most people are unlikely to join organization-specific social media spaces if all an organization tries to do is recreate its current social media advertising presence on Facebook and Twitter.

A second step is to consider ways to engage face-to-face with publics. Relationships are built in real time and require real knowledge about other people. Successful organizations and organizational communicators need access to more diverse people and diverse voices to gain more knowledge of their relationships with others.

A third step is to train organizational members and managers in ways to be dialogic (Kent & Taylor, 2014). Having dialogically trained professionals would allow communicators to build relationships and trust, and more effectively interact with stakeholders and publics.

Dialogic models really do work and there is a body of knowledge and practice that public relations scholars and practitioners can draw upon. One example is the Dialogue Project at the Massachusetts Institute of Technology (MIT). This Boston-based initiative draws on faculty expertise of professors in business, psychology, and leadership. Dialogue is facilitated around episodes of engagement and collective inquiry (Isaacs, 1999). Isaacs viewed dialogues as located in "containers" or spaces where interactions can take place. Participants are guided through a series of discussions where they share their views, build trust, work through conflict, and then come up with new understandings of the situation. MIT's Dialogue Project provides facilitation services to government, educational institutions, and businesses.

We have also seen a growing number of college and university campuses attempting to use dialogic theory to structure discussions about race, diversity, and political disagreements. Ramasubramanian, Sousa, and Gonlin (2017) explored how a campus brought the topic of race to public dialogue. Intergroup dialogues may offer many students one of their first meaningful opportunities to explore difficult or taboo topics in a safe group setting. Because dialogue proceeds from a positive orientation toward others, it is a useful framework to structure discussions around topics of race, stereotypes, justice, and systemic inequities. We have not seen a lot of businesses and corporations embracing dialogue yet. We accept that change is difficult. Change takes time. But, also accept that *understanding dialogue is part of the future of public relations and organization–public relationships.*

Major Topics/Questions Needing to Be Addressed by Public Relations Theorists Working in Dialogue in Organization–Public Relationships

There are two major topics that need to be addressed by public relations theorists working in dialogue. First, we need to move past the idea that websites and social media are inherently dialogic. Websites and social media platforms have the potential to facilitate interactions but they are the lowest level of dialogic potential.

Second, public relations theorists working in dialogue must be able to bring the concepts and processes of dialogue to the practitioner community. Theorists can make dialogue a relevant, useful, and effective framework to structure public relations practice by teaching dialogue in the public relations classroom. Dialogue can be embedded into classes such as PR Writing, Research, Cases and Campaigns. Student projects could help local nonprofit organizations engage in dialogue with community stakeholders. Another way to bring the concept of dialogue to the industry is to meet practitioners on their own turf. We can present dialogue at practioner conferences such as the annual or regional conferences of the Public Relations Society of America (PRSA). We can also write articles about dialogue for industry publications, blogs, and business outlets.

This is an exciting time in public relations practice and the dialogic turn suggests that public relations has significant contributions to make to organizations and society.

Suggested Cases to Explore That Demonstrate Dialogic Theory in Action

The Pearce and Pearce article, "Extending the theory of coordinated management of meaning (CMM) through a community dialogue process" (2000b) and Shawn Spano's book *Public dialogue and participatory democracy: The Cupertino Community Project* provide a great case study of the power of dialogue to help communities. As founders of the Public Dialogue Consortium (PDC), Barnett Pearce, Kimberly Pearce, and Shawn Spano have worked with the City of Cupertino, California for many years. The Cupertino Community Project: Voices and Visions used a dialogic approach to foster community discussions.

Cupertino, California, is a small town located outside of San Jose. It experienced a rapid change in demographics in the 1980s as the Asian population grew to approximately 66% of the community, and the Caucasian population felt threatened and many left the community. The PDC facilitations began in 1996, in an uncomfortable climate described as "a powder keg, waiting to go off" (Krey, 1999, p. 4). Through structured dialogues in community venues, the city has increased its capacity to address community concerns on intercommunal relationships and other topics. The PDC employed a variety of dialogic activities, including public meetings in which residents discussed how issues relating to ethnicity should be handled in the future, local government promotion of multiculturalism, and a perception of shared ownership of the Cupertino Community Project: Voices and Visions by residents and city officials (see Pearce & Pearce, 2000a; Spano, 2001).

Another case study that is useful for learning about how dialogic processes can empower communities occurred in Aqaba, Jordan. Maureen Taylor's article "Building social capital through rhetoric and public relations" (2011) observed how a local nonprofit group, the Jordan River Foundation (JRF), applied dialogic principles to bring citizen concerns and priorities to the local governing agency. This is an interesting case study because it provides a glimpse into the ways in which culture shapes dialogue. Jordanian culture has traditional roles for men and women and in rural areas the two groups rarely interact in public settings. To listen to the voices of both men and women, JRF created a culturally appropriate, dialogic facilitation model for the community discussion groups.

JRF publicized community meetings through mosques, schools, and health centers. The meetings took place in a large tent, similar to those used by the local Bedouin to engage guests and discuss tribal issues. To increase the participation of women, JRF encouraged women to bring their children to the meeting. When women entered, JRF members offered them seats in circles with other women. When married men arrived, they were escorted to sit in circles with other men. When young, unmarried men arrived, they were placed in their own group of seats. Seats were organized into circles of eight people and in the middle of each grouping of chairs, there was a large flip chart.

The JRF facilitators welcomed everyone with appropriate cultural and religious greetings, and explained the rules for the community dialogue. They then showed a list of community priorities that had emerged from a previous meeting with community members and explained each topic on the large flip chart. At the end of the discussion, each circle talked about the topics, which included road improvement, pest control, parks, and local education. These were quality-of-life issues that the local government had not addressed. Each person identified his or her priorities within the group. The group members spent time talking about the topics, adding personal anecdotes. JRF provided each participant with three stickers and asked them to place the stickers on the topics that they believed were most in need of improvement in the neighborhood. Eventually the individual priorities were tabulated to represent a group list, and then one member of each group reported his or her group's priorities to the entire neighborhood. A JRF facilitator tabulated the choices and then publicly counted the times a priority was selected. At the end of the session, the neighborhood had discussed and voted for their priorities to be brought to the government in a transparent, dialogic manner.

These two case studies show that dialogue can be facilitated to improve people's lives. The use of clear, transparent rules and process helps people to participate in dialogic activities where all voices are given a chance to articulate their position.

Discussion Questions

1   What are the best practices in a dialogic approach to creating and maintaining organization–public relationships?

2   What are some of the antecedents of dialogue?

3   What are some of the consequences of a dialogic approach to public relations for the organization and for the public?

4   How do we measure dialogue or dialogic public relations?

5   Is it possible to achieve a dialogic relationship between an organization and its public in social media platforms? If yes, please elaborate the rules that should be applied. If no, why?

6   What is the difference between dialogue and other conceptual frameworks discussed in this book?

7   How can you apply the dialogic features and principles to your own life, to your organization or group?

8   What are some of the limitations of dialogue? Under which circumstances would a dialogic approach not be appropriate?

9   What is the link between dialogue and civic discourse?

Suggested Readings

Kent, M. L., & Lane, A. B. (2017). A rhizomatous metaphor for dialogic theory. *Public Relations Review, 43*, 568–578.

Kent, M. L., & Taylor, M. (1998). Building dialogic relationships through the World Wide Web. *Public Relations Review, 24*, 321–334.

Kent, M. L., & Taylor, M. (2002). Toward a dialogic theory of public relations. *Public Relations Review, 28*, 21–37.

Taylor, M., & Kent, M. L. (2014). Dialogic engagement: Clarifying foundational concepts. *Journal of Public Relations Research, 26*, 384–398.

Theunissen, P., & Noordin, W. N. W. (2012). Revisiting the concept "dialogue" in public relations. *Public Relations Review, 38*, 5–13.

References

Adams, A., & McCorkindale, T. (2013). Dialogue and transparency: A content analysis of how the 2012 presidential candidates used twitter. *Public Relations Review, 39*, 357–359.

Arpan, L. M., & Pompper, D. (2003). Stormy weather: Testing "stealing thunder" as a crisis communication strategy to improve communication flow between organizations and journalists. *Public Relations Review, 29*, 291–308.

Bhattacharya, C. B., & Sen, S. (2004). Doing better at doing good: When, why, and how consumers respond to corporate social initiatives. *California Management Review, 47*, 9–24.

Botan, C. H., & Taylor, M. (2004). Public relations: The state of the field. *Journal of Communication, 54*(4), 645–661.

Briones, R. L., Kuch, B., Liu, B. F., & Jin, Y. (2011). Keeping up with the digital age: How the American Red Cross uses social media to build relationships. *Public Relations Review, 37*, 37–43. doi:10.1016/j.pubrev.2010.12.006

Buber, M. (1958). *I and Thou* (R. G. Smith, Trans.). Edinburgh: T & T Clark.

Buber, M. (1965). *Between man and man* (R. G. Smith, Trans.). New York: Macmillan.

Cissna, K. N., & Anderson, R. (1998). Theorizing about dialogic moments: The Buber-Rogers position and postmodern themes. *Communication Theory, 8*(1), 63–104.

Cormode, G., & Krishnamurthy, B. (2008). Key differences between Web 1.0 and Web 2.0. *First Monday, 13*(6).

Duhé, S. (2012). Introduction: A thematic analysis of 30 years of public relations literature addressing the potential and pitfalls of new media. In S. Duhé (Ed.), *New media and public relations* (pp. xiii–xxvi). New York: Peter Lang.

Gordon, J., & Berhow, S. (2009). University websites and dialogic features for building relationships with potential students. *Public Relations Review, 35*(2), 150–152. doi:10.1016/j.pubrev.2008.11.003

Holtzhausen, D. R., & Voto, R. (2002). Resistance from the margins: The postmodern public relations practitioner as organizational activist. *Journal of Public Relations Research, 14*, 57–84.

Huang, J., & Yang, A. (2015). Implementing dialogic communication: A survey of IPR, PRSA, and IABC members. *Public Relations Review, 41*, 376–377.

Hutton, J. G. (1999). The definition, dimensions, and domain of public relations. *Public Relations Review, 25*, 199–214.

Isaacs, W. (1999). *Dialogue: The art of thinking together*. New York: Doubleday.

Kelleher, T. (2009). Conversational voice, communicated commitment, and public relations outcomes in interactive online communication. *Journal of Communication, 59*, 172–188.

Kent, M. L. (2011). Public relations rhetoric: Criticism, dialogue, and the long now. *Management Communication Quarterly, 25*(3), 550–559.

Kent, M. L. (2013). Using social media dialogically: Public relations role in reviving democracy. *Public Relations Review, 39*, 337–345.

Kent, M. L. (2014). Rethinking technology research and social media. *Public Relations Review, 40*(1), 1–2.

Kent, M. L., & Lane, A. B. (2017). A rhizomatous metaphor for dialogic theory. *Public Relations Review, 43*, 568–578.

Kent, M. L., & Taylor, M. (1998). Building dialogic relationships through the World Wide Web. *Public Relations Review, 24*, 321–334.

Kent, M. L., & Taylor, M. (2002). Toward a dialogic theory of public relations. *Public Relations Review, 28*, 21–37.

Kent, M. L., & Taylor, M. (2014). Problems with social media in public relations: Misremembering the past and ignoring the future. *International Journal of Interdisciplinary Research, 3*(2), 23–37.

Kent, M. L., & Taylor, M. (2016). From *Homo economicus* to *Homo dialogicus*: Rethinking social media use in CSR communication. *Public Relations Review, 42*, 60–67.

Kent, M. L., & Theunissen, P. (2016). Elegy for mediated dialogue: Shiva the Destroyer and reclaiming our first principles. *International Journal of Communication, 10*, 4040–4054.

Krey, D. (1999). Cupertino asks, "Can we talk about diversity?" *Western City, 75*, 4–8.

Kuhn, T. S. (1970). *The structure of scientific revolutions.* Chicago: University of Chicago press.

Lane, A. B. & Bartlett, J. (2016). Why dialogic principles don't make it in practice – and what we can do about it. *International Journal of Communication, 10*, 4074–4094.

Lane, A., & Kent, M. L. (2018). Dialogic engagement. In K. Johnston & M. Taylor (Eds.), *The handbook of communication engagement* (pp. 61–72). Medford, MA: Wiley Blackwell.

L'Etang, J. (2006). Public relations and propaganda: Conceptual issues, methodological problems and public relations discourse. In J. L'Etang & M. Pieczka (Eds.), *Public relations: Critical debates and contemporary practice* (pp. 23–40). Mahwah, NJ: Lawrence Erlbaum.

Macnamara, J. (2013). Beyond voice: Audience-making and the work and architecture of listening as new media literacies. *Continuum, 27*(1), 160–175.

McAllister, S. M. (2012). How the world's top universities provide dialogic forums for marginalized voices. *Public Relations Review, 38*(2), 319–327. doi:10.1016/j.pubrev.2011.12.010

McAllister-Spooner, S. M., & Kent, M. L. (2009). Dialogic public relations and resource dependency: New Jersey community colleges as models for web site effectiveness. *Atlantic Journal of Communication, 17*(4), 220–239.

Paquette, M., Sommerfeldt, E. J., & Kent, M. L. (2015). Do the ends justify the means? Dialogue, development communication, and deontological ethics. *Public Relations Review, 41*(1), 30–39.

Pearce, W. B., & Pearce, K. A. (2000a). Combining passions and abilities: Toward dialogic virtuosity. *Southern Journal of Communication, 65*, 161–175.

Pearce, W. B., & Pearce, K. A. (2000b). Extending the theory of coordinated management of meaning (CMM) through a community dialogue process. *Communication Theory, 10*, 405–423.

Pearson, R. (1989a). Business ethics as communication ethics: Public relations practice and the idea of dialogue. In C. H. Botan, & V. Hazleton (Eds.), *Public relations theory* (pp. 111–131). Hillsdale, NJ: Lawrence Erlbaum.

Pearson, R. (1989b). *A theory of public relations ethics* (Unpublished doctoral dissertation). Ohio University, Athens, OH.

Ramasubramanian, S., Sousa, A., & Gonlin, V. (2017). Facilitated difficult dialogues on racism: A goal-based approach. *Journal of Applied Communication Research, 45*, 537–556.

Rogers, C. (1992). The necessary and sufficient conditions of therapeutic personality change. *Journal of Consulting and Clinical Psychology, 60*(6), 827–832.

Rybalko, S., & Seltzer, T. (2010). Dialogic communication in 140 characters or less: How Fortune 500 companies engage stakeholders using Twitter. *Public Relations Review, 36*, 336–341.

Saffer, A. J., Sommerfeldt, E. J., & Taylor, M. (2013). The effects of organizational Twitter interactivity on organization–public relationships. *Public Relations Review, 39*, 213–215.

Smith, B. G. (2010). Socially distributing public relations: Twitter, Haiti, and interactivity in social media. *Public Relations Review, 36*, 329–335.

Spano, S. J. (2001). *Public dialogue and participatory democracy: The Cupertino Community Project.* New York: Hampton.

Taylor, M. (2011). Building social capital through rhetoric and public relations. *Management Communication Quarterly*, *25*, 436–454.

Taylor, M. (2012). Corporate social responsibility communication campaigns. In R. E. Rice & C. Aiken (Eds.), *Communication campaigns* (4th ed.) (pp. 261–274). Thousand Oaks, CA: Sage.

Taylor, M., & Kent, M. L. (2014). Dialogic engagement: Clarifying foundational concepts. *Journal of Public Relations Research*, *26*, 384–398.

Theunissen, P. (2014). Co-creating corporate identity through dialogue: A pilot study. *Public Relations Review*, *40*, 612–614.

Theunissen, P., & Wan Noordin, W. N. (2012). Revisiting the concept "dialogue" in public relations. *Public Relations Review*, *38*, 5–13.

Toledano, M. (2017). Dialogue, strategic communication, and ethical public relations: Lessons from Martin Buber's political activism. *Public Relations Review*, *44*, 131–141.

7

Social Media and Emerging Media

Theoretical Foundations

Karen Freberg

When 16-year-old teenager Carter Wilkerson reached out to the official Wendy's Twitter account in April 2017 about how many retweets he would need to get their chicken nuggets free for a year, he showed the world the power of social media. Wendy's surprisingly reached out to Carter and said he would need 18 million retweets to get this incentive. With this single tweet, the rest is history. Since then, Carter's initial tweet has gone viral, getting mainstream media coverage around the world and even surpassing Ellen DeGeneres's popular Oscar selfie tweet to become the most retweeted tweet ever in Twitter's history. In addition to this accomplishment, the #NuggsForCarter campaign was even showcased and entered for consideration to the Cannes Lions Festival of Creativity for PR work.

Without social media, Carter may not have gotten the exposure and engagement for this exchange with a brand like Wendy's. Other brands have experienced both the positive and negative consequences of not using social media proactively, as in crisis situations. When United Airlines experienced its April 2017 crisis where a passenger was dragged off one of its flights from Chicago to Louisville, it showed audiences the power of video and the importance of understanding the medium and first impressions that arise from what is shared and posted. The United Airlines case, along with its CEO, Oscar Munoz, also realized the response that is necessary on social media needs to be tailored and framed for the appropriate audiences. However, other brands like Always and its campaign #LikeAGirl helped build a community surrounding a clear message that resonated with audiences and won several awards in the process.

All of these cases show an important distinction. Social media are not like traditional media outlets. For example, social media are not just for official spokespeople, brands, or gatekeepers. Everyone has a distinct voice, influence, and presence in the digital space. Brands, along with public relations professionals, are constantly learning and adapting their practices to fulfill the growing expectations for having mutually beneficial relationships with key audiences and effective message strategies for each situation, and to assess the overall financial and emotional impact of the community and network on the reputation of the parties involved.

Social media have transformed public relations both in research and in practice. With each advance that occurs in the social media industry, public relations research adapts and explores these various changes and discusses their implications for the field, society, and practice. This chapter will discuss the core characteristics of what social media are, some of the theoretical frameworks that are incorporated in public relations research, and future challenges and opportunities to note for scholars and practitioners studying social media.

Public Relations Theory: Application and Understanding, First Edition. Edited by Brigitta R. Brunner.
© 2019 John Wiley & Sons, Inc. Published 2019 by John Wiley & Sons, Inc.

Defining the Concepts: What Are Social Media?

Social media have been at the forefront of bringing both pain and delight for brands, organizations, and public relations professionals over the past decade. They are the focus of some of the more recognizable campaigns, as well as crises, in the public relations profession. One case, in particular, first started with content that was shared and immediately spread like wildfire. Social media played a significant role in the response as well as perception of the brand, which is still recovering. Samsung is one of the most established brands in the world and experienced a significant crisis in 2016 when malfunctions with the batteries of its Note 7 devices started being reported. Malfunctions soon turned to sparks that caused fires, which were shared online and spread virally on social media. Samsung in turn had to order an immediate recall of the devices, responding online as well as in other channels. The sentiment and spread of the news for Samsung first began on social media, which have become a powerful hub of community and information to be created, shared, and disseminated at a rapid speed, breaking down barriers in time and location.

Social media have transformed how people are able to consume, disseminate, and engage with news and other forms of information in society. These new communication technology tools allow individual users and organizations to engage with, reach, persuade, and target key audiences more effectively across multiple platforms. Pew Research Center surveys found that, in 2017, 7 out of 10 Americans used social media, a dramatic increase from the 5% reporting social media use in 2005 (Smith, 2017).

Industry professionals, scholars, and social media users have contributed a number of different definitions and conceptualizations for the concept of social media. Social media are sometimes referred to as "new media" to capture the association of social media with the advanced integration, strategy, and application of new communication technologies. Freberg (2016) described social media as providing the ultimate personalized online networked hub of information, dialogue, and relationship management. Essentially, social media combine the use of innovative strategies with digital communication technology platforms, enabling the user to share knowledge, engage in digital storytelling through conversations and visual components, collaborate with others, engage in crowdsourcing tasks and contribute ideas to solve problems, conduct strategic monitoring and analytic analysis online, and build relationships within a community sharing common interests, investments, and needs.

Other conceptualizations emphasize the role of social media as a toolkit that allows users to create and share content. Still others focus on how social media extend Web 2.0 technologies to bring communities together. Social media platforms serve as gateways where content and conversations are created and ignited between individuals, brands, organizations, and nations. In addition, social media platforms provide first impression management tools for corporations and individuals to showcase their own brands and reputations. These virtual platforms allow user-generated content to be shared in highly dynamic and interactive communities in real time, which allows for co-creating of content, crowdsourcing of ideas and perspectives, and even the editing and extending of conversations and ideas within a respective platform and with a particular community.

Many definitions have focused on specific platforms (Mangold & Faulds, 2009), construction of profiles to build digital connections (boyd & Ellison, 2008), application of tools (Lariscy, Avery, Sweetser, & Howes, 2009), or building communities virtually through user-generated content (Mulhern, 2009; Waters, Burnett, Lamm, & Lucas, 2009). While useful for understanding social media, this textbook takes a broader view of social media, incorporating the vast opportunities and actions that can be incorporated strategically in campaigns and strategic communication plans.

How and Why Are Social and Emerging Media of Concern to Public Relations?

Social media have changed the face of public relations for the twenty-first century. Public relations has had its own evolution over the years with its modernized definition from the Public Relations Society of America: "Public relations is a strategic communication process that builds mutually beneficial relationships between organizations and their publics" (PRSA, 2018).

The importance of social media to practice is reflected in the rise of social media research over the past decades (Duhé, 2015). Researchers are working together to explore growing issues, challenges, and opportunities in their work. The power that individuals have been given to create, curate, and share content, becoming their own media outlets in the process while engaging with businesses in real time, is unlike any other form of interactive or emerging technologies previously available in society. As public relations agencies are trying to become more relevant in their stance with social media, they are moving backwards into more tactical roles rather than strategic thought leader roles (Kent & Saffer, 2014).

Social media and public relations have become intimately connected. Social media have shifted from being simple, entertaining platforms (such as MySpace) to channels of communication for scholars, researchers, businesses, and other entities, used to create networking connections and relationships. Social media in essence offer more than just a platform where people congregate and engage in dialogue, but also provide a way to express oneself in a virtual space in multiple formats and frameworks.

Social media within public relations are not a new phenomenon, but they have brought forth novel opportunities to engage, share knowledge, use strategic storytelling, and break down the barriers between the organization and their key publics. There are many similarities between what public relations does and what social media offer. Both focus on creating and maintain meaningful relationships. Both share a correspondence with the traditional media. While social media have allowed more access and transparency between public relations and journalists, there are still some challenges for using social media for fact checking, using user-generated content, and bypassing the traditional media altogether and going directly to the source (Meltwater, 2014).

As Taylor and Kent (2010) noted, public relations focuses on building relationships and understanding between organizations and their key publics. Public relations seeks to create meaning in conversations among different parties, which can take place in person or on social media. The dominant view is that "social media are good" for the public relations profession, but there are challenges to this view. Valentini (2015) argues that the ability of anyone to post an update online does not guarantee the health or sustainability of the community or conversation. However, what it does provide is a solid documentation that is posted for all to see, breaking down the barriers of time and location as well as helping create a transparent view for others to witness. We should not rely too much on individual platforms (or "rented space") on social media or else we will lose track of the overall purpose and meaning of being part of these platforms. Ideally, building relationships and the health of communities will translate into offline interactions and behaviors (Valentini, 2015).

Public relations professionals are able to use social media in a variety of different ways to conduct their businesses and formulate relationships. Social media tools and platforms have allowed public relations professionals to initiate conversations and queries that lead to real-time correspondence and customer service options. This process transforms a customer from an inactive audience member to an active audience member. In addition, social media have impacted the customer service sector – so much so that there is now an established specialized area called social care. Customer support, for both positive circumstances and negative ones such as crisis communications, has become a key part in establishing the image and overall reputation for a public relations function for an organization or business.

While social media and public relations are interconnected and aligned, some distinct differences between the two areas remain. Social media management engages in the strategic planning of the right time, platform, and circumstance to send out a message for the community in question, whereas public relations identifies the right relationships in which to invest to have the right impact for the long term.

Social media allow real-time interactions and conversations to emerge, while adapting to evolving parties, communities, and influencers. Before engaging with communities, public relations professionals must understand the management and health of the relationships within each community. Consumers often have strong views regarding how they do and do not want to engage with organizations and what they want in terms of communication and relationships. Public relations professionals must account for these preferences and strategically plan for optimum engagement in advance.

As social media continue to evolve, the field of public relations must also adapt in response to changes to maintain relevancy.

How, When, and Why Is Theory Applied to Social Media?

The Challenges Social Media Pose for Public Relations Theory

To assist public relations professionals as they navigate the new world of social media, researchers have turned their attention to the identification of best practices in the strategic use of social media. Most of the literature that focuses on social media has used established theories from public relations, but has borrowed approaches from other fields as well such as marketing, advertising, business communications, and even social psychology. Social media research has extended past discipline and professional boundaries for research and practice, which has allowed more opportunities for transdisciplinary research and collaborative projects.

One line of research has explored the extent of public relations professionals' use of social media (Wright & Hinson, 2014, 2015). Social media management has been a key duty and responsibility task for public relations professionals for some time now (SCPRC, 2014; Wright & Hinson, 2014, 2015). The *GAP VIII* study from the University of Southern California (SCPRC, 2014) found that surveyed practitioners spent 83% of their time dedicated to social media, making social media activities an essential part of their positions.

Additional theoretical work attempts to guide the practitioner in using social media to best advantage under precise circumstances.

Determining Behavioral Actions to Take

Two prominent theories have been used on social media to look at behavioral actions to take in response to messages, but they have been primarily focused within the crisis communications area of public relations research. The situational crisis communication theory (SCCT; Coombs, 1995) and the social-mediated crisis communication model (SMCC) have both been implemented and applied in social media contexts in crisis communication situations. Most of the literature focuses on the overall message responses that are needed in order to reduce uncertainty and provide action steps for users and others to take.

Researchers are also exploring the impact of messaging on intended behavior (Freberg, 2012). For example, the platforms that are being used more frequently will most likely impact the likelihood of achieving behavioral goals for a specific campaign, initiative, or strategy for a public relations effort (Paek, Hove, Jung, & Cole, 2013).

Determining the Channels for Dialogue to Emerge

Communication is one of the fundamental functions that social media serve for public relations professionals. One of the dominant theories that has been used to evaluate and determine the nature of communication online has been dialogic theory, which is interconnected between public relations and social media. Kent and Taylor (2002) discussed the role of public relations in building dialogues on established channels. These channels have evolved over the years from websites and blogs (Seltzer & Mitrook, 2007), to social networking sites (Bortree & Seltzer, 2009), and finally to microblogs like Twitter (Rybalko & Seltzer, 2010). Each platform explored in each of these studies has focused on communities. Communities may be in a particular geographic location, be based on similar interests, or may be based on affiliation or identify. While some communities are only online, with members never or seldom meeting each other in person, they are no less robust than the physical communities in which we live, and in many ways more robust from the simple fact that the barriers barriers of time and location are removed.

While most of the studies have looked at the way in which organizations have created these networks and communities within individual channels, organizations have yet to really foster and establish a sustainable community where dialogue truly emerges authentically among the individual users. Theunissen and Wan Noordin (2012) noted that dialogue is an ongoing process that needs to be authentic among the community in question and the content being created needs to be supported by the organization or business in question.

Determining Best Strategies for Using Social Media

There have been discussions of how social media focus on strategic planning or if these practices are emerging from the industry (Charest, Bouffard, & Zajmovic, 2016). Social media are naturally a field where practices, strategies, and applications come from both planning and research capabilities for businesses, organizations, and other public relations efforts like campaigns. A strong line of research has evaluated the use of social media for campaigns (Wright & Hinson, 2015; Paek et al., 2013; Briones, Kuch, Liu, & Jin, 2011). Specifically, Paek et al. (2013) analyzed a social media campaign using different messages across the different social media platforms of blogs, Twitter, and Facebook, while looking at user engagement. One of the ways in which campaigns are explored is through the evaluation of how they are taught in current public relations curricula. Social media pedagogy research has explored large projects like campaigns (Melton & Hicks, 2011) as well the implementation of specific platforms or tactics online such as Twitter (Anderson & Swenson, 2013; Carpenter & Krutka, 2014; DeGroot, Young, & VanSlette, 2015; Forgie, Duff, & Ross, 2013; Fraustino, Briones, & Janoske, 2015) and Facebook (McCorkindale, DiStaso, & Fussell Sisco, 2013). While most of these are focused primarily on applying these tools in the classroom, the theoretical foundations that are prominently used in this line of work for public relations education are experiential learning and evidence-based practice.

Evidence based practices (EBP) is an approach focused on integrating three perspectives together, namely the practitioner's expertise, the client's situation, and proven best practices. Shlonsky and Gibbs (2004) define EBP as involving "a well-built practice question, an efficient search for best evidence, a critical appraisal of that evidence, and action based on the interchange between client preferences, practice experience, and the best evidence" (p. 137). The first perspective takes into account the individual knowledge and expertise of the practitioner, a role that may be defined as that of a manager, technician, or some hybrid of these two functions. The second model focuses on client expectations. The third part of the model is best evidence. In medicine, social work, clinical psychology, and public health, EBP focuses on systematically comparing various scenarios and treatment options to help improve the impact of practice. That means drawing upon evidence from applied research, the expertise and educational training of the practitioner involved, and the expectations and needs of the client (Shlonsky & Gibbs, 2004). All of these elements are interconnected and rely on each other to formulate the most effective approach for the client or organization in question (Shlonsky & Gibbs, 2004). While this approach has been explored in other public relations related studies (Freberg, Remund, & Keltner-Previs, 2013), there needs to be more studies in public relations that address the theory, research, and applied practices in social media specifically. Social media as a discipline and field is still in its infancy, but it is becoming more scientifically oriented, so the studies and theories used in public relations work need to evolve concurrently.

Determining Quality of Engagement and Consumption of Information

The quality of social media content, messages, and relationships all play a part in how relationships and reputations are built online. Generally speaking, social media platforms and channels are open and dynamic in span and presence. While traditional media appear to be focused on one-way forms of communication, social media content is emerging in real time with multiple parties involved. The barriers to entry for establishing one's presence on social media are much lower and easier to overcome than those involved in establishing a presence in traditional media. In addition to the barriers of entry, barriers of time and location are also overcome by social media, where users and can engage in conversation and dialogue in a matter of seconds in widely different locations. Users of social media vary in their levels of active participation and voice. Users can range from being very vocal on issues that are important to them, while others take the roles of observers and lurkers in social media discussions.

Li (2016) distinguished between active and passive users on social media, which is important when evaluating the message strategies and overall activity related to the timing and channels being utilized for public relations purposes. In either case, there has to be the ability to be part of the conversation, be connected, and to be able to share relevant information for those who are part of the community (Li, 2016). However, researchers have noted that the level of engagement as well as the characteristics attributed to each platform are somewhat different (Paek et al., 2013).

Social media not only provide users with an opportunity to engage people in their local community, but motivate their engagement a world away. Anyone with a computer, tablet, or smartphone can use social media platforms to inform, educate, and engage others. In essence, social media give users the opportunity to communicate in a different way. These channels have changed the way individuals communicate by allowing them to have access to a variety of different platforms to consume and create knowledge, with the accessibility to share these insights with their local and global communities. The use of these technologies to their fullest potential assists in the improvement of community engagement overall. Linking individuals, organizations, and governments across multiple platforms, including social media and other mobile as well as web-based platforms, allows better communication and sharing of information, which is important in understanding engagement. Engagement can arise in different ways, from sharing information (contribution), to consuming information (consumption), to creating information (creation), as discussed by Sisson (2016). Tsai and Men (2013) discussed how social media creation elicited the most engagement, because it allowed others to view the content, consume it, and provide their own feedback and insights to the original piece of content.

It is important to note that connecting the terms community with engagement seems to be a shift in itself for public relations professionals. When discussing engagement, we are looking at specific users rather than a group, and if we go down this path of community, we are bypassing the individual connections and one-to-one communication efforts we may want to have with our audiences. Community engagement is a separate entity in itself, and has to have a strong place within the public relations strategy to make sure it is defined as a specific group that is characterized based on location, interest, affiliation, or membership.

Determining Relevance in Trust and Credibility

The level of trust in what is being shared on social media often depends on its source, as well as the timeliness of the message given the situation. Social media users are able to bypass traditional media gatekeepers who attempt to set the narrative and frame the stories from their point of view. Social media present widely diverse points of view, and allow the individual users or consumers to make the ultimate decision about the information they want, how they want it, and whether or not the information fits their overall needs and expectations.

The overall functions of social media are not limited to communicating messages designed by professionals for audiences, in parallel to message construction in traditional media. In addition, social media allow the user to participate to an extent not seen previously in traditional media. Increased empowerment of the individual stakeholder leads to greater feelings of control over a situation and a willingness to help others in the community, which could potentially be used by brands and corporations to engage with audiences, formulate message strategies, and evaluate their own reputation in the eyes of their online audience members. With these new shifts in power and breakdown in barriers, brands are expected to listen and to respond to stakeholder concerns in new ways. Recognizing the influence of social media provides professionals with the opportunity to use social media strategically to discover potential issues relevant to their stakeholders, to prepare for different scenarios and situations, to implement online communication strategically, and to evaluate results of communications in real time.

Trust and credibility of sources is a large part of what influences behavior and action taken in a given situation. Freberg (2012) questioned the impact of the level of trustworthiness and credibility of messages from a social media platform compared to other forms of media as a function of age cohort. Younger consumers were more influenced by social media messages than older consumers.

Examples of Theory Used with Social Media

How Can Public Relations Theories Inform Social and Emerging Media?

One of the important elements to keep in mind when it comes to social media theory development is the fact that it is not limited to just public relations. Theoretical frameworks for social media are advancing from diverse disciplines such as communication, psychology, marketing, and many others.

Many theories used in social media and public relations research have a strong connection back to psychology (for example, the theory of planned behavior; Fishbein & Azjen, 2010), while others have been adapted from public relations into the new space. Dialogic theory has been a stronghold for understanding conversations and their impact between an organization and its key publics. Other specific theories focus on particular specializations like crisis communication. Theories need to be able to inform and predict outcomes that can be transferred from situation to situation.

Table 7.1 outlines some of the dominant theories that have been used to explore and examine different aspects of social media activities and specializations (for example, crisis communications) in the public relations literature.

Table 7.1 Dominant theoretical perspectives for social media research

Theory	Researchers using theory	Summary
Agenda setting theory	Kiousis et al., 2016; Waters, Tindall, & Morton, 2010	Traditional mass media theory focusing on the ability of the news media to influence the stories and essential agenda for their intended audiences. This has become a primary focus for research due to the increased perception and use of social media as a way to receive news and updates on local, national, and global events.
Critical theory	Valentini, 2015	Critical theory is a fundamental approach in the social sciences, but this approach looks at social phenomena happening in society and in our environment and critiques how it impacts our human interactions and practices. With social media, this discusses how access to the tools of communication has been beneficial (or not) to our relationships, identity, and how we practice in our field.
Convergence theory	Saffer, 2016	Focuses on how the intersection between traditional and social media comes together online in the various networks and platforms.
Dialogic theory	Sommerfeldt, Kent, & Taylor, 2012; Kent, 2014; McCorkindale & Morgoch, 2013; Rybalko & Seltzer, 2010; Kent & Taylor, 2016; Watkins & Lewis, 2014; Watkins, 2017	Main focus for this theory is that dialogue is about the exchange of ideas and perspectives, and channels are needed in which these conversations can be used for organizations with their publics.
Organization–public relationship (OPR) (Ledingham & Bruning, 1998)	Saffer, Sommerfeldt, & Taylor, 2013 Engagement: Men & Tsai, 2012, 2013, 2015, 2016; Sweetser & Kelleher, 2016	One of the fundamental perspectives in the public relations field. The primary focus is on the management of mutually beneficial relationships between the key publics and the organization in question (Ledingham & Bruning, 1998). Many of the studies have explored this on social media by adding in the component of interaction on these platforms, otherwise known as engagement.
Situational crisis communication theory	Freberg, 2012; Ott & Theunissen, 2015; Roshan, Warren, & Car, 2016; Schultz, Utz, & Goritz, 2011	An established crisis communication theory focusing on which responses to use in a given crisis situation based on legitimacy and attribution of responsibility.
Social-mediated crisis communication model (Jin & Liu, 2010)	Jin & Liu, 2010; Liu, Austin, & Jin, 2011; Jin, Liu, & Austin, 2014; Austin, Liu, & Jin, 2014	Specific to crisis situations emerging on social media, this theory evaluates the source of the information and how to respond to the situation.
Social capital theory	Saffer, 2016; Sommerfeldt, 2013a, 2013b	Theory focuses on utilizing resources to facilitate actions and resources based on collective actions and responses. Primary focus in the research utilizing this theory looks at the networks and associations available online.
Social network theory	Kent, Sommerfeldt, & Saffer, 2016	Social media is a vehicle that links sites, resources, and people in social networks that have been built to build and maintain relationships.

Table 7.1 (Continued)

Theory	Researchers using theory	Summary
Theory of planned behavior	Kinsky et al., 2015; Lee, Park, Lee, & Cameron, 2010	A traditional psychology theory (linked with the theory of reasoned action) which connects attitudes, subjective norms, and perceived behavioral control together. This has been tested in social media research in various situations and determines the intention to comply with messages that appear in various scenarios and channels.
Uses and gratification theory	Krishna & Kim, 2015; Woo, An, & Cho, 2008; Chen, 2011	Theory focusing on why individuals seek out specific channels and media for particular needs. Understanding the rationale and reasoning for why users choose certain platforms is critical for public relations professionals to determine whether or not they are sending out the right messages on the right channels for their audiences.

Major Topics/Questions Needing to Be Addressed by Public Relations Theorists Working with Social Media

There is a range of challenges facing social media scholarship:

- the rise of anonymity on social media and the impact this has on relationships, influence, and the quality of messages and content being shared;
- the move from examining reactive to predictive innovative strategies;
- behavioral intent to comply with messages and formulate sustainable relationships online;
- the rise of the influencer as a source to engage with in terms of organization–public relationships;
- how to foster participation and development of online communities that are sustainable and actionable;
- exploring the "negative" features of what social media can do to impact public relations, but connecting this back to proactive strategies.

There also seems to be an apparent rush and pressure to publish research about social media due to the rapid evolution of each of the platforms. There has to be a balance between timely applied uses for public relations and social media strategies, and enough time to be able to sit back and understand the psychological, philosophical, and behavioral differences happening across the different platforms. Public relations theory has to develop further as well (Theunissen & Wan Noordin, 2012) to make sure there are key differences between each of the theories already being explored in studies that are not focused on social media.

The focus of theoretical scholarship and creative applications of social media should be explored not only in public relations, but also through the lens of other associated disciplines. More transdisciplinary work needs to happen rather than isolated work within the public relations field. The field of social media scholarship is not limited to just public relations. Opportunities exist for scholars to move to the forefront of innovation with thought leadership that explains behavior and underlying message comprehension and intention rather than exploring tactical behavior that is relevant for a specific segment in time.

Furthermore, new advances in social media theory and application research need to position themselves more centrally within the public relations discipline. Of the research literature that has examined social media as a core concept and focus, most concentrate on specific platforms, with more global cross-cutting theory coming second. Instead of being able to explain why things happened the way they did for a social media campaign or a social media experiment within a classroom, current examples of social media research often stop without exploring how these experiments and campaigns would do in the real world.

Theory needs to be focused on explaining behavior as well as being able to predict behavioral actions by others. Social media theoretical research has been more along the lines of applying other theories from other disciplines rather than solidifying unique and specific theories that are applied and integrated within the platforms themselves. In addition, there has been a limited number of articles in the public relations field that have tried to push the envelope from just applying traditional public relations theories to social media rather than exploring new innovative ways of evaluating, testing, and explaining phenomena arising on these various platforms. Many current studies have just scratched the surface of the underlying behavioral measures driving the conversations, attitudes, and behavior we are seeing online among brands, organizations, and key stakeholders.

With that being said, most of the research focuses on testing ideas, concepts, and cases with students, most who have grown up with social media. In order to move forward, research in social media needs to expand beyond one age cohort and look at universal trends happening across different groups. Participant samples – whether they are student samples or participants in services like Amazon MTurk – do not always tell us what our audiences will do in a given situation, especially on social media. If researchers want to use these tools as a pilot test or for a Study 1 perhaps, then these have some benefit. Study 1 could be used as a preliminary test to explore key concepts before testing these at a larger scale with a bigger pool of participants. We have to push ourselves to be stronger both theoretically as well as in methodology to be able to be in the same room as disciplines like marketing, psychology, and even computer science, not only for the research community, but in the applied circles. The more rigorous we are in our research and theoretical standards when it comes to social media, the better.

The other growing concern with current social media research in public relations is the issue of measurement, as well as the methods that are used to evaluate the various concepts being explored. Public relations researchers should expand their horizons with new ways of evaluating behaviors, attitudes, and other concepts on social media, and include additional methods. The studies that have focused on social media in particular have used perhaps one specific method (survey or interviews, for example), but in order to advance the theoretical foundation of social media theory within public relations, the methods also have to be more advanced to tie into the questions researchers are waiting to test in their work.

Social media have become a mainstream communication platform for businesses, organizations, and public relations professionals. This is one of the rising specializations and focuses we are seeing both in research and for public relations practice. With the rise of these digital platforms, more research needs to be conducted in the public relations discipline. More research is not only needed to explore the strategic social media applications within public relations practices, but designated theories can provide a better understanding of the impact messages, information, and actions have on offline interactions. Public relations professionals must explore new ways to answer these questions with methods that are appropriate for addressing these points. Public relations scholarship and the profession need to come together to create a more stable and sustaining bridge to answer and address these challenges for the twenty-first century.

Suggested Cases to Explore to Demonstrate Theory at Work with Social Media

Within the public relations field, there are several places where public relations scholars can witness theory being applied effectively. Several cases showcase how certain theories can be strategically applied to social media.

One of the cases that can be applied in the context of social media is the Samsung Note 7 crisis in 2016. Samsung Notes were reported to have a tendency to explode at random. This phenomenon was first reported by users on social media. Individual users came together to engage in the conversation surrounding an ongoing issue. Only later did the traditional and social media outlets pick up the story based on the conversation. While dialogue was emerging among users during this case, Samsung took the traditional approach in addressing it through their own media outlets and with the traditional media.

Another case is related to the power of utilizing social media to build relationships and stories. Clemson University Athletics used social media to engage with fans, university students, and the media in their pursuit of a 2017 National Championship run for their football team. The social media team (Jonathan Gantt, Jeff Kallin, and Nik Conklin) implemented visual storytelling strategies in the hope of engaging with active audience members, reaching out to emerging audiences, and motivating latent audiences to participate in this campaign with the team. This particular case study example can be examined and evaluated by using some of the established theories that were discussed earlier. For example, when exploring the prominence of the community, public relations researchers can look at the online network Clemson Athletics has established on their social media platforms to determine the state of the relationship, the connection they have to individual and media accounts, and the frequency of these exchanges. In addition, the dialogue that emerges from their respective communities online could provide us with indications of effective message strategies to help not only to build community, but to engage in virtual dialogues to influence behavior and perceptions for a brand, organization, or in this case, team.

Discussion Questions

1   How would you define social media? How has this definition changed or adapted over time for public relations professionals?

2   What are the underlying similarities and differences among the studies that have explored social media?

3   What theories could help guide future research studies into the application and understanding of social media within public relations?

4   What methods could help guide future research studies into emerging areas of social media within public relations?

5   Based on this chapter's reading, what are the future theoretical opportunities and practical challenges that need to be addressed in social media research?

Suggested Readings

Charest, F., Bouffard, J., & Zajmovic, E. (2016). Public relations and social media: Deliberate or creative strategic planning. *Public Relations Review, 42*(4), 530–538.

Freberg, K., Graham, K., McGaughey, K., & Freberg, L. A. (2011). Who are social media influencers? A study of public perceptions of personality. *Public Relations Review, 37*(1), 90–92.

Jiang, H., Luo, Y., & Kulemeka, O. (2016). Social media engagement as an evaluation barometer: Insights from communication executives. *Public Relations Review, 42*(4), 679–691.

Kent, M. L., & Saffer, A. J. (2014). A Delphi study of the future of new technology research in public relations. *Public Relations Review, 40*(3), 568–576. http://dx.doi.org/10.1016/j.pubrev.2014.02.008

References

Anderson, B., & Swenson, R. (2013). What should we be teaching our students about digital PR? Collaborating with top industry bloggers and PR Twitter chat professionals. *Teaching Public Relations, 87*, 1–4.

Austin, L. L., Liu, B. F., & Jin, Y. (2014). Examining signs of recovery: How senior crisis communicators define organizational crisis recovery. *Public Relations Review, 40*(5), 844–846. http://dx.doi.org/10.1016/j.pubrev.2014.06.003

Bortree, D. S., & Seltzer, T. (2009). Dialogic strategies and outcomes: An analysis of environmental advocacy groups' Facebook profiles. *Public Relations Review, 35*(3), 317–319. http://dx.doi.org/10.1016/j.pubrev.2009.05.002

boyd, d. m., & Ellison, N. B. (2008). Social network sites: Definition, history, and scholarship. *Journal of Computer-Mediated Communication, 13*, 210–230.

Briones, R. L., Kuch, B., Liu, B. F., & Jin, Y. (2011). Keeping up with the digital age: How the American Red Cross uses social media to build relationships. *Public Relations Review, 37*(1), 37–43. http://dx.doi.org/10.1016/j.pubrev.2010.12.006

Carpenter, J. P., & Krutka, D. G. (2014). How and why educators use Twitter: A survey of the field. *Journal of Research and Technology in Education, 46*(4), 414–434.

Charest, F., Bouffard, J., & Zajmovic, E. (2016). Public relations and social media: Deliberate or creative strategic planning. *Public Relations Review, 42*(4), 530–538.

Chen, G. M. (2011). Tweet this: A uses and gratifications perspective on how active Twitter use gratifies a need to connect with others. *Computers in Human Behavior, 27*, 755–762.

Coombs, W. T. (1995). Choosing the right words: The development of guidelines for the selection of the "appropriate" crisis-response strategies. *Management Communication Quarterly, 8*(4), 447–476.

DeGroot, J. M., Young, V. J., & VanSlette, S. H. (2015). Twitter use and its effect on student perception of instructor credibility. *Communication Education, 64*(4), 419–437.

Duhé, S. (2015). An overview of new media research in public relations journals from 1981 to 2014. *Public Relations Review, 41*(2), 153–169. http://dx.doi.org/10.1016/j.pubrev.2014.11.002

Fishbein, M., & Azjen, I. (2010). *Predicting and changing behavior: The reasoned action approach.* New York: Psychology Press.

Forgie, S. E., Duff, J. P., & Ross, S. (2013). Twelve tips for using Twitter as a learning tool in medical education. *Medical Teacher, 35*(1), 8–14. doi:10.3109/0142159X.2012.746448

Fraustino, J. D., Briones, R., & Janoske, M. (2015). Can every class be a Twitter chat? Cross-institutional collaboration and experiential learning in the social media classroom. *Journal of Public Relations Education, 1*(1).

Freberg, K. (2012). Intention to comply with crisis messages communicated via social media. *Public Relations Review, 38,* 416–421. doi:10.1016/j.pubrev.2012.01.008

Freberg, K. (2016). Social media. In C. Carroll (Ed.), *Encyclopedia of corporate reputation.* Thousand Oaks, CA: Sage.

Freberg, K., Remund, D., & Keltner-Previs, K. (2013). Integrating evidence based practices into public relations education. *Public Relations Review, 39*(3), 235–237. doi:10.1016/j.pubrev.2013.03.005

Jin, Y., & Liu, B. (2010). The blog-mediated crisis communication model: Recommendations for responding to influential external blogs. *Journal of Public Relations Research, 4,* 429–455.

Jin, Y., Liu, B., & Austin, L. (2014). Examining the role of social media in effective crisis management: The effects of crisis origin, information form, and source on publics' crisis responses. *Communication Research, 41*(1), 74–94. doi:10.1177/0093650211423918

Kent, M. L. (2014). Rethinking technology research and social media. *Public Relations Review, 40,* 1–2.

Kent, M. L., & Saffer, A. J. (2014). A Delphi study of the future of new technology research in public relations. *Public Relations Review, 40*(3), 568–576. http://dx.doi.org/10.1016/j.pubrev.2014.02.008

Kent, M. L., Sommerfeldt, E. J., & Saffer, A. J. (2016). Social networks, power, and public relations: *Tertius iungens* as a cocreational approach to studying relationship networks. *Public Relations Review, 42*(1), 91–100. http://dx.doi.org/10.1016/j.pubrev.2015.08.002

Kent, M. L., & Taylor, M. (2002). Toward a dialogic theory of public relations. *Public Relations Review, 28,* 21–37.

Kent, M. L., & Taylor, M. (2016). From *Homo Economicus* to *Homo dialogicus*: Rethinking social media use in CSR communication. *Public Relations Review, 42*(1), 60–67. http://dx.doi.org/10.1016/j.pubrev.2015.11.003

Kinsky, E. S., Drumheller, K., Gerlich, R. N., Brock-Baskin, M. E., & Sollosy, M. (2015). The effect of socially mediated public relations crises on planned behavior: How TPB can help both corporations and nonprofits. *Journal of Public Relations Research, 27*(2), 136–157. doi:10.1080/1062726X.2014.976826

Kiousis, S., Kim, J. Y., Kochhar, S. K., Lim, H.-J., Park, J. M., & Im, J. S. (2016). Agenda-building linkages between public relations and state news media during the 2010 Florida Senate Election. *Public Relations Review, 42*(1), 240–242. http://dx.doi.org/10.1016/j.pubrev.2015.07.009

Krishna, A., & Kim, S. (2015). Confessions of an angry employee: The dark side of de-identified "confessions" on Facebook. *Public Relations Review, 41*(3), 404–410. http://dx.doi.org/10.1016/j.pubrev.2015.03.001

Lariscy, R. W., Avery, E. J., Sweetser, K. D., & Howes, P. (2009). An examination of the role of online social media in journalists' source mix. *Public Relations Review, 35*(3), 314–316. http://dx.doi.org/10.1016/j.pubrev.2009.05.008

Ledingham, J. A., & Bruning, S. D. (1998). Relationship management in public relations: Dimensions of an organization–public relationship. *Public Relations Review, 24*(1), 55–65. http://dx.doi.org/10.1016/S0363-8111(98)80020-9

Lee, H., Park, S.-A., Lee, Y., & Cameron, G. T. (2010). Assessment of motion media on believability and credibility: An exploratory study. *Public Relations Review, 36*(3), 310–312. http://dx.doi.org/10.1016/j.pubrev.2010.04.003

Li, Z. (2016). Psychological empowerment on social media: Who are the empowered users? *Public Relations Review, 42*(1), 49–59. http://dx.doi.org/10.1016/j.pubrev.2015.09.001

Mangold, W. G., & Faulds, D. J. (2009). Social media: The new hybrid element of the promotion mix. *Business Horizons, 52,* 357–365.

McCorkindale, T., DiStaso, M. W., & Fussell Sisco, H. (2013). How millennials are engaging and building relationships with organizations on Facebook. *Journal of Social Media in Society, 2*(1), 66–87.

McCorkindale, T., & Morgoch, M. (2013). An analysis of the mobile readiness and dialogic principles of Fortune 500 mobile websites. *Public Relations Review, 39,* 193–197.

Melton, J., & Hicks, N. (2011). Integrating social and traditional media in a client project. *Business and Professional Communication Quarterly, 74*(4), 494–504.

Meltwater. (2014, July 14) Social media impact on public relations and news: Infographic. Retrieved from https://www.meltwater.com/test/social-media-impact-public-relations-infographic/

Men, L. R., & Tsai, W.-H. S. (2012). How companies cultivate relationships with publics on social network sites: Evidence from China and the United States. *Public Relations Review, 38*(5), 723–730. http://dx.doi.org/10.1016/j.pubrev.2011.10.006

Men, L. R., & Tsai, W.-H. S. (2013). Beyond liking or following: Understanding public engagement on social networking sites in China. *Public Relations Review, 39*(1), 13–22. http://dx.doi.org/10.1016/j.pubrev.2012.09.013

Men, L. R., & Tsai, W.-H. S. (2015). Infusing social media with humanity: Corporate character, public engagement, and relational outcomes. *Public Relations Review, 41*(3), 395–403. http://dx.doi.org/10.1016/j.pubrev.2015.02.005

Men, L. R., & Tsai, W.-H. S. (2016). Public engagement with CEOs on social media: Motivations and relational outcomes. *Public Relations Review, 42*(5), 932–942. http://dx.doi.org/10.1016/j.pubrev.2016.08.001

Mulhern, F. (2009). Integrated marketing communications: From media channels to digital connectivity. *Journal of Marketing Communications, 15*(2/3), 85–101. doi:10.1080/13527260902757506

Ott, L., & Theunissen, P. (2015). Reputations at risk: Engagement during social media crises. *Public Relations Review, 41,* 97–102.

Paek, H.-J., Hove, T., Jung, Y., & Cole, R. T. (2013). Engagement across three social media platforms: An exploratory study of a cause-related PR campaign. *Public Relations Review, 39*(5), 526–533. http://dx.doi.org/10.1016/j.pubrev.2013.09.013

PRSA. (2018). *About public relations.* Retrieved from Public Relations Society of America website: https://apps.prsa.org/AboutPRSA/PublicRelationsDefined/#.WLs07RLyugQ

Roshan, M., Warren, M., & Carr, R. (2016). Understanding the use of social media by organizations for crisis communication. *Computers in Human Behavior, 63,* 350–361.

Rybalko, S., & Seltzer, T. (2010). Dialogic communication in 140 characters or less: How Fortune 500 companies engage stakeholders using Twitter. *Public Relations Review, 36*(4), 336–341. http://dx.doi.org/10.1016/j.pubrev.2010.08.004

Saffer, A. J. (2016). A message-focused measurement of the communication dimension of social capital: Revealing shared meaning in a network of relationships. *Journal of Public Relations Research, 28*(3–4), 170–192. doi:10.1080/1062726X.2016.1228065

Saffer, A. J., Sommerfeldt, E. J., & Taylor, M. (2013). The effects of organizational Twitter interactivity on organization–public relationships. *Public Relations Review, 39*(3), 213–215. http://dx.doi.org/10.1016/j.pubrev.2013.02.005

Schultz, F., Ultz, S. & Goritz, A. (2011). Is the medium the message? Perceptions of and reactions to crisis communication via Twitter, blogs, and traditional media. *Public Relations Review, 37*(1), 20–27.

SCPRC. (2014). *GAP VIII: Eighth Communication and Public Relations Generally Accepted Practices Study.* Strategic Communication and Public Relations Center (SCPRC), USC Annenberg School for Communication and Journalism, University of Southern California.

Seltzer, T., & Mitrook, M. A. (2007). The dialogic potential of weblogs in relationship building. *Public Relations Review, 33*(2), 227–229. http://dx.doi.org/10.1016/j.pubrev.2007.02.011

Shlonsky, A., & Gibbs, L. (2004). Will the real evidence-based practice please stand up? Teaching the process of evidence-based practice to the helping professions. *Brief Treatment and Crisis Intervention, 4*(2), 137–153.

Sisson, D. C. (2016). Control mutuality, social media, and organization–public relationships: A study of local animal welfare organizations' donors. *Public Relations Review.* http://dx.doi.org/10.1016/j.pubrev.2016.10.007

Smith, A. (2017, January 12). Record shares of Americans now own smartphones, have home broadband. Retrieved from Pew Research Center website: http://www.pewresearch.org/fact-tank/2017/01/12/evolution-of-technology/

Sommerfeldt, E. J. (2013a). The civility of social capital: Public relations in the public sphere, civil society, and democracy. *Public Relations Review, 39*(4), 280–289. http://dx.doi.org/10.1016/j.pubrev.2012.12.004

Sommerfeldt, E. J. (2013b). Networks of social capital: Extending a public relations model of civil society in Peru. *Public Relations Review, 39*(1), 1–12. http://dx.doi.org/10.1016/j.pubrev.2012.08.005

Sommerfeldt, E. J., Kent, M. L., & Taylor, M. (2012). Activist practitioner perspectives of website public relations: Why aren't activist websites fulfilling the dialogic promise? *Public Relations Review, 38*(2), 303–312. http://dx.doi.org/10.1016/j.pubrev.2012.01.001

Sweetser, K. D., & Kelleher, T. (2016). Communicated commitment and conversational voice: Abbreviated measures of communicative strategies for maintaining organization–public relationships. *Journal of Public Relations Research, 28*(5–6), 217–231. doi:10.1080/1062726X.2016.1237359

Taylor, M., & Kent, M. L. (2010). Anticipatory socialization in the use of social media in public relations: A content analysis of PRSA's *Public relations tactics. Public Relations Review, 36*(3), 207–214. http://dx.doi.org/10.1016/j.pubrev.2010.04.012

Theunissen, P., & Wan Noordin, W. N. (2012). Revisiting the concept "dialogue" in public relations. *Public Relations Review, 38*(1), 5–13. http://dx.doi.org/10.1016/j.pubrev.2011.09.006

Tsai, W.-H. S., & Men, L. R. (2013). Motivations and antecedents of consumer engagement with brand pages on social networking sites. *Journal of Interactive Advertising, 13*(2), 76–87. doi:10.1080/15252019.2013.826549

Valentini, C. (2015). Is using social media "good" for the public relations profession? A critical reflection. *Public Relations Review, 41*(2), 170–177. http://dx.doi.org/10.1016/j.pubrev.2014.11.009

Waters, R. D., Burnett, E., Lamm, A., & Lucas, J. (2009). Engaging stakeholders through social networking: How nonprofit organizations are using Facebook. *Public Relations Review, 35*(2), 102–106. doi:10.1016/j.pubrev.2009.01.006

Waters, R. D., Tindall, N. T. J., & Morton, T. S. (2010). Media catching and the journalist–public relations practitioner relationship: How social media are changing the practice of media relations. *Journal of Public Relations Research, 22*(3), 241–264. doi:10.1080/10627261003799202

Watkins, B. A. (2017). Experimenting with dialogue on Twitter: An examination of the influence of the dialogic principles on engagement, interaction, and attitude. *Public Relations Review, 43*(1), 163–171. http://dx.doi.org/10.1016/j.pubrev.2016.07.002

Watkins, B., & Lewis, R. (2014). Initiating dialogue on social media: An investigation of athletes' use of dialogic principles and structural features of Twitter. *Public Relations Review, 40*(5), 853–855. http://dx.doi.org/10.1016/j.pubrev.2014.08.001

Woo, C. W., An, S.-K., & Cho, S. H. (2008). Sports PR in message boards on Major League Baseball websites. *Public Relations Review, 34*(2), 169–175. http://dx.doi.org/10.1016/j.pubrev.2008.03.009

Wright, D. K., & Hinson, M. D. (2014). An updated examination of social and emerging media use in public relations practice: A longitudinal analysis between 2006 and 2014. *Public Relations Journal, 8*(2). Retrieved from https://www.prsa.org/intelligence/prjournal/vol8/no2/#.V22-_FcSPYA

Wright, D. K., & Hinson, M. D. (2015). Examining social and emerging media use in public relations practice: A ten-year longitudinal analysis. *Public Relations Journal, 9*(2). Retrieved from https://www.prsa.org/Intelligence/PRJournal/Vol9/No2/index.html#.V22_TlcSPYA

8

Nonprofits

Geah Pressgrove and Richard D. Waters

What do the Metropolitan Museum of Art, National Rifle Association of America, Harvard, Young Men's Christian Association, Chamber of Commerce, Bill & Melinda Gates Foundation, National Association of Realtors, and Feeding America have in common? While the missions and structures of these organizations are vastly different, each is part of the nonprofit sector. Also referred to as the third sector, voluntary sector, civil society or charitable sector, organizations in this sector operate outside of the government and for-profit sectors.

Nonprofits play a unique and vital role in society, providing critical services, enriching cultural life, offering an outlet for political expression, and contributing to quality of life. As examples of the unique role of nonprofits, consider that most of the social movements that have taken place in the last century (e.g. civil rights, woman's suffrage, antislavery) all operated through this sector. In America, over 90% of orchestras and operas, as well as over half of the nation's hospitals are part of the nonprofit sector (Salamon, 2015). Further, nonprofit organizations provide individuals with the venues to act on matters that concern them in coordination with other like-minded individuals. The significance of this last point is perhaps best illustrated by a report from the Corporation for National Community Service which found that over a quarter of Americans (62.8 million) volunteer an average of 32 volunteer hours per person, accumulating to an estimated value of $184 billion (Joseph, 2017). Further, approximately 71% of US charitable giving comes from individuals (MacLaughlin, 2016).

Beyond the important role the nonprofit sector plays in quality of life, the sector also represents an important cog in the national economy. Accounting for $1.7 trillion in revenue, nonprofits enhance local economic vitality, create jobs, and offer economic value (Salamon, 2012). In fact, in 2013, this sector included more than 1.4 million registered nonprofit organizations, accounting for approximately 5% of the gross domestic product and $634 billion in wages, and employing an estimated 14.4 million people or 10% of the domestic workforce (McKeever & Gaddy, 2016).

Defining the Concepts: What Is the Nonprofit Sector?

Domestically, a state has the authority to grant nonprofit status. Upon receiving this designation many organizations apply for federal tax-exempt designations from the Internal Revenue Service. While there are 29 types of nonprofit organizations, the most common are public charities and private foundations with a 501(c)3 designation. These organizations enjoy many benefits, including exemption from federal, state, and local taxes; the opportunity to receive

Public Relations Theory: Application and Understanding, First Edition. Edited by Brigitta R. Brunner.
© 2019 John Wiley & Sons, Inc. Published 2019 by John Wiley & Sons, Inc.

government and private foundation grants; and the ability to offer tax deductions to individual donors. Nonprofits that have this designation, however, may not engage in partisan activity, including intervening in political campaigns for candidates for public office. Additionally, these nonprofits are also prohibited from using funds attained from the government to lobby.

Around the world, the nonprofit sector encompasses a wide array of entities ranging from hospitals and universities, to day-care centers, cultural organizations, social welfare organizations, community groups, disaster assistance services, religious congregations and foundations, to name a few. While seemingly disparate, these nonprofit organizations share similar functional characteristics that differentiate them from other sectors of the economy. For instance, Billis and Glennerster (1998) argue that the nonprofit sector provides efficient and effective services for those who suffer financial, personal, societal, or communal disadvantage by mobilizing assets to address public problems. Putman (1995) asserts that this sector fosters social capital that promotes economic growth and contributes to the functioning operation of a democratic society. Auger (2013) advances that nonprofit organizations serve an important role in democratic society by offering the opportunity for people with diverse viewpoints to assemble and share ideas.

Perhaps the most commonly accepted comprehensive definition of the sector, however, was developed as part of the Johns Hopkins Comparative Nonprofit Sector Project, which empirically examines the scope, structure, funding bases, and special contributions of the sector in 42 countries in Western and Central Europe, Asia, Latin America, and North America. The "structural-operational definition" identifies five key characteristics that these organizations must share (Salamon et al., 1999, p. 3):

1) Organized: institutional presence and structure
2) Private: institutionally separate from government
3) Non-profit-distributing: do not return profits to managers or a set of owners
4) Self-governing: fundamentally in control of their own affairs
5) Voluntary: membership is not legally required and they attract some level of voluntary contribution of time or money

How and Why Are Nonprofits of Concern to Public Relations?

At the core of nonprofit mission fulfillment is effective negotiation of complex relationships. Often, these nonprofits have limited budgets for expensive outreach and communication campaigns, making the necessity of strategic positioning even more vital. Further the audiences that a nonprofit must connect with range from service recipients, donors, and volunteers, to advocates and government. Sustaining and cultivating mutually beneficial relationships with each of these audiences is the lifeblood of the sector.

While some nonprofit organizations are adapting to and embracing market practices for strategic communication planning, the potential risks to the sector's identity are considerable (Young & Salamon, 2002). As evidence of this, according to a report from Johns Hopkins University's Center for Civil Society Studies, the nonprofit sector has seven core values: to be productive contributors to the economy, empowering, effective, enriching, reliable, responsive, and caring (Salamon, Geller, & Newhouse, 2012). While there is general consensus in the sector that these are shared core values, there is a rising concern that these values are not understood by key stakeholders in government, media, and the general public. Further, it is felt that the consequences of this lack of understanding could be detrimental.

The importance of strategically aligned relationship cultivation and maintenance is further complicated by the unique challenges faced by the sector. For instance, there are fiscal stressors such as tax reform and the related implications for charitable giving; increasing competition for donor and volunteer contributions; pressure to incorporate technology despite limited resources for training, purchase costs, and upkeep; and the need to recruit and retain quality employees despite lower salaries and benefits (Salamon, 2002). In each of these instances, public relations could play a role in sustaining the sector by reconnecting stakeholders to the sector's mission and values, and enhancing public understanding of the function and role of the nonprofit sector (Salamon, 1999).

How, When, and Why Is Theory Applied within the Nonprofit Sector?

The National Center for Charitable Statistics identifies eight types of nonprofits. According to analysis conducted by Sisco, Pressgrove, and Collins (2013), nonprofit scholarship has explored each of these types, including research on arts; education; environment; health; human services; international issues; civil rights, social action, and advocacy; and other public benefit organizations (i.e. foundations). The authors also discovered that while much of nonprofit public relations scholarship focused on the public relations function, education of future practitioners, or solving practical problems faced by practitioners, research also included theory development and theory testing.

Theory-driven research is important to the nonprofit sector. While many of the foundational public relations theories and paradigms have been used to predict outcomes in the nonprofit sector, the literature also suggests that the relationship between for-profit and nonprofit publics is often quite different (Frumkin, 2002; M. O'Neill & Young, 1988). Thus, research has sought to shine light on some of the most pressing issues facing nonprofits, including increasing fiscal challenges (e.g. Hall, 2002; J. O'Neil, 2007), decreasing public confidence (e.g. McDougle & Lam, 2014), rapid technology changes (e.g. Hether, 2014), and human resource challenges (Swanger & Rodgers, 2013).

Reviewing nonprofit public relations research from the last decade further highlights the importance of theory in understanding how nonprofits might sustain and improve relationships with publics on whom the viability of the organization hinges. Among the most common theory-building and theory-testing research in these areas are investigations of relationships with stakeholders, technology and communication, crisis management, and advocacy communication. The following highlights theory-based work in each area.

Relationships with Stakeholders

Perhaps the most robust area of theory-based scholarship in nonprofit public relations focuses on improving relationships with key internal and external organizational stakeholders. In this area of research, substantial focus has been on the donor–organization relationship, both domestically (Powers & Yaros, 2013; Shen, 2016; Sisson, 2017) and internationally (Kashif & De Run, 2015; Wiggill, 2014). Another important area of relationship management research has focused on the organization–volunteer relationship (Bortree & Waters, 2014; Hyde et al., 2016; Kang, 2016). Research on internal stakeholders has explored important topics, such as diversity in fundraising roles (Tindall, Waters, & Kelly, 2014; Waters, Kelly, & Walker, 2012). Other less commonly explored relationships included grantor–grantee (Auger, 2015) and university alumni (Bowen & Sisson, 2015) relationships. Much of the work in the area of relationship management highlights the importance of tailoring communication for particular audiences (e.g. Cao, 2016; Maxwell & Carboni, 2014), while other work focuses on key variables that stimulate support for the organization (e.g. Pressgrove, 2017), and improved models for assessing relationship quality (e.g. Pressgrove & McKeever, 2016; Sargeant, Ford, & West, 2006).

Technology and Communication

Advances in communication technology have provided a staggering array of choices, challenges, and opportunities for nonprofits. Therefore, it is not surprising that the recent years have seen an explosion of research in this area. Published scholarship has included how nonprofits use social media to engage the public (e.g. Auger, 2014; Bortree & Seltzer, 2009; Cho, Schweickart, & Haase, 2014; Ihm, 2015; Saxton & Waters, 2014), adopt social media within the organization (Nah & Saxton, 2013), and employ websites to fulfill organizational missions in domestic and emerging markets (Kirk, Ractham, & Abrahams, 2016; Patel & McKeever, 2014), as well as how nonprofits raise money through online fundraising and mobile campaigns (Weberling & Waters, 2012). While early research in the area of nonprofit new media communication highlighted ineffective use of online resources (e.g. Waters & Lord, 2009), an emerging body of theoretically grounded research is beginning to inform how these communication conduits can be used for mission fulfillment, relationship development, audience segmentation, and enhanced fundraising.

Crisis Management

Crisis management nonprofit public relations research falls primarily into to two overarching categories. The first category is research that focuses on how nonprofits manage crisis that effect their reputation and viability (Lee & Rim, 2016; Long, 2016; Rasmussen, 2015; Sisco, 2012), and the effects of these crises on future supportive stakeholder behaviors (Kinsky et al., 2015; Kinsky, Drumheller, & Gerlich, 2014). The second category of nonprofit crisis management research focuses on the role that nonprofits play in relation to crises that effect the public (Liu, Jin, Briones, & Kuch, 2012; Waters, 2013). In these studies, theory provides a lens through which to consider message and response approaches, audience segmentation, and the role of new media in crisis response strategies.

Advocacy

In communication research, advocacy has been defined as "the set of skills used to create a shift in public opinion and mobilize the necessary resources and forces to support an issue, policy, or constituency" (Wallack, Dorfman, Jernigan, & Themba, 1993, p. 27). While some public relations scholars eschew advocacy in public relations (see Edgett, 2002), ethical advocacy and nonprofit communications are inextricably linked. Thus, it makes sense that a portion of the theory-based research on nonprofit public relations would explore this important topic. To this end, research in this area has examined the role of traditional and online communication channels for engaging audiences (Rudov et al., 2017; Weberling, 2012), fundraising and organizational support for advocacy-based nonprofits (McKeever, 2013; McKeever, Pressgrove, McKeever, & Zheng, 2016), employing advocacy-based frames to shift public opinion (Benson & Reber, 2015), and activist mobilization and engagement (Curtin, 2016; Sommerfeldt, 2013).

Examples of Theory Used by Nonprofits

Numerous theories and paradigms from both within and outside of public relations scholarship have been used to explore the topics in nonprofit public relations outlined (for a summary of examples, see Table 8.1). While this section will not exhaust the theory-driven scholarship in the area, it will illustrate numerous approaches and identify key theory-testing and theory-building work.

Table 8.1 Examples of public relations theories used in nonprofit work

Topics	Examples of theory
Relationships with stakeholders	Organization–public relationship (OPR)
Technology and communication	Dialogic communication; technology acceptance model
Crisis communication	Situational crisis communication theory (SCCT); theory of planned behavior; organization–public relationship (OPR)
Advocacy and fundraising	Framing; agenda building; situational theory of publics

Given the prominence of relationship management theory more generally in public relations scholarship, it is not surprising that this paradigm offers a key framework for considering relationships with stakeholders. Initially work in this area explored the organization-public relationship (OPR) to evaluate the donor relationship based on dimensions including trust, commitment, satisfaction, and control mutuality (e.g. Waters, 2008, 2011). Building on this foundation, other researchers have expanded nonprofit OPR research to include volunteers. For instance, one study explored the role of inclusion in predicting relationship quality and future volunteerism for participants of diverse racial and ethnic backgrounds (Bortree & Waters, 2014). In the area of theory development, other scholars extended the OPR model to include other important nonprofit variables, including perceptions of stewardship and desired outcomes such as behavioral intent (donate, volunteer) and loyalty to the organization (Pressgrove & McKeever, 2016).

As outlined, another important area for scholarship has been to inform and understand the evolving role of technology in nonprofit public relations. Much of the work in this area has been theory testing in the realm of stakeholder engagement through online channels. For instance, numerous studies use dialogic theory to explore how nonprofits use social media to build relationships online (e.g. Briones et al., 2011; Hether, 2014). Other scholars have gone outside traditional public relations theories to find an appropriate lens for studying technology-driven communication. For instance, Weberling and Waters (2012) employ the technology acceptance model to gauge public preparedness for campaigns based on text alerts on mobiles.

In research that explores how nonprofits manage crisis communication, numerous theories emerge. To study the response of nonprofit organizations to crises that affect their reputation and future supportive behaviors, one commonly employed framework has been the situational crisis communication theory (e.g. Sisco, 2012; Sisco, Collins, & Zoch, 2010). To better understand public sentiment for organizations embroiled in a high-visibility crisis, other scholars have used the theory of planned behavior to predict donation behavior (Kinksy, Drumheller, & Gerlich, 2014; Kinsky et al., 2015). Still another study expanded the systems theory as it relates to decision-making and strategies for managing conflict with titled volunteers, those with a significant job title and autonomy, of a nonprofit organization (Gallicano, 2013).

Given the restrictions on lobbying and intervening in political campaigns that many nonprofits face, research on advocacy in public relations typically focuses on fundraising and mobilizing stakeholders to support mission-driven action. For instance, the situational theory of publics has been used to analyze communication and participation behaviors (McKeever, 2013). Agenda-building theory and framing have been employed to better understand involvement in advocacy and fundraising efforts (Weberling, 2012).

Major Topics/Questions Needing to Be Addressed by Public Relations Theorists Working with Nonprofits

Communication research on the nonprofit sector has increased in the last decade, but theory-driven scholarship in this area is far from reaching saturation. Thus, there is much room for emerging scholarship to empirically explore and expand theory in the area of nonprofit public relations at the organizational, community, and societal levels. As outlined, nonprofits often do not have the same structure and mission as corporate and government institutions, and therefore the measurement and predictive validity of existing models may not be the same for this sector. Further, the diversity of the stakeholders on whom the organization's success hinges, restrictions on lobbying, and competition in the sector lead to many distinctive challenges. For instance, a study of nonprofit communication challenges identified six common themes that nonprofits face: politics, law and regulation, media attention, evaluation, brand recognition, and employee engagement (Liu, 2012). Additionally, the *Chronicle of Philanthropy* reported that only 13% of Americans believe charities spend money wisely, 41% think leaders are paid too much, and 68% indicated that program effectiveness was a key factor in decisions to give (Perry, 2015). Further, for 20 years the Edelman Trust Barometer has indicated that trust in the nonprofit sector was unequaled by other institutions, but in 2016, trust in nonprofits dropped by 12% (Edelman, 2017).

These emerging and persistent challenges underscore the trials facing the nonprofit sector (both domestically and abroad) and provide a host of questions needing to be addressed by public relations theorists. While not a comprehensive list, the following issues highlight significant opportunities that would provide great value for practitioners, educators, researchers, and students:

- How can theory inform the renewal of the sector identity and increase public understanding?
- Can image and reputation management research inform a path forward in response to the crisis of trust in the sector?
- How can public relations add value to the relationship between a nonprofit and its many stakeholder types (e.g. government, volunteer, board, advocate, donor, employee)?
- In what ways might innovation and technology be effectively used to overcome challenges facing the sector?
- In what ways might research from the areas of ethics, political communication, international relations, and other interrelated fields inform nonprofit public relations domestically and internationally?
- What are the key antecedents to relationship cultivation and maintenance for both internal and external publics?

Suggested Cases to Explore to Demonstrate Theory at Work in the Nonprofit Sector

Numerous case studies highlight the value of public relations theory in nonprofit communication (e.g. Curtin, 2016; Sisco & McCorkindale, 2013; Kirk et al., 2016). As an example of how these case studies inform the intersection of theory and practice, Worley and Little (2002) examine the role of stewardship in fundraising by focusing on the Coaches vs. Cancer campaign. The campaign, a partnership between the American Cancer Society (ACS) and the National Association of Basketball Coaches, was created to tap into the college basketball audience to find new donors and volunteers. While the program successfully generated enough funds through sponsorship and in-kind donations to execute the campaign, the pledge drive did not meet its first-year goals and only received limited media coverage. Further, as the authors point out, evaluating a campaign solely on impressions and dollars donated misses an opportunity to cultivate long-term meaningful relationships.

A key aim of this case study was to use this campaign as a lens to highlight the limitations of current public relations models and advocate for the inclusion of stewardship as a final step in the campaign planning process. Fundraising experts and scholars alike agree that it is easier and more fiscally responsible to maintain a relationship with a supporter (e.g. donor) than recruit a new one (Kelly, 2001). Thus, public relations, with its focus on relationship management, potentially provides uniquely useful insight. Most students of the field are familiar with the RACE (research, action planning, communication, evaluation) and ROPE (research, objective development, programming, evaluation) models of communication. These models are intended to guide communicators through the processes for strategic public relations planning. However, these models are campaign-centric. To overcome this limitation, Kelly (2001) proposed that stewardship be added as a final step to make the process cyclical and promote ethical behavior by practitioners and their organizations. In Kelly's conceptualization, stewardship is comprised of four parts:

1) Reciprocity: demonstration of gratitude for supportive behaviors
2) Responsibility: acting in a socially responsible manner to supporters
3) Reporting: keeping publics informed and being accountable
4) Relationship nurturing: focusing on continuous relationship building

According to Worley and Little (2002), much of the Coaches vs. Cancer campaign's lack of success can be attributed to problems of stewardship. First, while the campaign aimed to engage a new audience, planners failed to understand who among the audience truly supported ACS, thus limiting opportunities for proper recognition and gratitude (reciprocity). Next, planners did not sufficiently identify and understand audience expectations in their initial research (responsibility), thus leading to extensive production of pledge cards and other materials that were not appropriate. Further, planners focused their message on donation, or what the audience could do for ACS, rather than keeping the public informed (reporting). Finally, campaign planners maintained the same solicitation-based message throughout the campaign without attempting to recognize or nurture prior relationships (relationship nurturing).

Discussion Questions

1   Reviewing the characteristics that define a nonprofit, what special considerations should be given when applying existing theories to the sector?

2   Do you believe existing public relations theories are sufficient to explore the myriad challenges and relationships in the nonprofit sector?

3   Advances in technology continue to affect the interplay between stakeholders and organizations. What theories might provide a relevant framework for considering the role of emerging innovations in the nonprofit sector?

4   How can theory inform the role of nonprofits, in the current political landscape, to mobilize and engage audiences?

5   What do you believe are the key areas for theory development and testing needed in the nonprofit sector?

Suggested Reading

For a deeper exploration of theory and applied studies in the sector, the following compendium of research in the area of nonprofit public relations is recommended as a starting point.
Waters, R. D. (Ed.). (2015). *Public relations in the nonprofit sector: Theory and practice*. New York: Routledge.

References

Auger, G. A. (2013). Fostering democracy through social media: Evaluating diametrically opposed nonprofit advocacy organizations' use of Facebook, Twitter, and YouTube. *Public Relations Review, 39*(4), 369–376.

Auger, G. A. (2014). Rhetorical framing: Examining the message structure of nonprofit organizations on Twitter. *International Journal of Nonprofit and Voluntary Sector Marketing, 19*(4), 239–249.

Auger, G. A. (2015). Building mutually beneficial relationships: Recommended best practices for online grant making procedures. In R. D. Waters (Ed.), *Public Relations in the nonprofit sector: Theory and practice* (pp. 154–166). New York: Routledge.

Benson, B., & Reber, B. H. (2015). The Cape Wind debate: Framing by energy activist groups and frame salience for active online audiences. In R. D. Waters (Ed.), *Public relations in the nonprofit sector: Theory and practice* (pp. 203–218). New York: Routledge.

Billis, D., & Glennerster, H. (1998). Human services and the voluntary sector: Towards a theory of comparative advantage. *Journal of Social Policy, 27*, 79–98.

Bortree, D. S., & Seltzer, T. (2009). Dialogic strategies and outcomes: An analysis of environmental advocacy groups' Facebook profiles. *Public Relations Review, 35*(3), 317–319.

Bortree, D. S., & Waters, R. D. (2014). Race and inclusion in volunteerism: Using communication theory to improve volunteer retention. *Journal of Public Relations Research, 26*(3), 215–234.

Bowen, S. A., & Sisson, D. C. (2015). Alumni commitment, organization–public relationships, and ethics. In R. D. Waters (Ed.), *Public Relations in the nonprofit sector: Theory and practice* (pp. 66–83). New York: Routledge.

Briones, R. L., Kuch, B., Liu, B. F., & Jin, Y. (2011). Keeping up with the digital age: How the American Red Cross uses social media to build relationships. *Public Relations Review, 37*(1), 37–43.

Cao, X. (2016). Framing charitable appeals: The effect of message framing and perceived susceptibility to the negative consequences of inaction on donation intention. *International Journal of Nonprofit and Voluntary Sector Marketing, 21*(1), 3–12.

Cho, M., Schweickart, T., & Haase, A. (2014). Public engagement with nonprofit organizations on Facebook. *Public Relations Review, 40*(3), 565–567.

Curtin, P. A. (2016). Exploring articulation in internal activism and public relations theory: A case study. *Journal of Public Relations Research, 28*(1), 19–34.

Edelman. (2017). 2017 Edelman Trust Barometer. Retrieved from https://www.edelman.com/trust2017/

Edgett, R. (2002). Toward an ethical framework for advocacy in public relations. *Journal of Public Relations Research, 14*(1), 1–26.

Frumkin, P. (2002). *On being nonprofit: A conceptual and policy primer*. Cambridge, MA: Harvard University Press.

Gallicano, T. D. (2013). Internal conflict management and decision making: A qualitative study of a multitiered grassroots advocacy organization. *Journal of Public Relations Research, 25*(4), 368–388.

Hall, M. R. (2002). Fundraising and public relations: A comparison of programme concepts and characteristics. *International Journal of Nonprofit and Voluntary Sector Marketing, 7*(4), 368–381.

Hether, H. J. (2014). Dialogic communication in the health care context: A case study of Kaiser Permanente's social media practices. *Public Relations Review, 40*(5), 856–858.

Hyde, M. K., Dunn, J., Wust, N., Bax, C., & Chambers, S. K. (2016). Satisfaction, organizational commitment and future action in charity sport event volunteers. *International Journal of Nonprofit and Voluntary Sector Marketing, 21*(3), 148–167.

Ihm, J. (2015). Network measures to evaluate stakeholder engagement with nonprofit organizations on social networking sites. *Public Relations Review, 41*(4), 501–503.

Joseph, M. (2017, January 31). America does not have enough volunteers. *Huffington Post.* Retrieved from http://www.huffingtonpost.com/marc-joseph/america-does-not-have-eno_b_9032152.html

Kang, M. (2016). Moderating effects of identification on volunteer engagement: An exploratory study of a faith-based charity organization. *Journal of Communication Management, 20*(2), 102–117

Kashif, M., & De Run, E. C. (2015). Money donations intentions among Muslim donors: An extended theory of planned behavior model. *International Journal of Nonprofit and Voluntary Sector Marketing, 20*(1), 84–96.

Kelly, K. S. (2001). Stewardship: The fifth step in the public relations process. In R. Heath (Ed.), *Handbook of public relations* (pp. 279–289). Thousand Oaks, CA: Sage.

Kinsky, E. S., Drumheller, K., & Gerlich, R. N. (2014). Weathering the storm: Best practices for nonprofits in crisis. *International Journal of Nonprofit and Voluntary Sector Marketing, 19*(4), 277–285.

Kinsky, E. S., Drumheller, K., Gerlich, R. N., Brock-Baskin, M. E., & Sollosy, M. (2015). The effect of socially mediated public relations crises on planned behavior: How TPB can help both corporations and nonprofits. *Journal of Public Relations Research, 27*(2), 136–157.

Kirk, K., Ractham, P., & Abrahams, A. (2016). Website development by nonprofit organizations in an emerging market: A case study of Thai websites. *International Journal of Nonprofit and Voluntary Sector Marketing, 21*(3), 195–211.

Lee, S. Y., & Rim, H. (2016). Negative spillover in corporate–nonprofit partnerships: Exploring the effects of company–cause congruence and organization–public relationships. *Public Relations Review, 42*(4), 710–712.

Liu, B. F. (2012). Toward a better understanding of nonprofit communication management. *Journal of Communication Management, 16*(4), 388–404.

Liu, B. F., Jin, Y., Briones, R., & Kuch, B. (2012). Managing turbulence in the blogosphere: Evaluating the blog-mediated crisis communication model with the American Red Cross. *Journal of Public Relations Research, 24*(4), 353–370.

Long, Z. (2016). Managing legitimacy crisis for state-owned non-profit organization: A case study of the Red Cross Society of China. *Public Relations Review, 42*(2), 372–374.

MacLaughlin, S. (2016, October 17). 50 fascinating nonprofit statistics. *npEngage.* Retrieved from https://npengage.com/nonprofit-news/50-fascinating-nonprofit-statistics/

Maxwell, S. P., & Carboni, J. L. (2014). Stakeholder communication in service implementation networks: Expanding relationship management theory to the nonprofit sector through organizational network analysis. *International Journal of Nonprofit and Voluntary Sector Marketing, 19*(4), 301–313.

McDougle, L. M., & Lam, M. (2014). Indvidual- and community-level determinants of public attitudes toward nonprofit organizations. *Voluntary and Nonprofit Sector Quarterly, 43*(4), 672–692.

McKeever, B. W. (2013). From awareness to advocacy: Understanding nonprofit communication, participation, and support. *Journal of Public Relations Research, 25*(4), 307–328.

McKeever, B. & Gaddy, M. (2016, October 24). The nonprofit workforce: By the numbers. *Nonprofit Quarterly.* Retrieved from https://nonprofitquarterly.org/2016/10/24/nonprofit-workforce-numbers/

McKeever, B. W., Pressgrove, G., McKeever, R., & Zheng, Y. (2016). Toward a theory of situational support: A model for exploring fundraising, advocacy and organizational support. *Public Relations Review, 42*(1), 219–222.

Nah, S., & Saxton, G. D. (2013). Modeling the adoption and use of social media by nonprofit organizations. *New Media and Society, 15*(2), 294–313.

O'Neil, J. (2007). The link between strong public relationships and donor support. *Public Relations Review, 33,* 99–102.

O'Neill, M. & Young, D. R. (Eds.). (1988). *Educating managers of nonprofit organizations.* New York: Praeger.

Patel, S. J., & McKeever, B. W. (2014). Health nonprofits online: The use of frames and stewardship strategies to increase stakeholder involvement. *International Journal of Nonprofit and Voluntary Sector Marketing, 19*(4), 224–238.

Perry, S. (2015, October 5). 1 in 3 Americans lacks faith in charities, *Chronicle* poll finds. *Chronicle of Philanthropy.* Retrieved from https://www.philanthropy.com/article/1-in-3-Americans-Lacks-Faith/233613

Powers, E., & Yaros, R. A. (2013). Cultivating support for nonprofit news organizations: Commitment, trust and donating audiences. *Journal of Communication Management, 17*(2), 157–170.

Pressgrove, G. (2017). Development of a scale to measure perceptions of stewardship strategies for nonprofit organizations. *Journalism & Mass Communication Quarterly, 94*(1), 102–123.

Pressgrove, G. N., & McKeever, B. W. (2016). Nonprofit relationship management: Extending the organization–public relationship to loyalty and behaviors. *Journal of Public Relations Research, 28*(3–4), 193–211.

Putnam, R. D. (1995). Bowling alone: America's declining social capital. *Journal of Democracy, 6,* 65–78.

Rasmussen, L. (2015). Planned Parenthood takes on Live Action: An analysis of media interplay and image restoration strategies in strategic conflict management. *Public Relations Review, 41*(3), 354–356.

Rudov, L., McCormick-Ricket, I., Kingsmill, D., Ledford, C., & Carton, T. (2017). Evaluation recommendations for nonprofit social marketing campaigns: An example from the Louisiana Campaign for Tobacco-Free Living. *International Journal of Nonprofit and Voluntary Sector Marketing, 22*(1), e1570.

Salamon, L. M. (1999). The nonprofit sector at a crossroads: The case of America. *Voluntas: International Journal of Voluntary and Nonprofit Organizations, 10*(1), 5–23.

Salamon, L. M. (2002) *The state of nonprofit America.* Washington, DC: Brookings Institution Press.

Salamon, L. M. (2012). *America's nonprofit sector* (3rd ed.). New York: Foundation Center.

Salamon, L. M. (2015). *The resilient sector revisited: The new challenge to nonprofit America* (2nd ed.). Washington, DC: Brookings Institution.

Salamon, L. M., Anheier, H. K., List, R., Toepler, S., Sokolowski, S. W., & Associates. (1999). *Global civil society: Dimensions of the nonprofit sector.* Baltimore: Johns Hopkins Center for Civil Society Studies.

Salamon, L. M., Geller, S. L., & Newhouse, C. L. (2012, December). *What do nonprofits stand for? Renewing the nonprofit value commitment.* Baltimore: Johns Hopkins Center for Civil Society

Studies. Retrieved from http://ccss.jhu.edu/wp-content/uploads/downloads/2012/12/What-Do-Nonprofits-Stand-For_JHUCCSS_12.2012.pdf

Sargeant, A., Ford, J. B., & West, D. C. (2006). Perceptual determinants of nonprofit giving behavior. *Journal of Business Research, 59*(2), 155–165.

Saxton, G. D., & Waters, R. D. (2014). What do stakeholders like on Facebook? Examining public reactions to nonprofit organizations' informational, promotional, and community-building messages. *Journal of Public Relations Research, 26*(3), 280–299.

Shen, A. (2016). First-year donation behavior and risk of supporter lapse. *International Journal of Nonprofit and Voluntary Sector Marketing, 21*(3), 212–224.

Sisco, H. F. (2012). Nonprofit in crisis: An examination of the applicability of situational crisis communication theory. *Journal of Public Relations Research, 24*(1), 1–17.

Sisco, H. F., Collins, E. L., & Zoch, L. M. (2010). Through the looking glass: A decade of Red Cross crisis response and situational crisis communication theory. *Public Relations Review, 36*(1), 21–27

Sisco, H. F., & McCorkindale, T. (2013). Communicating "pink": An analysis of the communication strategies, transparency, and credibility of breast cancer social media sites. *International Journal of Nonprofit and Voluntary Sector Marketing, 18*(4), 287–301.

Sisco, H. F., Pressgrove, G., & Collins, E. L. (2013). Paralleling the practice: An analysis of the scholarly literature in nonprofit public relations. *Journal of Public Relations Research, 25*(4), 282–306.

Sisson, D. C. (2017). Control mutuality, social media, and organization-public relationships: A study of local animal welfare organizations' donors. *Public Relations Review, 43*(1), 179–189.

Sommerfeldt, E. J. (2013). Online power resource management: Activist resource mobilization, communication strategy, and organizational structure. *Journal of Public Relations Research, 25*(4), 347–367.

Swanger, W., & Rodgers, S. (2013). Revisiting fundraising encroachment of public relations in light of theory of donor relations. *Public Relations Review, 39*, 566–568.

Tindall, N. T., Waters, R. D., & Kelly, K. S. (2014). A fractured glass ceiling in fundraising? Examining the careers of minority healthcare fundraisers using role theory. In R. D. Waters (Ed.), *Public relations in the nonprofit sector: Theory and practice* (pp. 3–18). New York: Routledge.

Wallack, L., Dorfman, J., Jernigan, D., & Themba, M. (1993). *Media advocacy and public health: Power for prevention.* Newbury Park, CA: Sage.

Waters, R. D. (2008). Applying relationship management theory to the fundraising process for individual donors. *Journal of Communication Management, 12*(1), 73–87.

Waters, R. D. (2011). Increasing fundraising efficiency through evaluation: Applying communication theory to the nonprofit organization–donor relationship. *Nonprofit and Voluntary Sector Quarterly, 40*(3), 458–475.

Waters, R. D. (2013). Tracing the impact of media relations and television coverage on US charitable relief fundraising: An application of agenda-setting theory across three natural disasters. *Journal of Public Relations Research, 25*(4), 329–346.

Waters, R. D., Kelly, K. S., & Lee Walker, M. (2012). Organizational roles enacted by healthcare fundraisers: A national study testing theory and assessing gender differences. *Journal of Communication Management, 16*(3), 244–263.

Waters, R. D., & Lord, M. (2009). Examining how advocacy groups build relationships on the internet. *International Journal of Nonprofit and Voluntary Sector Marketing, 14*(3), 231–241.

Weberling, B. (2012). Framing breast cancer: Building an agenda through online advocacy and fundraising. *Public Relations Review, 38*(1), 108–115.

Weberling, B., & Waters, R. D. (2012). Gauging the public's preparedness for mobile public relations: The "Text for Haiti" campaign. *Public Relations Review, 38*(1), 51–55.

Wiggill, M. N. (2014). Donor relationship management practices in the South African non-profit sector. *Public Relations Review, 40*(2), 278–285.

Worley, D. A., & Little, J. K. (2002). The critical role of stewardship in fund raising: The Coaches vs. Cancer campaign. *Public Relations Review, 28*(1), 99–112.

Young, D. R., & Salamon, L. M. (2002) Commercialization, social ventures and for-profit competition. In L. M. Salamon (Ed.), *The state of nonprofit America* (pp. 423–446). Washington, DC: Brookings Institution Press.

9

Globalization

Chiara Valentini

Especially in the last 30 years, globalization has emerged as a central concept in public, political, and managerial discourses dealing with its impact on societies, cultures, social policies, and the lives of people in general. As a historical and social phenomenon, globalization is associated with internationalization processes, social relations, and technological developments. In public relations, globalization is often related to the increased and widespread transnationalization of organizations, particularly large corporations, and how these organizations manage the complexity and ambiguity that come when operating in multiple and diverse types of market and with heterogeneous and often diverging public groups. This transnational process, occurring first, but not only, in large corporations, has posed several challenges to the public relations profession. By the late 1980s, many companies were actually multinational and multicultural organizations and had to respond to, and be accountable to international publics and shareholders to a greater degree (Valentini, 2012). Internationally, the economic boom of the 1980s and the revitalization of a capitalist and corporatist mentality in many postsocialist countries have contributed to the diffusion of public relations in non-Western countries (Bardhan & Weaver, 2011; Valentini, 2012).

Consequently, questions of how to address the specificities of these post-Soviet countries when conducting public relations have become even more compelling. Whether Western organizations had to enter new markets or new, non-Western markets relied more and more on public relations practices, an increasing need for communication addressing international concerns and thus of more global approaches in public relations arose among both practitioners and scholars. Globalization can thus be considered a major force in bringing about the transnationalization of organizations and the consequent expansion of public relations roles and functions. It has also been a key factor in promoting public relations as a central function in profit, nonprofit, and public organizations in non-Western countries. These two developments urged changes in how public relations has been conceptualized and conducted internally and externally in organizations to meet new environment conditions.

This chapter offers an introduction to the concept of globalization and how and why it impacts public relations. It then presents and reviews some theories, models, and concepts in public relations addressing globalization and discusses how these can be used to meet public relations challenges in global societies. It concludes with some reflections on major questions that need to be addressed by public relations theorists working in globalization.

Defining the Concepts: What Is Globalization?

According to sociologist Giddens (1991), globalization is "the intensification of worldwide social relations linking distant localities in such a way that local happenings are shaped by events occurring many thousands of miles away and vice versa" (p. 71). Globalization covers an increase both of interactions (liberalization and internationalization) and of integrations (universalization, Westernization, and deterritorialization) among people, organizations, and governments of different nations (Valentini, Kruckeberg, & Starck, 2016). It has been driven by international trade and investment and facilitated by digital technologies, but its effects go beyond economic ones. It is a complex, multidirectional process that touches upon different levels of agencies and structures in society in a continuous flux (Rittenhofer & Valentini, 2015; Scholte, 2005). Globalization is not a homogeneous and uniform process that occurs in all the parts at the world at the same time and at the same speed (cf. Dutta, 2012; Rittenhofer & Valentini, 2015; Shome & Hedge, 2002; Valentini et al., 2016).

Having this in mind, we can pinpoint four major aspects of globalization and its impact on societies. As a social phenomenon, globalization has been an intrinsic force in creating new opportunities to develop new forms of communications and technological structures that have facilitated the intensification of these social relations. The increased use and diffusion of digital technologies, including the phenomenon of social media, have accelerated and widened the means through which people can communicate, learn about distant phenomena, and share their own opinions with anyone. Today any person can influence or be influenced by what is happening in the world and can become an influential public for an organization at any time (Valentini et al., 2016).

From a cultural perspective, scholars have pointed out two opposite effects of globalization. It has prompted reactionary movements that reinforce parochial distinctions between people. For example, the increased popularity of extremist political parties and of movements defending local community interests, and the revival in "ethno-nations," such as the Basques, Scots, or Quebecois, are interpreted as antiglobalization reactions (Keating, 2001; Castells, 2004). But then again, globalization has also strengthened cosmopolitan attitudes by weakening the relevance of ethnicity, locality, or nationhood as sources of identification (Beck, 2006). As a result, individuals overcome the "in-group–out-group" tension of parochialism and experience a sense of common belonging merely by virtue of inhabiting the same planet (Cheah & Robbins, 1998; Scholte, 2005). For instance, global issues, such as climate change, human rights and humanitarian relief, and foreign aid to developing countries, are seen as a manifestation of this cosmopolitan conscience.

From an economic point of view, the most obvious aspect of increasing globalization is the expansion of a capitalist mind-set at international levels, with important effects on world global economies and on the international division of labor, according to Giddens (1991). These effects include the differentiation between more and less industrialized areas in the world. The fact that countries are able to trade with each other more freely has created an abundance of products and services that can be offered to the consumer. Yet, this situation can cause further issues. As Valentini (2017) noted:

> Research shows that operating across borders poses more challenges for organizations due to differences in economic standards, legislation, regulations, customs, and sociocultural matters. Among the different factors that organizations operating in international environments need to constantly monitor and be responsive to, scholars have pointed specifically to the level of bureaucracy, corruption, overall government stability, trade control,

competition regulation, employment law, discrimination law, data protection law, consumer protection law, tax policy, freedom of the press, and civil society and voluntary sector development. (p. 846)

From a civic/political point of view, the impact of globalization on industrialization takes many forms and shapes and is not simply limited to production, but affects many aspects of the day-to-day life of people and political relations. Multinational organizations, that is, organizations that produce, sell, and/or operate in several countries, have become important social actors in the world economy, since "corporations, especially globally active ones, can play a key role in shaping not only the economy but society as whole – if 'only' because they have it in their power to withdraw the material resources (capital, taxes, jobs) from society" (Beck, 2000, p. 2). Multinational companies are not just exploiting natural resources in third countries, but are actively contributing to social issues. By doing so, they take over traditional duties of the state (e.g. for providing clean water, proper sanitation infrastructure) and can leverage this social commitment in return for more favorable fiscal and market conditions.

Why and How Is Public Relations Impacted by Globalization?

Globalization impacts the environment, that is, the internal and external contexts in which public relations operates. Hence it affects the way public relations is conducted and approached by introducing different opportunities for the profession, but also by rendering the profession more complex as globalization enhances situational conditions and variables that can affect public relations outcomes. On the one hand, globalization has provided the public relations industry with new opportunities for expansion. Baskin and Aronoff (1992), for instance, underline three important opportunities to enlarge public relations competences as a result of globalization. First, public relations conducted on behalf of multinational organizations may include representative functions in host countries with the purpose of facilitating agreements with governments and local constituencies on questions related to international activities. Second, the bridging function of public relations can extend its scope to help the home management team and the local management team reach mutual and beneficial internal relationships between, often culturally diverse, groups of managers. Finally, the portfolio of activities of public relations generally increases to include more diversified actions that deal with developing and implementing local public relations initiatives. To these, Sriramesh (2010) adds that globalization has offered other professional, not corporate, opportunities to the field as well; public relations can play a key role in interactions among countries of the world at economic, political, and cultural levels through public diplomacy and cultural diplomacy activities, which typically deal with relationships among governments and publics around the world.

Globalization is also impacting the way public relations is conceptualized, from an organization-centric function to a societal one. Scholars critical of mainstream, managerial approaches in public relations posit that public relations should not just be conceptualized as an organizational function aiming to leverage the image and reputation of organizations through different communication activities, because the profession has "increasingly become a tool in shaping public policy and in instigating public debates, thereby playing an active role in shaping society and, ultimately, culture" (Banks, 1995 cited in Valentini, 2007, p. 119). Globalization has also influenced emergent understandings of public relations that take postcolonial and societal positions. Accordingly, public relations concerns activities and actions that shape globalization efforts and practices in countries that have historically experienced Western control.

Public relations becomes a communicative and relationship-building practice that can bridge the political- and cultural-economic spheres of globalization, recasting practice as a central tenet of a global social justice agenda (Curtin & Gaither, 2012).

Despite these positive effects on the public relations profession, globalization has destabilized its existing body of knowledge, which is still overly dominated by Western-centric theorizing (Rittenhofer & Valentini, 2015), by showing the limits of public relations theories in addressing professional questions at the global level. Sriramesh (2010) notes a general ethnocentrism in public relations, in that the public relations strategies of multinational organizations are still developed in home countries and implemented in different cultures with few or no changes to adjust to local social, economic, and political conditions. Generally, public relations has been following either a *global*, a *local*, or a *glocal* approach. A *global* approach assumes a certain level of homogeneity among the behaviors of key publics based on similarities in their interests regarding an organization, product, or brand despite their cultural, social, political, and economic differences. Communication strategies are strategically planned and managed on the assumption that there is a global public who shares some values, norms, and opinions. Often this approach is decided centrally, in the home country, and then implemented locally. There is a high level of control, coordination, and management of communication activities across the different regions, and the organization is capable of maintaining consistency in its diverse communication activities under the credo "one voice, one communication" (Valentini, 2012). This approach, however, does not help organizations reaching out to specific publics, and overall, it can be seen as top-down, asymmetric management approach, because it is centrally decided and does not consider the diversity of publics' needs.

Conversely, the *local* approach consists of ad hoc strategies created, developed, and implemented in local communities. Communication messages are crafted and delivered in a manner that resonates well with local publics, having in mind local values and norms. In a local approach, public relations activities typically reflect the peculiarities and the strategic objectives of each region or country, and these can be highly different one from another. Because strategies are tailored to the different social, cultural, political, and economic conditions of the context and of publics, they are more effective in reaching public relations goals, yet they require more resources than a global approach and can create unwanted effects, such as communicative cacophonies across regions and the emergence of diverse public opinions on what an organization represents. On the other hand, a local approach is more effective for particular types of public relations actions, for instance those addressing particular interests, such as lobbying governments and legislators who operate under different legislative frameworks.

Finally, a *glocal* approach consists of having a global strategy but adapting the tactics to local contextual conditions. Adaptation may consist in creating variations of the same campaign, initiative, or event, or contributing to philanthropic initiatives that are of major relevance for the host country without altering the overall organizational objectives and corporate values. The glocal approach is sensitive to local differences and thus is better suited to address contextual aspects and to answer publics' concerns more precisely than a global approach. It is also better than a local approach in maintaining consistency across the different communication activities of an organization because it is grounded on general principles. The three approaches describe the extent to which public relations are contextualized, but do not offer answers to questions about when and how public relations should be contextualized.

When best practices do not seem to work, several public relations scholars and practitioners impute the shortcomings to matters of cultural differences. Culture clearly plays an important role in addressing how publics of different regions perceive and interpret public relations actions. Yet, culture is not the only variable explaining disparities, as other factors influence public relations outcomes. In short, globalization has raised a lot of questions among professionals who daily experience its effects in different situations and contexts.

How, When and Why Is Theory Applied with Globalization?

Main Theories of Public Relations and for Public Relations Addressing Globalization

Despite the great relevance of globalization for the public relations profession, theorizing in global public relations has slowly though continuously grown in the last 15 years. Most of the studies engage in country-specific investigations to showcase situations in which consolidated theories and models are tested to confirm or refute their suitability in explaining a phenomenon in different parts of the world. Literature stresses the importance of formative research to learn about a country-specific profile before planning communication activities. Culture is typically considered one of the major factors influencing communication activities in international settings. Global public relations professionals are typically depicted as cultural intermediaries, that is "mediators between producers and consumers who actively create meanings by establishing an identification between the products or issues and publics" (Curtin & Gaither, 2007, p. 41). Hence most global public relations theorizing has taken as its point of departure the concept of culture and how culture can influence public relations outcomes.

Examples of Theory Used with Globalization

Table 9.1 shows an overview of some of the main theories and models offering insights on how to address the impact of globalization in public relations by summarizing their theoretical objectives (normative, descriptive, or instrumental) and their theoretical perspectives (professional, public, or conceptual), that is, whether such theories address the point of view of the public relations profession, publics, or a more general conceptual discussion of the relevance of a specific concept/postulation for global public relations.

Perhaps one of the most adopted and tested global public relations theories across the world is the *theory of generic principles and specific applications*. The theory suggests the role public relations should have and how it should be practiced in organizations in general, including multinational, transnational, and international organizations, so that it can help them in fulfilling their strategic objectives. This middle-range theory originates from early work by Verčič, Grunig, and Grunig (1996), L. A. Grunig, Grunig, and Verčič (1998), and Wakefield (1996). These and other scholars have contributed to providing empirical evidence for its normative foundations. This theory substantially supports a glocal approach in conducting public relations since it proposes that "some universally applicable principles of public relations are harmonized to develop communication strategies that suit local cultures" (Sriramesh, 2009, p. 4). The theory proposes a normative approach to conducting global public relations activities by suggesting professionals follow 10 generic principles and adapt them to five key contextual variables found to influence the environment of public relations. These variables are a country's culture (societal and organizational), media environment, the political system, the economic system and level of development, and activism. The 10 principles proposed in this theory, which are essentially the same principles as those elaborated in the excellence study (J. Grunig, 2008), suggest that public relations contributes to the achievement of organizational goals when it is part of or has direct access to the decision-making management team, is independent from other organizational functions and offers both managerial and technical expertise, is

Table 9.1 Overview of major theories addressing globalization

Theories	Proponents	Theoretical objectives	Theoretical perspectives
Theory of generic principles and specific applications	Sriramesh & Verčič, 2001; L. A. Grunig, Grunig, & Verčič, 1998; Verčič, Grunig, & Grunig, 1996; Wakefield, 1996	Normative	Public relations: interprets the function of public relations in global contexts.
Rhetorical generic theory	Kent & Taylor, 2007	Normative	Conceptual: interprets the normative characteristics of effective communications in intercultural settings and their significance for global public relations.
Circuit of culture	Curtin & Gaither, 2007	Descriptive	Conceptual: describes how particular aspects (i.e. moments) of meaning creation play a role in effective international public relations communications.
Third-culture building model	Casmir, 1978, 1993; Bardhan, 2011	Normative	Public relations and public: interprets the role of public relations professionals and of publics regarding reaching a common understanding (i.e. third culture).
In-awareness framework	Zaharna, 2001	Instrumental	Public relations: analyzes the connection between contextual, situational, and public-specific communication factors and how they impact the effectiveness of public relations communications in global contexts.

integrated in all its sub-areas of application, and promotes symmetrical communications inside and outside the organizations.

The application of this theory to the context of globalization is twofold. The generic principles in this theory can be used as indicators for how to structure and set up a public relations function in any type of organization in any part of the world. Yet, one should be cautious not to become overly obsessed in observing them. In many organizations around the world, there is no specific public relations function in the organizational structure, but public relations activities are embedded in others, and performed accordingly to internal versus external scopes. So, external communications may be handled by professionals in marketing and PR and internal communications by human resources professionals, and there can be a chief communication officer who manages the whole set of communications and relational activities, and whose educational background is not in public relations. Still these can be successful organizations from a public relations point of view. The second contribution of this theory consists in its contextual factors, which can serve as a starting point for deciding which elements of the public relations function, roles, or activities need to be adjusted. Yet, given its normative nature, this theory does not offer many insights into how a professional should use the information on the specific contextual factors obtained through formative research in a particular country to set up local strategies and tactics and adjust diverse public relations processes.

Another theory that has been influenced by the excellence study is the *rhetorical generic theory* by Kent and Taylor (2007). Conceptually this theory stands on the same premises as the theory of generic principles and specific applications, considering that contextual factors can be seen as generic factors describing most of the salient features of public relations across the world, but the generic principles as illustrated by the excellent project show several limitations. Kent and Taylor (2007) suggest to replace them with other generic principles from rhetorical studies, arguing that a normative theory of global public relations should guide professionals in handling global public relations issues, rather than focusing on suggesting what features and characteristics excellence in public relations should have. This theory's focus is on understanding the role of language in shaping communication dynamics among organizations and key publics, having in mind the contextual factors.

The six rhetorical principles of this theory suggest public relations professionals should (1) identify key features of a situation, (2) identify the intended audience effects, (3) clarify the motivational intent of the organization and publics, (4) examine how meaning is created through language, (5) examine professionals' strategic considerations, and (6) use communication principles and theory to understand how cultures influence organizations and communication (Kent & Taylor, 2007, pp. 11–12). The approach of this theory is very broad and normative. The rhetorical generic theory can be applied to any communication situation in a global context, yet because of its generic and universal nature, it does not offer clear parameters to make global comparisons.

Similarly, Curtin and Gaither (2007) propose a model that takes its point of departure from the role of language as a cultural device. According to these scholars, culture influences how publics think and act toward organizations and how they interpret and understand their communications. Hence, one must start from studying how language is expressed in diverse forms and shapes and represents the culture of the publics and how they respond to the organizations' public relations activities. Based on an early cultural model, Curtin and Gaither (2007) suggest the *circuit of culture* as a global public relations model addressing cultural differences that emerge in public relations communication activities. The model stands on the supposition that culture does not simply define the meaning of reality, but is itself a signifier of reality. In other words, meanings are socially constructed, and continuously change and adapt. To study how meanings form, evolve, and change, we need to look at five moments of meaning construction. These moments are regulation, production, consumption, representation, and identity. Each of these moments contributes to the creation, shape, and modification of meanings. In addition, each interacts with the others in a synergistic manner with no specific beginning or end.

This model systematically analyses how publics may form a certain understanding of an organization, brand, product, service, or experience based on an understanding of how public relations initiatives are produced by the organization. Members of the organization's publics encode specific representations, based on their understanding of the legal and regulatory context in which the messages are diffused. The model can be particularly useful during formative assessments of international communication campaigns as it helps in understanding publics' responses in the different stages of the meaning creation process. One of the strengths of this model is that it offers a central role of publics in the meaning creation process. Publics are not simply considered receivers and consumers of public relations communications, but instead they become integral elements of the construction of a shared meaning of a message or campaign.

Another cultural model that offers interesting insights for global public relations is the *third-culture building model* by the intercultural communication scholar Casmir (1978). This model differs from other models and theories that have been used in global public relations in suggesting the development of a new third culture among individuals who come together. This new culture becomes the common ground for all participants – a kind of cognitive space that incorporates elements of both cultures and yet remains separate and distinct. Essentially the model departs from adoption (the process of taking on the cultural mores of another) or adaptation (modifying one's cultural mores to better fit those of another) to create something unique to the specific communication context. The new third culture is achieved through deliberate developments in an extended process, during which all participants gain an understanding and appreciation of one another. According to Casmir (1993), the coexistence between different cultures must not imply the abandonment of own's cultural identity, but rather it should help develop a cultural interface that functions as a cultural bridge among different cultures, which facilitates relationship-building initiatives.

This model is considered a truly intersubjective and co-creational one because it focuses on the process of negotiating people's cultural differences when communicating together (Bardhan, 2011). It also offers insights into the power dynamics among people communicating one to another. The applicability of this model to the context of globalization is, however, limited to those consolidated and stable relationships that organizations may have with specific key publics. It is very difficult to negotiate a third culture with adversarial publics or publics who have no intention of negotiating their own stances. Similarly, professionals need to assess to what extent they are capable and willing, and what values (business, professional, or personal ones) they can set aside, to be able to understand and relate profoundly with their key publics. Public relations professionals are daily confronted with a complex system of values and beliefs, some prescribed by their organizations, others by their professional codes of ethics, and finally by their moral, social, and cultural stances. Deciding what to negotiate may be difficult.

Intercultural communication reflection and cultural awareness are also the central tenets in the *in-awareness framework* proposed by Zaharna (2001). This framework essentially summarizes and integrates early reflections on contextual and situational factors impacting the communicative interactions between organizations and publics from other cultural settings with intercultural scholarship. The framework is based on three variables: country profile, cultural profile, and communication profile. As Zaharna (2001) states: "The country profile provides a broad outline of what may be feasible within a particular country, while the cultural profile speaks to what may be effective in that country. The communication profile further refines cultural generalities by delineating culturally-based communication behaviors that underlie common public relations practices" (p. 135).

The country profile is based on similar contextual factors as other theories and models. The culture profile comprises elements related to the context of communicative interactions by assessing the extent to which a culture is (1) high/low in context, that is, if it relies on tacit or explicit knowledge; (2) monochronic or polychromic, that is, if it prefers to handle one or multiple activities at one time; (3) doing or being, that is, if it is focused on acting, achieving something, or reinforcing status quo and ranks; (4) future-tense or past-tense, that is, if it is interested in moving forward or rather maintaining continuity with the past; and (5) linear or nonlinear, that is, if it is focused on beginnings and ends and stresses unitary themes or has multiple themes and follows unorganized paths (Zaharna, 2001). Finally, the communication profile emphasizes the communication preferences of publics and their major communication behaviors based on their verbal, oral, and visual communications, use of gestures and communicative space, rhetorical style, and their communication matrix, which consists of how the different components of communication fit together in a particular culture.

Compared to earlier theoretical propositions, this framework offers more precise instrumental insights on how to address communicative interactions between public relations professionals and key publics, particularly in the situation of agency–client relations. Yet its applicability to other initiatives, such as global communication campaigns, is hard to foresee as it is impossible to analyze and include all elements of the communication profile into a strategic plan that addresses mass publics.

Major Topics/Questions Needing to Be Addressed by Public Relations Theorists Working with Globalization

To some extent it can be argued that globalization challenges public relations in at least four major respects: (1) definition of publics, (2) choice of strategies and tactics, (3) handling global issues and complexity, and (4) dealing with ethical responsibilities and moral considerations.

Perhaps a first question for professionals is the definition of key publics, that is, those groups of individuals who can affect an organization's strategic objectives. Given that the main role of public relations is to create and maintain mutual and beneficial relationships between organizations and publics, especially the strategic ones, the definition and identification of key publics is a central component for the creation and implementation of specific relational and communication plans addressing this objective.

There exist many models and theories that can help the profession in identifying and prioritizing publics that draw on public relations theories, such as J. E. Grunig's situational theory of publics (1966, 1997) or those in stakeholder management literature such as Mitchell, Agle, and Wood's (1997) stakeholder salience model.[1] What these, and other theories and models, have in common is their urge to categorize groups of individuals into public groups on the basis of specific parameters, such as the type of relationship that these groups of individuals possess with an organization, their interest in and level of involvement with the organization, their power in influencing an organization's behavior, the resources they possess, and their communicative behaviors, to mention a few. Based on the selected parameters, public relations professionals identify key publics, assess their level of relevance in respect to the situation and/or organizational objectives, and develop specific actions for them. These classifications are typically situational and contextual, and are often left to the discretion of a manager who performs the assessment. When organizations operate transculturally or internationally, this process becomes more complex. One cannot expect a key public, say consumers, to possess the same type of parameters and act homogeneously if this public group is, in fact, based in Bangladesh or in Brazil while the organization is housed in Europe or North America. Neither should one expect that all current and potential Bangladeshi or Brazilian consumers can be treated as if their purchasing power and income disposal were similar, and nor should one assume these consumers' interests and concerns in relation to the organization are alike. Existing approaches are short in reflecting on the influencing dynamics of inter- and intrapublic groups since they typically address linear relations between organizations and their key publics and tend to oversimplify how public groups form, interact, and influence each other. Accordingly, a multinational organization would have to perform multiple public analyses by regions, if not by nations, in order to identify key publics in the countries where it operates. However, these analyses would likely not capture the interrelations among public groups and the complexity of communication flows.

Research shows a general fluidity of public groupings; publics do not live in silos, isolated one from another, but rather affect each other across groups and borders. A typical example is that of investors and shareholders. These public groups do not simply make investment decisions on the basis of corporate reporting on financial performance; they are also highly influenced by extrafinancial information, such as disclosures on governance and environmental issues, news media coverage, etc., obtained from other sources, that is, other influential publics. Based on the premise that different publics influence each other, one would assume that organizations operating internationally could expect to see the rise of a global public, "a group of individuals or organizations whose primary interests and concerns are pursuing the world as a whole beyond their own national and cultural boundaries" (Lee, 2005, p. 15). However, Valentini (2007) has argued that even if public groups share similar attitudes toward some issues, it does not mean their interests and ways to solve those issues are similar, nor that they share similar norms and mores. Hence, scholars such as Kruckeberg and Vujnovic (2010) wonder whether the whole idea of public definition, identification, and prioritization is actually relevant today, especially considering how globalization has brought about numerous "volatile publics that can form immediately and unpredictably and can act seemingly chaotically and with unforeseen power" (p. 124). But if organizations cannot clearly identify their key publics, how can they strategically contribute to developing mutual and beneficial relationships for their organizations?

A second question that globalization has brought to public relations theorizing is related to the choice of strategies and tactics. The literature offers several suggestions of strategies and tactics, and illustrations of best practices, in relation to specific situations depending on the strategic publics' communicative behaviors and relational history. However, public relations strategies and tactics proposed so far are not entirely capable of responding to global questions and to diversified sets of publics because they do not take into consideration the complexity of inter- and cross-relations. Thus, it is up to the professional, relying on experience in matching, assembling, and disassembling consolidated strategies and tactics, to create a good mix that fits within the context, situation, and the specific public relations objective. With little theoretical direction on how to do this, the risk of failures increases, leaving early career professionals under a lot of pressure.

So far, fruitful theoretical propositions for how to address public relations strategies and tactics that address globalization have remained at the very generic level on one side, such as global, glocal, or local, or too specific to sub-areas, such as research on international consumers in international marketing and marketing public relations. While mainstream global public relations approaches tend to follow the glocal approach, this approach is not without shortcomings, and is still too hegemonic in its fundamental postulations. Critical scholars argue that a glocal approach still presumes that the core standards directing public relations actions, which have been primarily influenced by an Anglo-Saxon thinking of what excellence means, are valid and acceptable parameters in conducting communication activities in all parts of the world. Following these specific standards in host countries, however, may result in unsuccessful public relations outcomes. There is, thus, a need for more and diversified middle-range and micro theories in global public relations.

A third question is the handling of global issues and the general complexity and instability of the external environment. When organizations become international and enter new and diverse markets, they are expected to comply with local regulations and conduct proper business activities. They expect to produce benefits for themselves and for the host country, for example in the form of increasing their profits by reaching more consumers and customers, reducing production costs due to more competitive salary schemes, obtaining essential raw materials, but also increasing local employment opportunities, supporting the local community directly via diverse community initiatives and via corporate taxes, increasing the gross domestic product of the country, and even indirectly influencing further foreign investments in the area. Yet multinational companies are expected to take more and more responsibilities for diverse sets of global issues and not simply local issues that are highly important in the markets in which they operate. Neither existing theories of corporate social responsibility, nor existing global public relations theories are sufficient to help professionals.

A fourth question is related to an increased global expectation of organizations and their ethical responsibilities and moral considerations. This last challenge is related to the previous one but goes far deeper into the conduct of organizations and how public relations is practiced in that it does not simply address an organization's stance toward global issues. It questions the whole foundation of organizational values, norms, and cultures and the duties of public relations in this process. Consumer skepticism has increased toward corporate organizations and so has the general public's perception of political authorities' capabilities in handling social, political, and economic issues (Valentini & Kruckeberg, 2011). Publics have diverse channels for voicing their discontent and, unless oppressed by authoritative regimes, they are capable of reaching and mobilizing a large group of other individuals with different activist actions for many different reasons. Research on investor activism shows an increased interest by the financial community in socially responsible investments (Wen, 2009) and expects corporations to adjust business practices accordingly. Yet research shows that neither investors nor consumers are willing to pay the price for making organizations more responsible toward society and the environment. Research is also inconclusive on the actual economic benefits for businesses when engaging in moral actions (Clark & Hebb, 2005; Guyatt, 2005).

Normative ethical theories stress that organizations have moral duties toward different stakeholders and society. Yet what does an organization do if its publics' interests are contrasting or contradictory? Are all organizations compelled to take on ethical responsibilities or could they simply show some moral consideration? There is a substantial difference between ethics and morality. Ethics refers to rules provided by an external source, such as codes of conduct in workplaces or principles in religions. Morals refer to an individual's own principles regarding right and wrong. Codes of ethics in public relations function as a general principle governing good practices in public relations, which are often about acting according the rules of law, being transparent in intent, and not distorting or manipulating information. One of the main functions of public relations is to advise organizations on the best actions to take to meet publics' and societal concerns. Yet, as a result of globalization, publics expect organizations to display high moral standards when making decisions that transcend codes of ethics. The code of ethics in public relations does little to help professionals with addressing morality. These situations are very difficult to tackle because they belong to so-called "duties of beneficence," which refer to moral obligations "to act for the others' benefit, helping them to further their important and legitimate interests, often by preventing or removing possible harms" (Beauchamp, 2013, para. 1). By definition they cannot be controlled via legislation or sanctioned by professional authorities because they are based on an individual's or organization's self-constraint and thus they are voluntary, since an individual or organization can decide if they want to contribute to the happiness of someone else (cf. Mansell, 2013). Hence, in global public relations, professionals have more responsibilities in advising their organizations on questions that can have moral implications for large groups of people across the globe without having at their disposal precise theoretical instruments beyond their own personal judgments and experiences.

In this chapter, it has been argued that globalization is a continuous process impacting sociocultural, economic, and political aspects of people, organizations, and societies in general. It is not a new phenomenon nor a phenomenon that will cease to exist. For the profession of public relations, globalization has created new opportunities to extend its own contribution and reshape existing competences. Organizations operating internationally and/or transculturally should pay particular attention to their environments and should continuously address the conditions that affect effective communications with publics through research and formative assessments. Organizations, to be effective, should also develop a certain level of cultural sensitivity and awareness of cultural differences when relating to and communicating with publics from other countries (Valentini, 2017).

This chapter has also underlined the compelling need to develop more and new global public relations theories that can address globalization and its challenges. As critical scholars noted, the dominant thinking in public relations is still too hegemonic in that it tries to dictate what should be considered the best public relations practices in very different societies, with little consideration of the specificities of the contexts and situations in which they are applied (Bardhan & Weaver, 2011). To address these limits, there is thus a need to develop a more sensitive understanding of local differences and imprint theory with new approaches and perspectives that can better capture the fluidity, complexity, and ever-changing nature of globalized and globalizing societies. We need to move theory a step forward by challenging our existing epistemological and ontological theses, and enter "new lands" of discoveries to develop some new thinking and new ways to respond to globalization. Only through theoretically and methodologically sound approaches can scholarship help in answering those questions that professionals in public relations have, and will continue to have, when operating in international and multicultural environments.

Suggested Case to Explore to Demonstrate Theory at Work with Globalization

The recent refugee crisis is an exemplary case of how globalization is affecting organizations' involvement in handling a global humanitarian issue. The United Nations High Commissioner for Refugees reported that there were 65.3 million people displaced worldwide in 2016 (UNHCR, 2017). Political leaders around the world urged nations and private entities to take a stance on this global crisis (Kluge, 2016). Several political authorities responded to this call by working on legislative solutions that could support the integration of refugees in their countries and by seeking public and corporate assistance, too. In the United States, the Obama presidency issued a call for action to the American private sector and received the commitment of at least 50 large American companies in supporting refugees' education, employment, and enablement (Kluge, 2016). Similarly, in Germany several large companies joined together to promote the integration of refugees through diverse initiatives (DW, 2016, December 3), and so did other companies from other countries.

Global issues such as the refugee crisis bring a lot of challenges to multinational organizations. If organizations decide to take a stance on these, they need to consider the priorities of their existing corporate social responsibility programs, how these initiatives could include aspects that address global issues, and their budgeting, among other factors. They also need to assess how they can align their corporate values and their related communications to show a genuine commitment in the management of global issues. They need to evaluate the potential risks in addressing global issues that are far away from an easy solution, and for which different, even contrasting, positions among influential publics and/or inconsistencies in legislations exist. These and other questions make organizations' efforts in handling global issues rather a difficult and complex activity.

Discussion Questions

1 How would you describe globalization? Can you think of particular ways in which globalization has changed the public relations function, activities, and processes in organizations?

2 Can you describe at least two strengths and two weaknesses of the *glocal* approach in addressing contemporary global transformations and the complexity and fluidity of organization–public relations?

3 Can you think of an example where an organization has been successful in handling a global issue? What type of public relations activities did it develop to address the global issue? What strategic approach did it use?

4 In this chapter, five main theories of and for global public relations were presented; can you think of other public relations theories that could be used in global settings? Explain your view on this with clear rationales and references to theory and its application.

Note

1 While J. E. Grunig (1992) differentiates the concept of public from that of stakeholder, the latter being considered a generic group of individuals with some interest in an organization, whereas a public is often a specific group of individuals with active communicative behaviors, recent public relations literature interchangeably uses these terms to refer to groups of individuals who are affected by or affect an organization. Management literature consistently uses "stakeholder" even when some groups of individuals could be considered publics. Both literatures contribute to the definition, identification, and prioritization of the public/stakeholder concept, although from different theoretical premises.

Suggested Readings

Allagui, I., & Harris Breslow, H. (2016). Social media for public relations: Lessons from four effective cases. *Public Relations Review*, *42*(1), 20–30.

Ampuja, M. (2012). *Theorizing globalization: A critique of the mediatization of social theory*. Leiden, The Netherlands: Brill.

Bardhan, N., & Weaver, K. (2011). *Public relations in global cultural contexts. Multi-paradigmatic perspectives*. New York: Routledge

Coleman, W., & Sajed, A. (2013). *Fifty key thinkers on globalization*. New York: Routledge.

Curtin, P. A., & Gaither, T. K. (2012). *Globalization and public relations in postcolonial nations: Challenges and opportunities*. Amherst, NY: Cambria Press

Edwards, L., & Hodges C. E. M. (2011). *Public relations, society & culture: Theoretical and empirical explorations*. London: Routledge

Sriramesh, K., & Verčič, D. (2012). *Culture and public relations: Links and implications*. New York: Routledge

Sriramesh, K., & Verčič, D. (2018). *The global public relations handbook* (3rd ed.). New York: Routledge.

Theodossopoulos, D., & Kirtsoglou, E. (2010). *United in discontent: Local responses to cosmopolitanism and globalization*. New York: Berghahn Books

Turk, J. V., & Valin, J. (2017). *Public relations case studies from around the world* (2nd ed.). New York: Peter Lang

References

Banks, S. P. (1995). *Multicultural public relations: A social-interpretive approach*. London: Sage

Bardhan, N. (2011). Culture, communication and third culture building in public relations within global flux. In N. Bardhan & C. K. Weaver (Eds.), *Public relations in global cultural contexts. Multi-paradigmatic perspectives* (pp. 77–107). New York: Routledge

Bardhan, N., & Weaver, C. K. (Eds.). (2011). *Public relations in global cultural contexts. Multi-paradigmatic perspectives.* New York: Routledge

Baskin O., & Aronoff, C. (1992). *Public relations: The profession and the practice.* Dubuque, IA: Wm. C. Brown.

Beauchamp, T. (2013, October 3). The principle of beneficence in applied ethics. In E. N. Zalta (Ed.), *The Stanford encyclopedia of philosophy.* Retrieved from https://plato.stanford.edu/archives/win2016/entries/principle-beneficence

Beck, U. (2000). *What Is globalization?* Cambridge: Polity

Beck, U. (2006). *The cosmopolitan vision.* Cambridge: Polity.

Casmir, F. (1978). A multicultural perspective on human communication. In F. Casmir (Ed.), *Intercultural and international communication* (pp. 241–257). Washington, DC: University Press of America.

Casmir, F. (1993). Third-culture building: A paradigm shift for international and intercultural communication. *Communication Yearbook, 16,* 407–428.

Castells, M. (2004). *The power of identity* (2nd ed.). Malden, MA: Blackwell.

Cheah P., & Robbins, B. (1998). *Cosmopolitics: Thinking and feeling beyond the nation.* Minneapolis: University of Minnesota Press.

Clark, G., & Hebb, T. (2005). Why should they care? The role of institutional investors in the market for corporate global responsibility. *Environment and Planning, 37*(11), 2015–2031.

Curtin, P. A., & Gaither, T. K. (2007). *International public relations. Negotiating culture, identity, and power.* London: Sage.

Curtin, P. A., & Gaither, T. K. (2012). *Globalization and public relations in postcolonial nations: Challenges and opportunities.* Amherst, NY: Cambria Press

Dutta, M. J. (2012). Critical interrogations of global public relations. In K. Sriramesh & D. Verčič (Eds.), *Culture and public relations: Links and implications* (pp. 202–217). New York: Routledge.

DW. (2016, December 3). Businesses and refugees come together: One thousand companies are already involved in refugee initiatives. *Deutsche Welle.* Retrieved from http://www.dw.com/en/businesses-and-refugees-come-together/a-36629714

Giddens, A. (1991). *The consequences of modernity.* Cambridge: Polity Press.

Grunig, J. E. (1966, December). The role of information in economic decision making. *Journalism Monographs, 3.*

Grunig, J. E. (1992). *Excellence in public relations and communication management.* Hillsdale, NJ: Lawrence Erlbaum.

Grunig, J. E. (1997). A situational theory of publics: Conceptual history, recent challenges and new research. In D. Moss, T. MacManus, & D. Verčič (Eds.), *Public relations research: An international perspective* (pp. 3–48). London: International Thomson Business Press

Grunig, J. E. (2008). Excellence theory in public relations. In W. Donsbach (Ed.), *The international encyclopaedia of communication.* Malden, MA: Wiley-Blackwell.

Grunig, L. A., Grunig, J. E., & Verčič, D. (1998). Are the IABC's excellence principles generic? Comparing Slovenia and the United States, the United Kingdom and Canada. *Journal of Communication Management, 2*(4), 335–356.

Guyatt, D. (2005). Meeting objectives and resisting conventions: A focus on institutional investors and long term responsible investing. *Corporate Governance, 5*(3), 139–150.

Keating, M. (2001). *Nations against the state: The new politics of nationalism in Quebec, Catalonia, and Scotland.* Basingstoke, UK: Palgrave.

Kent, M. L., & Taylor, M. (2007). Beyond excellence: Extending the generic approach to international public relations: The case of Bosnia. *Public Relations Review, 33*(1), 10–20.

Kluge, J. (2016, September 20). Over 50 US businesses step up for refugees. *Forbes Business.* Retrieved from https://www.forbes.com/sites/johnkluge/2016/09/20/u-s-businesses-step-up-for-refugees/#1d4bcd3e3a9e

Kruckeberg, D., & Vujnovic, M. (2010). The death of the concept of publics (plural) in 21st century public relations. *International Journal of Strategic Communication, 4*(2), 117–125.

Lee, S. (2005). The emergence of global public and international public relations. *Public Relations Quarterly, 50*(2), 14–16.

Mansell, S. (2013). Shareholder theory and Kant's "duty of beneficence." *Journal of Business Ethics, 117*(3), 583–599.

Mitchell, R. K., Agle, B. R., & Wood, D. J. (1997). Toward a theory of stakeholder identification and salience: Defining the principle of who and what really counts. *Academy of Management Review, 22*(4), 853–886.

Rittenhofer, I., & Valentini, C. (2015). A "practice turn" for global public relations: An alternative approach. *Journal of Communication Management, 19*(1), 2–19.

Scholte, J. A. (2005). *Globalization: A critical introduction.* New York: Palgrave Macmillan.

Shome, R., & Hedge, R. (2002). Culture, communication, and the challenge of globalization. *Critical Studies in Media Communication, 19*(2), 172–189.

Sriramesh, K. (2009). Globalisation and public relations: An overview looking into the future. *PRism, 6*(2). Retrieved from http://www.prismjournal.org/fileadmin/Praxis/Files/globalPR/SRIRAMESH.pdf

Sriramesh, K. (2010). Globalization and public relations. Opportunities for growth and reformulation. In R. L. Heath (Eds.), *The handbook of public relations* (2nd ed.) (pp. 691–707). Thousand Oaks, CA: Sage.

Sriramesh, K., & Verčič, D. (2001). Globalizing public relations research: A conceptual framework. *Journal of Communication Management, 6*(2), 103–117.

UNHCR. (2017). *Global trends: Forced displacement in 2016.* Retrieved from the website of the United Nations High Commissioner for Refugees: http://www.unhcr.org/5943e8a34.pdf

Valentini, C. (2007). Global versus cultural approaches in public relationship management: The case of the European Union. *Journal of Communication Management, 11*(2), 117–133.

Valentini, C. (2012). Le relazioni pubbliche internazionali. In E. Invernizzi & S. Romenti (Eds.), *Relazioni pubbliche e corporate communication: La gestione dei servizi specializzati* (Vol. 2, pp. 215–248). Milan: McGraw-Hill.

Valentini, C. (2017). Environment. In C. R. Scott & L. K. Lewis (Eds.), *International encyclopedia of organizational communication* (Vol. 2, pp. 839–860). Malden, MA: Wiley-Blackwell.

Valentini, C., & Kruckeberg, D. (2011). Public relations and trust in contemporary society: A Luhmannian perspective of the role of public relations in enhancing trust among social systems. *Central European Journal of Communication, 4*(1), 89–107.

Valentini, C., Kruckeberg, D., & Starck, K. (2016). The global society and its impact on public relations theorizing: Reflections on major macro trends. *Central European Journal of Communication, 9*(2), 229–246.

Verčič, D., Grunig, L. A., & Grunig, J. E. (1996). Global and specific principles of public relations: Evidence from Slovenia. In H. M. Culbertson & N. Chen (Eds.), *International public relations: A comparative analysis* (pp. 31–65). Mahwah, NJ: Lawrence Erlbaum.

Wakefield, R. I. (1996). Interdisciplinary theoretical foundations for international public relations. In H. M. Culbertson & N. Chen (Eds.), *International public relations: A comparative analysis* (pp. 17–30). Mahwah, NJ: Lawrence Erlbaum.

Wen, S. (2009). Institutional investor activism on socially responsible investment: Effects and expectations. *Business Ethics: A European Review, 18*(3), 308–333.

Zaharna, R. S. (2001). "In-awareness" approach to international public relations. *Public Relations Review, 27*, 135–148.

10

Community

Marina Vujnovic and Dean Kruckeberg

In a world in which market values and profit-driven practices rule decision-making on every level of society, proposals to consider the impact of our actions on community are considered to be naive. However, through the processes of globalization in the past several decades, our lives have become more interconnected. Because of the impact of new technologies, our actions (if not always, then at least often) impact the lives of people and communities throughout the globe. Many organizations in the private and nonprofit sectors are beginning to recognize the immense need to acknowledge the impact that they have on various stakeholders worldwide. When organizations do acknowledge their impact, they nevertheless seldom understand how they can and should become active participants in their communities through community-building or by fostering deliberation and influencing change by building *organic* relationships with stakeholders everywhere. The idea of social capital and working for the common good are often seen in stark opposition to market capitalism. For those reasons, nonprofit organizations have historically played a larger role in advocating for the common good than have for-profit organizations. However, we believe that it is the responsibility of every organization to view society as that organization's ultimate stakeholder.

Recently, community-building has been used as synonym for community development, community relations, and brand communities. Although all these in some form advocate for the common good, or even social change, their ultimate goal is to create community for the organization, to support organizational existence, to build the brand, or especially to increase profit. That's particularly true for those organizations that use community-building as their term to engage in building brand communities online. It is usually quite obvious, however, that such impetus to engage with community members is not actually to create a sense of belonging, but rather the intent is brand-building and customer loyalty. For example, Starbucks launched a community forum, called "My Starbucks idea," for coffee enthusiasts in March 2008. People could provide ideas for products, but also were able to engage online through an interactive web interface. However, in May 2017, Starbucks changed the interface to "What's your Starbucks idea?" (Starbucks, 2018), in which individual users could submit their ideas. The community interaction part was removed. This illustrates that even providing platforms for community engagement is a commitment that many companies aren't willing to undertake. As Starbucks new pitch suggests, "Revolutionary or simple, we want to hear it," indicating that seeking feedback is simple, but building communities is not. In fact, we would argue that there are few examples of true community-building in the way that we conceptualize it, that is, in which the organization as an intrinsic part of the community demonstrates a keen interest in and responsibility for the community that will sometimes trump narrow organizational interests. Community-building could necessitate investment that might not show a direct return on that investment in terms of dollar value added to the profit margins. The key here is to create the organization for the community, and not the community for the organization, as has been the case with the majority of examples that we have found under the umbrella of community-building. Therefore, it is essential that we revisit some basic concepts in community-building and its successor, the organic theory of public relations, in the way that we conceptualize it, beginning with the idea of community itself.

Defining the Concepts: What Is Community?

During the past 40 years, the concept of community has been embraced by sociologists, historians, anthropologists, and other social scientists. However, some scholars have rejected it as a viable concept. As Macfarlane had famously argued, community, similarly to the concept of culture, is nearly impossible to define. The fundamental criticism is that scholars, particularly in sociology, have failed to agree on what is community. Macfarlane (1977) observed that community, as commonly defined as a group of people having common objectives who share the same territory, makes "belief in such 'communities' … one of the most powerful … [and] controlling myths of our time" (p. 632). He suggested that a community might exist only in the eye of the beholder. He further proposed that the loss of community is, in fact, a myth that leads scientists to attempt to find communities and thus create objects of study. One of Calhoun's (1978) main criticisms of Macfarlane's conceptualization of community was that Macfarlane had failed to "see community in historical perspective, as a phenomenon undergoing change, but rather as a rigid category" (p. 370).

Cohen (1985) similarly argued that attempts to abandon the concept of community in the study of sociology could be attributed to frustration in trying to provide an agreed-upon definition that would serve as a conceptual and methodological foundation for the study of social relationships. Many of the tensions in the conceptualization of community stem from the divide that has been created between those who subscribe to the more idealized focus of Ferdinand Tönnies on the "inner qualities of community life" (Calhoun, 1978, p. 369) versus those who focus on the reality of social relationships and human interaction, the approach that was offered by Émile Durkheim (Brint, 2001). According to Brint (2001), "Durkheim's conceptual breakthrough was to see community not as a social structure or physical entity but as a set of variable properties of human interaction" (p. 3). Calhoun (1978) argued that it is precisely this organization that makes a community a community, rather than the "mere aggregation of people" (p. 370).

Calhoun (1978) argued that a community is not a static entity. Thus, community encompasses, not only an organized set of social relationships, but also the structures that order them. All of these should be studied if we wish to understand society. Hamilton (1985), discussing Cohen's (1985) work, argued that Cohen had focused on the concept of community more through its symbolic dimension, values, and moral codes that provide meaning and identity to its members. This emphasis on meaning takes away the definitional difficulties of focusing on the structural dimension of the community that we are attempting to define. However, because structures are not capable of creating meanings, this likewise suggests that "organizations designed to create 'community' as palliatives to anomie and alienation are doomed to failure" (Hamilton, 1985, p. 9). This contention becomes particularly relevant in public relations practice, with its longstanding attempts at fostering engagement and building communities, especially around brands. From an examination of the public relations literature, both community relations and community-building in earlier public relations writings fall into the trap of structural definitions of community in worrying whether the structural dimensions of public relations can withstand societal changes, rather than what Cohen (1985) had suggested, as interpreted by Hamilton (1985): "Rather than being the sign of a traditional and outmoded social structure, the cultural experience of community as a bounded symbolic whole is something virtually universal in both non-industrial and industrial societies, transcending even the macro-social forces of capitalism and socialism in their many variations" (p. 9).

How and Why Is Community of Concern to Public Relations?

Even though community hasn't held a central place in public relations scholarship, several theoretical approaches position community and discussions surrounding it as central themes, for example community-building, communitarianism, community relations, and corporate social responsibility. Hallahan (2005) argued that theories that deal with communication symmetry and two-way communication, although not explicitly using the term community, in many ways are "consistent with the notion of community" (p. 173). Table 10.1 summarizes examples of public relations theories involving concepts of community.

Community-building first emerged under the influence of the writings of the Chicago School of Social Thought (Kruckeberg & Starck, 1988) and was further developed as a grand theory of public relations that argues that community and society must have a central place in public relations practice (Kruckeberg & Starck, 2004; Valentini, Kruckeberg, & Starck, 2012). For Kruckeberg and Starck (1988), the ultimate stakeholder is society. They argued, "Corporations must recognize that the greatest stakeholder – the ultimate environmental constituency – is

Table 10.1 Examples of public relations theories used in research involving concepts of community

Topics	Examples of theory	Type
Creating relationships with communities.	Community relations	Tactical theory
Addressing the needs of the communities and engaging with development projects.	Community development	Tactical theory
Providing space for engagement with communities, mostly online, with the primary goal to build a brand.	Community building (Building brand communities)	Tactical theory
The role of public relations in the creation, restoration, and maintenance of the linkages that exist among various stakeholders in society.	Community building (Social theory of public relations)	Social theory
Approach in which the organization participates, dialogues, and listens to the concerns of the community of which the organization is a part. Public relations emphasis on community and responsibility as an ethical base for *public relations* includes engaging in the critique of existing sociopolitical relations, seeing its practitioners as potential agents for change.	Organic theory of public relations	Social theory
Taking responsibility for organizational impact on communities and building relationships with these communities, with perceived benefits to organizations that practice it.	Corporate social responsibility	Tactical theory
Emphasis on community and responsibility as an ethical base for public relations.	Communitarianism	Social theory

society itself, to which such corporations are ultimately and irrefutably answerable" (Starck & Kruckeberg, 2001, p. 59). Hallahan (2005) suggests that community-building can take three forms: community involvement, community nurturing, and community organizing (pp. 173–174). This definition relates community-building more closely to community relations. The latter is a more strategic function of public relations. In other words, through strategic communication efforts, community relations targets specific groups that are identified as communities and tries to engage them in a meaningful relationship with an organization. This benefits not only the community, but the organization as well. Many scholars in PR have developed an interest in examining what community relations (CR) would mean for public relations (Grunig & Hunt, 1984; Heath & Palenchar, 1997; Jackson, 1999; Wilcox & Cameron, 2009; Heath & Ni, 2010). Grunig and Hunt (1984) defined community relations as "specialized public relations programs to facilitate communication between an organization and publics in its geographic locality" (p. 267), while Wilcox and Cameron (2009) defined it as a "planned activity with a community," emphasizing mutual benefits that these organizational efforts could bring to the organization and its community. Neff (2005) defined community relations as a strategic effort that should not be merely cosmetic. Burke (1999) described community relations based on the principle of the neighbor of choice, using corporations as the main agent. He argued that paying taxes and providing employment is no longer enough. People want corporations to be partners in solving community problems.

Heath and Ni (2010) categorized community relations activities as nice neighbor (organizations work to demonstrate that they add value to the community); good or generous neighbor (for example, strategic philanthropy); and reflective/responsive neighbor (encompassing risk management, crisis management, and issues management). Heath and Ni (2010) further defined CR as "not merely a communication activity," but also as an activity that is driven by management and policy and that is characterized by "the desire to be a constructive member of each community where it operates: local, regional, national and global" (p. 567). Even so, questions could be posed as to whether an organization has an expressed interest in the benefit of the community or whether community relations might simply be seen as that organization's return on the investment. Heath and Ni (2010) connected community relations with corporate social responsibility. Rawlins (2005) said corporate social responsibility "simply means that organizations have responsibilities to society that extend beyond the traditional contract to produce goods and services" (p. 211). For instance, Heath and Ni (2010) argued that organizations' corporate social responsibility literature often states that these companies profit from corporate social responsibility, which, "at a minimum ... feature the company as a nice neighbor" (p. 566).

Finally, communitarianism has had a significant impact on discussions of ethics in public relations (K. Leeper, 1996). Communitarianism as such emphasizes responsibilities that individuals have toward their communities, and not the other way around, as communitarianism often has been a dominant societal paradigm under the influence of liberalism. Communitarianism has been suggested as a metatheory for public relations (R. Leeper, 2001) and as a foundation for communication symmetry (Culbertson & Chen, 1996). Luoma-aho (2009) connected the communitarian term of social capital to public relations by arguing that public relations practitioners need to better understand the process of creating social capital and that practitioners should be instrumental in familiarizing organizations with the importance of social capital. Willis (2012) showed interest in social capital as an important aspect for promoting community engagement. In that sense, Willis (2012) sees the need for public relations to be associated more "with societal good rather than the exclusive pursuit of organisational interests" (p. 116).

All of these theoretical approaches deal in one way or another with organizations' role in society and the impact that organizations have on their various communities. Although community relations remains very much a strategic communication endeavor that is tied to management and policy and that is still very much a geographically bound practice, community-building provides a more holistic view of organizations' place in society.

If we could draw a major distinction in the way in which we theorize community-building versus other theoretical perspectives that include the notion of community in public relations, it would be in the strategic communication realm. Community-building is not about a focus on a specific group of people; rather, it's about all people who are joined in a society that includes various communities, symbolic and real. Community-building reminds us that public relations practice needs to be mindful of its impact on society at large. If we take, as an example, hurricanes such as Harvey and Maria in 2017 and Florence in 2018, their collective impact has to be measured not only by the local destruction they caused, but also through an examination of the damage that society collectively has done to the environment and the responsibility that we have to help and to find solutions together.

Community-Building: Then and Now

St. John (1998) provided a historical view of the development of community-building in the role that public relations had in nation-building as Americans moved westward. He argued that, with railroad expansion and the impact of the reform-minded crusading "muckraker" journalists of the late nineteenth and early twentieth centuries, public relations efforts of that time had moved toward corporate advocacy. He observed that, in contrast, public journalism today has assumed a community-building role by fostering and facilitating dialogue, while public relations has largely remained in its role of information dissemination. Community-building has been used to describe various attempts by organizations and their public relations practitioners to foster engagement and to help build social relationships that exist in a given social context. Community-building has been equated with nation-building and often is used interchangeably with community relations, where the goal is to increase organizations' standing and visibility within a particular social context. Hallahan (2004) defined community-building as "the integration of people and the organizations they create into a functional collectivity that strives toward common or compatible goals" (p. 245).

How, When, and Why Is Theory Applied to Community?

Community-building as a theoretical proposal first appeared in the work of Kruckeberg and Starck (1988). In their book *Public relations and community: A reconstructed theory*, these authors had argued that the main reason that public relations practice exists today is because of the loss of the sense of community, a loss that has been created by the evolution of communication and transportation technology. Kruckeberg and Starck (2004) concluded that public relations is best practiced "as the active attempt to restore and maintain a sense of community" (p. 136), which they argued should be the "highest calling of public relations practice" (p. 137). Their focus on the restoration of a sense of community is predicated on the scholarship of the Chicago School of Social Thought, and placing information and communication technology in the center of Kruckeberg and Starck's (1988) argument was inspired, in part, by the work of John Dewey.

However, some issues with the Chicago School's definition of community have been identified by scholars in various disciplines. Mainly, these criticisms have focused on the link between community and geographical location that the Chicago School, as well as communitarians, have espoused in their definitions of community. Even though both the Chicago School and communitarians have claimed that community is not static, they didn't define community as a social process and fell victim to a functionalist view of community (Walsh & High, 1999). Kruckeberg and Tsetsura (2008), in their concept of a community, revised Kruckeberg and Starck's (1988) original community-building theory to exclude this reliance on geographic space. They declared that this aspect of the definition of community has become obsolete due to the existence of today's virtual communities. Anderson (1983), in the first edition of his seminal work *Imagined communities: Reflections on the origin and spread of nationalism*, invoked cultural and imagined aspects of community formation. For those reasons, we wish not to add yet another definition of community, but rather we agree with historians Walsh and High (1999) that the following elements should be taken into account when examining the concept of community: "community as imagined reality, community as social interaction, and community as process" (p. 257). These elements further redefine community as it relates to community-building and the practice of public relations. Such definition of community includes components of space and indicates that community is embedded within other elements of power in society, which makes community both real and imagined. If those elements aren't considered, any attempt to describe community and to understand society then becomes simply an oratorical abstraction.

Community-building theory has more recently been developed into an "organic model" of public relations (for example, Kruckeberg, 2007; Vujnovic & Kruckeberg, 2010, 2012). In this model, organizations, rather than focusing on building communities, are constituent parts of these communities. Their destiny is that of their communities themselves. Kruckeberg and Starck (1988) insightfully argued that the ultimate stakeholder for any organization is society. In that sense, public relations practice is not subsumed into designing or manufacturing communities so that organizations' products and services could become recognizable brands; rather, organizational public relations efforts are tools to facilitate dialogue, enabling interaction and even enabling criticism so that the cultures of their communities are able to transform and to be a part of social change.

Example of Theory Used with Community

Organic Theory of Public Relations

An "organic theory" of public relations was originally conceptualized by Vujnovic and Kruckeberg (2005) and Kruckeberg and Vujnovic (2006). As a critical theory of public relations, it proposes organic interrelationships among elements in social systems that are mutually constituted (Vujnovic, Kumar, & Kruckeberg, 2007). This theory draws on the work of critical political economists of communication such as Mosco (2009, 2012), who argued that any study of communication must be seen in the context of society – with links between elements such as economics, geography, and cultural and policy studies. Similarly, we see the examination of public relations as a discipline to be impossible without a broader and more inclusive approach than is currently being offered by the dominant organization-centric public relations theory and practice. We go a step further to argue that an "organic theory" of public relations is, in itself, a critique of neoliberal capitalism because we see large social disruptions and gaps between those who gain and those who lose in current capitalist social organization, that is, a neoliberal global economy that public relations must address through its theory and practice.

Traditionally, public relations scholarship hasn't been thoroughly devoted to a critique of capitalism, if at all. However, critical public relations scholarship is a growing area of focus that examines public relations theory and practice from a variety of perspectives, for example, postmodern – Holtzhausen (2007); cultural – L'Etang (2004, 2005, 2007); sociopolitical – Brunton and Galloway (2016); and Marxist – Weaver (2016). We wish to place an "organic theory" of public relations into the context of this critical public relations scholarship that has identified public relations as a practice that often drives capitalist relations, panders to corporate interests (Davis, 2013; L'Etang, 2005; Miller & Dinan, 2008), and is the bard for policies that often prioritize narrow organizational interests over the interests of all individuals, that is, society at large.

Ideas and conceptualization of public relations as a theory of society can be traced back to the work of Kruckeberg and Starck (1988) and its "community-building" approach to the practice of public relations that had argued that the primary stakeholder of public relations is society itself. This approach was also born from a critique of the narrow and dominant public relations theory that puts organizations, rather than society, at the center of its arguments. More recently, in the context of globalization, Kruckeberg and Valentini (2014) argued for the need to rethink community relations as simply public relations for an organization's geographically proximate community. Additionally, the term community for public relations practice has been explicated by Hallahan (2005), who argued that "communities differ from publics because they organize around common interests, not issues, and are apolitical" (p. 172).

Community-building theory values the role of public relations in the creation, restoration, and maintenance of the linkages that exist among various stakeholders in society. An "organic theory" of public relations values community-building and is an approach in which the organization participates, dialogues, and listens to the concerns of the community of which the organization is a part. This, of course, has been a longtime premise in traditional public relations literature, notably Grunig and Hunt's (1984) two-way symmetrical model of practice. But, in addition, an "organic theory" of public relations argues that the role of public relations includes engagement in the critique of existing sociopolitical relations, that is, viewing society and all of its constituents as stakeholders, as well as its practitioners as potential agents for change. In that sense, change that can emanate from a critique of sociopolitical and economic relations is as important, if not more important, than is the maintenance of certain aspects of the existing system, that is, the existing networks and communities. As this theory had emerged through the examination of the "community-building" approach in some of our early writings, we have argued that public relations should focus on developing guidance for social and cultural policy that is designed to maintain healthy democratic and capitalist societies (Kruckeberg, 2007).

However, shortly after having made this argument, we have rethought the idea of the value of the building and maintenance of communities as something that should be applied to the capitalist system itself (Vujnovic et al., 2007); thus, we have later argued, from the perspective of a critical political economy of communication (Calabrese, 2003; Gibson-Graham, 2006), that the true value of public relations theory and practice lies in the critique of neoliberal global capitalist society because of neoliberalism's tremendous capacity for creating inequalities and inflicting suffering among communities across the globe. We still maintain, as one of the co-authors had asserted, "The model gives special emphasis to the humane protection of the weak and powerless as well as to the preservation of the physical environment" (Kruckeberg, 2007, p. 24). This concern with the preservation, or rather protection, of the environment and the inclusion of those individuals on the margins of the society is becoming increasingly important, considering current processes of globalization and reverse globalization (de-globalization) as well as the strengthening of a neoliberal corporate and profit-driven ideology that often demonstrates little or no regard for people and the physical environment. Thus, the ramifications of this ideology are exacerbated within the context of today's disturbing global demographic of an extremely young population (in some countries with a median age of 17 years or even less).

In many parts of the world, they remain uneducated or undereducated, and unemployed with little prospect of sustainable employment, but they are marketed to relentlessly by purveyors of consumer goods and services that this young population cannot afford, while most of them enjoy the empowering use of smartphones that have become essential, or at least a high priority, to be able to function in today's world.

Thus, the "organic theory" of public relations was born out of a constant rethinking of the prevailing public relations scholarship that privileges the strategic, organization-centered, managerial function of public relations. Vujnovic (2004) identified this organization-centered, primarily corporate emphasis of dominant public relations theoretical approaches as worrisome because such a perspective takes communicative agency out of the hands of public relations as a professionalized occupation by celebrating its managerial function within organizations. Vujnovic (2004) saw the role of the public relations practitioner more in line with that of an impartial ombudsman. She emphasized that the narrow identification of just certain segments of society as organizational stakeholders – particularly those that pose a threat as activist publics – misses the opportunity to cast public relations practitioners as a voice for all individuals, rather than restricting its practice to those whom organizations have strategically identified as voices that matter, that is, who could pose a threat to the organization and its mission. Celebrating public relations as a solely managerial function in the dominant public relations scholarship has been criticized by many (for example, Holtzhausen, 2007), and critical public relations scholarship has offered, as an alternative, a more socially responsible role for public relations practice. In that sense, Vujnovic et al. (2007) have argued: "As the world has become inextricably and irreversibly interdependent through the process of globalization, social actors such as governments, nongovernmental organizations (NGOs), and capitalist-based institutions, i.e., corporations, have an increasingly important role in the construction of a sense of responsibility for societies as cultural creations as well as for the preservation of the physical environment."

As critical public relations scholars have argued, relations of power are of utmost importance for the study of public relations, both within and outside the organizational context (Berger, 2005; Berger & Reber, 2006; L'Etang, 1996). In our view, the concerns of public relations practice should include an examination of power relations that pose questions about organizational behavior and social capital, but, more importantly, must prioritize the examination of interactions and the complex system of power relations among all social constituents. These interactions and interrelations are influenced by historical, economic, social, and cultural processes. In that sense, society is an amalgamation of all publics having various capacities to exert power and to influence change, including those on the margins. Importantly, the totality of social relations must include those who cannot speak for themselves, for example, marginalized people as well as animals and the physical environment, all of which must be recognized and respected as "stakeholders."

As we previously argued (Vujnovic et al., 2007), "These *organic* interrelations among elements in social systems that are mutually constituted is an essential premise of the 'organic theory' of public relations." Organizations, as they are narrowly defined in the dominant public relations scholarship, identify their stakeholders based on whether those stakeholders obviously (and sometimes formally) do or potentially could interact relationally with that organization. But, we argue, this approach fails to see the vast number of social constituents who might not be immediately visible to, and certainly have no formal relationship with, organizations. They also must be recognized "stakeholders," even though these invisible stakeholders, as social components, *organically* interact and change under the influence of historical, social, economic, and cultural conditions of the society of which organizations are a part and, we argue, to which organizations have a responsibility.

It is our belief that an organization-centered approach to public relations fails to fully grasp the importance of all social actors and, in terms of corporate organizational behavior, fails to adequately address the ramifications of these organizations' profit-seeking motives (Bakan, 2004). Dominant public relations scholarship that stems from the work of Grunig and Hunt (1984) is based on the premise of segmented publics and is predicated on a concern with systems that have perceived consequences on the organization. These publics are considered "strategic," and, in that sense, public relations is a strategic organizational function. Even though Grunig (1992) and Grunig, Grunig, and Dozier (2002) have argued that excellent organizations do monitor the effect of organizational behavior on society at large, their focus on segmenting publics into categories that have or may have consequences for an organization fails to recognize all social constituents as *strategic* by simply being members of society at large. We have argued (Vujnovic & Kruckeberg, 2016) that a focus on *strategic communication* in public relations tends to see communication as instrumental, that is, as simply a tool, and fails to recognize communication's moral/ethical responsibility and potential. In that sense, as Kruckeberg (1995–1996) had argued, public relations must be recognized as practice that "not only represent ideologies" but rather is highly ideological "value-laden ... with a concomitant set of professional beliefs and worldview" (p. 38). This introspective, self-critical approach to public relations practice is needed if one wishes to imagine "better public relations" that benefits most, if not all, members of society; thus, public relations isn't simply an extended arm of narrow organizational self-interests. We see such a narrow organization-centered approach to public relations as being ultimately detrimental to public relations itself, and as a threat to society at large.

In the global environment of the twenty-first century, we argue that organizations must be "participants" in the social media environment. However, community-building and community-maintenance that use social media especially require an "organic" perspective that does not place the practitioner's organization at the hub of its universe. Rather, within a three-dimensional model of a community, the organization must recognize itself as only one community member that must be equally concerned about stakeholders' relationships with one another within the community as well as with the organization itself (Vujnovic & Kruckeberg, 2015). Thus, we consider relationship *management* to be a limiting, and thereby an inappropriate, term; rather, we prefer relationship *building* and *maintenance* and, if and when required, relationship *change*. Organizations must be "participants" in today's social media environment, in which the goal should not be relationship *management*, suggesting control, but rather participation in community-building and community-maintenance in the furtherance of a healthy "organic" community, as well as fostering change when and if change is needed.

Uses and Applications of "Organic Theory"

We believe that this "organic theory," which was preceded by Kruckeberg and Starck's (1988) community-building theory, is neither naive nor doomed to rejection or a lack of traction. Many public relations scholars have acknowledged the heuristic value of an "organic theory" for theoretical examination and practical application. For instance, Galloway and Lynn (2007–2008) champion the value of an "organic theory" of public relations when outlining questions of global climate change. They argue that an "organic," rather than an organization-centered approach, is better suited to address climate change as a risk to the planet, because such change has potentially adverse effects on indigenous communities throughout the globe as well as to society at large. Rather than prioritizing client interests, they argue that facilitation by public relations of community conversations and collaborations around issues of climate change could result in the betterment of many societies worldwide. In that sense, we see this contention in synchronization with our "organic theory" that emphasizes giving voices to individuals about issues of concern to them, encouraging community conversations no matter how large those communities or conversations might be. These conversations could ultimately result in changes in thinking, behavior, and policy to benefit more or even all people.

Brunton and Galloway (2016) have embraced our critique of multiple publics that are dominant in public relations scholarship, finding value in the more inclusive concept of a *general public*, especially as this public (which most public relations literature argues does not exist) relates to their topic of examination, public health. What they call "wicked problems" with public health issues include communication, which they argue must be addressed by a more inclusive theoretical approach, that is, an "organic theory" of public relations. The narrow focus on so-called *strategic publics*, with which we take issue, is nicely explicated by Brunton and Galloway (2016): "Those impacted may be individuals and groups with whom dialogue is needed, whose engagement and action is required; perhaps also those whose behavior may need to change and whose very definitions of the problem may need to be reconciled if coordinated strategies are to be considered" (p. 163). Further in their article, Brunton and Galloway (2016) espoused: "Organic PR is well-situated to help establish a strong foundation to negotiate outcomes between social actors and healthcare organizations, through acknowledging not only that the answers to wicked problems are elusive, but also that a morally defensible greater good is at stake" (p. 163).

Major Topics/Questions Needing to Be Addressed by Public Relations Theorists Working with Community

To reiterate, we believe that this "organic theory," which was preceded by Kruckeberg and Starck's (1988) community-building theory, is neither naive nor doomed to rejection or a lack of traction, even in today's "America First" political climate and a global environment of neoliberalism. Although difficult to monitor in its practice among organizations worldwide, the public relations scholarly community unquestionably has paid attention to this theoretical perspective ever since publication of Kruckeberg and Starck's (1988) book. Today, many public relations scholars are rightly focusing on social media; furthermore, contemporary public relations research oftentimes is examining narrower and narrower meso and micro scholarly questions (which, of course, is the mark of an evolving body of knowledge and literature). However, the public relations scholar/educator/practitioner community must also step back to examine broader issues, not only in relation to globalism and neoliberalism, but also to reconsider the fundamental educational foundations that assure liberally educated and empathetic practitioners who are capable of understanding the world latitudinally (in its geographic breadth) and longitudinally (in its historical depth). Predicated on such a foundation, they will be equipped not only to identify, examine, and resolve public relations problems that affect organization-centric social actors of corporations, governments, and nongovernmental and civil society organizations, but also to contemplate and participate in the resolution of societal problems that affect those who are not presently identified by organizations as strategic publics. Public relations theories and practices of the twentieth century were not sufficiently heuristic to provide practitioners with this needed theoretical foundation to bring value, not only to their organizations, but importantly to everyone, that is, to society at large, which requires macro perspectives that are essential at this time.

Suggested Cases to Explore to Demonstrate Theory at Work within Community

The following cases exemplify both positive outcomes of community-building and negative outcomes when companies have disregarded the good of the community for their own gains. We provide the examples of the effort of MassMutual (Massachusetts Mutual Life Insurance Company) to support communities, and the impact of GM (General Motors) on Flint, Michigan, and an example of private money working against community members' efforts to retain their community garden in South Los Angeles, California. The final case is of Standard Oil (Indiana) and the city of Sugar Creek, Missouri, on which Kruckeberg and Starck (1988) based their book.

Case 1: MassMutual "Supporting our Communities" Program

As we have already argued, it is difficult to find organizations that were not primarily founded to act as charities, foundations, or nonprofits that engage with community-building in a meaningful way. However, some examples of organizations and companies that recognize the importance of community-building exist. A MassMutual commercial in 2018, "I'll stand by you," drew attention to the idea of community and the way in which neighbors can stay together, regardless of their differences, and build and rebuild communities (MassMutual, 2018a). MassMutual's website featured a site whose heading, "Supporting our Communities," we deem to be, at least in intent, a community-building endeavor. The company stated: "In the communities where we operate, we're more than employers. We're neighbors, colleagues, parents and friends. And we believe we can help those communities become better places to live, work and play. The focus of our commitment to our communities is to broaden economic opportunity by leveraging our financial resources and human capital."

What is relevant here is that MassMutual recognizes not only how the company impacts community, but that it is a part of the community. Those at MassMutual are themselves parents, friends, and neighbors. For example, the company put that in practice through its community investment program, "Mutual Impact," which is is completely employee-driven (MassMutual, 2018b). The company argues that employees are empowered to find community issues and members of the community who are in need. In addition to donating funds, employees volunteer their time working with various groups to collectively impact the communities in which they live and work. This case exemplifies a way in which a company recognizes that it is an intrinsic part of the community. Community-building is exemplified in the belief that the company is more than employers and employees but that the company itself makes a fabric of the community.

Case 2: General Motors and Flint, Michigan

Andrew Highsmith, a professor of history at the University of California Irvine, published a book in 2015, titled *Demolition means progress: Flint, Michigan and the fate of the American metropolis*, outlining the history of GM's impact and the impact of public policy on the industrial city of Flint, Michigan. In 1997, GM demolished factory complexes under the slogan "Demolition Means Progress." This corporate slogan was meant to suggest that Flint's new greatness could not begin until remnants of the old factories were gone. Even though it is believed that the problems for Flint, Michigan, began in the 1980s with the outsourcing of jobs, Highsmith poignantly points out that problems had begun long before then.

Between 1940 and 1960, GM built eight new industrial complexes in the Flint metropolitan area. All of these were built in the suburbs. Corporate leadership since the 1930s had pushed for profit-making policies, disregarding the potentially disastrous impact on the working-class community of Flint, Michigan. At the beginning of the twentieth century, the auto industry was an essential part of building working-class communities in places such as Detroit and Flint; however, once managers discovered the suburbs for their families, they slowly began moving their business there too. Corporate abandonment, coupled with other sociological forces such as economic and racial divisions, deindustrialization, and suburbanization, as well as failed public policies, led Flint to become one of most racially segregated and economically divided cities in the United States. Therefore, it is important to discuss corporate or organizational abandonment and its adverse effect on community in the context of community-building. Organizations with massive economic power can have both an extremely positive impact and, as this example shows, an extremely negative impact on a community.

Case 3: South Central Community Garden and "South Central Farmers Feeding Families": South Los Angeles, California

This case, described by Hoffmann (2007), Lee (2014), and Sulaiman (2017), is about one of the largest urban farms (community gardens) that has ever existed in the United States. It was 13.3 acres, or 5.4 hectares, in size and was located in the South Los Angeles area (4051 South Alameda Street). The farm was operated between 1994 to 2006 by a self-governing organization called the South Central Farmers, which consisted of approximately 350 families who were mostly lower income. Before the creation of the garden, the land belonged to nine different owners, the largest of which was Alameda-Barbara Investment Company, a real-estate firm that purchased its share in 1980.The City of Los Angeles acquired this land through eminent domain in 1986 for a project that was later abandoned. It sold the property to the Los Angeles Harbor Department in 1994. The final order of condemnation under eminent domain included a right of the largest landowner, Alameda-Barbara Investment Company, to repurchase the land.

In July 1994, the Harbor Department granted a permit to the Los Angeles Regional Food Bank to use this land for a community garden. However, one of the partners of Alameda-Barbara Investment Company, Ralph Horowitz, made claim to the land in 2003 and ordered eviction in 2004. In 2006, he put the purchasing price at over 16 million dollars, three times what he had acquired it for in 2003. Farmers managed to fundraise enough money to purchase the land, but Horowitz refused to sell it to them. After a long fight by farmers, the farm was bulldozed in 2006. The lot is still empty, although in 2017 there were discussions of establishing industrial buildings on the site. The City of Los Angeles provided alternative land at 110th and Avalon for the farmers, of which three acres are now being used for community gardening. Farmers also acquired land and a farm in Buttonwillow, some hundred miles from Los Angeles.

This case is what we could call an anti-community-building example. The investment company, in this case, acted against the interest of the community and waged a "war" against the South Central farmers. While the farmers continued feeding over 10,000 families, this company, as of late 2017, is still trying to turn the lot into a profitable business. This example also shows a company that shows a complete lack of value for the community, and, even though the garden was bulldozed a decade ago, business isn't materializing easily. Some of the problem is a result of legal battles that the farmers pursued afterwards, but some of it is a result of the difficulties that companies and organizations face when they choose to destroy, rather than to help build, communities.

Standard Oil (Indiana) and Sugar Creek, Missouri

Kruckeberg and Starck (1988) describe the case of Standard Oil (Indiana), which had an oil refinery in the city of Sugar Creek, Missouri. In fall 1903, company officials selected a refinery site three miles north of Independence and about 10 miles east of Kansas City, where a a break in the bluffs provided about 2,000 feet of frontage on the Missouri River. The refinery closed in 1982. During much of its history, the Standard Oil (Indiana) refinery was an ideal community member of this city of about five thousand. The authors observed, "Oil refineries, the one in Sugar Creek included, do not lend themselves to pastoralism" (p. 92). But the authors noted:

> Yet one lifelong resident expressed the sentiments of the majority when he said that Sugar Creek had always been a good place to live and to bring up children. The town had nice parks and a large community swimming pool, and the atmosphere was that of a friendly and family-oriented town. Tax structures and levies were extremely reasonable. (p. 92)

One resident noted that residents would prefer to be left alone, and they didn't like intruders (Kruckeberg & Starck, 1988). When intruders came in, they got rather violent. But he added: "There has never been any trouble down here; we have always taken care of our own problems. There is no rough and toughness down here; we won't allow it to happen" (p. 93).

Despite being a refinery town having a tough reputation, many activities revolved around the church. Although many young people had left in the late 1960s and early 1970s, later many returned, taking an active part in church and community activities. In many ways, Sugar Creek was a community that had an excellent relationship with its refinery, and Kruckeberg and Starck (1988) considered it to be an ideal case that exemplifies the community-building efforts of a large corporation.

Discussion Questions

1 How do you define a community as a concept? Identify specific examples of communities.

2 Is an "organic theory" of public relations likely, or even feasible, other than as an idealistic normative model that could replace today's positive models of public relations that are organization-centric and managerial? If so, what changes would be needed for organizations and their public relations practitioners to adapt such a theoretical grounding and perspective?

3 Are predominant public relations theories compatible with an "organic theory" of public relations? In what ways are they alike and in what ways are they different?

4 How would you define and describe communitarianism? How would you define neoliberalism? How could an organic three-dimensional model of organizations' relationships with stakeholders, in particular society at large, be practiced? Provide examples, both of what would be possible applications of practice and of what is already being practiced today by organizations.

5 What can or should organizations, including the social actors of governments, nongovernmental organizations and civil society organizations, and corporations, do to address today's

global challenges, for example, a global demographic of an extremely young population that includes significant numbers of uneducated or undereducated and unemployed people who nevertheless are empowered by the communication technology that is needed to be able to function in today's world?

Suggested Readings

Anderson, B. (1983) *Imagined communities: Reflections on the origin and spread of nationalism.* London: Verso.

Kruckeberg, D., & Starck, K. (1988). *Public relations and community: A reconstructed theory.* New York: Praeger.

Mosco, V. (2009). *The political economy of communication* (2nd ed.). Thousand Oaks, CA: Sage.

References

Anderson, B. (1983) *Imagined communities: Reflections on the origin and spread of nationalism.* London: Verso.

Bakan, J. (2004). *The corporation: The pathological pursuit of profit and power.* London: Constable.

Berger, B. (2005). Power over, power with, and power to relations: Critical reflections on public relations, the dominant coalition, and activism. *Journal of Public Relations Research, 17*(1), 5–28.

Berger, B., & Reber, B. (2006). *Gaining influence in public relations: The role of resistance in practice.* Mahwah, NJ: Lawrence Erlbaum.

Brint, S. (2001). Gemeinschaft revisited: A critique and reconstruction of the community concept. *Sociological Theory 19*(1), 1–23.

Brunton, M. A., & Galloway, C. J. (2016). The role of "organic public relations" in communicating wicked public health issues. *Journal of Communication Management, 20*(2), 162–177.

Burke, E. (1999). *Corporate community relations: The principle of the neighbor of choice.* Westport, CT: Praeger.

Calabrese, A. (2003). Toward a political economy of culture. In A. Calabrese & C. Sparks (Eds.), *Toward a political economy of culture: Capitalism and communication in the twenty first century* (pp. 1–13). Lanham, MD: Rowman and Littlefield.

Calhoun, C. J. (1978). History, anthropology and the study of communities: Some problems in Macfarlane's proposal. *Social History, 3*(3), 363–373.

Cohen, A. P. (1985). *The symbolic construction of community.* London: Routledge.

Culbertson, H. M., & Chen, N. (1996). Communitarianism: A foundation for communication symmetry. *Public Relations Quarterly, 42*(3), 36–41.

Davis, A. (2013). *Promotional cultures: The rise and spread of advertising, public relations, marketing and branding.* Cambridge: Polity Press.

Galloway, C., & Lynn, M. (2007–2008). Public relations and climate change impacts: Developing a collaborative response. *PRism, 5*(1–2). Retrieved from http://www.prismjournal.org/fileadmin/Praxis/Files/Journal_Files/Galloway_Lynn.pdf

Gibson-Graham, J. K. (2006). *The end of capitalism (as we knew it): A feminist critique of political economy.* Minneapolis: University of Minnesota Press.

Grunig, J. E. (Ed.) (1992). *Excellence in public relations and communication management.* Hillsdale, NJ: Lawrence Erlbaum.

Grunig, J. E., Grunig, L. A., & Dozier, D. M. (2002). *Excellent public relations and effective organizations: A study of communication management in three countries.* Mahwah, NJ: Lawrence Erlbaum.

Grunig, J. E., & Hunt, T. (1984). *Managing public relations.* New York: Holt, Rinehart and Winston.

Hallahan, K. (2004). "Community" as the framework for public relations theory and research. *Communication Yearbook, 28,* 233–279.

Hallahan, K. (2005). Community and community building. In R. L. Heath (Ed.), *Encyclopedia of public relations* (pp. 171–174). Thousand Oaks, CA: Sage.

Hamilton, P. (1985). Foreword. In A. P. Cohen, *The symbolic construction of community* (pp. 7–9). London: Routledge.

Heath, R. L., & Ni, L. (2010). Community relations and corporate social responsibility. In *The Sage handbook of public relations* (2nd ed.) (pp. 557–568). Thousand Oaks, CA: Sage.

Heath, R. L., & Palenchar, M. J. (1997). *Strategic issues management: Organizations and public policy challenges.* Thousand Oaks, CA: Sage.

Highsmith, A. (2015). *Demolition means progress: Flint, Michigan and the fate of the American metropolis.* Chicago: University of Chicago Press.

Hoffmann, J. (2007, April 27). History of the South Central Farm: How the community has used the land since 1985. *New Standard.* Retrieved from http://newstandardnews.net/content/index.cfm/items/3028

Holtzhausen, D. R. (2007). A postmodern critique of public relations theory and practice. *Communicatio, 28*(1), 29–38.

Jackson, P. (Ed.) (1999). Community relations becoming more strategic but companies are contributing less $$. *PR Reporter, 42*(19), 2–3.

Kruckeberg, D. (1995–1996). The challenge for public relations in the era of globalization. *Public Relations Quarterly, 40*(4), 36–39.

Kruckeberg, D. (2007). An "organic model" of public relations: The role of public relations for governments, civil society organizations (CSOs) and corporations in developing and guiding social and cultural policy to build and maintain community in 21st-century civil society. In the Administration of Ulan-Ude Committee of Social Politics (Ed.), *Municipal social politics and the publics: Realities and perspectives: Materials of the international/scientific conference* (pp. 17–25). Ulan-Ude, Buryatia, Russia: Buryatia Scientific Center of Russian Academy of Science.

Kruckeberg, D., & Starck, K. (1988). *Public relations and community: A reconstructed theory.* New York: Praeger.

Kruckeberg, D., & Starck, K. (2004). The role and ethics of community building for consumer products and services. In M.-L. Galician (Ed.), *Handbook of product placement in the mass media: New strategies in marketing theory, practice, trends and ethics* (pp. 133–146). New York: Best Business Books.

Kruckeberg, D., & Tsetsura, K. (2008). The "Chicago School" in the global community: Concept explication for communication theories and practices. *Asian Communication Research, 3,* 9–30.

Kruckeberg, D., & Valentini, C. (2014, November). *Conceptualization of community and community-building in a globalized world.* Paper presented at the 100th Annual Convention of the National Communication Association, Chicago.

Kruckeberg, D., & Vujnovic, M. (2006, March). *Toward an "organic model" of public relations in public diplomacy.* Paper presented at the 9th Annual International Public Relations Research Conference, Miami, FL.

Lee, S. S. (May 5, 2014). *Surviving South Central: The rise, fall, and rise of a Los Angeles urban garden.* uncube Magazine, blog comment. http://www.uncubemagazine.com/blog/12844525

Leeper, K. A. (1996). Public relations ethics and communitarianism: A preliminary investigation. *Public Relations Review, 22*(2), 163–179.

Leeper, R. (2001). In search of a metatheory for public relations: An argument for communitarianism. In R. L. Heath (Ed.), *Handbook of public relations* (p. 93–104). Thousand Oaks, CA: Sage.

L'Etang, J. (1996). Corporate responsibility and public relations ethics. In J. L'Etang & M. Pieczka (Eds.), *Critical perspectives in public relations* (pp. 82–105). London: International Thomson Business Press.

L'Etang, J. (2004). *Public relations in Britain: A history of professional practice.* Mahwah, NJ: Lawrence Erlbaum.

L'Etang, J. (2005). Critical public relations: Some reflections. *Public Relations Review, 31*(4), 521–527.

L'Etang, J. (2007). *Public relations: Concepts, practice and critique.* London: Sage.

Luoma-aho, V. (2009). On Putnam: Bowling together – applying Putnam's theories of community and social capital to public relations. In O. Ihlen, B. van Ruler, & M. Fredriksson (Eds.), *Public relations and social theory. Key figures and concepts* (pp. 231–251). New York: Routledge.

Macfarlane, A. (1977). Anthropology and the study of communities. *Social History, 2*(5), 631–652.

MassMutual. (2018a). *I'll stand by you.* Song in Superbowl commercial. Retrieved from https://www.nbcsports.com/video/super-bowl-mass-mutual-stand-you

MassMutual. (2018b). *Mutual Impact*SM. Retrieved from https://www.massmutual.com/about-us/corporate-responsibility/mutual-impact

Miller, D., & Dinan, W. (2008). *A century of spin: How public relations became the cutting edge of corporate power.* London: Pluto Press.

Mosco, V. (2009). *The political economy of communication* (2nd ed.). Thousand Oaks, CA: Sage.

Mosco, V. (2012) Marx is back, but which one? On knowledge labour and media practice. *Triple C: Communication, Capitalism & Critique, 10*(2), 570–576.

Neff, B. D. (2005) Community relations. In R. L. Heath (Ed.), *Encyclopedia of public relations* (pp. 174–177). Thousand Oaks, CA: Sage.

Rawlins, B. L. (2005). Corporate social responsibility. In R. L. Heath (Ed.), *Encyclopedia of public relations* (pp. 210–214). Thousand Oaks, CA: Sage.

Starbucks. (2018). *What's your Starbucks idea?* Retrieved from https://ideas.starbucks.com

Starck, K., & Kruckeberg, D. (2001). Public relations and community: A reconstructed theory revisited. In R. L. Heath (Ed.), *Handbook of public relations* (pp. 51–59). Thousand Oaks, CA: Sage.

St. John, B., III (1998, Spring). Public relations as community-building: Then and now. *Public Relations Quarterly, 43*, 34–40.

Sulaiman, S. (2017, March 7). *Today: Plans for industrial buildings on former South Central farm lot go before PLUM Committee.* StreetsBlog LA. Retrieved from https://la.streetsblog.org/2017/03/07/today-plans-for-industrial-buildings-on-former-south-central-farm-lot-go-before-planning-commission/

Valentini, C., Kruckeberg, D., & Starck, K. (2012). Public relations and community: A persistent covenant. *Public Relations Review, 38*, 873–879.

Vujnovic, M. (2004). *The public relations practitioner as ombudsman: A reconstructed model* (Unpublished master's thesis). University of Northern Iowa, Cedar Falls, IA.

Vujnovic, M., & Kruckeberg, D. (2005). Imperative for an *Arab* model of public relations as a framework for diplomatic, corporate and nongovernmental organization relationships. *Public Relations Review, 31*(3), 338–343.

Vujnovic, M., & Kruckeberg, D. (2010). The local, national, and global challenges of public relations: A call for an anthropological approach to practicing public relations. In R. L. Heath (Ed.), *Handbook of public relations* (pp. 671–678). Thousand Oaks, CA: Sage.

Vujnovic, M., & Kruckeberg, D. (2012, March). Public relations and community: A reconstructed theory revisited (once again). In *15th International Public Relations Research Conference: Using theory for strategic practice through global engagement and conflict research*. Miami, FL: University of Miami.

Vujnovic, M., & Kruckeberg, D. (2015). Conceptualization, examination, and recommendations for a normative model of community-building for organizations managing change using new media. In E-J. Ki, J-N. Kim, & J. Ledingham (Eds.), *Public relations as relationship management: A relational approach to the study and practice of public relations* (2nd ed.). New York: Routledge.

Vujnovic, M., & Kruckeberg, D. (2016). Pitfalls and promises of transparency in the digital age. *Public Relations Inquiry, 5*(2), 121–143.

Vujnovic, M., Kumar, A., & Kruckeberg, D. (2007, March). *An "organic theory" as a social theory of public relations: A case study from India*. Paper presented at the 10th Annual International Public Relations Research Conference, Miami, FL.

Walsh, J. C., & High, S. (1999). Rethinking the concept of community. *Social History, 32*, 255–273.

Weaver, C. K. (2016). A Marxist primer for critical public relations scholarship. *Media International Australia, 160*(1), 43–52.

Wilcox, D. L., & Cameron, G. T. (2009). *Public relations: Strategies and tactics* (9th ed.). Boston: Pearson.

Willis, P. (2012). Engaging communities: Ostrom's economic commons, social capital and public relations. *Public Relations Review, 38*, 116–122.

11

Activism

Erica Ciszek

> *Where there is power, there is resistance.*
> Michel Foucault

"Build bridges, not walls." "Love trumps hate." "Smash the patriarchy." On January 21, 2017, more than a million people around the world marched in the streets in opposition to the inauguration of Donald J. Trump, the 45th President of the United States. Public transit was packed, the streets were flooded, and social media ignited with images and videos from the global Women's March. Less than a week later, thousands of opponents of abortion from across the country gathered in Washington, DC, as part of the March for Life, joined by US Vice President Mike Pence.

"Hands up. Don't shoot." "White silence is violence." "Is my son next?" Black Lives Matter (BLM), a demonstration against violence and systemic racism toward African Americans, began as a social media movement in 2013. In the wake of deaths of numerous African Americans by police actions, activists took to social media as well as direct action to spark policy change. The phrases "all lives matter" and "blue lives matter" emerged as oppositional rhetoric to BLM, spurring countermovements.

#NoDAPL. More than 1 million people "checked in" on Facebook to the Standing Rock Indian Reservation in November 2016 to confuse law enforcement, who were believed to use geotracking services to monitor communications there. This geolocation tactic is among various moves employed by the Dakota Access Pipeline protestors, a grassroots movement that emerged in early 2016 in response to the construction of the Energy Transfer Partners' Dakota Access Pipeline in the northern United States.

Images of a three-year-old Syrian refugee trying to reach Europe, but lying drowned on the beach, echoed around the world in September 2015, as international media published a heartbreaking photo of the child. Nearly one year later, another image of a Syrian boy covered in dust and blood in the back of an ambulance circulated round social media. While the images went viral, the war continued. In Russia on November 3, 2016, a group of 25 activists from Syria Solidarity UK and the Syria Campaign dispersed more than eight hundred mannequin arms and legs near the entrance to the embassy to symbolize the murder of Syrians in Aleppo.

Public Relations Theory: Application and Understanding, First Edition. Edited by Brigitta R. Brunner.
© 2019 John Wiley & Sons, Inc. Published 2019 by John Wiley & Sons, Inc.

Defining the Concepts: What Is Activism?

As demonstrated in these examples, activism is a global phenomenon that varies across social, economic, and political landscapes and influences public relations theory and practice. Public relations scholars and practitioners cannot assume activism is a "homogeneous category"; activists range in scale and fall along an ideological spectrum, often in direct opposition to one another (L'Etang, 2016, p. 207).

Research suggests activists have been engaging in public relations for more than a century, and activism is a complex issue that requires a variety of theoretical and methodological perspectives. How one views and studies activism (by way of theory) depends on the lens through which the scholar views the world (paradigm), impacting the object of study (ontology), how it is studied (methodology), and what is valued about it (axiology).

While there are several conceptualizations of activism in public relations, L. A. Grunig's (1992) definition is one of the most common in PR literature: an activist organization is "two or more individuals who organize in order to influence another public or publics through action that may include education, compromise, persuasion tactics, or force" (p. 504). Activist organizations strive to raise awareness, change attitudes, and encourage or discourage certain actions (Taylor & Das, 2010). Additionally, activism is a process of exerting pressure on institutions or organizations to "change policies, practices, or conditions the activists find problematic" (M. E. Smith, 2005, p. 5). Jones and Chase (1979) suggest the role of activists is to create a "perceived need for reform" (p. 10), challenging the status quo, targeting social norms, practices, policies, and the dominance of social groups (Zoller, 2005).

Activist organizations have two main public relations goals: first, to influence public opinion and behavior to resolve the problematic situation; and, second, to create and maintain their efforts (M. E. Smith, 2005). In working to resolve issues they have identified, activist publics generally pursue three areas: (1) eliciting or resisting change on the part of an organization, industry, or field; (2) seeking public policy or regulatory changes that would effect institutional change or public behavior; and (3) changing social norms. These goals are not independent or mutually exclusive, and many activist organizations take up all three.

Activists employ various methods to affect socially or environmentally detrimental practices, leveraging a range of approaches to achieve this goal (Davis, McAdam, Scott, & Zald, 2005), most commonly contesting practices of prominent organizations in focal industries (Baron & Diermeier, 2007; den Hond & de Bakker, 2007; King, 2008; Lenox & Eesley, 2009; Rehbein, Waddock, & Graves, 2004). M. E. Smith (2005) identified three categories of strategies employed by activists: confrontational tactics, informational strategies, and relationship-building strategies. Confrontational tactics, which include boycotts, demonstrations, and symbolic events, are used to garner public attention through dramatization of an issue. Informational strategies are designed to raise awareness and understanding of a group's issue and suggestions for solving the concern. Finally, through relationship-building strategies, the goal is to negotiate a desirable outcome for all parties involved by building satisfactory relationships with the responsible institutions or organizations.

Activism is "essential to nourish democracy" (Demetrious, 2013, p. 53), and Heath and Waymer (2009) argued that "obtaining the democratic exchange long championed by public relations" required "seeing how and when activists engage in the dialogue that occurs on various issues" (p. 195). Activism requires the development of oppositional consciousness, contesting dominant ideologies, and providing "symbolic blueprints" for collective action and social change (Morris & Braine, 2001, p. 26). Activists rely on persuasive appeals to change attitudes and encourage action, employing various strategies and tactics to connect with publics, including pleas for social responsibility and appeals to fear, sympathy, morality, respect, or social justice. Activism employs a range of communicative actions – advocacy, stakeholder relations, fundraising, recruitment, internal and external engagement, and dialogue – and is not always confrontational.

How and Why Is Activism of Concern to Public Relations?

Public relations has had a complicated relationship with activism. "Historically activism justified organisational investment in PR services and personnel and apparently explained the emergence and development of the specialist areas of issue management and crisis management" (L'Etang, 2016, p. 207). Until fairly recently, however, public relations theory has failed to consider how its history emerged from the work of activists and how activists are on the forefront of communication that advances their strategic objectives (Coombs & Holladay, 2012b). In the 1960s and 1970s, new social movements played a central role in the relationship between activism and public relations, whereby organizations employed PR as a protective strategy against radical critiques:

> The dominant corporate-centric view of US public relations history often claims that public relations developed as a response to activists who attempted to interfere with business operations … By alternatively grounding US public relations history in the works of activists, we open possibilities for re-imagining the field and legitimizing activists' works as a positive, central component in public relations theory and research. (Coombs & Holladay, 2012b, p. 347)

This history resulted in the "formation of rather fixed identities" of activism and public relations, positioning them as binaries that "opposed each other" (L'Etang, 2016, p. 207).

Populist and progressive organizations challenged monopolies during the late nineteenth century (Coombs & Holladay, 2007), employing direct confrontation and advocating for workplace reform, women's suffrage, and reform in the food and drug sectors. During this time, abolitionists, suffragists, and labor organizers acted as strategic communicators, working toward corporate and governmental change by attracting the attention of "the corporate elite, developing and utilizing many of the modern tools of public relations" (Coombs & Holladay, 2007, p. 52). Antislavery groups created alliances, lobbied, raised money, mobilized resources, engaged in media and community relations, and advocated for policy reform (Heath & Waymer, 2009).

Now third-sector groups such as social collectives, community action groups, and nongovernmental organizations carry out activist public relations to foster public legitimacy for social change (Demetrious, 2008), and social movement organizations employ public relations and issues management practices to engage public spheres and impact issue outcomes (e.g. Crable & Vibbert, 1985; M. F. Smith & Ferguson, 2010; Weaver & Motion, 2002). Because garnering acceptance by segments of the public is part of the life cycle of an issue (Crable & Vibbert, 1985), activists must establish the legitimacy of their own issues while simultaneously challenging the legitimacy of target organizations and the values they represent (M. F. Smith & Ferguson, 2010).

Some scholars have argued that, while not typically as sophisticated in resources and scope as the organizations and institutions they target, activist groups use similar strategies and tactics to reach publics and achieve goals (Dozier, Grunig, & Grunig, 1995). J. E. Grunig and Grunig (1997) suggest that activist groups might practice public relations in the same way as other groups or organizations. Activist communication efforts, therefore, are driven by objectives that are "not that different" from other organizations that use public relations to pursue strategic goals and maintain the organization (M. E. Smith, 2005, p. 7). A challenge in positioning activism as public relations, however, lies in the "inescapable understanding of PR as an organizational function" (Edwards, 2012, p. 12). Therefore, shifting the definition of PR to account for "the flow of purposive communication on behalf of individuals, formally constituted and informally constituted groups, through their continuous transactions with other social entities" (Edwards, 2012, p. 21) allows activist groups to be considered, and this idea should be incorporated into public relations theory.

How, When, and Why Is Theory Applied to Activism

Public relations theory has had a "historical animosity" to activism (Demetrious, 2013, p. 26), and activism was understood as "the Other" (L'Etang, 2016, p. 208). Activists, however, are not always external to an organization (Greenwood, 2015), and they may be an internal public (Curtin, 2016) or part of the strategic communication team (Holtzhausen, 2012); public relations practitioners can be activists (Holtzhausen & Voto, 2002), and activists may also function as public relations practitioners (Taylor & Das, 2010). Although activism is central to public relations, scholars have not adequately dealt with activism (Demetrious, 2006). Activism is a key part of public relations past, present, and future.

Public relations is a multiparadigmatic discipline. Paradigms, or worldviews, are not theories; rather, within each paradigm, theory has a different meaning and function (Rakow, 2005). Public relations is comprised of competing paradigms embodying different questions (theories) about activism and employing diverse means (methods) to answer them. Within each paradigm, activism is theorized and examined differently (for more on public relations paradigms, see Curtin, 2012; Bardhan & Weaver, 2011). Public relations began as a functional discipline, such that the role of teaching and research worked to advance the profession. Conversely, nonfunctional perspectives work to explain, challenge, and deconstruct the practice. Since the end of the twentieth century, these ideological positions have existed in tension with one another. Fitting with Edward's (2011) analytic division, the following section is divided into functional and nonfunctional perspectives that emphasize the role of public relations from multiple perspectives.

Activism reflects the "contested terrain" (Cheney & Christensen, 2001) of the discipline and represents an instance of "semantic incommensurability" (Kuhn, 1996), where terminology from one paradigm does not neatly translate to another. Activism, therefore, is conceptualized, theorized, and examined in various ways depending on one's paradigm. The meanings surrounding activism vary paradigmatically, and the following section presents a brief overview of how activism is conceptualized within public relations scholarship. Table 11.1 draws from Curtin's (2012) communication paradigms and characteristics to contextualize activism within public relations.

Functional Perspectives

Functional perspectives are concerned with the effectiveness of an organization and its communication; as such, research and theory serve the interests of the professional practice. Public relations is defined and assessed within the limits of the organization and its objectives, and for functional scholars the context of theory and research is conceptualized within organizational terms. In functional approaches, organizational goals are "paramount," and systems of public relations (strategies, tactics, and evaluation) are aligned to work in the interest of

Table 11.1 Paradigmatic conceptualizations of activism in public relations

	Paradigm	Conceptualization of activism and public relations	Questions to consider	Role of theory	Examples of theory
Functional	Postpositivist	Activists are threats to organizations. The role of PR is to monitor and respond to activist groups.	How do we predict publics becoming activists? How does PR manage activists? How should practitioners deal with activists most effectively?	Theory is predictive.	Excellence
Nonfunctional	Constructivist	Activist groups are organizational stakeholders. Activism is socially constructed and is important for what it means and conveys in a culture.	What is the historical and social context in which activism and public relations intersect? What are the shared social realities?	Theory is explanatory.	Cocreational approach Ethnographic research Framing
	Critical	Activism is a manifestation of unequal power structures.	What role does ideology play in political and economic structures? How may activism contribute in changes to social power arrangements?	Theory is deterministic. Theory drives social change.	Political economy Feminist theory Critical race theory
	Postmodern	Activists and PR are not binary; they exist on a continuum and are constructed through discourse.	How does context impact the relationship between activism and PR? What role do power and discourse play?	Theory is illuminating.	Postcolonial theory Chaos and complexity theory Queer theory

organizational management (Munshi & Edwards, 2011, p. 355). In this sense, activists are obstacles to corporate goals and are problems or issues that managers need to learn to deal with (J. Grunig, 1989). Activists are conceptualized as "barriers to overcome or challenges to meet," and, regardless of the size of their group, are potentially damaging to organizations (Coombs & Holladay, 2007, p. 52; Mintzberg, 1983).

Postpositivist Paradigm

Postpositivism, which draws from the scientific method, drives much of the work in public relations research. According to postpositivism, theory is predictive, demonstrated by Ferguson's (1984) call for theory that "predict[s] future events based upon research findings" (p. 2). Employing statistical tests, researchers measure and analyze data to develop predictive theories. A functionalist foundation places issues management, excellence theory, and the situational theory of publics within the postpositivist paradigm.

In the late 1970s and early 1980s, *issues management* emerged as a way for organizations to preventatively confront matters affecting them, rather than reactively responding, by anticipating change, prioritizing opportunities, and avoiding or mitigating threats (Renfro, 1993). Issues management was born as a corporate business discipline (Chase, 1976), founded with the idea that corporations have the moral and legal right to participate in the formation of public policy – not merely to react or be responsive. Grounded in management processes, issues management is focused on strategic planning, policy, implementation, and evaluation as a way to balance opportunities and threats (Heath, 2010). According to Heath (1997), issues management is "centered on the ability of activists, business entities and government agencies to find common ground and create wise public policy" (p. ix). Ultimately, the goal is for public relations practitioners to identify an issue, mobilize resources, and develop and implement a strategic plan (Heath, 2010).

In his book *Excellence in public relations and communication management*, J. E. Grunig (1992) described the two-way symmetrical model, which can be traced back to J. E. Grunig and T. Hunt's (1984) four models of public relations (that is, press agentry/publicity, public information, two-way asymmetrical, and two-way symmetrical), as the *excellent model* for the practice of public relations. The two-way symmetrical model was deemed most effective when dealing with activist publics (Anderson, 1992; L. Grunig, 1986; Sha, 1995). This perspective was intended to inform practitioners and scholars on the best way to address activist publics in certain situations and to predict the uprising of groups of people. J. E. Grunig and L. A. Grunig (1997) hypothesized that activists would push organizations toward excellence in public relations: "Organizations that face activist pressure would be more likely to assign public relations a managerial role, include public relations in strategic management, communicate more symmetrically with a powerful adversary or partner, and develop more participative cultures and organic structures that would open the organization to its environment" (p. 10).

According to excellence, organizations are most likely to empower public relations when pressured by activists; activism pushes organizations toward excellence as they try to cope with the expectations of their constituency. Excellent PR departments develop programs to communicate effectively and symmetrically with activists. J. E. Grunig (2001) revised his original four-model typology to account for the activist need for asymmetrical strategies, stating that the two-way symmetrical model employs both symmetrical and asymmetrical, or mixed motive, elements. The adversarial relationship that activists establish, then, creates a "turbulent, complex environment" in which pressure from activist groups "stimulates organizations" to develop excellent public relations (L. Grunig, Grunig, & Dozier, 2002, p. 16).

Public relations scholarship has had a resulting "preoccupation" with activism because of the potential consequences of activist groups, which can "directly and immediately threaten the organization's goals or help to attain them" (Hallahan, 2000, p. 500). Organizations must anticipate activist pressures because activist groups can issue grievances, boycott an organization, participate in or encourage a strike, garner negative media attention, and take other actions that can severely harm the revenue of an organization (L. Grunig, 1992). The *situational theory of publics* (J. Grunig & Hunt, 1984) serves as a predictor of activism, categorizing publics as either active information seekers or passive information processors (J. Grunig, 1997). According to this theory, the communication behaviors of activist publics can be best understood by measuring how publics understand the situations in which they are impacted by organizations (J. Grunig & Hunt, 1984).

Nonfunctional Perspectives

Many scholars agree that the models, especially the two-way symmetrical stance, do not adequately explain activist public relations (Cancel, Cameron, Sallot, & Mitrook, 1997; Dozier & Lauzen, 2000; Leichty & Springston, 1993; Murphy & Dee, 1992, 1996). Scholars also contest the symmetrical model because they argue that mainstream organizations holding more power than activists will not realistically enact symmetrical strategies, especially if they stand to lose influence (Berger, 2005). Critics of the excellence approach point to the "enormous resource disparity" between activists and organizations (Dozier & Lauzen, 2000, p. 10; Karlberg, 1996), while noting at the same time that "groups without large reserves of professional and financial resources can still … effect change" (Stokes & Rubin, 2010, p. 27). Karlberg (1996) critiqued functionalist, organization-centered approaches that dominated public relations scholarship, arguing that asymmetry had situated "citizens and public interest groups to the periphery of public relations research" (p. 271). He called for "remembering the public in public relations research."

Historically, activism was marginalized and positioned as "the Other" by functionalism in public relations theory. Unlike functionalism, nonfunctional approaches are rooted in a sociocultural conceptualization of the discipline, creating theoretical space for considering the intersections between public relations and activism. The following addresses activism within constructivist, critical, and postmodern paradigms.

Constructivist Paradigm

Constructivism is an interpretive framework focused on meaning-making and sense-making of the phenomena under investigation. Drawing from anthropology (e.g. Geertz, 1973) and sociology (e.g. Blumer, 1969; Goffman, 1959; Mead, 1934), the goal of constructivism is to develop an understanding of the social world. Rather than postpositivism, which conceptualizes the researcher as outside or objective to the phenomena under investigation, constructivist researchers immerse themselves with the object of study, attempting to "see it from the inside" (Charmaz, 2011, p. 366).

Although not many public relations theories have stemmed from this paradigm, it has potential for building theories that have explanatory power. As it relates to activism, research could examine activist culture at formal and informal levels. With the professionalizing of activism since the latter half of the twentieth century, social movement organizations have hired full-time employees to run campaigns and strategic communication. Through ethnographic methods, research could examine organizational culture and how activists use framing to develop strategic communication to create shared realities.

Critical Paradigm

Critical theory moves away from the dichotomization of activism vs. public relations to explore the relationship between public relations and activism. Coombs and Holladay (2012a) argue that activism is the key to the next step in advancing the discussion of critical ideas in PR away from fringe and toward mainstream – critical theory allows us to move beyond a corporate-centric view to consider activism and public relations.

Within the critical paradigm, the researcher is an activist, putting forth social critique for social change: "the goal is not to learn more about the world but to change it, to revise history as given" (Curtin, 2012, p. 37). The goal is to develop research and theory that will bring to light the relationship between public relations and ideology, illustrating the role PR plays in creating, maintaining, or challenging power structures in society. Critical theory considers how power is symbolically and discursively deployed through public relations; organizations project certain goals and values to publics, thus practicing public relations discursively. Research on activism from this perspective has examined the use of strategic communication by groups to "promote, maintain, and resist dominant political and economic ideologies" (Motion & Weaver, 2005, p. 64). Recognizing that interactions take place in social, cultural, and political spaces, research considers how power is symbolically and discursively deployed through public relations; organizations project certain goals and values to publics, thus practicing public relations discursively. Organizations express symbolic power through public relations (Benoit & Czerwinski, 1997; Edwards, 2009; Maguire & Hardy, 2009; Motion, Leitch, & Brodie, 2003; Motion & Weaver, 2005), and activism often emerges as a result of ideological contests, drawing attention to inequality.

Postmodern Paradigm

Postmodernism developed as response to the determinism of critical perspectives (Curtin, 2012), focusing on context and the flow of power and discourse. It emphasizes multiple truths, deconstructing processes of power that impact social reality and questioning how and why knowledge comes to be (Holtzhausen, 2002). A postmodern approach challenges dominant narratives and ideologies, and, within public relations, it questions the role of consensus in symmetrical public relations (Holtzhausen, 2000). A handful of scholars have established a framework for a postmodern theorizing of public relations, including Mickey (1998), Holtzhausen (2000, 2002) and Kennedy and Sommerfeldt (2015), building the foundation for empirical research that applies chaos and complexity theories (e.g. Gilpin & Murphy, 2008; McKie, 2001; Murphy & Dee, 1996), dissensus (e.g. Ciszek, 2015), and postcolonialism (e.g. Bardhan, 2003; Dutta, 2009; Munshi, 2005).

Recognizing communication as both contextual and cultural, and recognizing identity as relational (Stewart, 1991), postmodern inquiry considers the importance of relationships and dialogue in public relations. It provides a space for "listening to the voices of the multiple publics that are complexly layered within and outside the organization" (Pal & Dutta, 2008, p. 171), including activists. Power is relative, and the relationship between activists and organizations is fluid and implicated in power relations. With an emphasis on nonbinary relationships and fluidity, postmodernism positions activists as both internal and external to an organization. A postmodern perspective "opens the door for public relations practitioners to act as community activists, an approach that is not only radical but also ethical and desirable" (Holtzhausen, 2000, p. 99).

Examples of Theory Used with Activism

Postpositivist Paradigm

An example of postpositivism is Hallahan's (2001) issues processes model, which provides insights into how activist publics form. Using Hallahan's model of issues processes, J. Kim and

Cho (2011) examine the protests against US in Seoul, South Korea, by focusing on an activist public: "stroller moms." J. Kim and Cho found that online community websites were critical in converting these women from an inactive public to an active public by enhancing their knowledge of and involvement in the issue. As J. Kim and Cho (2011) concluded, the unique characteristics of the internet (e.g. interactivity, duplicability, and ubiquity) allow active publics to "spread information immediately and extensively, with almost no limitations" (p. 19), impacting organizational reputation. The research concludes with theoretical considerations and strategic lessons for organizations and communicative entities.

Constructivist Paradigm

While public relations research has been slow to adopt constructivism, social movement scholars have embraced this perspective. Sociologist Alberto Melucci (1989) argues that a movement is "always a composite action system, in which widely differing means, ends and forms of solidarity and organization converge in a more or less stable manner" (p. 28). Constructivism recognizes that activists' interests are not fixed, representing the complex network of activists comprising a social movement and its corresponding organizations and collectives. According to constructivism, a social movement is "a result rather than a starting point," and solidarity and sovereignty cannot be assumed (Melucci, 1996, p. 40).

Critical Paradigm

In a study of internal activism, Curtin (2016) presents a critical examination of the Girl Scouts, exploring the emergence of competing discourses that arose during a campaign. The case surrounds an activist campaign over seven years mounted by two scouts who asked Girl Scouts USA to take palm oil out of their cookies because of its association with environmental damage. Curtin presents articulation theory to explore the processes and meaning of multiple discourses that emerged throughout the campaign, demonstrating individual-level and structural constructs, blurring organizational boundaries, and rejecting the organization/activist binary.

Postmodern Paradigm

Embracing postmodernism, Holtzhausen and Voto (2002) advocate for the emancipatory potential of public relations, arguing that practitioners are often the moral compass of an organization. Through in-depth interviews with public relations practitioners, findings reveal that practitioners can function as organizational activists, resisting dominant power and embracing a desire for change. Holtzhausen and Voto present dissensus and dissymmetry (Docherty, 1993; Lyotard, 1992, 1993) as alternatives to the consensus and symmetrical communication that have been heralded as the gold standard in public relations theory and practice.

Major Topics/Questions Needing to Be Addressed by Public Relations Theorists Working with Activism

While the paradigmatic landscape of public relations is diverse, postpositivist theories dominate much of the research on activism. Additional theory development is needed to provide a more robust account of the intersections between public relations and activism. To advance the theoretical landscape of activism, further research is needed that builds theory within public relations and draws from other disciplines. L'Etang (2016) recognized the opportunities for theory building and empirical exploration: "There is room for considerable theoretical expansion in terms of reflections upon the connections between societal change, social movements and activism and the role of communicative action" (p. 211).

Research is needed that explores activism and public relations at multiple levels: individual, discipline, social, and global. Future theorizing is needed in three main areas: (1) activism as public relations (conceptualizing social movement organizations as strategic communicators); (2) public relations as activism (conceptualizing public relations practitioners as organizational change agents); and (3) activism and strategic communication (considering how key stakeholders engage with communication materials aimed at them).

Suggested Cases to Explore to Demonstrate Theory at Work with Activism

The following are two short overviews of some cases involving activism. More than 160 corporations (including Apple, Time Warner Cable, Microsoft, Visa, and Google) condemned the passage of House Bill 2 (HB2) in North Carolina that effectively forces transgender people to use the bathroom that corresponds with the sex they were assigned at birth, rather than with their gender identity. In response to HB2, organizations and corporations became activists, taking a stand. Deutsche Bank announced a freeze on its plan to create 250 jobs at its Cary, North Carolina facility, and PayPal pulled out of a $3.8 million deal to expand in Charlotte, North Carolina. The National Basketball Association pulled the 2017 All-Star Game from Charlotte, which would have had an estimated $100 million in regional economic impact.

On the heels of a new generation of public relations, Ripple Strategies, a strategic communication agency that engages in "PR with purpose," partnered with more than a hundred organizations nationwide to demand that Dollar Stores stop selling products containing chemicals known to cause cancer, learning disabilities, obesity, and other serious illnesses. Ripple (2015) released a report – *A day late and a dollar short* – resulting in two dozen TV stories and several nationwide high-profile online stories, over half of which appeared in the Spanish-language press. Two days after the campaign launch, the Consumer Product Safety Commission requested the product testing results, forcing Dollar Stores to respond.

Discussion Questions

1   What role has activism played in the development of public relations practice and theory?

2   What role do new media play in theorizing public relations, activism, and power?

3   How do activists practice public relations and strategic communication? How do public relations practitioners engage in activism?

4   How does a researcher's paradigm affect empirical and theoretical work?

5   What discourses surround activism in other disciplines (business, management, sociology, anthropology, etc.)? How does this compare with public relations?

6   What might an embrace of activism and public relations mean for the future of public relations theory and research?

Suggested Readings

Allagui, I. (2017). Towards organisational activism in the UAE: A case study approach. *Public Relations Review, 43*(1), 258–266.

Ciszek, E. L. (2016). Digital activism: How social media and dissensus inform theory and practice. *Public Relations Review, 42*(2), 314–321.

Curtin, P. A. (2016). Exploring articulation in internal activism and public relations theory: A case study. *Journal of Public Relations Research, 28*(1), 19–34.

Henderson, A. (2005). Activism in "Paradise": Identity management in a public relations campaign against genetic engineering. *Journal of Public Relations Research, 17*(2), 117–137.

Reber, B. H., & Berger, B. K. (2005). Framing analysis of activist rhetoric: How the Sierra Club succeeds or fails at creating salient messages. *Public Relations Review, 31*(2), 185–195.

Stokes, A. Q., & Rubin, D. (2010). Activism and the limits of symmetry: The public relations battle between Colorado GASP and Philip Morris. *Journal of Public Relations Research, 22*(1), 26–48.

Veil, S. R., Reno, J., Freihaut, R., & Oldham, J. (2015). Online activists vs. Kraft foods: A case of social media hijacking. *Public Relations Review, 41*(1), 103–108.

Weaver, C. K. (2010). Carnivalesque activism as a public relations genre: A case study of the New Zealand group Mothers Against Genetic Engineering. *Public Relations Review, 36*(1), 35–41.

References

Anderson, D. S. (1992). Identifying and responding to activist publics: A case study. *Journal of Public Relations Research, 4*(3), 151–165.

Bardhan, N. (2003). Rupturing public relations metanarratives: The example of India. *Journal of Public Relations Research, 15*(3), 225–248.

Bardhan, N., & Weaver, C. K. (Eds.). (2011). *Public relations in global cultural contexts: Multi-paradigmatic perspectives.* New York: Routledge.

Baron, D. P., & Diermeier, D. (2007). Strategic activism and nonmarket strategy. *Journal of Economics & Management Strategy, 16*(3), 599–634.

Benoit, W. L., & Czerwinski, A. (1997). A critical analysis of USAir's image repair discourse. *Business Communication Quarterly, 60*(3), 38–57.

Berger, B. K. (2005). Power over, power with, and power to relations: Critical reflections on public relations, the dominant coalition, and activism. *Journal of Public Relations Research, 17*(1), 5–28.

Blumer, H. (1969). Fashion: From class differentiation to collective selection. *Sociological Quarterly, 10*(3), 275–291.

Cancel, A. E., Cameron, G. T., Sallot, L. M., & Mitrook, M. A. (1997). It depends: A contingency theory of accommodation in public relations. *Journal of Public Relations Research, 9*, 31–63.

Charmaz, K. (2011). Grounded theory methods in social justice research. In N. K. Denzin & Y. S. Lincoln (Eds.), *The Sage handbook of qualitative research* (4th ed.) (pp. 359–380). Thousand Oaks, CA: Sage.

Chase, H. W. (1976). *Corporate public issues and their management.* Leesburg, VA: IAP.

Cheney, G., & Christensen, L. T. (2001). Public relations as contested terrain. In R. L. Heath (Ed.), *Handbook of public relations* (pp. 167–182). Thousand Oaks, CA: Sage.

Ciszek, E. L. (2015). Bridging the gap: Mapping the relationship between activism and public relations. *Public Relations Review, 41*(4), 447–455.

Coombs, W. T., & Holladay, S. J. (2007). *It's not just PR: Public relations in society.* Malden, MA: Blackwell.

Coombs, W. T., & Holladay, S. J. (2012a). Fringe public relations: How activism moves critical PR toward the mainstream. *Public Relations Review, 38*(5), 880–887.

Coombs, W. T., & Holladay, S. J. (2012b). Privileging an activist vs. a corporate view of public relations history in the US. *Public Relations Review, 38*(3), 347–353.

Crable, R. E., & Vibbert, S. L. (1985). Managing issues and influencing public policy. *Public Relations Review, 11*(2), 3–16.

Curtin, P. A. (2012). Public relations and philosophy: Parsing paradigms. *Public Relations Inquiry, 1*(1), 31–47.

Curtin, P. A. (2016). Exploring articulation in internal activism and public relations theory: A case study. *Journal of Public Relations Research, 28*(1), 19–34.

Davis, G. F., McAdam, D., Scott, W. R., & Zald, M. N. (Eds.). (2005). *Social movements and organization theory*. Cambridge: Cambridge University Press.

Demetrious, K. (2006). Active voices. In J. L'Etang & M. Pieczka (Eds.), *Public relations: Critical debates and contemporary practice* (pp. 93–107). Mahwah, NJ: Lawrence Erlbaum.

Demetrious, K. (2008). Corporate social responsibility, new activism and public relations. *Social Responsibility Journal, 4*(1/2), 104–119.

Demetrious, K. (2013). *Public relations, activism, and social change: Speaking up*. New York: Routledge.

Den Hond, F., & De Bakker, F. G. (2007). Ideologically motivated activism: How activist groups influence corporate social change activities. *Academy of Management Review, 32*(3), 901–924.

Docherty, T. (Ed.). (1993). *Postmodernism: A reader*. New York: Columbia University Press.

Dozier, D. M., Grunig, J. E., & Grunig, L. A. (1995). *Manager's guide to excellence in public relations and communication management*. Mahwah, NJ: Lawrence Erlbaum.

Dozier, D. M., & Lauzen, M. M. (2000). Liberating the intellectual domain from the practice: Public relations, activism, and the role of the scholar. *Journal of Public Relations Research, 12*, 3–22.

Dutta, M. J. (2009). On Spivak: Theorizing resistance – applying Gayatri Chakravorty Spivak in public relations. In Ø. Ihlen, B. Van Ruler, & M. Fredriksson (Eds.), *Public relations and social theory: Key figures and concepts* (pp. 278–299). New York: Routledge.

Edwards, L. (2009). Symbolic power and public relations practice: Locating individual practitioners within their social context. *Journal of Public Relations Research, 21*, 251–272.

Edwards, L. (2011). Critical perspectives in global public relations: Theorizing power. In N. Bardhan & C. K. Weaver (Eds.), *Public Relations in global cultural contexts: Multi-paradigmatic perspectives* (pp. 29–49). London: Routledge.

Edwards, L. (2012). Defining the "object" of public relations research: A new starting point. *Public Relations Inquiry, 1*(1), 7–30.

Ferguson, M. A. (1984, August). *Building theory in public relations: Interorganizational relationships as a public relations paradigm*. Paper presented at the meeting of the Association for Education in Journalism and Mass Communication, Gainesville, FL.

Geertz, G. (1973). *The interpretation of cultures: Selected essays*. New York: Basic Books.

Gilpin, D. R., & Murphy, P. J. (2008). *Crisis management in a complex world*. Oxford: Oxford University Press.

Goffman, E. (1959). *The presentation of self in everyday life*. New York: Doubleday.

Greenwood, C. A. (2015). Whistleblowing in the Fortune 1000: What practitioners told us about wrongdoing in corporations in a pilot study. *Public Relations Review, 41*(4), 490–500.

Grunig, J. E. (1989). Sierra Club study shows who become activists. *Public Relations Review, 15*(3), 3–24.

Grunig, J. E. (Ed.). (1992). *Excellence in public relations and communication management*. Hillsdale, NJ: Lawrence Erlbaum.

Grunig, J. E. (1997). A situational theory of publics: Conceptual history, recent challenges and new research. In D. Moss, T. MacManus, & D. Verčič (Eds.), *Public relations research: An international perspective* (pp. 4–48). London: International Thomson.

Grunig, J. E. (2001). Two-way symmetrical public relations: Past, present, and future. In R. L. Heath (Ed.), *Handbook of public relations* (pp. 11–30). Thousand Oaks, CA: Sage.

Grunig, J. E., & Grunig, L. A. (1997). *Review of a program of research on activism: Incidence in four countries, activist publics, strategies of activist groups, and organizational responses to activism.* Paper presented at the Fourth Public Relations Research Symposium, Bled, Slovenia.

Grunig, J. E., & Hunt, T. (1984). *Managing public relations.* New York: CBS College.

Grunig, L. A. (1986). *Activism and organizational response: Contemporary cases of collective behavior.* Public Relations Division, Association for Education in Journalism and Mass Communication.

Grunig, L. A. (1992). Activism: How it limits the effectiveness of organizations and how excellent public relations departments respond. In J. E. Grunig (Ed.), *Excellence in public relations and communication management* (pp. 503–530). Hillsdale, NJ: Lawrence Erlbaum.

Grunig, L. A., Grunig, J. E., & Dozier, D. M. (2002). *Excellent public relations and effective organizations: A study of communication management in three countries.* Mahwah, NJ: Lawrence Erlbaum.

Hallahan, K. (2000). Inactive publics: The forgotten publics in public relations. *Public Relations Review, 26*(4), 499–515.

Hallahan, K. (2001). The dynamics of issues activation and response: An issues processes model. *Journal of Public Relations Research, 13*(1), 27–59.

Heath, R. L. (1997). Strategic issues management: Organisations and public policy challenges. Thousand Oaks, CA: Sage.

Heath, R. L. (2010). Mind, self, and society. In R. L. Heath (Ed.), *Handbook of public relations* (2nd ed.) (pp. 1–4). Thousand Oaks, CA: Sage.

Heath, R. L., & Waymer, D. (2009). A case study of Frederick Douglass' Fourth of July address. In R. L. Heath, E. L. Toth, & D. Waymer (Eds.), *Rhetorical and critical approaches to public relations II* (pp. 195–215). New York: Routledge.

Holtzhausen, D. R. (2000). Postmodern values in public relations. *Journal of Public Relations Research, 12*(1), 93–114.

Holtzhausen, D. R. (2002). Towards a postmodern research agenda for public relations. *Public Relations Review, 28*(3), 251–264.

Holtzhausen, D. R. (2012). *Public relations as activism: Postmodern approaches to theory and practice.* New York: Routledge.

Holtzhausen, D. R., & Voto, R. (2002). Resistance from the margins: The postmodern public relations practitioner as organizational activist. *Journal of Public Relations Research, 14*(1), 57–84.

Jones, B. L., & Chase, W. H. (1979). Managing public policy issues. *Public Relations Review, 5*(2), 3–23.

Karlberg, M. (1996). Remembering the public in public relations research: From theoretical to operational symmetry. *Journal of Public Relations Research, 8*(4), 263–278.

Kennedy, A. K., & Sommerfeldt, E. J. (2015). A postmodern turn for social media research: Theory and research directions for public relations scholarship. *Atlantic Journal of Communication, 23*(1), 31–45.

Kim, J., & Cho, M. (2011). When the "stroller moms" take hold of the street: A case study of how social influence made the inactive publics active in anti-US beef protest in Seoul – an issues processes model perspective. *International Journal of Strategic Communication, 5*(1), 1–25.

King, B. G. (2008). A political mediation model of corporate response to social movement activism. *Administrative Science Quarterly, 53*(3), 395–421.

Kuhn, T. S. (1996) *The structure of scientific revolutions* (3rd ed.). Chicago: University of Chicago Press.

Leichty, G., & Springston, J. (1993). Reconsidering public relations models. *Public Relations Review, 19*, 327–339.

Lenox, M. J., & Eesley, C. E. (2009). Private environmental activism and the selection and response of firm targets. *Journal of Economics & Management Strategy, 18*(1), 45–73.

L'Etang, J. (2016). Public relations, activism and social movements: Critical perspectives. *Public Relations Inquiry, 5*(3), 207–211.

Lyotard, J.-F. (1992). Answering the question: What is postmodernism? In C. Jencks (Ed.), *The postmodern reader* (pp. 138–150). London: Academy.

Lyotard, J.-F. (1993). *Libidinal economy.* Bloomington: Indiana University Press.

Maguire, S., & Hardy, C. (2009). Discourse and deinstitutionalization: The decline of DDT. *Academy of Management Journal, 52*(1), 148–178.

McKie, D. (2001). Updating public relations: "New science," research paradigms, and uneven developments. In R. L. Heath (Ed.), *Handbook of public relations* (pp. 75–91). Thousand Oaks, CA: Sage

Mead, G. H. (1934). *Mind, self, and society* (Vol. 3). Chicago: University of Chicago Press.

Melucci, A. (1989). *Nomads of the present.* London: Hutchinson Radius

Melucci, A. (1996). *Challenging codes: Collective action in the information age.* New York: Cambridge University Press.

Mickey, T. J. (1998). Selling the internet: A cultural studies approach to public relations. *Public Relations Review, 24*(3), 335–349.

Mintzberg, H. (1983). The case for corporate social responsibility. *Journal of Business Strategy, 4*(2), 3–15.

Morris, A., & Braine, N. (2001). Social movements and oppositional consciousness. In J. J. Mansbridge & A. Morris (Eds.), *Oppositional consciousness: The subjective roots of social protest* (pp. 20–37). Chicago: University of Chicago Press.

Motion, J., Leitch, S., & Brodie, R. J. (2003). Equity in corporate co-branding: The case of Adidas and the All Blacks. *European Journal of Marketing, 37*(7/8), 1080–1094.

Motion, J., & Weaver, C. K. (2005). A discourse perspective for critical public relations research: Life sciences network and the battle for truth. *Journal of Public Relations Research, 17*(1), 49–67.

Munshi, D. (2005). Postcolonial theory and public relations. In R. L. Heath (Ed.), *Encyclopedia of public relations* (Vol. 2, pp. 631–632). Thousand Oaks, CA: Sage.

Munshi, D, & Edwards, L. (2011). Understanding "race" in/and public relations: Where do we start and where should we go? *Journal of Public Relations Research, 23*, 349–67.

Murphy, P., & Dee, J. (1992). DuPont and Greenpeace: The dynamics of conflict between corporations and activist groups. *Journal of Public Relations Research, 4*, 3–20.

Murphy, P., & Dee, J. (1996). Reconciling the preferences of environmental activists and corporate policymakers. *Journal of Public Relations Research, 8*, 1–33.

Pal, M., & Dutta, M. J. (2008). Public relations in a global context: The relevance of critical modernism as a theoretical lens. *Journal of Public Relations Research, 20*(2), 159–179.

Rakow, L. (2005). *A generative grammar of communication theories.* Paper presented at the annual meeting of the International Communication Association, New York.

Rehbein, K., Waddock, S., & Graves, S. B. (2004). Understanding shareholder activism: Which corporations are targeted? *Business & Society, 43*(3), 239–267.

Renfro, W. L. (1993). *Issues management in strategic planning.* Westport, CT: Quorum Books.

Ripple Strategies. (2015). A day late and a dollar short. Retrieved from https://www.ripplestrategies.com/2015/02/10/day-late-dollar-short/

Sha, B.-L. (1995). *Intercultural public relations: Exploring cultural identity as a means of segmenting publics* (Unpublished MA thesis). University of Maryland, College Park.

Smith, M. E. (2005). Activism. In R. L. Heath (Ed.), *Encyclopedia of public relations* (pp. 5–9). Thousand Oaks, CA: Sage.

Smith, M. F., & Ferguson, D. P. (2010). Activism 2.0. In R. Heath (Ed.), *Handbook of public relations* (pp. 395–408). Thousand Oaks, CA: Sage.

Stewart, K. (1991). Corporate identity: A strategic marketing issue. *International Journal of Bank Marketing, 9*(1), 32–39.

Stokes, A. Q., & Rubin, D. (2010). Activism and the limits of symmetry: The public relations battle between Colorado GASP and Philip Morris. *Journal of Public Relations Research, 22*(1), 26–48.

Taylor, M., & Das, S. S. (2010). Public relations in advocacy: Stem cell research organizations' use of the internet in resource mobilization. *Public Relations Journal, 4*(4), 1–22.

Weaver, C. K., & Motion, J. (2002). Sabotage and subterfuge: Public relations, democracy and genetic engineering in New Zealand. *Media, Culture & Society, 24*(3), 325–343.

Zoller, H. M. (2005). Health activism: Communication theory and action for social change. *Communication Theory, 15*(4), 341–364.

12

Media Relations and Challenges in a Digital Media Era

Samsup Jo

The following job opening announcement posted on www.salary.com describes the basic qualifications and the role of a media relations manager for a typical organization which could be found around the world.

> Develops and implements policies and procedures for the relations between the media and the organization. Works to expand understanding of the organization's business, performance, and strategy. Prepares summaries of media activity for senior management. May serve as the company's spokesperson. Requires a bachelor's degree. Typically reports to a head of a unit/department. Typically manages through subordinate managers and professionals in larger groups of moderate complexity. Provides input to strategic decisions that affect the functional area of responsibility. May give input into developing the budget. Capable of resolving escalated issues arising from operations and requiring coordination with other departments. Typically requires 3+ years of managerial experience.

As this job description shows, media relations has many facets; however, the core functions of media relations seem to be engaging in media management and resolving communication issues, especially those which might influence the bottom line.

Defining the Concepts: What Is Media Relations?

Media relations is a central part of public relations practice across countries and throughout public relations history. It also encompasses many forms and facets of interaction with traditional and nontraditional media. According to Zoch and Molleda (2006), media relations is defined as "an active process in which the public relations practitioner has, at the least, a modicum of control over the message she wishes to reach the public, its timing, the source of that information, and the effect on the media agenda of the issue presented" (p. 280). Furthering these thoughts, O'Brien (2014) adds that media relations "can be described as a company's interactions with editors, reporters and journalists. The media can be newspapers, radio, television and the internet. The goal is to communicate a client's newsworthy message, story or information using the appropriate media outlets." Therefore, media relations includes an array of activities such as pitching news stories, monitoring both online and offline media, responding to journalists' inquiries, gaining a favorable press, and reducing negative news coverage on behalf of an organization.

Public Relations Theory: Application and Understanding, First Edition. Edited by Brigitta R. Brunner.
© 2019 John Wiley & Sons, Inc. Published 2019 by John Wiley & Sons, Inc.

Traditionally, newspapers, magazines, trade publications, radio stations, and television channels were the main media with which public relations practitioners interacted to publicize their organization's stories. However, now the range of media needs to be extended beyond these traditional media to new media such as social media and new types of information producers such as independent power bloggers, YouTubers, and online influencers. The growth of the internet and omnipresence of social media combined with the smartphone platform has led to abundant digital platforms such as podcasts, video on demand (VOD) services, livestreams on Facebook, and livestreams on YouTube that were not seen previously. Therefore, bloggers, independent influencers, and other citizen journalists who post opinions and information in the online sphere are now also producing the news for the public to consume. Thus, the public has become increasingly accustomed to consuming news through digital platforms rather than relying only on traditional media, especially since traditional newsrooms are shrinking while the online sphere is booming. This situation has caused both significant challenges and opportunities for media relations professionals as they navigate working with both traditional journalists and online influencers in trying to relay their organizations' stories.

How and Why Is Media Relations of Concern to Public Relations?

In order to be effective, media relations professionals not only need to understand the news production process and the importance of deadlines, but they must also understand what information is newsworthy as well as what information is not. By providing relevant and newsworthy information to journalists and others, the media relations practitioner can establish herself as a trustworthy and reliable source.

Media relations can be practiced in either a proactive or a reactive manner (Smith, 2013). Public relations professionals continuously provide information such as press releases, media advisories, fact sheets, speeches, photos, and statistics to media outlets and on social media. These types of media relations activities would be considered proactive media relations because the organization is preemptively sharing information to generate interest and perhaps third-party endorsement for its news (Smith, 2013). In contrast, reactive media relations describes when an organization responds to inquiries and information requests from the media, as well as to social media posts (Smith, 2013). These responses could be simply providing basic facts or statistics. They could be working to schedule interview requests. They might also be attempts to explain organizational positions on hot topics or issues. Finally, they could be responses to crisis situations. Unlike proactive media relations, media inquiries can be unpredictable and unexpected; however, the practitioner must respond promptly no matter the situation.

One of the most critical aspects of media relations is working with the media in times of crisis. Although the necessary response to a crisis depends upon the severity of the issue and the amount of responsibility the organization has for the situation, responding promptly is key. The media relations department of the organization in crisis should establish itself as the source of information because multiple voices can cause confusion and undermine the organization's message and response. These media relations specialists should also anticipate the needs and questions of the media covering the crisis.

Reflecting upon the media environment paradigm, some classify the media into three categories: paid media, owned media, and earned media. Paid media refer to advertising and influencers paid by clients to use and publicize products and/or services. Owned media are the online and offline communication tools for which content is controlled. Some examples are websites, blogs, and social media. Earned media is online or offline endorsement given by a third party. Examples include power bloggers, news editorials, and online opinion leaders.

Not surprisingly, with growth, digital media have shifted to own and produce content for mass-mediated communication (Zerfass, Verčič, & Wiesenberg, 2016). More people trust the content of earned media due to its third-party endorsement, thereby lessening the impact of paid and owned media. Media relations professionals need to use owned and earned media in a balanced way. Using the Edelman Trust Barometer, scholars have found that the public is more likely to trust traditional media over social media across the United States, China, Japan, Germany, and France (Cacciatore, Meng, Boyd, & Reber, 2016).

How, When, and Why Is Theory Applied to Media Relations?

Building Relationships

At the most basic level, every media relations practitioner should have a list of journalists who are important to their organization and industry. This media list should include writers' and editors' names, e-mails, and cellular phones. The list could be organized alphabetically by journalist name or by media type and its relevance and importance to the organization at hand. Maintaining media lists can be time-consuming due to high turnover and frequent assignment changes in the news industry. However, the time spent cultivating media lists is time well spent.

There have been a number of studies examining the relationships that exists between public relations professionals and journalists (Turk, 1991; Griffin & Dunwoody, 1995). Unfortunately, it seems a high level of antagonism exists between journalists and public relations practitioners (DeLorme & Fedler, 2003; Sallot & Johnson, 2006). For example, some journalists believe public relations professionals are self-serving because they only provide favorable information about the organizations they represent to the media. Similarly, some public relations practitioners believe journalists are only interested in stories which cast the organizations for which they advocate in a negative light. However, it should be noted that journalists and media relations practitioners need each other; their relationships are symbiotic. Therefore, media relations practitioners should build and maintain relationships with journalists not only by understanding newsworthiness and deadlines, but also by getting to know journalists as people, anticipating their needs, understanding news consumers, and providing timely and relevant information.

Digital Communication

The evolution of digital technology has changed the landscape of media relations in recent years. First of all, communication between media relations professionals and reporters is driven more and more by online formats such as e-mail, personal chatting applications, and social media. Thus traditional mass-media communication yielded many more roles than digital media (Savič, 2016; Zerfass et al., 2016), and computer-mediated communication has become a more frequent mode of interaction than face-to-face communication. Therefore, media relations practitioners need to know how to use various tools such as owned media and social media. Furthermore, they also need to understand how journalists obtain news sources. For example, since journalists may visit websites, blogs, and social media managed by organizations to get information without contacting the public relations department, practitioners should update online content and check online information accuracy frequently. Savič (2016) states that "companies are transforming into products of owned media and media content" due to this mediatization trend (p. 607).

The increased use of digital technology, such as social media, has changed media relations in other ways, too. For example, the gatekeeping function of the media has been lessened due to organizations' ability to communicate directly with publics through Facebook, Twitter, and other online platforms. Social media have given media relations a very powerful function because practitioners no longer have to wait for the media to evaluate and place messages. Practitioners can place messages themselves using digital channels. However, while working around the gatekeeping process of traditional media has made placing information and messages easier, it has also taken away third-party endorsement, which may undermine the credibility of online content. Thus, media relations professionals need to be aware of the positive and negative aspects of direct communication channels. In fact, the public is still likely to trust the media news format rather than the content placed by owned channels since the public tends to distrust controlled content (Carah & Louw, 2015).

Another new aspect of media relations is managing relationships with online influencers in the digital media environment. Online influencers are independent individuals who post personal reviews and opinions on blogs and through other social media. Typically, influencers have thousands of followers and fans who share their opinions and reviews. Since online influencers often have expertise in a specific area such as politics, entertainment, brands, services, or controversial issues, the public is likely to trust and value their opinions and agree with the influencers' preferences and political standpoints. Many view influencers as experts and base their purchases and stances on issues on what influencers have said or done.

For example, a public relations practitioner who works for a cosmetics brand may spend a significant amount of time building favorable relationships with online influencers who broadcast cosmetics product reviews on YouTube channels and gain audiences. For example, hundreds of thousands of YouTube subscribers watch these videos rather than relying upon traditional media such as magazines or network TV to get news about the latest cosmetics on the market. These power bloggers wield a lot of influence. Although power bloggers are not journalists in principle, the impact of their opinions does matter to the public. Thus, media relations has increasingly shifted to the online sphere and has focused on building relationships with online influencers.

Finally, media relations specialists will have to monitor trending buzzwords on search engines such as Google, Yahoo, and Bing to determine if any of those trending terms relate to the organizations they represent. In order to manage online media relations, media relations specialists need to understand the algorithm of buzzword placement in the online sphere and handle inquiries from the media, especially in times of crisis.

Examples of Theories Used with Media Relations

The most common media relations theories come from mass communications and examine how sources work with media. Following are some summaries of theories typically used with media relations, and also see Table 12.1.

Information Subsidy and Agenda Setting

As has been stated, media relations manages the flow of information between sources and media. Gandy (1982) coined the term "information subsidy" to refer to any information that organizations hope will receive favorable placement in the media. Organizations benefit from third-party endorsement, which is when the media legitimize the sources' information. Conversely, the media benefit by acquiring newsworthy information subsidies from sources, which saves them the time and effort associated with news gathering. Thus, the relationship between sources and media is symbiotic.

Table 12.1 Media relations theories

Theory	Key features and attention point
Agenda building on media	Public relations practitioners continuously provide information to media, with efforts to influence the media agenda. The media agenda affects what people know about issues, brands, services, policies, and people related to the specific organizations.
Third-party endorsement	The public is more likely to believe news content endorsed by a third party, such as in the media, which is unbiased, objective, and maintains editorial independence. The public is less likely to believe first-party content and will perceive this content as self-serving and biased. Third-party endorsement is a distinguishing characteristic in comparing publicity to advertising messages. However, in the social media environment, where earned, owned, and paid media are presented on the same platform, third-party endorsement can be hard to discern.
Information subsidies	Sources, such as organizations, attempt to provide information subsidies to the media, whereas the media seek news information. Information subsidies can save media costs when producing news content. Therefore, sources and media have a symbiotic relationship.

The agenda-setting theory (McCombs & Shaw, 1972) explains the role of the media and how the media decide on and frame news content based on journalists' judgment. Basically, while the media do not tell the public what to think, the media tell the public what to think about, meaning that the issues and topics covered by the media are the ones people tend to talk about and know. Since the public receives news from the media and generally gives credence to the media, the news content covered (as well as the content not covered) affects the public's recognition and awareness of topics and issues. Therefore, no matter what a media relations practitioner's industry is, he should be aware of and recognize the power of the media.

In addition, framing theory (Goffman, 1974) is related to agenda-setting theory. Framing refers to the presentation and nuances that affect the public's perception. For example, if a CEO makes a decision that is viewed as a socially responsible response to a societal issue such as gun control, that CEO might be framed in a positive way. Similarly, if a CEO were to respond to an issue such as gender equality in an insensitive way, he might be framed in a negative fashion. Public relations practitioners need to pay attention to how news content is presented because that presentation can affect how publics come to know topics and issues.

Third-Party Endorsement Theory

A central premise of media relations can be explained by the third-party endorsement theory. Third party refers to an entity which is independent, objective, and not affiliated with the organization releasing information. Therefore, the third party is frequently the media. News organizations are considered credible because they are free from any influence by clients or sources. Since news coverage is filtered by objective journalistic judgment, news typically has third-party credibility. Therefore, any news content endorsed by the media affects the public's perception of issues, organizations, and people, meaning that if the objective media say something, it is credible because it is free from influence. In recent years, however, the digital media environment has lessened the value of third-party endorsement. Marketing content is often portrayed as objective news when presented on a digital platform. This disguised marketing material which only seems to have third-party endorsement blurs the line between advertising and news. For example, bloggers who do not disclose that they are paid, purchase replies that are secretly paid, and fake postings can appear in the online sphere and imitate the wording and presentation of third-party endorsements in the news. The issue then becomes ensuring the credibility of content found in the digital media environment.

Major Topics/Questions Needing to Be Addressed by Public Relations Theorists Working with Media Relations

Media Relations in Cross-Cultural Setting

The world is shrinking because communication across borders and time zones is so much easier than in the past. However, with these changes come challenges. For example, cultural differences sometimes affect aspects of media relations depending on the culture in which media relations is practiced. Eastern culture values collectivism while the West values individualism. Collectivism is defined as the degree to which individuals are integrated into groups; and in contrast, individualism is "the degree to which people in a country prefer to act as individuals rather than as members of groups" (Hofstede, 1994, p. 6).

Guanxi is defined as the interrelationship between individuals characterized by an intimate bond. For example, *Guanxi* in Taiwan and personal networks in South Korea based on school ties may affect the practice of media relations in Asian countries (Huang, 2000; Jo & Kim, 2004). To lose negative publicity about an organization in the news media, public relations practitioners often ask a journalist to remove the bad news as a favor by employing personal networks such as school ties. Thus, how media relations is practiced depends upon media systems, political systems, level of economic development, and culture (Sriramesh & Verčič, 2003). Media relations may be altered depending on the cultural context of each country. External factors such as the personal influence model may also influence the agenda setting of news content.

In Eastern cultures, the agenda-setting role of media is often encroached upon by external factors such as advertising subsidies, or personal networks such as school or hometown ties. Intimate interpersonal relationships between the sources and media journalists may affect news content. For example, public relations professionals are likely to rely on informal relationships to gain positive publicity and reduce negative publicity. Furthermore, the dramatic decline in newspaper subscriptions has forced many news media to secure profits by selling editorial space to clients. In some countries, this situation has led to a degradation of the integrity of journalism because the traditional relationship between sources and media has been replaced by economic motives (Jo, 2011; Jo & Bae, 2013). Therefore, future research needs to examine the changing nature of the source–media relationship in the global context to determine if current theory is adequate.

Ethical Issues of Media Relations

Negative perceptions of public relations can be traced back to historically unethical relationships between sources and media (Callison, 2004). The rapid growth of digital technology combined with the downsizing of media has created a number of ethical issues and challenges for the future of media relations. First, although bypassing the gatekeeping of traditional media allows organizations to communicate directly with their publics, it also challenges the credibility of owned and controlled news content (DiStaso & Brown, 2015). The value of third-party endorsement is lost when the gatekeeping function is bypassed.

Second, the plethora of fake news content and false posts, replies, and comments intended to sway public opinion on digital platforms also challenges traditional third-party endorsement by the media. At times, organizations hire bloggers without revealing that the bloggers have been paid for their product. Therefore, what seems like a nonbiased third- party endorsement is actually a paid-for endorsement. Similarly, paid advertising often imitates third-party endorsed content. These so-called news editorials and reviews where payment is not disclosed create ethical issues for both journalism and public relations, and these need to be examined further.

Finally, the economic constraints bearing upon the media can lead some news organizations to turn to new revenue streams. In the short term, news organizations can benefit from paid news placements such as advertising. Similarly, media can secure financial profit by selling their editorial content. However, in the long term, media could lose credibility, resulting in a loss of trust in journalism. These situations all have repercussions for media relations. More research needs to focus on the gray areas of online media relations and the adoption of digital communication technology in a new media landscape.

Suggested Case to Explore to Demonstrate Theory at Work with Media Relations

The case of media relations and *Cheong* culture in South Korea is interesting to examine in the international context. If any global organization wants to operate in South Korea, its media relations representatives must have personal relationships with the media in order to create *Cheong*. *Cheong* has its roots in the Confucianism of eastern Asia. Its main cultural characteristic resides the private domain of the human relationship. In this culture, the ties and personal connections built among people through schools, hometowns, friendship, and work relationships are often called upon. The issue with *Cheong*, however, is that it can influence media relations, which then affects what the public does and does not know.

The selection of news content is an intrinsic right of the media, and should not be influenced by external media relations practitioners. However, in South Korea, *Cheong* still affects media relations (Berkowitz & Lee, 2004; Jung, 2007). For example, large organizations will often hire male former journalists as public relations managers in order to use their connections with the media to their advantage. For example, in the case of negative publicity, the media relations practitioner will ask his media connections to remove any negative news about his organization so it does not become publicly known and does not spread. This process of removing negative news is an example of how the personal connections rooted in the *Cheong* culture can affect public relations. Thus, building and maintaining favorable relationships with journalists is regarded as a highly important skill for public relations professionals. This unique aspect of media relations in South Korea illustrates how the practice of media relations differs depending on country and cultural context (Taylor, 2001).

Discussion Questions

1   How does media relations practice change with the digital communication age? How do the interactions between sources and media evolve compared to those in the past driven by traditional media?

2   According to earlier studies, the relationship between public relations practitioners and journalists has not been positive. How does the relationship evolve given recent digital technology?

3   How does media relations differ depending on countries? How do cross-culture issues affect dimensions of media relations?

4   In Japan and South Korea, the existence of a press club (some organizations limit news reporting access to only a few in the media) provides pros and cons to media relations specialists. Discuss the pros and cons of a press club system.

5 How do you define media relations ethics?

6 Many public relations practitioners argue that the line between advertising and public relations has become blurred in a converging media environment. How do you perceive this issue? Do you favor this trend?

Suggested Readings

Bowen, S. A. (2016). Clarifying ethics in public relations from A to V, authenticity to virtue: BledCom special issue of PR review sleeping (with the) media: Media relations. *Public Relations Review, 42*, 564–572.

Charest, F., Bouffard, J., & Zajmovic, E. (2016). Public relations and social media: Deliberate or creative strategic planning. *Public Relations Review, 42*, 530–538.

Cheng, Y., Huang, Y., & Chan, C. (2017). Public relations, media coverage, and public opinion in contemporary China: Testing agenda building theory in a social mediated crisis. *Telematics and Informatics, 34*, 765–773.

Han, G. S. (2002). *Understanding Korean social psychology*. Seoul: Hakjisa.

Macnamara, J. (2014). Journalism–PR relations revisited: The good news, the bad news, and insights into tomorrow's news. *Public Relations Review, 40*, 739–750.

Macnamara, J. (2016). The continuing convergence of journalism and PR: New insights for ethical practice from a three-country study of senior practitioners. *Journalism and Mass Communication Quarterly, 93*(1), 118–141.

Toledano, M., & Avidar, R. (2016). Public relations, ethics, and social media: A cross-national study of PR practitioners. *Public Relations Review, 42*, 161–169.

Waters, R. (2013). Tracing the impact of media relations and television coverage on US charitable relief fundraising: An application of agenda setting theory across three natural disasters. *Journal of Public Relations Research, 25*, 329–346.

References

Berkowitz, D., & Lee, J. (2004). Media relations in Korea: Cheong between journalist and public relations practitioner. *Public Relations Review, 30*(4): 4531–437.

Cacciatore, M., Meng, J., Boyd, B., & Reber, B (2016). Political ideology, media-source preferences, and messaging strategies: A global perspective on trust building. *Public Relations Review, 42*(4), 616–626.

Callison, C. (2004). The good, the bad, and the ugly: Perceptions of public relations practitioners. *Journal of Public Relations Research, 16*(4), 371–389.

Carah, N., & Louw, E. (2015). *Media and society: Production, content and participation*. Thousand and Oaks, CA: Sage.

DeLorme, D. E., & Fedler, F. (2003). Journalists' hostility toward public relations: An historical analysis. *Public Relations Review, 29*, 99–124.

DiStaso, M., & Brown, B. (2015). From owned to earned media: An analysis of corporate efforts about being on Fortune lists. *Communication Research Reports, 32*(3), 191–198.

Gandy, O. H. (1982). *Beyond agenda setting: Information subsidies and public policy*. Norwood, NJ: Ablex.

Goffman, E. (1974). Frame analysis: an essay on the organization of experience. New York: Harper and Row.

Griffin, R., & Dunwoody, S. (1995). Impacts of information subsidies and community structure on local press coverage of environmental contamination. *Journalism and Mass Communication Quarterly, 72*(2), 271–284.

Hofstede, G. H. (1994). Management scientists are human. *Management Science, 40*(1), 4–13.

Huang, Y. H. (2000). The personal influence model and Gao Guanxi in Taiwan Chinese public relations. *Public Relations Review, 26,* 219–236.

Jo, S. (2011). Advertising as payment: Information transactions in the South Korean newspaper market. *Public Relations Review, 37*(4), 399–404.

Jo, S., & Bae, J. (2013). The study of relationship between sources and newspapers. *Korean Journal of Public Relations Research, 17*(2), 40–76.

Jo, S., & Kim, Y. (2004). Media or personal relations? Exploring media relations dimensions in South Korea. *Journalism and Mass Communication Quarterly, 81*(2), 292–306.

Jung, S. (2007). *Koreans' cultural grammar.* Seoul: Thinking Tree.

McCombs, M., & Shaw, D. (1972). The agenda-setting function of mass media. *Public Opinion Quarterly, 36*(2): 176–187.

O'Brien, A. (2014, September 19). Public relations vs. media relations. *Everything-PR.* Retrieved from http://everything-pr.com/public-relations-media-relations/52598/

Sallot, L. M., & Johnson, E. A. (2006). Investigating relationships between journalists and public relations practitioners: Working together to set, frame and build the public agenda, 1991–2004. *Public Relations Review, 32,* 151–159.

Savič, I. (2016). Mediatization of companies as a factor of their communication power and the new role of public relations. *Public Relations Review, 42*(4), 607–615.

Smith, R. (2013). *Strategic planning for public relations* (4th ed.). New York: Routledge.

Sriramesh, K., & Verčič, D. (2003). *The global public relations handbook.* Mahwah, NJ: Lawrence Erlbaum.

Taylor, M. (2001). International public relations: Opportunities and challenges for the 21st century. In R. L. Heath (Ed.), *Handbook of public relations* (pp. 627–637). Thousand Oaks, CA: Sage.

Turk, J. V. (1991). Public relations' influence on the news. In D. L. Protess and M. McCombs (Eds), *Agenda setting: Readings on media, public opinion, and policymaking* (pp. 211–222). Hillsdale, NJ: Lawrence Erlbaum.

Zerfass, A., Verčič, D., & Wiesenberg, M. (2016). The dawn of a new golden age for media relations? How PR professionals interact with the mass media and use new collaboration practices. *Public Relations Review, 42*(4), 499–508.

Zoch, L. M., & Molleda, J. (2006). Building a theoretical model of media relations using framing, information subsidies, and agenda-building. In C. Botan & V. Hazleton (Eds.), *Public relations theory II* (pp. 279–309). Mahwah, NJ: Lawrence Erlbaum.

13

Corporate Social Responsibility

Chun-Ju Flora Hung-Baesecke, Yi-Ru Regina Chen, Cindy Sing-Bik Ngai, and Minqin Ma

In recent decades, organizations have placed increasing emphasis on corporate social responsibility (CSR), either because of public demand or because of its contribution to corporate outcomes by triggering positive reactions from various stakeholders (e.g. consumers, employees, community leaders, and government officials) (Dawkins & Lewis, 2003). For example, 3,478 companies in Hong Kong were awarded the Caring Company logo in recognition of their CSR practices by the Caring Company scheme in 2016–2017 (Hong Kong Council of Social Service, 2017). The scheme is the longest standing and largest CSR recognition scheme in Hong Kong sponsored by the government. The number of corporate awardees was 12 times larger than it was 15 years ago when the scheme was founded (Hong Kong Council of Social Service, 2017). A recent CSR study found that Americans are more willing than before to reward companies for their responsible business practice and advocacy of social issues in line with their own concerns by doing business with them or making donations to charities the companies support (Cone, 2017). The study also found that Americans are more willing than before to punish corporations that fail to act responsibly by stopping their purchases of the company's products and boycotting them. These examples demonstrate why giving attention to CSR efforts is important.

Defining the Concepts: What Is CSR?

CSR is a multidisciplinary umbrella concept encompassing core corporate management domains such as business ethics, corporate citizenship, corporate sustainability, stakeholder management, environmental management, and corporate social performance (e.g. Carroll, 1991, 2004; Moon, 2002; Garriga & Mele, 2004; Van Marrewijk, 2003; Wheeler, Colbert, & Freeman, 2003). Previous studies have revealed the importance of CSR in the corporate sector by identifying positive relationships between CSR and corporate financial performance or firm productivity (e.g. Beurden & Gossling, 2008; Cochran & Wood, 1984; McGuire, Sundgren, & Schneeweis, 1988; Sun & Stuebs, 2013; Tsoutsoura, 2004; Waddock & Graves, 1997). Porter and Kramer (2006) suggested that CSR brings opportunities, innovations, and competitive advantages to companies, especially when a company establishes an affirmative CSR agenda and incorporates it into its business practice. Leonard and McAdam (2003) further proposed that good CSR practices give rise to business advantages that help "reducing and limiting litigation, protecting brand image, improving customer satisfaction, as well as reducing absenteeism

Public Relations Theory: Application and Understanding, First Edition. Edited by Brigitta R. Brunner.
© 2019 John Wiley & Sons, Inc. Published 2019 by John Wiley & Sons, Inc.

and employee turnover and increasing the ability to retain talented employees" (p. 30). Their studies confirmed the importance of CSR in stakeholder management as well as image and reputation management in the corporate sector (Kay, 1993; Vilanova, Lozano, & Arenas, 2009).

Corporate Stakeholder Management and CSR

The traditional view of CSR, especially in a capitalistic context, focuses mainly on "the conduct of a business so that it is economically profitable, law abiding, ethical and socially supportive" (Carroll, 1983, p. 608). Among these four pillars, profitability and obedience to the law were recognized by Carroll as the "foremost conditions" to be fulfilled (Carroll, 1983, p. 608). Similarly, Freeman (1984) attested that it is important for corporations to make profits while safeguarding the best interest of the primary stakeholders, shareholders in particular, without causing societal harm. Essentially, the early CSR approaches were mostly instrumental, oriented to profits and shareholders, and lacked an integrative, affirmative approach in examining the tension between business and society, and the statutory public responsibility of corporations to society at large (Bowie, 1991; Donaldson & Preston, 1995; Porter & Kramer, 2006).

Subsequently, CSR expanded to encompass a more dynamic and interactive view of advancing various stakeholders' interests by incorporating the concept of the social contract as the driving force in CSR strategies (Bowie, 1991; Donaldson & Preston, 1995). This socially progressive view has placed much emphasis on fundamental CSR values, including moral obligation and "individual rights and justice" (Bowie, 1991, p. 56) in stakeholder management of CSR. However, CSR strategies are still predominantly passive and reactive, focusing on the traditional economic model of promoting corporate citizenship to "generate profit, provide employment, follow the law, replenish the public coffers, and do no harm" (Vidaver-Cohen & Altman, 2000, p. 147).

Eventually, a more proactive, community-integrative mode of CSR emerged to highlight the importance of stakeholder management in CSR for driving corporate success. From the perspective of social issues management, Solomon (1992) suggested that corporate citizenship could only be realized through addressing stakeholder interests while advocating moral obligations to contribute to the local communities (Vidaver-Cohen & Altman, 2000). Subsequently, Carroll (2004) has revisited his CSR model to highlight the notion of stakeholders, where he redefined "economic responsibility" as "do what is required by global capitalism," "legal responsibility" as "do what is required by global stakeholders," "ethical responsibility" as "do what is expected by global stakeholders," and "philanthropic responsibility" as "do what is desired by global stakeholders" (p. 116). Stakeholder management was placed as the focal point of CSR development in the corporate sector by the European Commission (2012): enterprises "should have in place a process to integrate social, environmental, ethical, human rights and consumer concerns into their business operations and core strategy in close collaboration with stakeholders."

How and Why Is CSR of Concern to Public Relations?

Questions of corporate morality and reputation management make CSR of importance to public relations practitioners. Scholars have been using the concepts of intrinsic and extrinsic CSR in analyzing the purposes of corporations' CSR efforts. Du, Bhattacharya, and Sen (2010) posited that stakeholders usually view the motives of corporate CSR initiatives to be either intrinsic (corporations having genuine concern for social issues), or extrinsic (corporations having a profit-seeking motive in instigating CSR initiatives). Pistoni, Songini, and Perrone (2016) posited that corporations apply CSR principles for a combination of institutional (how a corporation gains legitimacy for its business in a society), organizational (how a corporation improve its adaptability in the business environment), and moral/ethical reasons. With the frequent occurrence of mixed motives for CSR practices, Looser and Wehrmeyer (2016) contended that corporate behavior that is attributed to extrinsic motives could be perceived as "dishonest and misleading" (p. 545), and extrinsic CSR behavior could crowd out morale and lead corporations to abandon intrinsic CSR motives and behaviors. There are many debates on corporations' various motives in performing CSR, be it for considerations of corporate reputation, profit-seeking, obtaining legitimacy in a society, or for genuine moral reasons. Therefore, it is essential for corporations to prioritize CSR outcomes which have positive impacts on society.

When a corporation's CSR efforts are perceived as genuine, it usually benefits the corporation's reputation. As revealed in the 2016 Global RepTrek 100, corporate reputation is defined and measured via seven vital dimensions: products and services, innovation, workplace, governance, citizenship, leadership, and performance (Reputation Institute, 2016). Among these reputation criteria, workplace, governance, and citizenship are closely related to CSR strategies and practices adopted by the companies studied. In the Global RepTrak 2017 report, the chief marketing officer further remarked that "companies with a strong sense of purpose who are committed to improving on all dimensions of reputation – especially governance and citizenship – tend to be the most highly regarded" (McLaughin, 2017). In other words, good CSR practices contribute to corporate reputation building and maintenance in these key aspects. In view of the positive connection found in prior studies among stakeholder management, corporate reputation, and CSR, the latter is expected to exert a growing influence on corporate management and performance in the global environment.

For the past decade, company reputation and CSR have been discussed and studied extensively in the corporate sector. Theoretical and empirical research studies have also identified a positive relationship between CSR activities/performance and corporation reputation (e.g. Fombrun & Shanley 1990; Hur, Kim, & Woo, 2014; Lev, Petrovits, & Radhakrishnan, 2010; Williams & Barrett, 2000). Specifically, recent studies have concluded that CSR activities help corporations to build corporate reputation and credibility with their stakeholders and publics (Pfau, Haigh, Sims, & Wigley, 2009). Previous studies have also confirmed that CSR can help corporations to reduce damage to their reputations during difficult times and crises (Fombrun & Gardberg, 2000; Vanhamme & Grobben, 2009).

The importance of stakeholder management in CSR is further supported by Branco and Rodrigues (2006), who argued that good CSR allows companies to improve reputation with various stakeholder groups, including customers, suppliers, bankers, and even competitors. Given the fact that good CSR can help strengthen corporate–stakeholder relationships and improve corporate reputation, many corporations have decided to invest heavily in CSR for reputation building (see KPMG International, 2011).

How, When, and Why Is Theory Applied to CSR?

CSR is a mainstream topic of public relations and a focus of theoretical development in academia and the industry for two reasons. First, the two disciplines have much in common. The primary similarity is that they both focus on setting organizational behaviors in line with public expectations (e.g. being socially responsible) (Bartlett, 2011; Clark, 2000). Second, CSR is often a responsibility of the public relations profession in various sectors because the professionals serve as a bridge between an organization and its publics. Public relations expertise in stakeholder knowledge, environmental scanning, communication management, and organization–public relationship management makes it an apt profession to handle CSR (Clark, 2000; Steyn, 2007). Empirical studies have identified five roles of public relations in CSR: CSR strategists, philanthropists, value advocates, CSR communicators, and no role. Each role will be discussed.

Public Relations in Strategizing CSR

The role of strategist is equivalent to the significant management role identified by S.-Y. Kim and Reber (2008) after surveying 313 public relations professionals in the United States. Public relations professionals in this role "strongly advise clients or advocate to management on behalf of CSR issues" (p. 339). Typically, these people are members of the dominant coalition or the CSR team in organizations or are senior public relations consultants at agencies. They usually engage in the following activities to contribute to the strategic development of CSR initiatives: (1) persuade management to adopt CSR within organizations (S.-Y. Kim & Reber, 2008); (2) inform ethical CSR decision-making that is situated in the local context by interjecting diverse stakeholder expectations, beliefs, and attitudes to the management discourse, foregrounding marginalized internal voices, and advising on the impact of possible CSR initiatives (Dhanesh, 2013; Reeves, 2016); (3) negotiate new meanings where there is dissensus between organizations and their stakeholders (Dhanesh, 2013); (4) identity and establish strategic partnerships with stakeholders (e.g. governments, nonprofit organizations, and opinion leaders) that facilitate effective CSR performance (Reeves, 2016); (5) conduct a systematic environmental scanning function to detect threats to and opportunities for CSR programs (Heath, 1998; Zurita, 2006); (6) lead the processes for developing a vision statement and code of ethics (S.-Y. Kim & Reber, 2008). This CSR strategist role was the most common among those who participated in S.-Y. Kim and Reber's (2008) study, accounting for 32.9% of the group.

Public Relations in Philanthropy

Philanthropy is a kind of CSR (Carroll, 1991). As S.-Y. Kim and Reber's (2008) empirical data have shown, public relations often serves as the decision-maker in an organization's community or social philanthropic programs such as giving, employee volunteering, and community relations. An emerging trend in CSR shows that employee volunteering has become one of the fundamental CSR activities worldwide owing to its benefits to both the employee (e.g. skill improvement and job enrichment) and the corporation (e.g. reputation) (Cycyota, Ferrante, & Schroeder, 2016). Meanwhile, an effective CSR practice should go beyond giving money because such philanthropy usually would be "an ad-hoc project aimed at short-term social impact" (Zollo, 2004, p. 19). In addition, such philanthropic programs do not create shared experience between the organization and its publics (e.g. employees or nongovernmental organizations) that can result in benefits to the parties.

Public Relations in Value Advocacy

Public relations usually serves as the organization's conscience by safeguarding the organization's ethical standards, advocating CSR as a core value or serving as a role model in the organization (Bowen, 2008; Holtzhausen, 2000; S.-Y. Kim & Reber, 2008). Practicing CSR does not necessarily make an organization ethical. Because the duty of public relations as a profession is to serve the organization and the society, its professionals should engage employees at all levels in the complex ethical and political issues inherent in CSR from the stakeholder's perspective (L'Etang, 2003). This is because CSR should be a shared responsibility or activity conducted by the organization and its employees rather than those in public relations (Benn, Todd, & Pendleton, 2010). Public relations practitioners should also follow ethical guidelines when communicating CSR to avoid manipulative messages that harm the interest of the public or the beneficiary (L'Etang, 2003).

Another example of this role is the aggregator role of public relations identified by Reeves (2016) that focuses on cultivating CSR as an organizational culture and tradition by storytelling, such as publicizing volunteer work done by individual employees. This work would help cement CSR's importance as a core value and allow those employees featured in the publicity pieces to serve as role models for others. Furthermore, when public relations enacts a role in cultivating CSR culture in organizations, practitioners become more involved in the planning and implementation of CSR initiatives because of the leadership support (Reeves, 2016). Such involvement leads to public relations leadership in CSR, which in turn facilitates the development of public relations as a profession (Benn et al., 2010).

Other scholars have provided examples of public relations efforts in advocating CSR at the industrial or national levels. Byrd (2009) found international public relations agencies based in the United States had applied the 10 stipulated principles developed by the United Nations Global Compact to consult their clients on human and environmental issues. Therefore, public relations contributed to CSR development by advancing business adoption of global citizenship initiatives. Having said that, Byrd (2009) also argued that more effort was needed to integrate the principles into the internal functions, especially when dealing with ethical and diversity issues. White, Vanc, and Coman (2011) reported how corporations based in the United States performed their corporate citizenship (i.e. a CSR initiative) in Romania to advocate certain social and political issues using transitional public relations, a public relations function that helps the process of transition in postsocialist economies by adapting to the special conditions of those types of economies (Lawniczak, 2007).

Public Relations in CSR Communication

Practitioners in the role of CSR communicators provide communication to effectively plan, implement, and promote CSR initiatives for maximum positive impact on the organization and its involved stakeholders. They can act as publicist, strategic communicator, or both. A publicist publicizes CSR activities using various (online and offline) communication platforms, tactics, and content without overpromotion of the communicator. A strategic communicator recommends CSR communication strategies that support CSR activities (Reeves, 2016). Whether a public relations professional serves more as a strategic communicator or a publicist for CSR activities depends on the professional's understanding of the business management and the leadership of an organization (Benn el al., 2010).

In the early stage of CSR communication, public relations professionals were largely CSR communicators using external communication to gain positive publicity for CSR activities that address public demands (Bartlett, Tywoniak, & Hatcher, 2007; S.-Y. Kim & Reber, 2008). Later, public relations professionals became strategic communicators who supported CSR activities by shaping public opinion in favor of the organization's community relations and CSR performance using participatory, open processes of two-way communication (Bartlett et al., 2007; Dhanesh, 2013). At this stage, US public relations practitioners utilize "balanced reporting" as a CSR communication tactic to avoid overpromotion or greenwashing (Reeves, 2016). Balanced reporting refers to the use of stories and press releases surrounding a results-focused report; in other words, it is to "humanize" the disseminated CSR information while simultaneously supporting the information with statistics. Most recently, CSR communication has also taken on a form of transparency and engagement that aims to develop CSR initiatives in a collective process involving both the organization and its publics (S. Kim, 2017).

It is worth noting that a comparison of the results of research on public relations roles in CSR in 2008 and 2016 suggests an increasing weight of public relations in CSR communication efforts: 11% of the surveyed participants in 2008 pinpointed the public relations role of CSR communicators (S.-Y. Kim & Reber, 2008), while almost all of the interviewed participants in the 2016 research identified communication as the valuable contribution of public relations to CSR (Reeves, 2016). There are three possible explanations for this trend. First, increasing CSR expectations from the public make CSR communication throughout the entire CSR process – planning, implementation, evaluation, and post-CSR promotion – more significant to organizations in 2016 than it was in 2008. Second, as a result of the increasing CSR expectations, CSR reporting for transparency is now a common, if not required, practice of corporate communication. Lastly, the public relations professionals interviewed contended that with sustainability becoming rooted in every aspect of business, it also needs to be embedded in all internal and external corporate communications (Reeves, 2016).

Public Relations Playing No Role in CSR

Public relations scholars generally conceptualize significant contributions of public relations to CSR because both functions focus on cultivating mutually beneficial organization–public relationships by corporate performance that meets stakeholder expectations (Hung-Baesecke, Chen, & Boyd, 2016). However, some empirical data show that this theoretical argument does not always hold in practice. For example, S.-Y. Kim and Reber (2008) found that public relations played no role in CSR in some companies for several reasons, such as the companies' minimal CSR efforts or public relations practitioners' skepticism of the corporate motives of CSR initiatives. Even though most companies engage in CSR initiatives, Ruiz-Mora, Lugo-Ocando, and Castillo-Esparcia (2016) found no role of public relations in the CSR efforts of Spanish companies. This result is consistent with the finding of Argandoña, Fontrodona, Ramón, and García (2008, cited in Ruiz-Mora et al., 2016) that public relations was largely excluded from CSR in Spanish organizations. Ruiz-Mora et al. (2016) claimed that public relations is necessary in planning and implementing CSR programs because the function excessively involves professional communication to define CSR issues and to engage stakeholders. However, public relations was not involved in CSR in practice for three reasons: (1) public relations practitioners had limited understanding of business, corporate strategies, and sustainability, (2) CSR managers believed they could perform strategic communication despite their lack of skills and knowledge, and (3) CSR programs were largely unidirectional (Ruiz-Mora et al., 2016).

Examples of Theories Used in CSR Communication

There has been a surge of published research on CSR communication in public relations journals. In the past decade (2007 to 2017), there were a total of 60 CSR communication articles published in *Public Relations Review* (50 articles) and *Journal of Public Relations Research* (10 articles). After a thorough review of these articles, we have identified the major theories of research development on this topic in the public relations literature (see also the summary in Table 13.1).

Table 13.1 Examples of public relations theories used in CSR communication

Theories	Short description	Some key references
Stakeholder theory	Focuses on the relationship between an organization and its stakeholders.	Ansoff, 1965; Freeman, 1984; Hasnas, 1998; Carroll, 2004; Porter & Kramer, 2006
Legitimacy theory	Focuses on the corporation's responsibility to follow the expectations and norms of the society in which it operates.	Maignan, Ferrell, & Hult, 1999; Deegan, Rankin, & Tobin, 2002; Branco & Rodrigues, 2006; Arvidsson, 2010
Framing theory	Focuses on how media highlight certain aspects of a topic that they want the audience and/or stakeholder to perceive.	Goffman, 1974; Scheufele, 1999; Steltenpool & Verhoeven, 2012; Bortree, Ahern, Smith, & Dou, 2013

Stakeholder Theory

The stakeholder theory concerns the relationship between an organization and its stakeholders. This theory was first proposed by Ansoff (1965) and received wide attention in the mid-1980s (Freeman, 1984). Freeman (1984) contended that a stakeholder is "any group or individual who can affect or is affected by the achievement of the firm's objectives" (p. 49). Hasnas (1998) posited that organizations should manage the business for the benefit of all the stakeholders, regardless of whether any financial benefits can be generated. The stakeholder theory highlighted stakeholders' right to know about certain corporation behaviors. As a result, corporate social reporting serves as a mechanism for corporations to disclose whether corporations' business operations have met society's expectations, and this disclosure should be responsibility driven, rather than only provided when stakeholders request it (Gray et al., 1996).

Legitimacy Theory

The legitimacy theory argues that a corporation obtains legitimacy by following the expectations and norms of the society in which it operates (Arvidsson, 2010). Hence, Deegan, Rankin, and Tobin (2002) suggested that, in order to gain legitimacy with stakeholders, corporations voluntarily disclose information that is expected by the stakeholders, such as prevention of environmental damage and "employee health and safety issues" (p. 326).

Maignan, Ferrell, and Hult (1999) posited that, according to the rationale of legitimacy theory, when a corporation wants to be perceived as socially responsible, it should make its CSR activities visible to its internal and external stakeholders. Branco and Rodrigues (2006) stated that bigger corporations face more pressure from government and more media scrutiny to be socially responsible than smaller ones. Therefore, having their CSR efforts seen by the society and media is crucial for larger corporations, and this effort can be achieved via corporate communication (Arvidsson, 2010).

Studies employing the stakeholder theory and legitimacy theory in public relations research can be seen through the works of Golob and Bartlett (2007), who investigated CSR communication in Australia and Slovenia, and O'Connor, Shumate, and Meister (2008), who researched the definition and important attributes of CSR perceived by Active Moms (a stakeholder group of mothers aged between 25 and 49 with two or more kids). Their research explained how corporations handled the relationship with stakeholders and how they met stakeholders' expectations. In Golob and Bartlett's article in 2007, the results indicated that organizations' adoption of CSR reporting in both countries was facing market pressures, but due to the differences in foreign investments and social systems, the emergence of CSR reporting in Slovenia was much later than in Australia. Moreover, Australia was adopting a more international standard of CSR reporting, while in Slovenia there was no official standard. Unlike the discussion in Golob and Bartlett's article, which had a global perspective, O'Connor et al. (2008) took a local community as a basis and found that Active Moms perceived CSR as a contested term blending economic, social, rational, and emotional contexts. Moreover, Active Moms assumed CSR was different from, and more than philanthropy, and pointed out the attributes of corporate ethos (honesty, integrity, and character) and community ethos (compatibility, longevity, and accountability).

Framing Theory

Framing theory has been used extensively in research on communication, economics, sociology, psychology, and political science (Borah, 2011). This theory states that by using framing, the media highlight certain aspects of a topic that they want the audience and the stakeholder to know about, or to reinforce certain perceptions of a topic. Research using framing theory with CSR communication includes Bortree et al.'s (2013) study on environmental CSR advertising in *National Geographic* magazine, and Steltenpool and Verhoeven (2012), whose study used framing theory to understand the effect of differently framed CSR messages from various sectors on consumers. In their research, Bortree et al. (2013) tracked the trend, content, and types of environmental CSR communication from 1979 to 2008 in *National Geographic* and identified that a combination of a gain frame (positive message) with a focus on the current generation was the most common strategy. To be more specific, the messages presented in the magazine were mainly about how the readers would be affected personally by the benefits the organizations contributed to the environment. However, Bortree et al.'s study did not find many practices of using the loss frame (negative message) on the current generation, which was most likely to enhance future intended behavior toward the environment (Davis, 1995). In Steltenpool and Verhoeven's (2012) article, the research results indicated that sector/industry was a crucial factor for the effect of CSR communication. For an organization not socially stigmatized (such as an organization producing non-alcoholic drinks, e.g. orange juice), CSR framed messages generated a more positive attitude, better reputation, higher buying intentions, and less skepticism compared to no CSR messages. However, for a socially stigmatized organization (for instance, an organization that produces alcoholic drinks, e.g. Italian martini), the results suggested that CSR messages had adverse effects on customers' perceptions.

Other Related Theories

It is worth noting that since 2012 the research on CSR communication has expanded across geographical boundaries. The 60 CSR communication articles published in these two journals include studies in 20 countries from North and South America, Europe, Africa, and Asia. Besides finding that stakeholder theory is still widely used in CSR communication, we also found more theories emerging in the CSR communication research. For example, scholars tested attribution theory (Garcia, 2011; Shim & Yang, 2016), social identity theory (Ozdora-Aksak, 2015), storytelling (Gill, 2015), synergistic model of corporate communication strategy (e.g., S. Kim, 2011; Fraustino & Connolly-Ahern, 2015), persuasion knowledge model

(Bachmann & Ingenhoff, 2016), strategic issues management (Dhanesh, 2015), and institutional theory (Ozdora-Aksak & Atakan-Duman, 2015; Aksak, Ferguson, & Duman, 2016).

Major Topics/Questions Needing to Be Addressed by Public Relations Theorists Working with CSR

Trends in Topics in CSR Communication

There has been a significant increase of publications on the interaction of public relations and CSR since 2006, as noted by T. H. Lee (2017), who provided a systematic review of 133 peer-reviewed CSR studies published in 11 journals relevant to public relations scholarship from 1980 to 2015. The 133 journal articles included in the analysis could be divided into six research topics: description of CSR practices (n = 27); description of CSR communication (n = 25); effects of CSR (n = 32); conceptual framework (n = 21); role of public relations (n = 16); and stakeholders' perceptions, attitudes, and beliefs (n = 12). Roles of public relations in CSR initiatives and communication seem to be the second-least popular among the six research topics. Among the four time periods (1980–2000, 2001–2005, 2006–2010, and 2011–2015) of T. H. Lee's (2017) analysis, research into the role of public relations in CSR reached its climax in 2006–2010 (n = 10). However, the number of publications on this topic fell to five in 2011–2015. Despite that drop, the total number of CSR publications in public relations scholarship has increased from 50 in 2006–2010 to 73 in 2011–2015. In fact, public relations research in CSR and stakeholder perceptions, attitudes, and beliefs are the only topics that have received less attention in recent years.

Empirical research on the roles public relations assumes in CSR predominantly aims to answer two questions. The primary question asks about the contributions of public relations in planning, performing, and communicating CSR initiatives and comes from the perspective of public relations practitioners. The secondary question discusses the discrepancy between the importance of public relations in CSR theory and the marginalized role of public relations in CSR practice and its causes and implications (Benn et al., 2010; Dhanesh, 2013; S.-Y. Kim & Reber, 2008; Ruiz-Mora et al., 2016; Reeves, 2016).

In addition, we also analyzed CSR communication related topics published in two major public relations journals, *Journal of Public Relations Research* and *Public Relations Review*, for the trends of topics public relations scholars explored in the recent decade (2007–2017). From 2007 to 2011, the foci of CSR communication research were exploring the contents and channels of CSR communication, consumers' awareness of corporate CSR communication, and investigating the context of CSR communication. Most of the studies examined took place in the United States.

From 2012 to 2014, besides seeing more research exploring CSR communication topics in different countries, the most common topics in this field included CSR communication of small and medium-sized enterprises (M. Lee, Mak, & Pang, 2012; Coppa & Sriramesh, 2013; Pastrana & Sriramesh, 2014); CSR communication effects (Steltenpool & Verhoeven, 2012); and strategic CSR communication (Y. Kim, 2014). In the latter study, the topic of CSR skepticism was discussed in a public relations journal for the first time in the recent decade.

From 2015 to 2017, research on strategic CSR communication remained a popular topic (Ozdora-Aksak, 2015; Dhanesh, 2015). In addition, new topics included CSR and organization reputation (Shim & Yang, 2016), CSR fit (Aksak et al., 2016; Lunenberg, Gosselt, & De Jong, 2016), CSR and social media (Fraustino & Connolly-Ahern, 2015; Gaither & Austin, 2016; Uzunoglu, Turkel, & Akyar, 2017), CSR skepticism (Rim & Kim, 2016), and CSR disclosure (Bachmann & Ingenhoff, 2016; Devin, 2016).

Summarizing the trends of CSR communication topics in recent years, it is clear that researchers' focus has gone beyond exploring how corporations communicate their CSR initiatives.

The development of the research topic has evolved from an explanation of why corporations should engage in CSR communication, to how to communicate, to the benefits of CSR communication, and to communicating CSR in the digital era. Moreover, due to the public expectations for corporate disclosure, CSR communication research also reflects the importance of CSR reporting. Another development worth discussing is the skepticism people have about the motives of CSR communication. This topic has been discussed extensively in the business literature and is becoming a significant factor for the discussion of CSR fit.

A New Development: Creating Shared Values

Criticism of CSR motivations has received much attention. For example, publics will be skeptical of corporate CSR intentions if corporations cannot provide an ethical alignment in their operations (Hollender & Breen, 2010). Scholars also have suggested that CSR initiatives fail to accomplish corporate missions because of corporations' focus on short-term profits without attending to stakeholders' actual needs and concerns (Wójcik, 2016). Responding to the criticism of corporate motivations for performing CSR, Porter and Kramer (2011) proposed the new concept of creating shared values (CSV). CSV refers to "policies and operating practices which enhance the competitiveness of a company while simultaneously advancing the economic and social conditions in the communities in which it operates" (p. 66). Porter and Kramer (2011) also identified CSV as a new way of doing business by both gaining credibility from stakeholders and improving economic and social conditions of the market.

CSV differs from CSR in two ways. First, CSV is internally driven (Wójcik, 2016) inasmuch as CSV *increases total economic and social values* rather than redistributing "values already created by the firm" (D. Lee et al., 2014, p. 461). Furthermore, CSV *integrates social issues with the firm's core business innovation* through operational changes and/or technical support, while CSR initiatives can be separate from the business practice. Hence, CSV is integral to the corporate core business and strategy framework (Wójcik, 2016).

While this concept has gained attention in business scholarship, little has been explored in public relations research. The advantage of CSV is that it can help corporations reach a win-win business outcome because stakeholders' issues and concerns can be integrated into business operations. For example, the first two authors of this chapter adopted the CSV concept and explored publics' perceptions of this concept (Hung-Baesecke et al., 2018). The in-depth interviews conducted in the United States and China showed discrepancies in what people believe are the benefits of CSV. For example, Chinese publics interviewed tended to trust CSV-performing corporations, while their US counterparts trusted such corporations less. However, both US and Chinese publics had positive perceptions of CSV-performing corporations.

The CSV approach provides a direction for corporations to strategically integrate stakeholders' values and societal issues into their policies and strategies. The outcomes can be win-win because corporate behaviors, while directed at profit seeking, provide solutions toward resolving societal problems and at the same time enhance corporate competitive advantage in innovative ways. The context of CSV can be explained by the case of Starbucks in the next section.

In this chapter, we have discussed the importance of CSR, public relations roles in CSR, public relations theories used in CSR communication research, and trends of topics in CSR communication research, and offer a case study on a new trend of a corporation's combined motives in serving society. Many studies have illustrated the positive aspects of rewards when corporations perform CSR. The topics in CSR research have expanded to integrate multiple disciplines for evaluating the benefits and outcomes of CSR. Even though there is a debate as to whether public relations should have a role in CSR, it is essential for public relations to take advantage of being a corporate boundary spanner and be a strong advocate to corporations to be morally and socially responsible. We consider that by doing so, public relations can fulfill its role in the society.

Suggested Case to Explore to Demonstrate Theory at Work in CSR

Starbucks is an example of success through stakeholder engagement. The coffee shop, Starbucks, was founded on March 30, 1971, by Jerry Baldwin, Zev Siegl, and Gordon Bowker at Pike Place Market in Seattle. Over the years, the company has operated the business by following the corporate mission, which is "to inspire and nurture the human spirit – one person, one cup, and one neighborhood at a time." Moreover, Starbucks has been strongly positioning itself as a corporation committed to connecting with people and communities. For example, Starbucks shows respect to its employees by calling them "partners," and established a community website, My Starbucks Idea, for engaging with customers (Hung-Baesecke, 2014). In addition, by being a responsible corporate citizen and following the corporate mission, Starbucks has been dedicated to ethical sourcing, green retailing, community engagement, and partner career development.

However, with a rapid corporate expansion in different markets, Starbucks experienced two consecutive years of the slowest financial growth. Employees in the company felt they were not connected with it as the focus of the corporate operation was on business expansion. Worse, the company's stock price fell to its lowest on November 20, 2008 in the wake of the Lehman Brothers financial crisis. The company had overcome the crisis by the end of 2010, and then launched a global campaign to reconnect to the stakeholders and to demonstrate its healthy financial situation in the celebration of its fortieth anniversary in 2011. By working with the Edelman public relations firm, Starbucks linked stakeholders to some important events, such as the fortieth anniversary, developed a new brand logo, and organized special community and employee engagement events for five months.

The success of this campaign was clear: at the end of the campaign, Starbucks revenues had increased 11% compared with the previous year, reaching a record $11.7 billion for the fiscal year. In addition, there was a 40% rise in consumer favorability of the brand. Several factors contributed to the success of Starbucks in transforming the brand (and eventually winning the Holmes Report's Gold Sabre Award for 2012): engaging important stakeholders, for example, the customers, the partners (employees), the community, and financial influencers for better conveying the brand values; announcing a new brand evolution model and logo; and reinforcing to the stakeholders what Starbucks does best in promoting a quality coffee experience.

In January 2017, responding to the global refugee crisis, Howard Schultz, the CEO, announced that the company would employ ten thousand refugees in its coffee shops in its markets around the world in the following five years, although right after this announcement a hashtag, #boycottstarbucks, appeared on social media as American consumers considered Starbucks was not considering the employment problem in the United States. As a committed corporate citizen, Starbucks still incorporated this initiative in its community engagement efforts (Starbucks, 2017). Starbucks has long been advocated for its "people-oriented culture," and its case is well explained by Gregory's (2007) view on "negotiated brand," in which corporations work with stakeholders and respond to their inputs so as to help bring corporate and brand competitiveness. Furthermore, by utilizing the stakeholder theory, creating shared values, and legitimacy theory, the company's CSR engagements can be explained as follows.

The stakeholder theory states that corporate operations need to meet the expectations of stakeholders, instead of merely shareholders, and corporate behaviors should be accountable to the stakeholders. In its business pursuit before the 2008 financial crisis, Starbucks demonstrated corporations' ignorance of other stakeholders: employees and customers, for example. The price Starbucks paid was great financial loss in the stock market and disengagement from employees. By a series of actions taken in its global stakeholder engagement campaign in 2011, Starbucks was able to regain confidence from its employees and to maintain stable customer growth.

From the legitimacy theory perspective, organizations are able to continue operation and existence when social expectations are met. Therefore, organizations are expected to show that their business operations also benefit society. Starbucks, by its constant communications on social media, its corporate website, and annual reports on the corporation's CSR behavior, demonstrated that it was a corporation committed to giving back to society and making an effort to be recognized as a responsible corporate citizen.

From the perspective of creating shared values, Starbucks ensured that the way it behaved in its business operation conformed to social expectations through its ethical support for suppliers and the principle of inclusion by providing job opportunities to help refugees. At the same time, quality products from suppliers and contributions of refugee employees also benefit the company's bottom lines.

Discussion Questions

1   Examine and discuss the CSR objectives of corporations in various industrial sectors.

2   Discuss and evaluate the social issues addressed by multinational corporations in different regions.

3   Discuss the corporate social agenda and its related practices of corporations from the stakeholder perspective.

4   Examine the communication of CSR strategies and/or activities of corporations in their visual and/or behavioral aspects.

5   Evaluate the communication of CSR of corporations on social media platforms.

6   Discuss the different effects and outcomes of CSR communication.

7   Discuss the skepticism of corporate CSR initiatives.

Suggested Readings

Chatterji, A., & Levine, D. (2006). Breaking down the wall of codes: Evaluating non-financial performance measurement. *California Management Review, 48*(2), 29–51.

Lee, T. H. (2017). The status of corporate social responsibility research in public relations: A content analysis of published articles in eleven scholarly journals from 1980 to 2015. *Public Relations Review, 43*, 211–218.

Porter, M. E., & Kramer, M. R. (2011). Creating shared value. *Harvard Business Review, 89*(1/2), 62–77.

Reeves, H. (2016). Defining public relations' role in corporate social responsibility programs. *PR Journal, 10*(2). Retrieved from https://prjournal.instituteforpr.org/wp-content/uploads/reeves_nz3.pdf

White, C., Vanc, A., & Coman, I. (2011). Corporate social responsibility in transitional countries: Public relations as a component of public diplomacy in Romania. *International Journal of Strategic Communication, 5*, 281–292.

References

Aksak, E. O., Ferguson, M. A., & Duman, S. A. (2016). Corporate social responsibility and CSR fit as predictors of corporate reputation: A global perspective. *Public Relations Review, 42*, 79–81. doi:10.1016/j.pubrev.2015.11.004

Ansoff, I. (1965). *Corporate strategy.* New York: McGraw-Hill.

Argandoña, A., Fontrodona, J., Ramón, J. & Garcìa, P. (2008). *El perfil emergente del directivo de RSC* [The emerging profile of the CSR manager]. Barcelona: Documento de Investigación DI-756.

Arvidsson, S. (2010), Communication of corporate social responsibility: A study of the views of management teams in large companies. *Journal of Business Ethics, 96*(3), 339–354.

Bachmann, P., & Ingenhoff, D. (2016). Legitimacy through CSR disclosures? The advantage outweighs the disadvantages. *Public Relations Review, 42*, 386–394. doi:10.1016/j.pubrev.2016.02.008

Bartlett, J. L. (2011). Public relations and corporate social responsibility. In Ø. Ihlen, J. L., Bartlett, & S. May (Eds.), *The handbook of communication and corporate social responsibility* (pp. 67–86). Oxford: John Wiley & Sons.

Bartlett, J. L., Tywoniak, S., & Hatcher, C. A. (2007). Public relations professional practice and the institutionalisation of CSR. *Journal of Communication Management, 11*(4), 281–299.

Benn, S., Todd, L. R., & Pendleton, J. (2010). Public relations leadership in corporate social responsibility. *Journal of Business Ethics, 96*, 403–423.

Beurden, P., & Gossling, T. (2008). The worth of values: A literature review on the relation between corporate social and financial performance. *Journal of Business Ethics, 82*, 407–424.

Borah, P. (2011). Conceptual issues in framing theory: A systematic examination of a decade's literature. *Journal of Communication, 61*, 246–263.

Bortree, D. S., Ahern, L., Smith, A. N., & Dou, X. (2013). Framing environmental responsibility: 30 years of CSR messages in *National Geographic* magazine. *Public Relations Review, 39*, 491–496. doi:10.1016/j.pubrev.2013.07.003

Bowen, S. A. (2008). A state of neglect: Public relations as "corporate conscience" or ethics counsel. *Journal of Public Relations Research, 20*, 271–296.

Bowie, N. (1991). New directions in corporate social responsibility. *Business Horizons, 34*(4), 56–66.

Branco, M., & Rodrigues, L. C. (2006). Corporate social responsibility and resource-based perspectives. *Journal of Business Ethics, 69*, 111–132.

Byrd, L. S. (2009). Collaborative corporate social responsibility: A case study examination of the international public relations agency involvement in the United Nations Global Compact. *Corporate Communications, 14*(3), 303–319.

Carroll, A. B. (1983). Corporate social responsibility: Will industry respond to cut-backs in social program funding? *Vital Speeches of the Day, 49*, 604–608.

Carroll, A. B. (1991). The pyramid of corporate social responsibility: Toward the moral management of organizational stakeholders. *Business Horizons, 34*, 39–48.

Carroll, A. B. (2004). Managing ethically with global stakeholders: A present and future challenge. *Academy of Management Executive, 18*(2), 114–120.

Clark, C. E. (2000). Differences between public relations and corporate social responsibility: An analysis. *Public Relations Review, 26,* 363–380.

Cochran, R., & Wood, R. (1984). Corporate social responsibility and financial performance. *Academy of Management Journal, 27*(1), 42–56.

Cone. (2017). *2017 Cone Communications CSR study.* Retrieved from http://www.conecomm. com/research-blog/2017-csr-study?rq=CSR%20study

Coppa, M., & Sriramesh, K. (2013). Corporate social responsibility among SMEs in Italy. *Public Relations Review, 39,* 30–39. doi:10.1016/j.pubrev.2012.09.009

Cycyota, C. S., Ferrante, C. J., & Schroeder, J. M. (2016). Corporate social responsibility and employee volunteerism: What do the best companies do? *Business Horizons, 59,* 321–329.

Davis, J. (1995). The effects of message framing on response to environmental communication. *Journalism and Mass Communication Quarterly, 72*(2), 285–299.

Dawkins, J., & Lewis, S. (2003). CSR in stakeholder expectations: And their implication for company strategy. *Journal of Business Ethics, 44*(2/3), 185–193.

Deegan, C., Rankin, M., & Tobin, J. (2002). An examination of the corporate social and environmental disclosures of BHP from 1983–1997: A test of legitimacy theory. *Accounting, Auditing & Accountability Journal, 15*(3), 312–343.

Devin, B. (2016). Half-truths and dirty secrets: Omissions in CSR communication. *Public Relations Review, 42*(1), 226–228. doi:10.1016/j.pubrev.2015.09.004

Dhanesh, G. S. (2013). Building communities: The postmodern CSR practitioner as a dialectical activist-agent in India. *Public Relations Review, 39,* 398–402.

Dhanesh, G. S. (2015). The paradox of communicating CSR in India: Minimalist and strategic approaches. *Journal of Public Relations Research, 27*(5), 431–451. doi:10.1080/10627 26X.2015.1084583

Donaldson, T., & Preston, L. E. (1995). The stakeholder theory of the corporation: Concepts, evidence, and implications. *Academy of Management Review, 20*(1), 65–91.

Du, S., Bhattacharya, C. B., & Sen, S. (2010). Maximizing business returns to corporate social responsibility (CSR): The role of CSR communication. *International Journal of Management Reviews, 12*(1), 8–19.

European Commission. (2012). *Responsible business: a key to competitiveness.* Retrieved from https://ec.europa.eu/growth/content/responsible-business-key-competitiveness-0_en

Fombrun, C. J., & Gardberg, N. A. (2000). Opportunity platforms safety nets: Corporate citizenship and reputational risk. *Business & Society Review, 105*(1), 85–106.

Fombrun, C. J., & Shanley, M. (1990). What's in a name? Reputation building and corporate strategy. *Academy of Management Journal, 33*(2), 233–258.

Fraustino, J. D., & Connolly-Ahern, C. (2015). Corporate associations written on the wall: Publics' responses to Fortune 500 ability and social responsibility Facebook posts. *Journal of Public Relations Research, 27*(5), 452–474. doi:10.1080/1062726X.2015.1098543

Freeman, R. E. (1984). *Strategic management: A stakeholder approach.* New York: Oxford University Press.

Gaither, B. M., & Austin, L. (2016). Campaign and corporate goals in conflict: Exploring company–issue congruence through a content analysis of Coca-Cola's twitter feed. *Public Relations Review, 42,* 698–709. doi:10.1016/j.pubrev.2016.07.001

García, M. M. (2011). Perception is truth: How US newspapers framed the "Go Green" conflict between BP and Greenpeace. *Public Relations Review, 37,* 57–59.

Garriga, E., & Mele, D. (2004). Corporate social responsibility theories: Mapping the territory. *Journal of Business Ethics, 53*(1–2), 51–71.

Gill, R. (2015). Why the PR strategy of storytelling improves employee engagement and adds value to CSR: An integrated literature review. *Public Relations Review, 41*, 662–674. doi:10.1016/j.pubrev.2014.02.012

Goffman, E. (1974). *Frame analysis: An essay on the organization of experience.* Cambridge, MA: Harvard University Press.

Golob, U., & Bartlett, J. L. (2007). Communicating about corporate social responsibility: A comparative study of CSR reporting in Australia and Slovenia. *Public Relations Review, 33*, 1–9. doi:10.1016/j.pubrev.2006.11.001

Gray, R., Owen, D., & Adams, C. (1996). *Accounting and accountability: Changes and challenges in corporate social and environmental reporting.* London: Prentice Hall.

Gregory, A. (2007). Involving stakeholders in developing corporate brands: The communication dimension. *Journal of Marketing Management, 23*(1–2), 59–73.

Hasnas, J. (1998). The normative theories of business ethics: A guide for the perplexed. *Business Ethics Quarterly, 8*(1), 19–42.

Heath, R. L. (1998). New communication technologies: An issues management point of view. *Public Relations Review, 24*, 273–288.

Hollender, J., & Breen, B. (2010). *The responsibility revolution: How the next generation of business will win.* San Francisco: Jossey-Bass.

Holtzhausen, D. R. (2000). Postmodern values in public relations. *Journal of Public Relations Research, 12*(1), 93–114.

Hong Kong Council of Social Service. (2017). *3,478 companies in Hong Kong recognized by the 2016–2017 Caring Company scheme.* Press release. Retrieved from http://www.hkcss.org.hk/e/cont_detail.asp?type_id=9&content_id=3821

Hung-Baesecke, C. J. F. (2014). Success through stakeholder engagement: The Starbucks example. In J. V. Turk, J. Paluszek, & J. Valin (Eds.), *Public relations case studies from around the globe.* New York: Peter Lang.

Hung-Baesecke, C. J. F., Chen, Y. R., & Boyd, B. (2016). Corporate social responsibility, media source preference, trust, and public engagement: The informed public's perspective. *Public Relations Review, 42*, 591–599.

Hung-Baesecke, C. F. J., Chen, Y. R., Stacks, D. S., Coombs, W. T., & Boyd, B. (2018). Creating shared value, public trust, supportive behavior, and communication preferences: A comparison study in the United States and China. *Public Relations Journal, 11*(4). Retrieved from https://prjournal.instituteforpr.org/wp-content/uploads/Flora-Final.pdf

Hur, W. M., Kim, H., & Woo, J. (2014). How CSR leads to corporate brand equity: Mediating mechanisms of corporate brand credibility and reputation. *Journal of Business Ethics, 125*(1), 75–86.

Kay, J. (1993). *Foundations of corporate success.* Oxford: Oxford University Press.

Kim, S. (2011). Transferring effects of CSR strategy on consumer responses: The synergistic model of corporate communication strategy. *Journal of Public Relations Research, 23*(2), 218–241.

Kim, S. (2017). The process model of corporate social responsibility (CSR) communication: CSR communication and its relationship with consumers' CSR knowledge, trust, and corporate reputation perception. *Journal of Business Ethics.* https://doi.org/10.1007/s10551-017-3433-6

Kim, S.-Y., & Reber, B. H. (2008). Public relations' place in corporate social responsibility: Practitioners define their role. *Public Relations Review, 34*, 337–342.

Kim, Y. (2014). Strategic communication of corporate social responsibility (CSR): Effects of stated motives and corporate reputation on stakeholder responses. *Public Relations Review, 40*, 838–840.

KPMG International. (2011). *KPMG International survey of corporate responsibility reporting 2011.* Amstelveen, The Netherlands: KPMG International.

Lawniczak, R. (2007). Public relations role in global competition "to sell" alternative political and socio-economic models of market economy. *Public Relations Review, 33*, 377–386.

Lee, D., Moon, J., Cho, J., Kang, H.-G., & Jeong, J. (2014). From corporate social responsibility to creating shared value with suppliers through mutual firm foundation in the Korean bakery industry: A case study of the SPC Group. *Asia Pacific Business Review, 20*(3), 461–483.

Lee, M. H., Mak, A. K., & Pang, A. (2012). Bridging the gap: An exploratory study of corporate social responsibility among SMEs in Singapore. *Journal of Public Relations Research, 24*(4), 299–317.

Lee, T. H. (2017). The status of corporate social responsibility research in public relations: A content analysis of published articles in eleven scholarly journals from 1980 to 2015. *Public Relations Review, 43*, 211–218.

Leonard, D., & McAdam, R. (2003). Quality and ethics: Corporate social responsibility. *Quality Progress, 36*(10), 27–32.

L'Etang, J. (2003). The myth of the ethical guardian: An examination of its origins, potency and illusions. *Journal of Communication Management, 8*(1), 53–67.

Lev, B., Petrovits, C., & Radhakrishnan, S. (2010). Is doing good good for you? Yes, charitable contributions enhance revenue growth. *Strategic Management Journal, 31*(2), 182–200.

Looser, S., & Wehrmeyer, W. (2016). Ethics of the firm, for the firm or in the firm? Purpose of extrinsic and intrinsic CSR in Switzerland. *Social Responsibility Journal, 12*(3), 545–570.

Lunenberg, K., Gosselt, J. F., & De Jong, M. D. T. (2016). Framing CSR fit: How corporate social responsibility activities are covered by news media. *Public Relations Review, 42*(5), 943–951. doi:10.1016/j.pubrev.2015.11.016

Maignan, I., Ferrell, O. C., & Hult, G. T. M. (1999). Corporate citizenship: Cultural antecedents and business benefits. *Journal of the Academy of Marketing Science, 27*, 455–469.

McGuire, J., Sundgren, A., & Schneeweis, T. (1988). Corporate social responsibility and firm financial performance. *Academy of Management Journal, 31*(4), 854–872.

McLaughlin, J. (2017). Rolex, Lego, and Disney top Reputation Institute's 2017 Global RepTrak® 100 – the world's largest corporate reputation study. Retrieved from http://www.prweb.com/releases/2017/03/prweb14104502.htm

Moon, J. (2002). Business social responsibility and new governance. *Government and Opposition, 37*(3), 385–408.

O'Connor, A., Shumate, M., & Meister, M. (2008). Walk the line: Active moms define corporate social responsibility. *Public Relations Review, 34*(4), 343–350. doi:10.1016/j.pubrev.2008.06.005

Ozdora-Aksak, E. (2015). An analysis of Turkey's telecommunications sector's social responsibility practices online. *Public Relations Review, 41*, 365–369. doi:10.1016/j.pubrev.2015.01.001

Ozdora-Aksak, E., & Atakan-Duman, S. (2015). The online presence of Turkish banks: Communicating the softer side of corporate identity. *Public Relations Review, 41*, 119–128. doi:10.1016/j.pubrev.2014.10.004

Pastrana, N. A., & Sriramesh, K. (2014). Corporate social responsibility: Perceptions and practices among SMEs in Colombia. *Public Relations Review, 40*, 14–24. doi:10.1016/j.pubrev.2013.10.002

Pfau, M., Haigh, M., Sims, J., & Wigley, S. (2009). The Influence of corporate social responsibility campaigns on public opinion. *Corporate Reputation Review, 11*(2), 145–154.

Pistoni, A., Songini, L., & Perrone, O. (2016). The how and why of a firm's approach to CSR and sustainability: A case study of a large European company. *Journal of Management Governance, 20*, 655–685.

Porter, M. E., & Kramer, M. R. (2006). The link between competitive advantage and corporate social responsibility. *Harvard Business Review, 84*(12), 78–92.

Porter, M. E., & Kramer, M. R. (2011). Creating shared value. *Harvard Business Review, 89*(1/2), 62–77.

Reeves, H. (2016). Defining public relations' role in corporate social responsibility programs. *PR Journal*, *10*(2). Retrieved from https://prjournal.instituteforpr.org/wp-content/uploads/reeves_nz3.pdf

Reputation Institute (2016). *7 dimensions of reputation.* Retrieved from https://www.reputationinstitute.com/why-reputation-institute

Rim, H., & Kim, S. (2016). Dimensions of corporate social responsibility (CSR) skepticism and their impacts on public evaluations toward CSR. *Journal of Public Relations Research*, *28*(5–6), 248–267. doi:10.1080/1062726X.2016.1261702

Ruiz-Mora, I., Lugo-Ocando, J., & Castillo-Esparcia, A. (2016). Reluctant to talk, reluctant to listen: Public relations professionals and their involvement in CSR programmes in Spain. *Public Relations Review*, *42*, 402–407.

Scheufele, D. A. (1999). Framing as a theory of media effects. *Journal of Communication*, *49*(1), 103–122.

Shim, K., & Yang, S. (2016). The effect of bad reputation: The occurrence of crisis, corporate social responsibility, and perceptions of hypocrisy and attitudes toward a company. *Public Relations Review*, *42*, 68–78. doi:10.1016/j.pubrev.2015.11.009

Solomon, R. C. (1992). *Ethics and excellence.* New York: Oxford University Press.

Starbucks. (2017). Starbucks makes global commitment to hire 10,000 refugees by 2022. Retrieved from https://www.starbucks.com/responsibility/community/refugee-hiring

Steltenpool, G. J., & Verhoeven, P. (2012). Sector-dependent framing effects of corporate social responsibility messages: An experiment with non-alcoholic and alcoholic drinks. *Public Relations Review*, *38*, 627–629. doi:10.1016/j.pubrev.2012.06.008

Steyn, B. (2007). Contribution of public relations to organisational strategy formulation. In E. L. Toth (Ed.), *The future of excellence in public relations and communication management* (pp. 137–172). Mahwah, NJ: Lawrence Erlbaum.

Sun, J., & Stuebs, M. (2013). Corporate social responsibility and firm productivity: Evidence from the chemical industry in the United States. *Journal of Business Ethics*, *118*(2), 251–263.

Tsoutsoura, M. (2004). *Corporate social responsibility and financial performance: The "virtuous circle" revisited.* Working Paper, University of California at Berkeley.

Uzunoglu, E., Turkel, S., & Akyar, B. Y. (2017). Engaging consumers through corporate social responsibility messages on social media: An experimental study. *Public Relations Review*, *43*(5), 989–997. https://dx.doi.org/10.1016/j.pubrev.2017.03.013

Vanhamme, J., & Grobben, B. (2009). "Too good to be true!" The effectiveness of CSR history in countering negative publicity. *Journal of Business Ethics*, *85*, 273–283.

Van Marrewijk, M. (2003). Concept and definitions of CSR and corporate sustainability: Between agency and communion. *Journal of Business Ethics*, *44*(2/3), 95–105.

Vidaver-Cohen, D., & Altman, B. W. (2000). Corporate citizenship in the new millennium: Foundation for an architecture of excellence. *Business and Society Review*, *105*(1), 145–169.

Vilanova, M., Lozano, J., & Arenas, D. (2009). Exploring the nature of the relationship between CSR and competitiveness. *Journal of Business Ethics*, *87*, 57–69.

Waddock, S., & Graves, S. (1997). The corporate social performance: Financial performance link. *Strategic Management Journal*, *18*(4), 303–319.

Wheeler, D., Colbert, B., & Freeman, R. E. (2003). Focusing on value: Reconciling corporate social responsibility, sustainability and a stakeholder approach in a network world. *Journal of General Management*, *28*(3), 1–27.

White, C., Vanc, A., & Coman, I. (2011). Corporate social responsibility in transitional countries: Public relations as a component of public diplomacy in Romania. *International Journal of Strategic Communication*, *5*, 281–292.

Williams, R. J., & Barrett, J. D. (2000). Corporate philanthropy, criminal activity and firm reputation: Is there a link? *Journal of Business Ethics, 26*(4), 341–350.

Wójcik, P. (2016). How creating shared value differs from corporate social responsibility. *Journal of Management and Business Administration: Central Europe, 24*(2), 32–55.

Zollo, M. (2004). Philanthropy or CSR: A strategic choice. In European Business Forum (Ed.), *EBF on ... corporate social responsibility* (pp. 18–19). London: European Business Forum. Retrieved from http://johnelkington.com/archive/ebf_CSR_report.pdf

Zurita, P. C. (2006). *We are socially responsible: A framing analysis of corporate public relations and their corporate social responsibility messages* (master's thesis). University of Georgia, Athens, GA.

14

Health Public Relations

Shelley Aylesworth-Spink

A dog licks its owner's face on a cardiac rehabilitation clinic website, illustrating how pets can reduce the risk of heart disease. A new sunscreen product launches on social media and in local media outlets with a search for a region's most family-friendly beach. A hospital president speaks at a press conference about measures to stop a virus raging among patients and worrying the community.

Such tactics are found in the growing field of health public relations, a specialization that involves the disciplines of public relations and health communication.

This chapter focuses on health public relations, an area of practice and theory driven by the specific motivations and interests of organizations. Health public relations has been defined as the strategic planning, implementation, and evaluation of communication tactics for purposes of influencing health attitudes, knowledge, behaviors, and decision-making (Aldoory & Austin, 2011). While health communication may be more broadly defined as the ways in which people perceive and act on information about their overall health and health chances, health public relations focuses on achieving objectives and goals specific to the sponsoring business, nonprofit, governmental, or nongovernmental organization.

Unquestionably, both fields impact people's lives through communication.

Defining the Concepts: What Is Health Public Relations?

Health communication tends to promote informed decision-making that improves health. With its focus on theory, research, and practice, health communication analyzes and refines the relationship between communication and health, health beliefs, and health and risk behavior (Cline, 2011). Regardless of whether that information intends to affect health outcomes, health communication is a process through which an individual or an audience engages, either directly or indirectly, with information that can influence health-relevant beliefs and actions (Stephenson, Southwell, & Yzer, 2011).

As a broad field, health communication can involve health educators, health communication practitioners, and public relations practitioners, some of whom have medical or health-related education and training. Most areas of focus in health communication promote health information, such as public health campaigns, health education, and improved or targeted communication between doctors or health professionals and patients. Health promotion campaigns, for example, often use communication strategies to disseminate relevant and compelling information that can help at-risk populations resist serious health threats (Kreps, 2011).

Public Relations Theory: Application and Understanding, First Edition. Edited by Brigitta R. Brunner.
© 2019 John Wiley & Sons, Inc. Published 2019 by John Wiley & Sons, Inc.

Immunization campaigns target influenza or childhood diseases, while other health promotions seek to limit the spread of sexually transmitted diseases, reduce alcohol and drug use, or promote mental health awareness and resources.

Health public relations also seeks to inform individuals and audiences. However, tactics and strategies aim to change behavior in specific ways to use certain medications or treatments, adopt health practices, or use and trust specific health providers. Public relations campaigns here are in support of business or organizational needs.

Health public relations is a rapidly expanding field that has had its place within the health industry for more than 40 years (R. Thomas, 2006) and within hospital practice specifically since the 1960s (Gordon & Kelly, 1999). Health public relations practitioners work in health and medical public relations agencies; in-house for pharmaceutical and research companies or health organizations; in the public sector such as for hospitals, charities, academic and research institutes, or government departments of health; for advocacy groups and organizations; or for nongovernmental organizations.

Public relations activities range from supporting the promotion of new health and medical treatments and services, to advancing the reputation of a health-care or medical research organization, campaigning for patient rights groups or government campaigns to communicate health policy changes, or establishing the advocacy position for health regulatory bodies.

Health communication and health public relations professionals often coexist. For example, in a hospital, a patient may receive information from a nurse practitioner or dietician about managing a new diagnosis of diabetes. In the same hospital, a public relations professional focuses on the hospital's reputation and overall communication strategies. The public relations practitioner works to convince the local press to write a feature story about the hospital's innovative approach to diabetes education by providing media access to the nurse practitioner who designed the program and their patient.

This chapter reviews theories that relate to health public relations. Given the complexities and deep societal implications of health, health care and disease, drawing from a range of not only public relations but social theories offers the wide scope needed to analyze the ways that health public relations shapes the world around us. Such an interdisciplinary approach helps scholars examine and question the role of public relations as a rapidly changing social force.

The following theories are reviewed with examples of studies and practices to illustrate each: risk communication theory, cultural theory of risk communication, relationship theory of risk, uncertainty management theory, uncertainty reduction theory, problem integration theory, narrative theory, organization–public relationship theory, and situational theory of publics. The chapter ends with discussion questions and suggested further reading.

How and Why Is Health Communication of Concern to Public Relations?

Health and human well-being affect everyone. No sector is untouched by interests in biological matters, and thus the ways in which information is shaped, appears, is missing, or changes is a vast field of operations and concern for health public relations scholars and practitioners.

The global landscape is also increasingly challenging. Myriad publics, interests, and multisector organizations churn around matters of health, many of which have messages specific to their concerns. Around the world, people are living longer and sicker lives, increasing the burden on health services, budgets, and the workforce (Chan, 2017). Unparalleled attention comes during times of ill-health or widespread threats to health, and for good reason. In this century, new human pathogens have emerged such as severe acute respiratory syndrome, commonly known as SARS, and several influenza viruses, and older diseases have reappeared, including Ebola and Zika virus disease (Chan, 2017). In the United States alone, a leading priority of the Centers for Disease Control and Prevention is to improve health security at home and around the world (CDC, 2016). The CDC recognizes the enormous suffering, deaths, and economic implications of the spread of infectious disease, with foodborne illnesses alone numbering 48 million and costing more than $15.5 billion each year (CDC, 2016).

Shifting demographic, economic, and geopolitical realities give rise to public relations considerations targeting aging populations or the relationship between lifestyle and health as it affects obesity or cardiovascular disease. The World Health Organization finds that while 800 million people are chronically hungry worldwide, some countries have adult populations of whom more than 70% are obese or overweight (Chan, 2017).

The capacity of public relations scholars and practitioners to understand cultural concerns around the world is made more necessary by the intensification of migration and the related health effects. All the while, access to disease prevention, diagnosis, and treatment confounds and threats companies, governments, and states alike.

This section outlines several problematics that result from deepening interests in health: increasing and competing actors; changing health interventions; expanding and shifting knowledge of human health; the use of communication technologies among mobilizing publics; and the wider ethical implications when public relations theory and practice involves life itself.

Unrelenting Somatic Interests

Health issues are personal, often demanding immediate and high levels of interaction and information. People view their health circumstance as unique and personal, yet health public relations can involve strategies and practices that apply across publics or audiences with many common traits. This tension between the individual experience of health and the state of health among populations often shifts the definition and perspectives of risk, for example.

Above all, interests are shared about the possibility of health discovery, cure, treatment, or prevention. Medical science holds promise. People now operate in a hopeful state, one that features human suffering as "knowable, mutable, improvable, eminently manipulable" (Rose & Novas, 2005, p. 442). To be human is to endure, always knowing that one's biology is fragile yet capable of protection and treatment.

This hopeful state, and adding a unique dimension to the study and practice of health public relations, contains the framework of "biological citizenship." What counts as citizenship now includes novel practices and new identities (Bakardjieva, 2009). As noted by a remarkable number of scholars, our citizenship is now encased in our very existence as biological forms (Agamben, 1998; Epstein, 2007; Foucault, 1991; Isin, 2002, 2004; Rose, 2007; Petryna, 2004). Thus, our biological identities, in addition to political identities, increasingly ground claims to the idea of citizenship.

The biological citizen is the emerging identity, a new citizen who sees claims to rights prioritized on a cycle of creating, problematizing, and resolving issues of bodily experience as they link to their fellow citizens and distinguish themselves from others on biological terms (Rose & Novas, 2005; Rose, 2007). These claims involve people expressing their connection to a nation, and to each other, for their health needs, practices, and desires.

Most importantly, states have become highly visible as biopolitical by taking an active interest in population health. In turn, the rise in the number of health-related technologies continues to increase the scope and scale of diagnostic and therapeutic interventions. Citizens respond by turning their gaze toward concerns for their own health. This interest leads to claims to certain biological rights, including health-care systems, treatment, and healthier standards of living. Thus, biological concerns have become a shared point of both interrogation and concern among the state, related companies, and its citizens. In this evolving landscape, for example, the role of the media and public relations practices intensifies the focus by all interested parties.

Mobilizing Online around Health Concerns

Just as people demand certain health rights based on their biology, they also mobilize as disease- and illness-related groups and forums, actions made simple through digital communications. Social media suit health concerns well, for example. And people favor immediate information online when faced with a troubling health condition (Avery et al., 2010).

It is no surprise, then, that health information is one of the most riveting topics for news consumers (Brodie et al., 2003). In 2013, 72% of US internet users said they had looked online for health information within the past year (Fox & Duggan, 2013). The most commonly researched topics are specific diseases or conditions, treatments, or procedures and doctors or other health professionals. Most adults turn to a medical professional, family, or friends when faced with a serious health issue. However, those living with chronic and rare conditions are much more likely to go online to find others with similar health problems (Fox, 2011).

"Health information seeking behaviors" is a phenomenon that can be traced to several trends. Patients are increasingly active in treatment choices, self-monitoring, and self-care. Some have argued that health blogs allow patients to deal with their illness just as they inform and influence others (Sundar, Edwards, Hifeng, & Stavrositu, 2007). Integrated and cross-promotional health public relations efforts are another trend influencing this behavior. For example, one study found that the likelihood of people changing their online search behavior can be associated with media coverage of public figures or celebrities with similar health problems (Abedi et al., 2015). Another found that health websites that include blogs and wikis are vibrant forums of discussion and viewed as credible sources of information (Kovic, Lulic, & Brumini, 2008).

Ethical Considerations

Rising interests in health concerns among many actors strengthen the need for more scholarship and reflection about the ethical considerations of practice in this specialized area of public relations.

Key ethical dilemmas involve, for example, the role of public relations in persuading publics to adopt certain treatments or modalities to diagnose, treat, or prevent illness or injury. Such persuasion always seeks to instill confidence and trust in organizations, or actors, involved in health such as hospitals, health-care facilities, governments, and medical device manufacturers and pharmaceutical firms.

Tensions flourish among these health actors related to motivations and interests. For example, a clinic promotes its diagnostic imaging – x-rays, computerized tomography (CT) scans or medical resonance imaging – for people to gain insight about their health. However, the medical community gets concerned when CT examinations are used without a proven clinical rationale, when alternative modalities could be used with equal worth, or when CT scans are repeated unnecessarily (Hall & Brenner, 2008). Physicians are also influenced by pharmaceutical companies. From the mid-1950s, pharmaceutical companies began thinking systematically about nurturing key opinion leaders such as physicians and other respected medical researchers to speak and write positively in articles and books about their products (Sismondo, 2013). These activities now stretch around the world.

We may also question the ethics of persuasive appeals related to health. Is it ethical to slightly exaggerate risk to persuade people to avoid potentially unsafe practices? Related, are highly emotional appeals moral, such as stories or images of disease victims?

How journalists construct media stories about health can involve public relations decisions about the use, or absence, of certain information. Public relations tactics happen in an environment where, as noted by Hinnant, Len-Ríos, and Young (2013), journalists tend to select examples to inform, inspire, or sensationalize a health issue or product. An additional ethical concern is the use of information subsidies, or information from public relations sources and others, among journalists. General assignment journalists depend on subsidies because they may know less about the story subject, and specialty reporters may use them to meet deadline pressures (Len-Rios et al., 2009).

How, When, and Why Is Theory Applied to Health Public Relations?

No one theory explains the study or practice of health public relations. Instead, and perhaps most interestingly, questions and dilemmas faced in health public relations forge pathways for theory development and the use of existing theories from across several fields.

For instance, viewing health public relations through the lens of social and public relations theories offers unique and challenging perspectives about the role, focus, and consequences of this work. Scholars have also explored health public relations in a critical frame, questioning the role of power, discourse, and societal implications.

The section explores public relations, social, and critical theories relevant to health public relations. Because theories involving risk are central to the field, outlined here are risk communication, the cultural theory of risk communication, the relationship theory of risk, uncertainty management theory, and uncertainty reduction theory (with the related problematic integration theory). Three further theories – falling more squarely into the overall study of public relations – are also discussed: narrative theory, organization–public relationship theory, and the situational theory of publics. For a summary of the theories, see Table 14.1.

Risk Communication

Risk surrounds us. We make sense of threats based on our beliefs and the tone, type, and sources of information received. Risk communication as a field of study and practice finds its foundation in this subjectivity because health risk includes factors that can be calculated but not always. These factors include genetics, other health problems, age, lifestyle, and environmental exposure. However, an individual's perception of risk is crucial to how they determine their course of action.

Risk communication is a body of communication theory that offers insights into how crises and worrisome situations alter the usual rule of communication (Covello, Peters, Wojtecki, & Hyde, 2001). Risk communication as a practice and area of theory development and study offers principles and tools to communicate effectively during times when publics or individuals are most worried about their health and well-being.

However, the study of risk communication theories is more than understanding how people process immediate concern in the face of a health threat. We should take a more proactive view of publics as informed, involved, interested, and solution oriented. Success is measured by people's ability to make sound decisions. Most often, the communication process is characterized by the receiver's perspective, the message perspective, and how to communicate risk numerically and visually (Turner, Skubisz, & Rimal, 2011).

Table 14.1 Summary of theories used in health public relations

Theory	Summary
Risk communication	A body of theory that offers insights into how threatening situations alter the usual rules of public relations. Theories include the social amplification of risk framework which describes the news media as one "amplification station" that processes signals about risk.
Cultural theory of risk communication	A politicized view that sees all societal actors as interpreters of risk. It provides public relations scholars a view of information receivers as powerful actors who actively shape the types of communication they need.
Relationship theory of risk	This theory views the framing of an object or practice as capable of shifting perceptions of risk. Scholars use this theory to study how to consider key messages when objects or practices related to health are perceived as both helpful and dangerous.
Uncertainty management theory	Challenges scholars to take a neutral stance about the strength or weakness of ambiguous information. Uncertainty is viewed as neither positive nor negative.
Uncertainty reduction theory/problematic integration theory	Uncertainty reduction theory asserts that people need to reduce uncertainty about others by gaining information about them. Related, problematic integration theory helps us understand that people will fail to respond to public relations activities when their expectations about something happening do not match the outcome.
Narrative theory	This theory provides a perspective about why all stories are not equally powerful. Criteria include coherence, how much sense the story makes, and the degree to which the story fits with our views and experiences.
Organization–public relationship theory	OPR emphasizes the relationship between publics and organizations as the unit of study. The theory helps scholars in health public relations consider and understand the qualities of the best relationships.
Situational theory of publics	As a central public relations theory, this theory recognizes that publics can be identified and classified according to their passive or active situation. It helps us understand the segmentation of publics into four key types: active, aware, latent, and nonpublic.

Within the body of risk communication theory, the social amplification of risk framework offers a window to examine the role of public relations in communicating levels of threats to health (Kasperson et al., 1988). This framework calls for the study of how hazards interact with psychological, social, institutional, and cultural processes in ways that may amplify or attenuate public responses to the risk or risk event. Risk is amplified at two stages: the transfer of information about the risk and the response mechanisms of society. The news media, for instance, are one "amplification station" that processes signals about risk.

Cultural Theory of Risk Communication

The cultural theory of risk communication is a politicized view because all societal actors are seen as interpreters of risk. The meaning of risk is negotiated across institutional and organizational levels under a "risk democracy" perspective (Coman, 2013).

Risk is socially constructed with a host of meanings attached to various individuals. Public relations practice in health is informed by this theory to analyze population segments based on their experiences and perspectives of risk. A new waste treatment facility, for example, may be perceived as a source of jobs to some members of the community or the cause of a worrying cough in local children. Depending on the perspective, the cultural theory of risk communication gives us pause to think about those who may be seen as creating or bearing the risk.

Anthropologist Mary Douglas broke ground by using cultural theory to research risk as a cultural phenomenon. Risks are crises and often scientific events, but are also political and cultural. In her later work, Douglas (1992) links risk to a "blaming system," a process where blame is aimed at villains such as large corporations while scientists and technicians whose work may have initially produced the risk remain blame-free.

This theory is a way of interpreting how and why people make decisions about threats to their health. Such judgments are part of an evolving social debate about rights to know, justice for those likely to be affected by damage or loss of peace of mind, and about blame, responsibility, and liability (Tansey & O'Riordan, 1999).

Cultural theory provides health public relations scholars the opportunity to view receivers of information as powerful actors who actively shape the type of communication they need. The theory is based on the presumption that those receiving risk messages are active and that those creating the messages interpret the information to suit their interests. Meanings of health risks are constantly negotiated between the organization and its publics, with power at the center of these deliberations. The levels and types of health risks are inherently political and controversial among these active publics.

This social theory is important for health public relations because it considers different meanings of risk in terms of its construction and relevance. For example, journalists have different views about the risks of a new health product based on interviews with families than members of the medical profession. The cultural theory of risk communication reminds us to analyze wide groups and individuals when dealing with health risks, to understand how risk is translated and moderated.

Relationship Theory of Risk

Another social theory useful in the study of health public relations is the relationship theory of risk. According to this theory, a perception of risk results from the same object or practice being framed as threatening or useful. Our perceptions are shaped by the associations made in communications between dangers and benefits.

In their study of antibacterial silver, Boholm et al. (2015) noted that although the material is increasingly used in health-care products such as bandages, clothing, household products, and makeup, it is also controversial because of its risks. The controversy over antibacterial silver was constructed from two adversarial positions, using the relational theory of risk. Silver is a risk object, endangering organisms, public health, the environment, and sewage treatment. However, the association between silver and objects at risk is obstructed by referring to it as "safe" and characterizing it as suitable for consumer and health-care products. Their study highlights that the actual concerns of stakeholders should be considered in risk communication.

The same could be said about communications involving the risks of radiation. Radiation saves lives in medical diagnosis and treatment, yet high doses of radiation can damage health and kill. This theory is instructive for the study of messages with respect to the uses of radiation as both curative and dangerous.

Uncertainty Management Theory

Uncertainty management theory challenges scholars to take a neutral stance about the strength or weakness of ambiguous information. At its core, it is rooted in the assumption that uncertainty is appraised for its meaning and is not inherently negative (Brashers, 2001). Only the appraisal of uncertainty influences subsequent behaviors, such as seeking information or taking other actions (Rains & Tukachinsky, 2015).

Illness is unpredictable and people cope with these uncertainties through communication. Just as wrong or contradictory information can raise more questions than it answers, too much information can create uncertainty and concern. However, minimizing uncertainty may not be the only solution to deal with doubt. Instead, according to this theory, we should examine the free will of people to determine how they want to cope with uncertainty. For example, people facing a terminal illness may maintain or increase their uncertainty, particularly if this option means that they can stay hopeful about their chances of living longer.

For health public relations, this theory reminds us of the costs of communication actions. Too much information may overwhelm people, while information that forecasts disease may be counterproductive if it decreases rather than increases people's attention to health and well-being (Brashers, 2001).

Uncertainty Reduction Theory and Problematic Integration Theory

Reducing uncertainty must surely be a goal for health public relations scholars and practitioners. Two related theories in interpersonal communication, uncertainty reduction theory and problematic integration theory, provide a foundation to study, analyze, and strategize in public relations related to health.

Uncertainty reduction theory asserts that people need to reduce uncertainty about others by gaining information about them (Berger & Bradac, 1982). Information comes from observation, asking others, and direct interaction. In public relations, we can theorize that uncertainty is inherent in health matters and that these three modes of information gathering inform and reduce the ambiguity. The landscape of health public relations is variable due to changing perceptions of disease and illness, medical treatments and technologies, and health outcomes. Even though total reduction of uncertainty is impossible to achieve, uncertainty reduction theory reminds us that relationships can be managed and considered.

On the other hand, and as a complement to uncertainty reduction theory, problematic integration theory helps us understand how messages are received, processed, and made sense of. Two kinds of orientations are found in this theory: assessment of how something will happen, and whether we feel positive, negative, or neutral about the outcome. We experience problematic integration when these orientations do not match.

Using problematic integration theory could help health public relations scholars theorize why certain campaigns fail or succeed. For example, messages about the importance of safe sex practices may misalign with an infrequent occurrence of sexually transmitted diseases among certain populations.

Uncertainty has a powerful place in health public relations as an ethical imperative. For example, a drive to reduce uncertainty about the state of health and illness has led to a culture of chronic illness (Brashers, 2001). Public relations plays a role in this culture. In particular, society operates within a "political economy of hope" that links many actors, including patients, families, medical practitioners, states, markets, scientists and researchers, with therapeutic practices, research funding, and the search for treatments and care (Rose, 2007).

Narrative Theory

Above all, health public relations surrounds stories, narratives that describe human experiences of struggle, demand, resistance, and triumph. Public relations theorists and scholars help explain this storytelling phenomenon.

Knowledge of the basic elements and purposes of narratives is foundational to health communication scholarship (Sharf, Harter, Yamasaki, & Haidet, 2011). The story of someone escaping health danger by taking measures and precautions is a cautionary tale for people suspicious of immunization for their family. An improved quality of life from a new regimen of antidepressant treatment offers others hope.

Public relations scholarship examines the field as a bridge for health-care providers who often know the plot of the story yet struggle to adequately impart this to their patients. On the other hand, public relations can give voice to patients and worried members of the population to tell their stories as the ignored or powerless in health systems.

Narrative theory provides a perspective about why all stories are not equally powerful. Two criteria determine a story's strength: coherence, how much sense the story makes, and fidelity, the degree to which the story fits with our views and experiences (Fisher, 1987).

Kent (2015) dissects narrative theory into 20 "master story plots." Three of these plots are most useful for health public relations scholarship: the transformation, metamorphosis, and underdog plots.

According to the "transformation" plot, complete change happens when someone experiences a life-changing event like the loss of a loved one from heart disease, a patient dies waiting for treatment in a hospital emergency ward, or a child hears for the first time because of cochlea implant technology.

The "metamorphosis" plot involves an about-face change from one form to another. Health technologies enable these physical transformations, while activist organizations and others communicate, for instance, about emotional changes to people resulting from greater discussion and understanding about transgendered identities.

The "underdog" plot involves stories about a fight against a larger entity, a person or a group who struggles yet wants little spotlight on their concerns. The underdog narrative brings focus on ignored or unknown health issues and concerns, helps raise funds for charities, and fights for causes.

Organization–Public Relationship Theory

Organization–public relationship theory emphasizes the relationship as a unit of study (Ki, 2014) and has been regarded as one of the most critical concepts in public relations. The premise is that an organization will increase the likelihood of achieving certain goals if its public relations efforts emphasize building and maintaining mutually beneficial relationships with publics (Bruning & Ledingham, 1999). Mutual benefit can be economic, social, political, and cultural, involve all parties, and is characterized by mutual positive regard.

While the field of public relations inherently involves publics, or the public, organization–public relationship theory explicitly defines and studies what constitutes these relationships themselves (Broom, Casey, & Ritchey, 1997). One key element of this theory is that public relations researchers and practitioners can study relationships as phenomena that are separate from the perceptions held by the individuals, groups, or organizations in the relationships.

Time and again, scholars have proven that the strength and quality of organization–public relationships depends on organizational effectiveness, recovery from crisis, public attitude and behavior, and the organization's reputation.

Nowhere is this transformation more obvious than in health. The application of the dimensions within organization–public relationship theory to health public relations is crucial to understanding how and why quality relationships are built and cultivated to achieve goals and objectives.

As a theory focused on the qualities of the best relationships, this theory provides great flexibility for the study of health public relations. For example, one study of the organization–public relationship in a hospital emergency department found that structural barriers and an overreliance on asymmetrical communication strategies fostered a culture of mistrust, cynicism, and noncompliance among internal publics (Seltzer, Gardner, Bichard, & Callison, 2012). The study suggests that the relationship management perspective could extend to include organizational culture. Here, the use of organization–public relationship theory in a health-care setting allowed for study of how the quality of internal relationships could affect the relationship with publics depending on health services.

Situational Theory of Publics

The situational theory of publics reasons that publics can be identified and classified to the extent that they are aware of the problem and do something about the problem.

Grunig (1997) describes three factors that influence whether a public passively takes in information or actively seeks further information and then is more likely to change its attitudes and behaviors: problem recognition, constraint recognition, and level of involvement. These factors are relevant to health public relations with its inherent focus on bodily issues, risk, and the need for involvement among often large publics and audiences.

The situational theory of publics is useful because it helps segment publics into four types that allow for greater communication effects: active, aware, latent, and nonpublic (Grunig, 1997). This theory could be used to develop distinctive messages for different publics and leaders, for example, as they prepare for a health outbreak. Here, communication effort would target community leaders with high involvement and medium-to-high problem recognition but potentially constrained by a lack of knowledge about how to prepare. Focus groups could pinpoint how leaders perceive the problem, their levels of involvement, and limitations, research that could shape information for these leaders.

Examples of Theory Used in Health Public Relations

Risk Communication

Risk communication theories help us understand how people process health threats and opportunities.

For example, a case study of public relations strategies among "downwinders" exposed to releases of radioactive iodine from the Hanford Nuclear Reservation in the 1940s and 1950s found that having the right message in an appropriate format is an important element of risk communication (G. Thomas, Smith, & Turcotte, 2009). Public relations about this potentially life-threatening health concern worked better than advertising owing to mistrust among the target audience. "Downwinders" received key messages from existing and trusted community networks and opinion leaders. Those affected were part of two-way interactions with public relations tactics that considered how these key publics preferred to receive personal or sensitive health information.

Cultural Theory of Risk Communication

The cultural theory risk communication allows us to analyze an expanse of groups and individuals to understand how health risk is translated and moderated.

In one study, US Congressional testimony was examined concerning regulation of tobacco advertising by three policy factions representing industry, government, and lay activists (Murphy, 2001). Using the cultural theory of risk, the study analyzed the ways these three groups framed the tobacco advertising issues. It found that testimony by each of the three groups reflected their cultural biases toward health risk. Some of the discourse patterns involved seeing tobacco advertising for the public health issues it raises, the challenges of regulating such advertising, and government intrusions into people's decisions about their uses of tobacco.

The cultural theory of risk communication here highlights that cultural biases that underlie positions taken by groups often present the greatest barriers to negotiation. Using cultural theory to analyze health public relations efforts and results can reveal group concerns and similarities and differences.

Uncertainty Management Theory

Uncertainty management theory calls for scholars to take a nonjudgmental stance about the strengths or weaknesses of ambiguity. This theory holds considerable appeal for health public relations scholars because of its neutrality about the role of uncertainty. When uncertainty produces anxiety or other negative emotions, it is viewed as a threat, but when uncertainty excites or offers hope, it is appraised as an opportunity. For example, individuals diagnosed with a life-threatening illness, such as AIDS, might fear the unknown and desire certainty, or they might prefer uncertainty to the inevitability of death.

Several case studies highlight the use of information to manipulate uncertainty. For example, the US Postal Service produced a prostate cancer awareness stamp to elevate public understanding of the disease. Instead, the stamp led to confusion, anxiety, and an unhealthy preoccupation with illness (Woloshin & Schwartz, 1999). Considering the public relations implications of employing stamps to achieve a certain health awareness did not foresee the effects of increasing uncertainty about the likelihood of cancer.

In another case, uncertainty management theory was used to study which participants were primed to feel and want more or less uncertainty about skin cancer (Rains & Tukachinsky, 2015). Participants were given the opportunity to search for skin cancer information on the internet. Findings highlight the complex relationship between information seeking and uncertainty management. The results show that the depth of information people seek relates to their desired level of uncertainty. Use of this theory in this case offers insights about the degree to which people will seek information to manage how much uncertainty they want.

Situational Theory of Publics

The situational theory of publics argues that publics can be segmented to determine whether they will passively take information or actively seek further information.

A study of Text4baby, a large national texting health initiative, uses the situational theory of publics to explain its success (Aldoory, Roberts, Bushar, & Assini-Meytin, 2018). Text4baby aimed to lower the risk of infant mortality by responding to the information needs of pregnant women.

The study used this theory to analyze Text4baby messages and interview data with the project content developers. They used the situational theory of publics to understand the types of publics that might emerge from Text4baby's audiences of pregnant women. Text4baby demonstrates how cues to pregnant women can allow them to become aware and active publics in their prenatal health-care practices.

In another use of this theory, Meng, Pan, and Reber (2016) reviewed award-winning public health communication campaigns from the National Public Health Information Coalition from 2010 to 2012. Among award-winning campaigns that did mention health risk, about two-thirds of them recognized situational problems relevant to unique public health issues. The emphasis on situational factors reinforces the value of the situational theory of publics in the public health arena.

Major Topics/Questions Needing to Be Addressed by Public Relations Theorists Working with Health Public Relations

Health public relations theorists face increasingly vexing questions because of unrelenting global pressures around health and health care. As health is an encompassing societal matter, worldwide trends and issues shape the work of health public relations and drive an enormous need for greater theory development and the advancement of existing theories.

These pressures arise from the demands and needs of a predominantly aging global population and increasing middle classes in developing nations. Related, we see a rise in chronic diseases and conditions.

Other health trends are just as present and distressing. How can public relations scholars mobilize existing theories and forge theory development to address, for example, drug overdose and deaths involving opioids? In the United States, such deaths have increased by more than five times in less than 10 years, involving men and women of all races and adults of nearly all ages (CDC, 2017).

Some trends facing health public relations scholars find their basis in the rise in consumer involvement and activism alongside issues of trust about health systems, providers, and products. The demand for transparency and accountability is growing along with the public need for empowerment.

In this environment of increasing expectations, we find a societal rise in the use of technology and data to prevent and treat health problems. The theory of artificial intelligence (AI) and other emerging theoretical frameworks related to it could weave with the work of health public relations to help put the human touch back into health. For example, AI, with its focus on reducing bureaucracy and administrative duties that can take time away from personalized care, could certainly be studied using a health public relations lens.

Suggested Case to Explore to Demonstrate Theory at Work in Health Public Relations

Ebola strikes fear into people's hearts. This virus first appeared in 1976 near the Ebola River in the Democratic Republic of Congo (WHO, 2016). It is transmitted to people from wild animals and spreads in the human population through human-to-human transmission. About half of those who contract Ebola die; however, fatality rates vary from 25% to 90% during outbreaks.

In September 2014, Texas Health Presbyterian Hospital began treating the country's first Ebola case in a patient – a case that the hospital had previously misdiagnosed as sinusitis. The hospital had a major public relations problem, not only because of the presence of the deadly disease, but because it had provided false information that, although later corrected, fueled an adversarial media environment. Texas Health appeared through the media locally, nationally, and internationally as incompetent and dangerous to its patients and community.

Public relations worked swiftly. The hospital accepted responsibility, corrected any inaccurate media coverage, and secured strategic media interviews with national media outlets. Video clips showed nurses praising others who cared for the patient who died of Ebola and the hospital flooded social media with the hashtag #PresbyProud. Social media were blanketed with information about efforts and commitments to high-quality care and protection of patient care staff. A rally among nurses promoted their pride in the efforts at Texas Health, with local television news broadcasters capturing footage.

These efforts resulted in improved patient confidence, and elective surgeries returning to pre-Ebola levels, as Texas Health reshaped the story of a hospital and an industry "trying to address potential hysteria" (PR Week, 2016).

Public relations in this case demonstrates several theories at work, including the relationship theory of risk, organization–public relationship theory, and narrative theory.

The relationship theory of risk views the framing of an object or practice as capable of shifting perceptions of risk. In this case, the hospital became a site of danger and risk owing to its initial mishandling of the public communications about the Ebola case. Public relations switched the frame, positioning Texas Health instead as a caring organization, one capable of providing care through its vocal and supportive nursing staff. Previous risk was overshadowed by key messages of the organization as contrite and, importantly, helpful and trustworthy.

Giving voice to nurses rising to support their hospital – a strategy explained through narrative theory – was another key to the success of the public relations approach. Publics expect health-care organizations, particularly hospitals, to work above all in their interests. The story of the hospital rising to the enormous challenge of fighting a deadly virus and doing so with its patient care staff completely on side is powerful and engaging. This became a story of the underdog winning in the face of adversity, with the enemy being the Ebola virus, and one of transformation as the hospital admitted its earlier mistakes to become a winning organization.

Discussion Questions

1   The relationship theory of risk teaches us that the same objects and practices involved in public relations can be perceived as completely different by publics. How does this theory inform both the study and practice in health public relations?

2   What are the chief ethical considerations and dilemmas involved with the practice of health public relations? How can practitioners keep these considerations in the forefront of their study and practice?

3   Narrative theory describes several key "plots" that can apply to how we understand the power of stories. Given discussions about identities as they relate to gender, how could the metamorphosis plot, with its focus on a change from one form to another, shape our study of health public relations?

4   How can the situational theory of publics be applied in a health-care situation?

5   Why are risk theories appropriate ones for the health-care context?

Suggested Readings

Douglas, M. (1992). *Risk and blame: Essays in cultural theory*. New York: Routledge.
Ihlen, Ø., van Ruler, B., & Fredriksson, M. (Eds.) (2009). *Public relations and social theory: Key figures and concepts*. New York: Routledge.
Thompson, T., Parrot, R., & Nussbaum, J. (2011). *The Routledge handbook of health communication* (2nd ed.). New York: Routledge.

References

Abedi, V., Mbaye, M., Tsivgoulis, G., Male, S., Goyal, N., Alexandrov, A., & Zand, R. (2015). Internet-based information seeking behavior for transient ischemic attack. *Stroke, 46* (Suppl. 1).

Agamben, G. (1998). *Homo sacer: Sovereign power and bare life*. Stanford, CA: Stanford University Press.

Aldoory, L., & Austin, L. (2011). Relationship building and situational publics: Theoretical approaches guiding today's health public relations. In T. L. Thompson, R. Parrott, & J. F. Nussbaum (Eds.), *Routledge handbook of health communication* (pp. 132–145). New York: Routledge.

Aldoory, L., Roberts, E. B., Bushar, J., & Assini-Meytin, L. (2018). Exploring the use of theory in a national text message campaign: Addressing problem recognition and constraint recognition for publics of pregnant women. *Health Communication, 33*(1), 41–48.

Avery, E., Lariscy, R., Amador, E., Ickowitz, T., Primm, C., & Taylor, A. (2010). Diffusion of social media among public relations practitioners in health departments across various community population sizes. *Journal of Public Relations Research, 22*(3), 336–358.

Bakardjieva, M. (2009). Subactivism: Life and politics in the age of the internet. *Information Society, 25*(2), 91–104.

Berger, C. R., & Bradac, J. J. (1982). *Language and social knowledge: Uncertainty in interpersonal relations*. London: Arnold.

Boholm, M., Arvidsson, R., Boholm, Å., Corvellec, H., & Molander, S. (2015). Disagreement: The construction and negotiation of risk in the Swedish controversy over antibacterial silver. *Journal of Risk Research, 18*(1), 93–110.

Brashers, D. (2001). Communication and uncertainty management. *Journal of Communication, 51*(3), 477–497.

Brodie, M., Hamel, E. C., Altman, D. E., Blendon, R. J., & Benson, J. M. (2003). Health news and the American public, 1996–2002. *Journal of Health Politics, Policy & Law, 28*(5), 927.

Broom, G. M., Casey, S., & Ritchey, J. (1997). Toward a concept and theory of organization–public relationships. *Journal of Public Relations Research, 9*(2), 83–98.

Bruning, S., & Ledingham, J. (1999). Relationships between organizations and publics: Development of a multi-dimensional organization–public relationship scale. *Public Relations Review, 25*(2), 157–709.

CDC (Centers for Disease Control and Prevention). (2016). *Centers for Disease Control and Prevention's strategic framework FY 2016–FY 2020*. Retrieved from the CDC website: https://www.cdc.gov/about/organization/strategic-framework/index.html

CDC (Centers for Disease Control and Prevention). (2017). *Overview of the drug overdose epidemic: Behind the numbers*. Retrieved from the CDC website: https://www.cdc.gov/drugoverdose/data/index.html

Chan, M. (2017). *Grand challenges for the next decade in global health policy and programmes*. Address by the director-general of the World Health Organization at the University of Washington's department of global health. Retrieved from http://www.who.int/dg/speeches/2017/address-university-washington/en/

Cline, R. (2011). Everyday interpersonal communication and health. In T. L. Thompson, R. Parrott, & J. F. Nussbaum (Eds.), *Routledge handbook of health communication* (pp. 377–396). New York: Routledge.

Coman, I. A. (2013). Cultural theory of risk communication. In R. L. Heath (Ed.), *Encyclopedia of public relations* (Vol. 2, pp. 237–238). Thousand Oaks, CA: Sage.

Covello, V. T., Peters, R. G., Wojtecki, J. G., & Hyde, R. C. (2001). Risk communication, the West Nile virus epidemic, and bioterrorism: Responding to the communication challenges posed by the intentional or unintentional release of a pathogen in an urban setting. *Journal of Urban Health, 78*(2), 382–391.

Douglas, M. (1992). *Risk and blame: Essays in cultural theory.* New York: Routledge.

Epstein, S. (2007). *Inclusion: The politics of difference in medical research.* Chicago: University of Chicago Press.

Fisher, W. R. (1987). *Human communication as narration: Toward a philosophy of reason, value, and action.* Columbia: University of South Carolina Press.

Foucault, M. (1991). Governmentality. In G. Burchell, C. Gordon, & P. Miller (Eds.), *The Foucault effect: Studies in governmentality.* Brighton, UK: Harvester Wheatsheaf.

Fox, S. (2011, February 28). *Peer-to-peer healthcare.* Retrieved from website of the Pew Research Center: http://www.pewinternet.org/2011/02/28/peer-to-peer-health-care-2/

Fox, S., & Duggan, M. (2013). *Health online 2013.* Retrieved from website of the Pew Research Center: http://www.pewinternet.org/2013/01/15/health-online-2013/

Gordon, C., & Kelly, K. (1999). Public relations expertise and organizational effectiveness: A study of US hospitals. *Journal of Public Relations Research, 2*(2), 143–165.

Grunig, J. E. (1997). A situational theory of publics: Conceptual history, recent challenges and new research. In D. Moss, T. MacManus, & D. Verčič (Eds.), *Public relations research: An international perspective* (pp. 3–48). London: International Thomson Business Press.

Hall, E. J., & Brenner, D. J. (2008). Cancer risks from diagnostic radiology. *British Journal of Radiology, 81*(965), 362–378.

Hinnant, A., Len-Ríos, M. E., & Young, R. (2013). Journalistic use of exemplars to humanize health news. *Journalism Studies, 14*(4), 539–554.

Isin, E. F. (2002). *Being political: Genealogies of citizenship.* Minneapolis: University of Minnesota Press.

Isin, E. F. (2004). The neurotic citizen. *Citizenship Studies, 8*(3), 217–235.

Kasperson, R. E., Renn, O., Slovic, P., Brown, H. S., Emel, J., Goble, R., … Ratick, S. (1988). The social amplification of risk: A conceptual framework. *Risk Analysis, 8*(2), 177–187.

Kent, M. L. (2015). The power of storytelling in public relations: Introducing the 20 master plots. *Public Relations Review, 41*(4), 480–489.

Ki, E. (2014). Organization–public relations theory. In T. L. Thompson (Ed.), *Encyclopedia of health communication* (Vol. 3, pp. 1006–1007). Thousand Oaks, CA: Sage.

Kovic, I., Lulic, I., & Brumini, G. (2008). Examining the medical blogosphere: An online survey of medical bloggers. *Journal of Medical Internet Research, 10*(3), e28.

Kreps, G. (2011). Translating health communication research into practice: The influence of health communication scholarship on health policy, practice and outcomes. In T. L. Thompson, R. Parrott, & J. F. Nussbaum (Eds.), *Routledge handbook of health communication* (595–609). New York: Routledge.

Len-Rios, M., Hinnant, A., Park, S., Cameron, G., Frisby, C., & Lee, Y. (2009). Health news agenda building: Journalists' perceptions of the role of public relations. *Journalism & Mass Communication Quarterly, 86*(2), 315–331.

Meng, J., Pan, P., & Reber, B. H. (2016). Identify excellent features and situational factors in public health communication. *Public Relations Review, 42*(2), 366–368.

Murphy, P. (2001). Framing the nicotine debate: A cultural approach to risk. *Health Communication, 13*(2), 119–140.

Petryna, A. (2004). Biological citizenship: The science and politics of Chernobyl-exposed populations. *Osiris, 19*, 250–265.

PR Week. (2016, March 18). *Crisis or issues management campaign of the year 2016.* Retrieved from http://www.prweek.com/article/1387096/crisis-issues-management-campaign-year-2016

Rains, S. A., & Tukachinsky, R. (2015). An examination of the relationships among uncertainty, appraisal, and information-seeking behavior proposed in uncertainty management theory. *Health Communication, 30*(4), 339–349.

Rose, N. (2007). *Politics of life itself: Biomedicine, power and subjectivity in the twenty-first century.* Princeton, NJ: Princeton University Press.

Rose, N., & Novas, C. (2005). Biological citizenship. In A. Ong & S. J. Collier (Eds.), *Global assemblages: Technology, politics, and ethics as anthropological problems* (pp. 439–463). Oxford: Blackwell.

Seltzer, T., Gardner, E., Bichard, S., & Callison, C. (2012). PR in the ER: Managing internal organization–public relationships in a hospital emergency department. *Public Relations Review, 38*(1), 128–136.

Sharf, B., Harter, L., Yamasaki, J., & Haidet, P. (2011). Narrative turns epic: Continuing developments in health narrative scholarship. In T. L. Thompson, R. Parrott, & J. F. Nussbaum (Eds.), *Routledge handbook of health communication* (2nd ed.) (pp. 36–51). New York: Routledge.

Sismondo, S. (2013). Key opinion leaders and the corruption of medical knowledge: What the Sunshine Act will and won't cast light on. *Journal of Law, Medicine & Ethics, 41*(3), 635–643.

Stephenson, M., Southwell, B., & Yzer, M. (2011). Advancing health communication research: Issues and controversies in research design and analysis. In T. L. Thompson, R. Parrott, & J. F. Nussbaum (Eds.), *Routledge handbook of health communication* (pp. 560–577). New York: Routledge.

Sundar, S., Edwards, H. H., Hifeng, H., & Stavrositu, C. (2007) Blogging for better health: Putting the "public" back in public health. In M. Tremayne (Ed.), *Blogging, citizenship and the future of media*. New York: Routledge.

Tansey, J., & O'Riordan, T. (1999). Cultural theory and risk: A review. *Health, Risk & Society, 1*(1), 71–90.

Thomas, G. D., Smith, S. M., & Turcotte, J. A. (2009). Using public relations strategies to prompt populations at risk to seek health information: The Hanford community health project. *Health Promotion Practice, 10*(1), 92–101.

Thomas, R. (2006). *Health communication.* New York: Springer.

Turner, M. M., & Skubisz, C. R., & Rimal, R. N. (2011). Theory and practice in risk communication: A review of the literature and visions for the future. In T. L. Thompson, R. Parrott, & J. F. Nussbaum (Eds.), *Routledge handbook of health communication* (2nd ed.) (pp. 146–164). New York: Routledge.

WHO (World Health Organization). (2016). *Ebola virus disease.* Fact sheet. Retrieved from http://www.who.int/mediacentre/factsheets/fs103/en/

Woloshin, S., & Schwartz, L. M. (1999). The US postal service and cancer screening: Stamps of approval? *New England Journal of Medicine, 340*(11), 884–887.

15

Investor Relations

Alexander V. Laskin

Gatorade, a sports drink created in 1965 at the University of Florida to help Florida Gators athletes replenish electrolytes, carbohydrates, and water during sport activities, is the leading brand among consumers. In fact, Gatorade accounts for about three fourths of all sports drinks sales. It is no surprise that it was a prominent target for acquisition by large drink companies. In 2000, it looked like Gatorade would become a part of the Coca-Cola family. The acquisition deal was pioneered by Douglas Daft, who at the time was both the CEO of Coca-Cola and the chairman of its board of directors. With his support, the deal seemed set in stone. All the due diligence and formalities were completed, press releases were drafted, and even a conference call with analysts was already scheduled to announce the acquisition. Yet, at the last second, Coke investors through their representatives on the board of directors led by Warren Buffett, cancelled the deal. The *Wall Street Journal* concludes: "How Coke's biggest acquisition attempt ever was fumbled is the story of a CEO who couldn't – or wouldn't – force his will on his board" (McKay, Deogun, Spurgeon, & Eig, 2000). But it is also a story of a growing power of investors that in turn makes investor relations, a function responsible for managing relations with investors, shareholders, financial analysts, and other members of the financial community, top priority for corporations around the world.

Defining the Concepts: What Is Investor Relations?

The well-known scholarly definition of public relations describes the profession as "a management function that establishes and maintains mutually beneficial relationships between an organization and the publics on whom its success or failure depends" (Broom & Sha, 2013, p. 5). Here, the word "publics" is used generically and can be replaced with a specific public depending on the function – for example, for employee relations, it would be employees, and the definition then would become "a management function that establishes and maintains mutually beneficial relationships between an organization and the employees on whom its success or failure depends"; for media relations, it would be media and the definition would say a "management function that establishes and maintains mutually beneficial relationships between an organization and the media on whom its success or failure depends," and so on. As a result, if one wanted to create a definition of investor relations as a public relations function, that definition might read: "Investor relations is a management function that establishes and maintains mutually beneficial relationships between an organization and the investors on whom its success or failure depends."

Public Relations Theory: Application and Understanding, First Edition. Edited by Brigitta R. Brunner.
© 2019 John Wiley & Sons, Inc. Published 2019 by John Wiley & Sons, Inc.

In addition to this scholarly definition, professional associations offer their own takes on public relations and investor relations. The Public Relations Society of America (PRSA) defines public relations as "a strategic communication process that builds mutually beneficial relationships between organizations and their publics" (PRSA, 2018). Once again the generic word "public" can be replaced with the particular publics for various public relations subfunctions. In case of investors as the target public, the definition could be changed to this: Investor relations is a strategic communication process that builds mutually beneficial relationships between organizations and their investors.

The leading professional association of investor relations, the National Investor Relations Institute (NIRI), provides a more elaborate definition. Investor relations is defined as "a strategic management responsibility that integrates finance, communication, marketing and securities law compliance to enable the most effective two-way communication between a company, the financial community, and other constituencies, which ultimately contributes to a company's securities achieving fair valuation" (NIRI, 2018).

All three of these definitions have a lot in common, but there is an important difference in the final goal of the investor relations function. The first definitions that come from the public relations realm state the final goal is a relationship, building and maintaining it. The investor relations definition from NIRI, however, states the overall goal as the share price – to contribute to company's fair valuation. However, recent studies of investor relations practitioners showed that those who actually practice investor relations on a daily basis are not happy with either one of these metrics. In fact, Ragas, Laskin, and Brusch (2014) state that the respondents in their study "strongly rebuked … the notion of using company share price as a valid measure of the success of investor relations (p. 186). At the same time, respondents in Laskin's (2011) study doubted that relationship can be an objective measure of investor relations as it is difficult to measure and evaluate the quality of a relationship.

Most recently, Laskin (2018) proposed that the overall goal of investor relations should not be relationships or a share price, but expectations about them, and the function becomes a function of managing expectations. This transforms the long-known equation ROE from *return on equity* to *return on expectations*. This is also in line with the efficient market hypothesis, the key theoretical proposition governing the financial markets (Fama, 1970). The efficient market is a market in equilibrium: all securities are fairly priced – no investors can consistently outperform, or beat, the market. The efficient market hypothesis, however, requires key assumptions to be met: all relevant information about the company and its performance is publicly available, all market participants have equal access to such information on a timely basis, and all investors are rational and capable of evaluating the information available to them. Much attention in the financial world has been devoted to access to information as a key requirement for the efficient market – in order for all prices to fully and fairly reflect the underlying value of securities, all market participants must have full and fair access to information about such value. This led to promulgation of Regulation Fair Disclosure (Reg. FD or Regulations FD) in August 2000. The US Securities and Exchange Commission (2014) explains that "Regulation FD aims to promote the full and fair disclosure" by eliminating the practice of selective disclosure and enabling all investors, large and small, to access the same information.

But is access to information enough? Several studies by Laskin (2009, 2010, 2011, 2014a, 2016b) claim full and fair disclosure is not sufficient. For the efficient market hypothesis to work, in addition to access to information, investors need comprehension and understanding of this information. This means that investor relations officers, in addition to disclosing information, must also help investors understand what was disclosed, what this information means, and what reasonable expectations could be developed based on this information. In other words, investor relations officers educate investors about the company and its value. Laskin

(2018) concludes: "As a result, for the investor relations officers to be successful in the context of the efficient market hypothesis they must do significantly more than just put the information out there – they are also responsible for making sure their messages are received, understood, processed, and acted upon."

How and Why Is Investor Relations of Concern to Public Relations?

As shown, investors are one of many publics that organizations need to build and maintain relationships with. As a result, there is little doubt that public relations should be concerned with investor relations. In fact, the Body of Knowledge Task Force of the PRSA included investor relations as one of the seven subfunctions of public relations, along with media, internal/employee, consumer, community, government, and fundraising/donor relations (PRSA Task Force, 1988). Most recently, Laskin (2014a) claimed that investor relations is a public relations function: "Investor relations [is placed] directly into the public relations domain" (p. 201).

Furthermore, investor relations may not be just one of the functions of public relations – it may be one of the most important functions. Specifically, Grunig, Grunig, and Dozier (2002) suggested that investors have significant power over corporations, which makes them a very influential type of public. As a result, investor relations practitioners are more likely to practice the two-way symmetrical model in comparison with other public relations functions.

The importance of investors as a public may also suggest that investor relations takes priority over other functions – with more resources devoted to the function. Allen (2002) notes that investor relations is right at the top of the corporate agenda. A BNY Melon (2011) study concludes that a large publicly traded company spends approximately $1 million or more annually on investor relations. Ragas et al. (2014) state: "the corporate sector as a whole invests hundreds of millions of dollars per year in this function" (p. 177). Investor relations practitioners are also often ranked as the highest paid out of all public relations professionals (PRWeek, 2006; Laskin, 2014a).

Finally, the importance of investors as a public may suggest that investor relations practitioners are more likely to have a proverbial seat at the table – in other words, be part of the top management team of the organization – in comparison with other public relations functions, such as media relations or community relations (Ragas et al., 2014).

How, When, and Why Is Theory Applied to Investor Relations?

As explained, companies spend millions of dollars on investor relations. As a result, companies expect some kind of a return from this investment. Consequently, a significant part of theory-driven research in investor relations focuses on measuring this contribution. Measurement and evaluation are very important in investor relations, yet investor relations is not easy to measure (Ragas et al., 2014; Laskin, 2011; van Riel & Fombrun, 2007; Cole, 2004). On one hand, unlike other public relations functions, investor relations seems to have a ready-to-go quantitative metric – a share price. On the other hand, a direct link between share price and investor relations is difficult, if not impossible, to establish, as a company's valuation can be influenced by a variety of internal and external factors. What, then, can be considered a proper metric for measuring investor relations?

Another growing theoretical area is relationship management. In 1984, Ferguson famously proclaimed that for public relations "the unit of study should not be the organization, nor the public, nor the communication process. Rather the unit of study should be the relationships between organizations and their publics" (p. ii). This proclamation spurred a strong body of research on relationship management – Sallot, Lyon, Acosta-Alzuru, and Jones (2003) rank relationship management as one of the most researched perspectives in public relations. For investor relations practitioners building and maintaining relationships with their publics is of vital importance – institutional investors, financial analysts, buy-side and sell-side, retail share-holders, stock exchanges, regulatory organizations, media, activists, as well as internal publics, such as management teams, boards of directors, employees – each one of these publics may have a forceful effect on the investor relations job, pushing the share price sky high or destroying all the value in the company (Laskin, 2010). Relationships, however, are not easy to evaluate. Thus, research often focuses on trying to better understand relationships in investor relations.

A third area where theory is often applied in investor relations focuses on various com-munications produced in the context of performing investor relations tasks. Investor relations officers are responsible for producing earnings releases as well as quarterly and annual reports (Heath & Phelps, 1984; Hutchins, 1994; Lord, 2002). These are important documents that talk about past and future performances of companies and shape expectations of a variety of publics (Kohut & Segars, 1992; O'Donovan, 2001; Sidle, 2009; Rosenkranz & Pollach, 2016; Laskin, 2018). In addition to written communications, investor relations officers are responsible for a variety of oral communications – conference calls, investor conferences and investor days, roadshows, and so on. Much research has been devoted to analyzing these texts and the rhetorical devices employed to frame the company's performance (Subramanian, Insley, & Blackwell, 1993; Kwon & Wild, 1994; Anderson & Epstein, 1995; Abrahamson & Amir, 1996; Laskin & Samoilenko, 2014).

Finally, a significant part of investor relations scholarship focuses on analyzing investor relations as a profession. These introspective studies evaluate the role and place of investor relations departments within organizations, discuss the educational and professional back-grounds of investor relations officers, study budgets, activities, and chain of command, and similar (Petersen & Martin, 1996; Laskin, 2009, 2014a).

Examples of Theory Used with Investor Relations

Probably the earliest theories used in investor relations are part of the rhetorical paradigm. The first documented study actually focused on readability of annual reports and dates back to 1952 (Pashalian & Crissy, 1952). Many of these early studies use the Flesch readability formula as their theoretical foundation. The Flesch readability formula combines measures of sentence length and syllable count of individual words in order to evaluate difficulty (or ease) of reading textual material (Flesch, 1951). It was originally developed to evaluate elementary reading abilities but was eventually expanded to a variety of reading materials, including corporate communica-tions, as an "easy, objective, and reliable alternative" (Jones, 1988). Readability originally was considered a measure for effectiveness of investor relations communications, specifically as it relates to communicating financial information: "The communication of accounting information to external users is of fundamental importance to published accounting reports" (Jones, 1988, p. 300). Today, even more so, disclosure of financial information is regarded as an important contributor to corporate value (Argenti, 2007; Laskin, 2016b).

Over time this type of research grew exponentially. In fact, Stanton and Stanton (2002) and Rutherford (2005) note that there were more studies on readability than all other types of rhe-torical studies put together. Among these studies are Soper and Dolphin (1964); Smith and Smith (1971); Healy (1977); Barnett and Leoffler (1979); and Clatworthy and Jones (2001). Such studies typically conclude that the reading level of disclosure is prohibitive and incomprehensible. In fact, Jones and Shoemaker (1994) note that such disclosure can be categorized as inaccessible to a large proportion of the shareholders.

The research also became more sophisticated – from one Flesch index more than 30 various readability formulas were developed. For example, Thomas (1997), when studying letters to shareholders, analyzed several linguistic instruments in each document: transitivity, thematic structure, context, cohesion, and condensation. Arguably, the most complex and sophisticated approach to such an analysis was developed by Hart. Having reviewed a variety of literature applying rhetorical theory to analysis of political, managerial, organizational, and other texts, Hart (2000, 2001) identified 35 narrative strategies that can be applied to analyzing texts. The narrative strategies can be defined as ways of "argumentation as individuals seek to convince an audience of a construction of reality congruent with their interests (through justification) yet undermining of others (through criticism)" (Symon, 2008, p. 78). The 35 strategies identified by Hart are organized into five categories, called composite strategies: certainty, optimism, activity, realism, and commonality. Most recently, Laskin and Samoilenko (2014) applied Hart's methodology to studying annual reports.

In addition to complexity of data analysis, the studies became more sophisticated in terms of their explanation. Relying on research by Habermas (1984, 1987), Yuthas, Rogers, and Dillard (2002) proposed that corporate disclosure may be "used to transparently communicate performance information or to instrumentally influence stakeholders to act in the interests of the company" (p. 142). Laskin (2010, 2018) advances this claim and proposes that financial communication and investor relations are never a mere disclosure. Instead, they are a complex strategic function of managing expectations: organizations rely on communications to their investors, financial analysts, and other financial audiences to shape perceptions of organizational outcomes. This managing of expectations is done through rhetorical means. As a result, readability and other narrative strategies are now compared with such corporate metrics as net profit, return on capital, share price, or overall industry performance. Several studies actually proposed that difficulty in reading and understanding financial disclosure may be not in error or by accident, but by design (Keusch, Bollen, & Hassink, 2012). Adelberg (1979), Baker and Kare (1992), Courtis (1998), Bloomfield (2002), and Laskin and Samoilenko (2014) have suggested that managers may, in fact, have incentives to obfuscate information in the disclosure documents, especially in cases where firm performance is exceptionally poor. This became known as an obfuscation theory. Others suggested that the opposite should also be true – when firms perform exceptionally well the disclosure documents should become easy to read and understand (Schrand & Walther, 2000; Li, 2008).

Of course, this stream of research drew its share of criticism as well. Courtis (1986, 1998), having reviewed the usage of readability formulas and concerns whether such formulas can, in fact, measure the readability difficulty of narrative disclosures, summarizes:

> Readability formulas are simplistic in that they enable a passage of selected text to be represented by a single summary score, which at best is merely a general estimate of difficulty. The formulas concentrate on only those aspects of sentence construction which can be conveniently measurable, such as the attributes of word and sentence construction, i.e., number of syllables in a passage, number of polysyllabic words, number of words with seven or more letters, and sentence length. Other important matters such as syntax, style, format, graphic design, logic, conceptual density, human interest, organization and reinforcement are not considered. Moreover, formulas pay no heed to the way new concepts are introduced, nor to the motivational nature of the materials. (Courtis, 1998, p. 460)

Nevertheless, research on readability remains an important and popular contributor to the investor relations scholarship. In fact, scholars, professionals, and regulators continue to view text quality as one of the most important issues. The US Securities and Exchange Commission even released plain language guidelines for corporate disclosure with specific recommendations on how such disclosure should look: "short sentences; definite, concrete, everyday language; active voice; tabular presentation of complex information; no legal or business jargon; and no multiple negatives" (Glassman, 2005, para. 20).

Another important stream of research in investor relations focuses on analyzing the profession itself. Petersen and Martin (1996) surveyed CEOs in order to find out their views on investor relations. Although descriptive in nature, the research relied on the excellence study (Grunig, Grunig, & Dozier, 2002) as its theoretical foundation, specifically focusing on roles theory, to find out if CEOs viewed investor relations as a managerial or technical function. The study found that in practice investor relations rarely reports to public relations and people who practice investor relations rarely have any public relations training.

Laskin (2009, 2014a) continued this type of research, also analyzing the profession and the role of practitioners, with similar results: in the United States at least, investor relations is dominated by financial rather than communication expertise. But perhaps the most theoretically driven study was the research conducted by Kelly, Laskin, and Rosenstein (2010), where the practice of public relations was analyzed using the four models of public relations (press agentry/publicity, public information, two-way asymmetrical, and two-way symmetrical) as well as four dimensions of public relations (asymmetrical effects, symmetrical effects, one-way communication, and two-way communication). This research was the first study to find a predominant use of the two-way symmetrical model across its sample: "This study shows that the two-way symmetrical model does exist in the real world, and it can be found in the bastion of capitalism – publicly owned corporations in the United States" (p. 205). This refutes common criticism of models of public relations that symmetrical communications are a "utopian ideal' (Pieczka, 1996).

Research on investor relations has not been limited to the profession in the United States alone. Hoffmann, Tutic, and Wies (2011) studied investor relations professionals at Euronext 100 companies; Marston (1996) and Dolphin (2004) studied the investor relations function in companies in the United Kingdom; Tuominen (1997) studied investor relations in Finland; Laskin and Koehler (2012) conducted comparative research looking at both European and US investor relations practices, and Koehler (2014) studied companies from the United States, the United Kingdom, France, Germany, and Japan. Overall, however, studies on financial communication and investor relations outside of the United States or Europe are quite rare.

Measuring the impact of investor relations is a fast-growing area of research. And it is not surprising: "Vague assurances of goodwill and its invisible long-term impact can no longer persuade vigilant CEOs and upper management" (Kim, 2001). Thus, it becomes important to show and actually measure the contribution to the company's bottom line (Laskin, 2016a). Much of this research is grounded in the efficient market theory and agency theory – specifically, claiming that a function of investor relations should be to decrease the information asymmetry between shareholders and managers as their agents, who also may have different self-interests (Jensen & Meckling, 1976; Farraghe, Kleiman, & Bazaz, 1994; Brennan & Tamarowski, 2000; Healy & Palepu, 2001; Bushee, Jung, & Miller, 2011; Dimitrov & Jain, 2011; Laskin, 2011; Ragas & Laskin, 2014; Ragas et al., 2014).

The efficient market hypothesis primarily associated with research by Fama (1970) states: "A market in which prices always 'fully reflect' available information is called 'efficient'" (p. 383). Such a market is in equilibrium: all securities are fairly priced, according to their risks and returns. No investors can consistently outperform, or beat, the market, and thus there is no reason to constantly buy and sell shares of companies to try to outperform the average market return.

The efficient market hypothesis, however, requires key assumptions to be met: all relevant information about the company and its performance is publicly available, all market participants have equal access to such information on a timely basis, and all investors are rational and capable of evaluating the information available to them. Fama (1970) talked about three levels of market efficiency – weak, semi-strong, and strong. In the weak form of market efficiency, not all information is available to all market participants and, as a result, some investors can outperform others by taking advantage of better or faster access to information. In the semi-strong form of efficiency, all public information is equally available to everyone and, as a result, already reflected in the stock price; however, there may be other, nonpublic information that is not reflected in the stock price and, as a result, somebody with access to such information through, for example, insider trading can beat the market. And, finally, in strong market efficiency, all information is reflected in the stock price and all investors – internal and external – have the same access to information and the same knowledge and understanding of the company. Once again, investor relations, a function charged with providing information about the company to shareholders, financial analysts, and other market participants, is at the very foundation of the efficient market hypothesis. So, Laskin (2016b) proposes that investor relations officers must engage in educational efforts with the goal of educating investors, "essentially outsiders, to fully grasp the value" of the company and its business model (p. 378).

Finally, an important theoretical area of investor relations research focuses on relationships between organizations and their many financial publics, including trying to better understand these publics and their diverse needs. In fact, one of the earliest studies of investor relations from the public relations standpoint is based on applying the situational theory of publics in the investor relations context (Cameron, 1992). Penning (2011) studied retail shareholders in order to understand their informational preferences by applying uses and gratifications theory and the situational theory of publics, while Arvidsson (2012) analyzed financial analysts as a target public for investor relations. Koehler (2014) studied relationship building in investor relations on a theoretical foundation of dialogic communications.

The call for a relationship focus that was initially made by Ferguson (1984) was greatly supported and expanded by a variety of scholars. Already in 1997, Broom, Casey, and Ritchey (1997) claimed: "Many scholars and practitioners say that public relations is all about building and maintaining relationship" (p. 83). They also made an important contribution to the field by trying to define what relationship actually is by reviewing relationship definitions from other fields: interpersonal communications, psychotherapy, organizational behavior, and systems theory. Ledingham and Bruning (1998) defined relationship as a public relations concept as "the state which exists between an organization and its key publics, in which the actions of either can impact the economic, social, cultural or political well-being of the other" (p. 62). Finally, Hon and Grunig (1999) described the specific dimensions of relationships between organizations and their publics as control, mutuality, trust, commitment, and satisfaction, and identified as well two types of relationships: the exchange relationship and the communal relationship. Chandler (2014) studied CEOs' views on investor relations using relationship management theory and found support for these four dimensions in the investor relations context.

Major Topics/Questions Needing to Be Addressed by Public Relations Theorists Working in Investor Relations

Despite a variety of research described above (and see also Table 15.1), there are many areas of investor relations still understudied. In fact, Laskin (2014b) points to the lack of theory-building and theory-testing research in investor relations, claiming that most "simply provide descriptions

Table 15.1 Summary of public relations theories used in investor relations

Area	Examples of theories used
Communications	Flesch index; lexicosemantics; rhetorical theory; narrative strategies; obfuscation theory
Profession	Models of public relations; dimensions of public relations; roles theory; encroachment
Relationship	Relationship management; uses and gratifications; situational theory of publics; dialogic communications
Measurement and evaluation	Efficient market hypothesis; agency theory

of the current status of the field" (p. 127). For example, investor relations is often regarded as one of the most regulated areas of public relations, so research on laws and regulations and how companies adapt to them is of paramount importance. Some studies have been done in this area – for example, Pompper's (2014) study of the impact of the Sarbanes-Oxley Act based on a theory of planned behavior – but more research is needed.

Public relations has seen a significant growth of scholarship in social media and new media technologies over recent years. Although investor relations officers are less active on social media than, for example, consumer relations practitioners, new media still have a significant impact on investor relations. A few studies conducted in this area show that new media tools "are being embraced" in investor relations (Arvidsson, 2012, p. 109), but theory-based research in this area is very limited. Social media, meanwhile, whether investor relations professionals use it or not, can have a strong effect on their jobs and their company's operations. For example, a study of Twitter found that the sentiment of posts on Twitter about 30 stock companies had a strong correlation with abnormal stock returns during the peaks of Twitter volume (Ranco et al., 2015). Similarly, Sprenger, Tumasjan, Sandner, and Welpe (2014), using computational linguistics, discovered an "association between tweet sentiment and stock returns, message volume and trading volume, as well as disagreement and volatility" (p. 926). Investor relations officers need to know how to monitor, analyze, and respond to what is being said about the company on social media. Thus, research on social media in investor relations is needed.

Finally, as mentioned earlier, investor relations research is primarily limited to the United States and Europe. The world of finance, however, is truly global – a company can have investors from all parts of the world. So, future research in investor relations should expand to cover other regions of the world: Asia, South America, Africa, and Australia, including such fast-growing countries as China, India, Brazil, Russia, and South Africa. In addition to regional research, global investor relations should study investor relations in the context of global corporations and global investment strategies.

Suggested Case to Explore to Demonstrate Theory at Work in Investor Relations

An excellent opportunity to study investor relations arises when a company is dealing with investor activism – this is when investor relations can make or break the corporation. In fact, Rao and Sivakumar (1999) suggest that investor relations was recognized as a profession primarily due to the growth of social movement activists with strong antimanagement bias.

One of the recent cases of shareholder activism involves CONSOL Energy and New York City Public Pension Funds (Uysal, 2014; see also Sanzillo & Kunkel, 2014). NYC Pension Funds is in a unique position – on one hand, as a pension fund, it must make money for its clients, on the other hand, as an organization representing the City of New York, its investments must adhere to higher ethical standards than the standards of a regular mutual fund. Specifically, NYC Pension Funds is committed to "pressuring many of America's largest companies to improve workplace conditions, protect the environment, promote human rights abroad, and adhere to accepted corporate governance standards" (quoted in Uysal, 2014, p. 221). Such a position is known as social shareholder activism, when organizations are held accountable for not just making profits but also for making the world better and bringing about social change.

In the case of CONSOL Energy, particularly in relation to its coal operations, NYC Pension Funds filed a shareholder resolution on corporate response to climate change. CONSOL Energy then had three possible responses: *block*, exclude a resolution from the annual meeting materials; *settle*, engage in a dialogue with the fund to find a solution that would satisfy both parties; *fight*, let the resolution go for a vote and try to win this vote. The first and third options, *block* and *fight*, are adversarial options, while the second option, engaging in a dialogue, can be considered a cooperative response.

Analyzing this case presents a great opportunity for evaluating theories in investor relations as it highlights several of them: agency theory, efficient market hypothesis, dialogic communications, situational theory of publics, relationship management, and, in this case, in studying the actual texts of the resolutions, rhetorical and lexicosemantic theories.

Discussion Questions

1 Why do you think investor relations became "one of public relations' most unfortunate paradoxes" with high importance but little research (Kelly et al., 2010)?

2 Why are some areas of investor relations more developed and have seen more research than others?

3 What area of investor relations research in your opinion is the most important for practitioners?

4 Why do you think some say that if the efficient market hypothesis were true, there would be no stock trading?

Suggested Readings

Laskin, A. V. (2010). *Managing investor relations: Strategies for effective communication*. New York: Business Expert Press.

Laskin, A. V. (2018). *Handbook of financial communication and investor relations*. New York: Wiley.

Lev, B. (2012). *Winning investors over*. Boston: Harvard Business Review Press.

Marcus, B. W., & Wallace, S. L. (1997). *New dimensions in investor relations: Competing for capital in the 21st century*. New York: Wiley.

References

Abrahamson, E., & Amir, E. (1996). The information content of the president's letter to shareholders. *Journal of Business Finance and Accounting, 23*(8), 1157–82.

Adelberg, A. H. (1979). Narrative disclosures contained in financial reports: Means of communication or manipulation? *Accounting and Business Research, 9*(35), 179–189.

Allen, C. E. (2002). Building mountains in a flat landscape: Investor relations in the post-Enron era. *Corporate Communications, 7*(4), 206–211.

Anderson, R., & Epstein, M. (1995, April). The usefulness of annual reports. *Australian Accountant*, 25–28.

Argenti, P. A. (2007). *Corporate communication* (4th ed.). New York: McGraw-Hill.

Arvidsson, S. (2012). The corporate communication process between listed companies and financial analysts. *Corporate Communications, 17*(2), 98–112.

Baker, H. E., & Kare, D. D. (1992). Relationship between annual report readability and corporate financial performance. *Management Research, 15*, 1–4.

Barnett, A., & Leoffler, K. (1979). Readability of accounting and auditing messages. *Journal of Business Communication, 16*, 49–59.

Bloomfield, R. J. (2002). The "incomplete revelation hypothesis" and financial reporting. *Accounting Horizons, 16*, 233–243.

BNY Mellon. (2011). *Global trends in investor relations: Seventh edition, a survey analysis of IR practices worldwide*. New York: BNY Mellon.

Brennan, M. J., & Tamarowski, C. (2000). Investor relations, liquidity, and stock prices. *Journal of Applied Corporate Finance, 12*(4), 26–37.

Broom, G. M., Casey, S., & Ritchey, J. (1997). Toward a concept and theory of organization–public relationships. *Journal of Public Relations Research, 9*(2), 83–89.

Broom, G. M., & Sha, B.-L. (2013). *Cutlip and Center's effective public relations* (11th ed.). Harlow, UK: Pearson Education.

Bushee, B. J., Jung, M. J., & Miller, G. S. (2011). Conference presentations and the disclosure milieu. *Journal of Accounting Research, 49*(5), 1163–1192.

Cameron, G. T. (1992). Memory for investor relations messages: An information-processing study of Grunig's situational theory. *Journal of Public Relations Research, 4*(1), 45–60.

Chandler, C. S. (2014). Investor relations from the perspective of CEOs. *International Journal of Strategic Communication, 8*(3), 160–176.

Clatworthy, M., & Jones, M. J. (2001). The effect of thematic structure on the variability of annual report readability. *Accounting, Auditing & Accountability Journal, 14*, 311–326.

Cole, B. M. (2004). *The new investor relations: Expert perspectives on the state of the art*. New York: Bloomberg Press.

Courtis, J. K. (1986). An investigation into annual report readability and corporate risk return relationships. *Accounting and Business Research, 17*, 285–294.

Courtis, J. K. (1998). Annual report readability variability: Tests of the obfuscation hypothesis. *Accounting, Auditing & Accountability Journal, 11*(4), 459–472.

Dimitrov, V., & Jain, P. C. (2011). It's showtime: Do managers report better news before annual shareholder meetings? *Journal of Accounting Research, 49*(5), 1193–1221.

Dolphin, R. (2004). The strategic role of investor relations. *Corporate Communication, 9*(1), 25–42.

Fama, E. F. (1970). Efficient capital markets: A review of theory and empirical work. *Journal of Finance, 25*(2), 383–417.

Farraghe, E. J., Kleiman, R., & Bazaz, M. S. (1994). Do investor relations make a difference? *Quarterly Review of Economics and Finance, 34*(4), 403–412.

Ferguson, M. A. (1984, August). *Building theory in public relations: Interorganizational relationships.* Paper presented at the annual convention of the Association for Education in Journalism and Mass Communication, Gainesville, FL.

Flesch, R. (1951). *The art of clear thinking.* New York: Harper.

Glassman, C. A. (2005, November 4). *Does SEC disclosure eschew obfuscation? Res ipsa loquitur!* Speech by SEC Commissioner, US Securities and Exchange Commission. Retrieved from https://www.sec.gov/news/speech/spch110405cag.htm

Grunig, L. A., Grunig, J. E., & Dozier, D. M. (2002). *Excellent public relations and effective organizations.* Mahwah, NJ: Lawrence Erlbaum.

Habermas, J. (1984). *The theory of communicative action. Volume 1: Reason and the rationalization of society.* Boston: Beacon Press.

Habermas, J. (1987). *The theory of communicative action. Volume 2: Lifeworld and system: A critique of functionalist reason.* Boston: Beacon Press.

Hart, R. P. (2000). *DICTION 5.0: The text analysis program.* Thousand Oaks, CA: Sage.

Hart, R. P. (2001). Redeveloping DICTION: Theoretical considerations. In M. West (Ed.), *Theory, method, and practice of computer content analysis* (pp. 43–60). New York: Ablex.

Healy, P. (1977). Can you understand the footnotes to financial statements? *Accountants' Journal,* 219–222.

Healy, P., & Palepu, K. G. (2001). Information asymmetry, corporate disclosure, and the capital markets: A review of the empirical disclosure literature. *Journal of Accounting and Economics, 31,* 405–440.

Heath, R. L., & Phelps, G. (1984). Annual reports II: Readability of reports vs. business press. *Public Relations Review, 10*(2), 56–62.

Hoffmann, A. O. J., Tutic, A., & Wies, S. (2011). The role of educational diversity in investor relations. *Corporate Communication, 16*(4), 311–327.

Hon, L. C., & Grunig, J. E. (1999). *Guidelines for measuring relationships in public relations.* Gainesville, FL: Institute of Public Relations

Hutchins, H. R. (1994). Annual reports: Earning surprising respect from institutional investors. *Public Relations Review, 20,* 309–317.

Jensen, M. C., & Meckling, W. H. (1976). Theory of the firm: Managerial behaviour, agency costs, and ownership structure. *Journal of Financial Economics, 3*(4), 305–360.

Jones, M. J. (1988). A longitudinal study of the readability of the chairman's narratives in the corporate reports of a UK company. *Accounting and Business Research, 18*(72), 297–305.

Jones, M. J., & Shoemaker, P. A. (1994). Accounting narratives: A review of empirical studies of content and readability. *Journal of Accounting Literature, 13,* 142.

Kelly, K. S., Laskin, A. V., & Rosenstein, G. A. (2010). Investor relations: Two-way symmetrical practice. *Journal of Public Relations Research, 22*(2), 182–208.

Keusch, T., Bollen, L. H. H., & Hassink, H. F. D. (2012). Self-serving bias in annual report narratives: An empirical analysis of the impact of economic crises. *European Accounting Review, 21*(3), 623–648.

Kim, Y. (2001). Measuring the economic value of public relations. *Journal of Public Relations Research, 13*(1), 3–26.

Koehler, K. (2014). Dialogue and relationship building in online financial communications. *International Journal of Strategic Communication, 8*(3), 177–195.

Kohut, G. F., & Segars, A. H. (1992). The president's letter to stockholders: An examination of corporate communication strategy. *Journal of Business Communication, 29,* 7–21.

Kwon, S. S., & Wild, J. J. (1994). Informativeness of annual reports for firms in financial distress. *Contemporary Accounting Research, 11,* 331–352.

Laskin, A. V. (2009). A descriptive account of the investor relations profession: A national study. *Journal of Business Communication, 46*(2), 208–233.

Laskin, A. V. (2010). *Managing investor relations: Strategies for effective communication.* New York: Business Expert Press.

Laskin, A. V. (2011). How investor relations contributes to the corporate bottom line. *Journal of Public Relations Research, 23*(3), 302–324.

Laskin, A. V. (2014a). Investor relations as a public relations function: A state of the profession in the United States. *Journal of Public Relations Research, 26*(3), 200–214.

Laskin, A. V. (2014b). Strategic financial communication. *International Journal of Strategic Communication, 8*(3), 127–129.

Laskin, A. V. (2016a). Levels of evaluation: An agency's perspective on measurement and evaluation. *Public Relations Journal, 10*(2), 1–31.

Laskin, A. V. (2016b). Nonfinancial information in investor communications. *International Journal of Business Communication, 53*(4), 375–397.

Laskin, A. V. (2018). Investor relations and financial communication: The evolution of the profession. In A. V. Laskin (Ed.), *Handbook of financial communication and investor relations* (pp. 3–22). Malden, MA: Wiley-Blackwell.

Laskin, A., & Koehler, K. (2012). Investor relations: The state of the profession. In D. Verčič, A. T. Verčič, K. Sriramesh, & A. Zerfass (Eds.), *Proceedings of the 19th international public relations research symposium BledCom* (pp. 115–129). Lake Bled, Slovenia: Pristop.

Laskin, A. V., & Samoilenko, S. (2014). The investor communication strategies of newspaper corporations: A computerized content analysis. *International Journal of Strategic Communication, 8*(3), 196–214.

Ledingham J. A., & Bruning, S. D. (1998). Relationship management in public relations: Dimensions of an organization–public relationship. *Public Relations Review, 24*(1), 55–65.

Li, F. (2008). Annual report readability, current earnings, and earnings persistence. *Journal of Accounting & Economics, 45*, 221–247.

Lord, H. L. (2002). Annual reports: A literature review (1989–2001). *Journal of Technical Writing and Communication, 32*(4), 367–389.

Marston, C. (1996), The organization of the investor relations function by large UK quoted companies. *Omega, 24*(4), 477–488.

McKay, B., Deogun, N., Spurgeon, D., & Eig, J. (2000, November 30). Behind the Coke board refusal to let CEO Daft buy Quaker Oats. *Wall Street Journal* (Eastern ed.), B1.

NIRI (National Investor Relations Institute). (2018). *Definition of investor relations.* Retrieved from NIRI website: https://www.niri.org/about-niri

O'Donovan, G. (2001). Environmental disclosures in the annual report: Extending the applicability and predictive power of legitimate theory. *Accounting, Auditing & Accountability Journal, 15*(3), 344–371.

Pashalian, S., & Crissy, W. J. E. (1952). Corporate annual reports are difficult, dull reading, human interest value low, survey shows. *Journal of Accountancy, 94*, 215–219.

Penning, T. (2011). The value of public relations in investor relations: Individual investors' preferred information types, qualities, and sources. *Journalism and Mass Communication Quarterly, 88*(3), 615–631.

Petersen, B. K., & Martin, H. J. (1996). CEO perceptions of investor relations as a public relations function: An exploratory study. *Journal of Public Relations Research, 8*, 173–209.

Pieczka, M. (1996). Paradigms, systems theory and public relations, In J. L'Etang & M. Pieczka (Eds.), *Critical perspectives in public relations* (pp. 124–156). London: International Thomson Business Press.

Pompper, D. (2014). The Sarbanes-Oxley Act: Impact, processes, and roles for strategic communication. *International Journal of Strategic Communication, 8*(3), 130–145. doi:10.1080/1553118X.2014.905476

PRSA (2018). *About public relations*. Retrieved from Public Relations Society of America website: https://www.prsa.org/aboutprsa/publicrelationsdefined/

PRSA Task Force. (1988). Public relations body of knowledge task force report. *Public Relations Review, 14*(1), 3–40.

PRWeek (2006). *Salary survey 2006*. New York: Public Relations Society of America.

Ragas, M. W., & Laskin, A. V. (2014). Mixed-methods: Measurement and evaluation among investor relations officers. *Corporate Communications, 19*(2), 166–181.

Ragas, M. W., Laskin, A. V., & Brusch, M. (2014). Investor relations measurement: An industry survey. *Journal of Communication Management, 18*(2), 176–192.

Ranco, G., Aleksovski, D., Caldarelli, G., Grcar, M., & Mozetic, I. (2015). The effects of Twitter sentiment on stock price returns. *PLoS ONE, 10*(9), e0138441.

Rao, H., & Sivakumar, K. (1999). Institutional sources of boundary spanning structures: The establishment of investor relations departments in the Fortune 500 industrials. *Organizational Science, 10*, 27–42.

Rosenkranz, J., & Pollach, I. (2016). The framing and reframing of corporate financial results: How corporate earnings releases become news. *Corporate Communications, 21*(1), 103–119.

Rutherford, B. (2005). Genre analysis of corporate annual report narratives. *Journal of Business Communication, 42*(4), 349–378.

Sallot, L. M., Lyon, L. J., Acosta-Alzuru, C., & Jones, K. O. (2003). From aardvark to zebra: A new millennium analysis of theory development in public relations academic journals. *Journal of Public Relations Research, 15*(1), 27–90.

Sanzillo, T., & Kunkel, C. (2014). *NYC and NYS pension funds should divest coal stocks: A shrinking industry, weak upside, and wrong on climate change*. Institute for Energy Economics and Financial Analysis. Retrieved from http://www.ieefa.org/wp-content/uploads/2014/05/NYCNYS-pension-funds-should-divest-coal-stocks-IEEFA-Final58141.pdf

Schrand, C. M., & Walther, B. R. (2000). Strategic benchmarks in earnings announcement: The selective disclosure of prior-period earnings components. *Accounting Review, 75*, 151–177.

Sidle, S. D. (2009). Explaining performance in annual reports: Are American or Japanese executives more self-serving? *Academy of Management Perspectives, 23*(1), 81–82.

Smith, J. E., & Smith, N. P. (1971). Readability: A measure of the performance of the communication function of financial reporting. *Accounting Review, 46*, 552–561.

Soper, F. J., & Dolphin, R. (1964). Readability and corporate annual reports. *Accounting Review, 39*, 358–362.

Sprenger, T. O., Tumasjan, A., Sandner, P. G., & Welpe, I. M. (2014). Tweets and trades: The information content of stock microblogs. *European Financial Management, 20*(5), 926–957.

Stanton, P., & Stanton, J. (2002). Corporate annual reports: Research perspectives used. *Accounting, Auditing & Accountability Journal, 15*(4), 478–500.

Subramanian, R., Insley, R. G., & Blackwell, R. D. (1993). Performance and readability: A comparison of annual reports of profitable and unprofitable corporations. *Journal of Business Communication, 30*, 49–61.

Symon, G. (2008). Developing the political perspective on technological change through rhetorical analysis. *Management Communication Quarterly, 22*(1), 74–98.

Thomas, J. (1997). Discourse in the marketplace: The making of meaning in annual reports. *Journal of Business Communication, 34*(1), 47–66.

Tuominen, P. (1997). Investor relations: A Nordic school approach. *Corporate Communications, 2*(1), 46–55.

US Securities and Exchange Commission (2014, October 27). *Fair disclosure, Regulation FD*. Retrieved from https://www.sec.gov/fast-answers/answers-regfdhtm.html

Uysal, N. (2014). The expanded role of investor relations: Socially responsible investing, shareholder activism, and organizational legitimacy. *International Journal of Strategic Communication, 8*(3), 215–230.

van Riel, C. B. M., & Fombrun, C. J. (2007), *Essentials of corporate communication: Implementing practices for effective reputation management.* New York: Routledge.

Yuthas, K., Rogers, R., & Dillard, J. F. (2002). Communicative action and corporate annual reports. *Journal of Business Ethics, 41*, 141–157.

16

Political Communication and Government Relations

Barbara Myslik and Spiro Kiousis

Many countries around the world have recently made some unexpected political decisions, which were widely commented on by international media. The United States of America has elected a president who is a businessman and a former TV show host and who, before his own campaign, had very little to do with politics. Shortly before that, the citizens of Great Britain rejected their European Union (EU) membership. It was a decision made in a referendum, therefore enabled by a democratic process and yet surprising for many, who think of democracy as the least conflict-prone or least controversial of political systems. Until now, the United Kingdom has been struggling with the aftermath of this decision, since apparently many voters didn't necessarily understand what they were voting for or against (as indicated by the next day's most popular Google search in the UK: "What exactly is the EU?") (Beres, 2016). Another surprising election result within the EU family found many international commentators confused. In 2016, Poland, the fourth largest country in Europe and the only EU member virtually untouched by the 2008 crisis, as well as one of the steadiest and fastest growing of the new European democracies, elected its new leader based on his promise to "rebuild the country from its current ruin" (Kulish, 2012; Duval Smith, 2015).

It is important to remember that all of these events were preceded by public relations campaigns. How are these campaigns managed? How does the inside and outside of political relations function? How does theory relate to practice in the political arena of public relations? An answer to these and similar questions is the focus of this chapter. When we think about public relations, we often think of corporations managing their relationships with different publics. However, public relations plays just as big a role in politics as it does in business. To name just a few, countries such as Russia, Zimbabwe, or Ecuador had or still have leaders at their helm who changed or denied constitutional rules of term limits to stay in power for years. While remaining controversial figures on the international scene, they continued to maintain sufficient support in their home countries and have stated repeatedly that they remain in power due to the will of their people.

This chapter will shed some light on how the practice of public relations impacts politics and how the theory and practice of public relations interacts in these, and many other areas of our public lives.

Public relations has experienced a lot of growth and change since its inception, both as a profession and as an academic discipline. However, as a relatively new field in academic research, it is still in the developmental stages of theory building – defining the field, conceptualizing its focal concepts, and finding the best way to distinguish itself from other fields – while not missing out on potential for interdisciplinary exchange. It is important to be aware of the

Public Relations Theory: Application and Understanding, First Edition. Edited by Brigitta R. Brunner.
© 2019 John Wiley & Sons, Inc. Published 2019 by John Wiley & Sons, Inc.

accomplishments made in other disciplines with overlapping topics in order to avoid redundancy and yet enrich those existing concepts within a public relations perspective. The purpose of this chapter is to introduce two such concepts and explain how they relate to public relations. The first is political communication and the second is government relations. Both concepts will first be defined and later on both will be examined in reference to the field of public relations. Particular emphasis will be placed on how they both contribute to political public relations, a new field emerging from public relations research, focused on strategic efforts of political actors to advance their goals. Finally, relevant public relations theories will be presented and connected to these topics. The chapter will conclude with presenting some important questions that remain unanswered by scholarship so far, and a reading list pointing toward more detailed considerations of the topics mentioned here.

Defining the Concepts: What Are Political Communication and Government Relations?

What Is Political Communication?

Political communication can be defined differently depending on whether the definition focuses on the process itself or the actors involved in it, whether it is aiming to be broad or specific, and whether the emphasis lies in its connection to psychology, political science, or sociology. Two definitions that demonstrate these conceptual differences well are from Pippa Norris (political scientist) and Brian McNair (media and communications scholar). Norris (2007) focuses on the transfer of information among politicians, news media, and the public. Three categories of political communication research she points out focus on the production, content, and effects of political messages. Research focused on production discusses how messages are generated. Content is everything regarding tone and the context of the messages. Effects examine exposure, impact, and particular groups being affected by messages. The last is the largest body of research in the political communication realm (Norris, 2007).

McNair (1999) prefaces his definition with mentions of many difficulties related to defining this field. Finally, he settles on "all purposeful communication about politics" (p. 8). In this conceptualization, McNair points to two important features of his definition. First is the fact that it encompasses all communication undertaken by any political actors, as well as any communication addressed to them and communication about them and their activities. Second, an important feature is using the word "purposeful" to describe the communicative act; it indicates that intentionality defines communication as political as much as its topic and parties discussing it or being discussed (McNair, 1999). Both definitions encompass communication reaching beyond verbal, and allow for visual and nonverbal communication to be analyzed. While Norris focuses on which characteristics of communication make it political, McNair focuses on actors involved in the process, and how their ties to politics make their communication political as well as the conscious nature of the communicative act. Both approaches define the process from different sides but both give a good idea in terms of how broad it is. Many scholars researching political communication provide their own definition of the field (C. Smith, 1990; Perloff, 2008; J. Miller & McKerrow, 2010; Campbell & Crilly, 2011; Rúas & Capdevila, 2017). Based on these definitions, however different, it becomes clear that the field of political communication can be very closely intertwined with public relations and is often influenced by theoretical knowledge and practice of that field (Schuetz, 2009). Interestingly, an international orientation, while central to communication science, and present in public relations as international PR, was not explored much in political communication until the 1990s

(Esser & Pfetsch, 2004). Even now, political communication works are often centered on the United States (Canel & Sanders, 2012).

What Is Government Relations?

The second concept discussed in this chapter and also related to political public relations is government relations. Government relations is considered a part of an organization's public relations efforts aimed at establishing, maintaining, and influencing relationships with legislative bodies in an effort to monitor and lobby on regulations that will affect their current and future operations (Taylor, 2013). There are four major stages in which organizations conduct government relations. In chronological order, organizational leaders have to be aware of the legislative agenda of the government in the area that is of interest to their organization. The second step is obtaining as much information as possible about how potential acceptance or rejection of legislative plans affect the short- and long-term operations of the organization. In an effort to disseminate information about the organization's position on the issue, the next step is often to distribute messages that outline the desired outcome from the organization's perspective. Lastly, in order to ensure good relationships with the legislative bodies, organizations cultivate personal relationships with representatives of the legislature in order both to gain access to information and in hopes of influencing decisions. In this aspect, lobbying is often considered part of government relations.

Taylor (2013) assumes that the issue of interest to the organization is already present in the legislative process and the goal of the government relations campaign is to obtain decisions favorable to the organization's interest. Berger (2001) offers an alternative to this scenario by differentiating between private and public issues and by the public, media, and policy agendas. In this interpretation, corporations can influence the policy agenda even with regard to issues which are not yet considered as attention-worthy by the media or by the public (private issues). By differentiating between pluralistic and elite theories of influencing policy decisions, Berger explains how corporate interest, by interacting with policy rather than the media or public agenda, can be influential not necessarily by omitting, but by preceding media attention to an issue. That model is considered elitist in contrast to a pluralistic one, where media attention is considered a necessary antecedent to salience of an issue.

Berger's view echoes that of Cobb and colleagues (Cobb & Elder, 1971; Cobb, Ross, & Ross, 1976), who called the arena of issue choice "the pressure system" (Cobb & Elder, 1971, p. 896) and disagreed with pluralistic theorists, saying that access to the pressure system is limited only to selected, elitist groups. According to Cobb, these groups face many fewer difficulties in directing legislators' attention toward issues they favor. Even though still far from being fully understood, corporate agenda-building mechanisms remain largely unexplored with the exception of a few studies (Kiousis, Popescu, & Mitrook, 2007; B. Miller, 2010; Kiousis & Strömbäck, 2010; Ragas, Kim, & Kiousis, 2011; S. Lee & Riffe, 2017). Interestingly, in comparison to political communication and even though related to the political sphere, government relations is not considered part of political science, but rather one component of organizational communication. The reason for this classification is that in the case of government relations, most often focus is on the organization's communication tactics, rather than on whom they are directed at – government. Therefore, government is seen as simply one of the communication partners, not as a unique determinant of the type of relationship. Similarly, issues management literature makes the process of managing the issues, rather than issue topic, the focus of its classification. Therefore, issues management, while possibly including political issues, is seen as part of organizational leadership communication strategies (Bowen 2005; Lauzen, 1997; R. Smith, 2013).

How and Why Are Political Communication and Government Relations of Concern to Public Relations?

How are political communication and government relations of concern to the field of public relations? To effectively answer this question, it is important to define public relations. There are two major ways in which this area is delineated and conceptualized. One tradition strongly rooted in the industry and professional application places the inception of public relations practice at the beginning of twentieth century (PRSA, 2017). This approach considers people and events preceding the 1900s as important antecedents to what is seen as the proper development of public relations as a profession (Cutlip, 2013). Many undergraduate texts when discussing PR history subscribe to that timeline, considering P. T. Barnum, Ivy Lee, and Edward Bernays pioneers of the "proper" discipline of public relations, and texts following this tradition tend to be corporate-focused and centered on the United States (Kelleher, 2018; Lattimore et al., 2011; Wilcox, Ault, & Agee, 2006). The Public Relations Society of America defines public relations as a "strategic communication process that builds mutually beneficial relationships between organizations and their publics." (PRSA, 2017).

Another approach, supported by theorists like Lamme and Russell (2009), emphasizes practice over profession and identifies elements of public relations practices as early as in the writings of Saint Paul. This orientation searches for public relations examples beyond the United States, and rather than naming a time of the inception of the profession seeks to uncover multiple examples of practice throughout history (Myers, 2014). Russell and Lamme (2016), in their intent to broaden the historical records of public relations, identified strategic intent and human agency as two key elements present in public relations actions. Based on these criteria, they identified events in four different arenas: religious, political, business, and education nonprofit and reform. Examples of such actions include Saint Paul serving as an intermediary for the budding Catholic faith in the first century (Brown, 2003); Pope Pius VI founding Polyglot Press in the sixteenth century as the Vatican's first publishing house (Kunczik, 1997); Cardinal Richelieu appointing a "minister for information and propaganda" in the seventeenth century (Kunczik, 1997, p. 159); a fundraising campaign for Harvard College in 1641 (Cutlip, 2013); the Spartans minimizing defeats and maximizing victories in their battles with Athenians (Kunczik, 1997), and many more examples of events, campaigns, and strategic communicative actions taking place long before any formal establishment of the public relations profession (Lamme & Russell, 2009; Russell & Lamme, 2016)

Both of these approaches emphasize different elements of public relations concepts, but both echo the same actions as examples of public relations efforts, regardless of what the name of the effort might have been at that time (I. Lee, 1925).

Keeping this perspective in mind, government relations is considered by some to be one type of public relations practice (Curtin & Gaither, 2007; Freitag & Stokes, 2009). In political systems where it is the government, and not public opinion or professional associations, that dictates most legal rules and business regulations, organizations and businesses can sometimes prioritize government relations over relations with their respective target publics. Examples of countries where government relations can make up a primary field of public relations practice are China, Russia, and many countries where democratic systems are challenged or dysfunctional. Strong ties between business and government force the businesses in those countries to adjust their PR strategies toward those who make up the rules (Remington, 2016; Lieberthal, Li, & Keping, 2014). Even in countries where public opinion is considered less important in the political system, government relations are still an important factor of public relations practice.

In a different way than government relations, political communication is also tied to public relations practice. While government relations can be considered a branch of public relations practice, political communication can encompass public relations strategies but as a discipline encompass a larger spectrum of behaviors. Interpersonal, informal conversation between two friends can be considered political communication if its topic is political, but it cannot be considered public relations. However, any time a political actor engages in actions that display all the characteristics of PR practice and pertain to the political arena, these actions are an example of political public relations. That term grew to signify any case in which a type of communication deemed political overlaps with actions deemed as driven by public relations. Strömbäck and Kiousis (2011, 2013), pioneers in theoretical and conceptual development of the field, define political public relations as "the management process by which an organization or individual actor for political purposes, through purposeful communication and action, seeks to influence and establish, build, and maintain beneficial relationships and reputations with its key publics to help support its mission and achieve its goals" (Strömbäck & Kiousis, 2011, p. 8). As both government relations and political communication deal with society, government, and a variety of organizational political actors, their subjects of interest often overlap. Both disciplines also often research media effects and the role of media in political processes. There is already an existing group of theories that can be applied to both fields, but scarcely any that would mirror the unique character of political public relations as a separate discipline.

How, When, and Why Is Theory Applied to Political Communication and Government Relations?

The majority of theories used in relation to political communication and government relations are media effects theories. Most of these are also applicable to the campaigning process, which is uniquely a political public relations effort and is worth mentioning as heavily media-dependent, now happening mostly through the media, both digital and social, as well as traditional (Bennett & Iyengar, 2008). Two major themes in theoretical consideration differ in their approaches to social and digital media. The key question brought up by these two perspectives concerns the influence of digital media on the human communication process as it is practiced in public relations. Themes differ in seeing social media as accelerating versus as fundamentally altering the process. One approach rooted in the agenda-setting tradition includes agenda setting, framing, and agenda building. This theoretical approach treats social media as part of the media landscape and seeks to expand the traditional view of the role of media while maintaining theoretical assumptions behind agenda setting as the construction of issue salience both made by and mirrored in public opinion.

The other approach seeks to provide new theories specific to digital media to explain the participation of publics and their voices in co-creating issue salience. This theme includes digital advocacy theories and some new political communication theories. Digital advocacy and its role in modern social movements is an example of an area in public relations where changes brought by social media warrant new theoretical contributions. (For a summary, see the theory chart in Table 16.1.)

To analyze the role of social media in mobilizing social movements, Hon (2015) used the grassroots campaign of protests and media attention created after unarmed teenager Trayvon Martin was shot in Florida by George Zimmerman, a man who was later acquitted using the "stand your ground" law. Many people all over the country found Zimmerman's acquittal problematic as they believed the murder happened due to racial bias, rather than being motivated

Table 16.1 Theory chart

Social media as part of the traditional media landscape	
Agenda setting theory	Issues (objects) often covered by the media are considered salient (most important) by public opinion.
Agenda building theory	Issues (objects) can be strategically presented on the political agenda and become salient as a result of these purposeful actions. Also, objects can be made salient in combination with frames, tone, and other objects.
Concept of framing	The way complex issues are often simplified and presented in the media will result in shaping publics' perception of these issues.
Concept of priming	Seen as a continuation of both agenda building and agenda setting since it can be both strategic and inadvertent. Priming is concerned with establishing the particular standards by which politicians are evaluated.
Hybrid media system	The dichotomy between media systems is exaggerated by perception and should be abandoned in favor of one hybrid media system incorporating all types of media.
Social media as a new element altering human communication	
Hyperlinked society	New media empower previously marginalized groups to take part in social dialogue.
Logic of connective action	Single-issue groups are able to form, utilize social media to help their cause, and dissolve much quicker than ever before.
Theory of spillover effects	Social media as a unique tool of agenda building by *spilling over* issue salience from social to traditional media.

by Zimmerman's concern for his safety, which he cited in his defense. The country-wide protest actions were organized, spurred on, and coordinated using largely social media. When digital media qualities are utilized to their full extent, they create what Earl and Kimport (2011) call leveraged affordances. That means the uses and actions are made qualitatively easier by digital technologies compared to all prior technologies. In the case of social movements, leveraged affordances can change the way participants join, stay active, and lead (for example, eliminating the need for central leadership, and allowing for flash activism), and that, in turn, results in model-level changes in social movements theory.

In the political realm, Blumler (2015) presents an overview of political communication theories which consider the influence of digital media as altering the political communication process. Among them are the hyperlinked society by Turow and Tsui (2008), the logic of connective action (Bennet & Segerberg, 2012), the theory of spillover effects (Pfetsch, Adam, & Bennett, 2013), and the concept of a hybrid media system (Chadwick, 2013). In the case of the hyperlinked society, Turow and Tsui (2008) pose that mediated digital technology enables previously marginalized groups to network and find better representation in social dialogue. The logic of connective action emphasizes new media affordances and a proliferation of single-issue cause groups impossible before digital media (Bennet & Segerberg, 2012). In the theory of spillover effects, agenda building's potential of online communication is examined as *spilling over* into the traditional media agenda and influencing public opinion as well as policy outcomes (Pfetsch et al., 2013). Finally, Chadwick's (2013) proposed theory of a hybrid media system urges scholars to abandon the dual perception of media as new and old and instead look at the interaction of traditional and digital media as one system. This brings some changes at the theoretical level, such as the information cycle replacing the news cycle, the interaction of new and traditional journalistic sources, and changed power relations between elites and non-elites. For a comprehensive review and new trends in political communication, see Blumler (2015) or Esser and Strömbäck (2014).

When discussing political public relations, it is more appropriate to analyze the first group of theories, ones that consider digital media part of a media landscape that alters, rather than fundamentally changes, the political communication process. The focus in these theories is put more on the strategic nature of efforts of actors rather than on the media type used in these efforts. The second group, while important in adding depth to considerations of the relationship between media and society, does not focus on strategic efforts, but rather shifts weight to new ways of communicating regarding political issues. This second group of theories does not differentiate between purposeful and inadvertent effects; therefore, while it is important to briefly mention it for a complete picture, this approach is beyond the scope of this chapter.

Two conclusions emerge from these considerations: first, that both government relations and political communication have visible and necessary ties to public relations; and second, that applying these two in a public relations framework needs a theoretical context within which both can find their place and contribute to a more coherent understanding of how government relations and political communication can both add to what we now understand to be political public relations. Political public relations is a welcome expansion of the traditional understanding of public relations as usually conducted by organizations. Most public relations definitions include organizations as actors (Kelleher, 2018; Lattimore et al., 2011; Wilcox et al., 2006). While this is often the case, organizations are definitely not the only subjects using strategic communication to form relationships. Just as in the case of government relations when organizations are seeking to build, maintain, and influence their relationship with legislative bodies, political actors are also seeking to do the same. Governments, countries, city councils, and individual politicians all use strategic communication to establish relationships with media, with the media's respective publics, and with each other.

Examples of Theory Used within Political Communication and Government Relations

The theories considered most applicable to the nature of political public relations include agenda building and agenda setting, stakeholder theory, and a variety of persuasion perspectives including framing and priming.

Agenda building is considered a fitting theoretical framework for political public relations because it demonstrates how actors use strategic communication to achieve goals that extend beyond just emphasizing certain events in their materials designed for the media. Agenda building is often described in its relation to agenda setting. Agenda setting, originally put forward by McCombs and Shaw (1972), implies that events, issues, and people that are considered important by public opinion are shaped by being presented as important by the media. It doesn't imply that the media try to push an opinion on their recipients, but it definitely points toward media shaping the range of subjects discussed. To use the words of Bernard Cohen (1963), one of the fathers of agenda setting theory: "Media might not be successful in telling us what to think, but they are successful in telling us what to think about."

Agenda building also considers media and their interaction with issues, people, and events (from now on called objects). But unlike agenda setting, this theory seeks to answer the question of who or what sets the agenda for the media to follow. In relation to agenda setting, agenda building takes one step back in the process of issues becoming salient in the minds of the publics. In the case of political public relations, actors using strategic communication to achieve their goals are attempting to shape public opinion by capturing the media's attention and promoting their preferred perspective (Cheng, Golan, & Kiousis, 2016; Kiousis et al., 2015; Parmelee, 2014; Schweickart, Neil, Kim, & Kiousis, 2016). It is important to note that this strategic approach is not limited to media agendas. The same intentional actions can be applied to shape other types of agendas such as that of a legislature or public opinion. What makes these efforts different from agenda setting is that they are purposeful rather than inadvertent such as in the case of journalists impacting public opinion.

Another characteristic of agenda building is that in analyzing objects that can be made important (or as researchers call them: salient), the theory goes beyond just objects but also looks at the object pairs, their mutual connections and the ways in which they are discussed (frames and tone). News is not created in a vacuum. In a flurry of media materials presented to journalists and press agencies by governments, nonprofits, politicians, nongovernmental organizations, press secretaries, etc., beyond the issues themselves, there is always tone (positive, negative, mixed, or neutral) and frame (way of talking about a particular object), and finally, sometimes certain objects continuously appear together in a narrative, or are always presented as opposites. An example of an object pair can be Iraq being mentioned together with weapons of mass destruction in the media rhetoric surrounding George W. Bush's reelection campaign (Kiousis, 2005). An example of objects presented as opposites can be Republicans and Democrats always presented as opposite sides of the political spectrum. When referring to these two parties working together the word used more often is bipartisan, but when mentioned by name the parties are more often presented as opposites.

In other words, objects are not only presented in a certain light, and with a particular tone, but also in relation to each other. Those three types of salience are called levels in agenda building theory. And so the first level means that the object (person, issue, or event) is made salient in the message we are examining. The second level considers the tone, frame, and/or attributes of the object. In other words, whether the object is discussed in a positive, negative, neutral, or mixed (both positive and negative) tone, what context is dominant in the message (frame), and what characteristics are consistently assigned to this object (attributes). Attributes are further divided into affective and substantive. Substantive attributes refer to characteristics of an object such as candidates' qualifications or biographical information of a CEO. Affective attributes refer to how the object is described overall: favorably, unfavorably, or in a neutral way (Kiousis, Mitrook, Wu, & Seltzer, 2006; McCombs, Lopez-Escobar, & Llamas, 2000). Finally, if these objects, attributes, pairs of both, or combinations are appearing in the same configurations (co-occur consistently), we are talking about a third level of agenda building theory (Guo, Vu, & McCombs, 2012; Zoch & Molleda, 2006). Many studies examine and explore agenda-building properties in the areas of politics, sports, social movements, and public diplomacy. Before agenda building became strongly tied to agenda setting, Cobb and Elder (1971) were using the term agenda setting to describe how some issues find their way to the agenda of the public and media because they belong to groups with more resources and connections, while other issues potentially equally deserving of representation are never made salient due to tight and restricted access to the "pressure system" or to the agenda marketplace.

Often seen as a continuation of agenda setting and agenda building (particularly at the second level) is priming. Priming, among other persuasion perspectives, suggests to audiences that the performance of politicians and governments should be evaluated using particular standards, or benchmark events (Scheufele & Tewksbury, 2006; Weaver, 2007). An example of such priming in American politics is evaluating the president in his first hundred days based on unemployment rates and economic growth (Liptak, 2017), even though it takes much longer for the president to have any actual influence on these numbers. He certainly can't influence these numbers in a significant way within the first three months in office. This priming mechanism causes the mass public to judge the president, at least in the beginning, largely based on the accomplishments or failures of his predecessor. An interesting quality of priming is that it can be both strategic and inadvertent and, therefore, belong to both agenda setting and agenda building theory. Priming is not the only persuasion mechanism important to notice when discussing these theoretical perspectives.

Framing is different from both priming and agenda setting because it does not rely on the accessibility of a construct in the minds of the public (Weaver, 2007). Instead, framing operates on the assumption that the way in which the concept is presented in the media influences the ways in which the public understands and evaluates this concept. Framing an issue means presenting it in reference to preexisting cognitive schemas in order to make complex constructs simpler and to emphasize key elements of a complicated structure. Framing is a process involving "inclusion and exclusion as well as emphasis" (Hallahan, 1999, p. 207). Journalists use framing as a necessary tool to present sophisticated topics in ways that will be better understood by their publics. However, since journalists use frames they think will be helpful to their audiences, sometimes framing and priming go hand in hand, particularly in the case of partisan media (N. Lee, McLeod, & Shah, 2008; Slothuus & De Vreese, 2010).

Among other theoretical perspectives which lend themselves to unique characteristics of political public relations, stakeholder theory is particularly relevant. Put forward by Edward Freeman in 1984, it emphasizes the strategic nature of communication and acknowledges that successful public relations efforts require managing relationships with multiple publics simultaneously. The key assumption of this theoretical perspective is that by forging successful relationships with multiple groups of stakeholders, rather than focusing on stockowners, organizations minimize uncertainty and acquire valuable resources (Freeman, 1994). Political public relations focuses on efforts reaching beyond the organizational realm, and therefore multiple stakeholder groups, with often conflicting needs, play a key role in that process (Tindall & Holtzhausen, 2012). By acknowledging challenges related to identifying stakeholders and introducing the need for compromise between the needs of multiple publics, Freeman opened the door to what later became corporate social responsibility. He reinforced claims made by contingency theory that public relations actions happen on a continuum that results from a strategic and precise change of perspective between stakeholders' needs and an organization's engagement level.

Political communication and government relations are both contributing to the theoretical and practical development of political public relations. Political public relations is a welcome addition to public relations research and practice as it focuses on new aspects of public relations potential in previously underresearched areas and functions. Many theoretical perspectives discussed in this chapter are continuing to grow and to gain wider applications thanks to being applied in political public relations. Finally, understanding the process of applying these theories in the real world of political strategies and campaigns aids better understanding of global and local changes that are dependent on the political process and on the media.

Major Topics/Questions Needing to Be Addressed by Public Relations Theorists Working in Government Relations and Political Communication

Among the main topics, future trends, or questions in need of being addressed by public relations theorists working in government relations and political communication is the ability to differentiate among three trends: agenda building, the role of new media, and transnational comparisons. Agenda building, particularly with digital media and its potential to alter the agenda-building processes, is still a rarely researched subject in public relations. Also, the second and third levels of agenda building and factors determining its effectiveness are open for investigation. When it comes to new media, one particularly interesting aspect of political public relations and digital media are the alternative ways of news consumption and their influence on how political actors produce and promote public relations content. Finally, political public relations represents a large and underdeveloped platform for comparisons among nations with regard to their practices. Three such areas where international comparisons of public relations practices are still largely underresearched are alternative media systems (government owned or controlled media, censored systems, systems in political transition), relations between government public relations efforts and publics' engagement in obtaining alternative sources of news, as well as transnational comparisons regarding political public relations tactics and intended and achieved results in different cultural environments.

Suggested Cases to Explore to Demonstrate Theory at Work in Government Relations and Political Communication

Strategic communication and the use of social media in crisis communication using agenda building theory on issue salience can be seen through a case involving football and tree poison (Waters, 2012). The football rivalry between two of the largest Alabama universities resulted in an act of ecological terrorism. Two old, symbolic, historical trees cherished as part of university culture were poisoned with a fatal amount of herbicide. Both the university that was the subject of the attack and the one in whose name the attack was carried out faced a lot of issue and reputation management, as well as fending off potential crisis. This strategic management of multiple stakeholder groups and media coverage is a great example of agenda building, priming, and strategic communication management at work.

A case about a little girl in need of a transplant and her (small) PR team's strategic efforts brings government relations into focus (Kruvand, 2014). A little girl waiting for a lung transplant is down on the list because her age (12) puts her on the adult transplant list rather than the children's list. Worrying that her daughter might not survive the wait, the mother, a former PR professional, enlists the help of a few of her closest friends, also PR executives. Together they launch a campaign that results in placing the issue prominently on the public agenda, and further in changing the official rules regarding organ transplants for children. This case is a fascinating example of political public relations, agenda building, and social media leveraged affordances in not only interacting with public opinion but also in influencing political regulations.

Finally, for a glimpse into managing stakeholder relationships through strategic communication in a potential crisis situation, look into Amazon's dispute with Hachette Book Group and Authors United (Dimar, Kuchar, & Ragas, 2016).

Discussion Questions

1   Should public relations theory build upon an "open system" of interdisciplinary collaboration but strive to develop theories specific to the field, or should agenda setting, agenda building, etc., be established as theories that exceed one field in their explanatory power and can explain processes happening in public relations as well as government relations and political communication?

2 How do recent events in world politics (the rise of nationalist parties in the European Union, Donald Trump's election in the United States, events happening in Venezuela or Ecuador) change theoretical explanations of government and media interaction with public opinion?

3 To what degree are social media able to challenge an elitist view of agenda building and enable previously excluded groups access to the "pressure system"?

4 Are there any ethical considerations that should be taken into account when conducting political PR? Professionals, governments, nonprofit organizations, and all other actors that engage in intentional agenda building are often seen as separate from professional PR associations and corporate PR professionals. Should that be the case or should they adhere to ethical standards universal for the profession?

5 In the era of fake news, and social media being a source of news for two thirds of American adults according to Pew Research (Matsa & Shearer, 2018), what changes are most prominent in the process of influencing public opinion through media?

Suggested Readings

For each of the areas discussed in this chapter two or three authors whose work greatly contributes to the subject are listed. Only few key publications are indicated for each area but you are encouraged to look in references for this chapter, and in the publications listed here, for more information.

Agenda Setting

McCombs, M. (2011). *The news and public opinion: Media effects on civic life*. Malden, MA: Polity Press.
McCombs, M. (2014). *Setting the agenda: The mass media and public opinion* (2nd ed.). Malden, MA: Polity Press.
Wanta, W., & Alkazemi, M. F. (2017). Agenda-setting: History and research tradition. In *The international encyclopedia of media effects*. Hoboken, NJ: John Wiley and Sons.

Agenda Building and Political Public Relations

Strömbäck, J., & Kiousis, S. (Eds.). (2011). *Political public relations: Principles and applications*. New York: Routledge.
Strömbäck, J., & Kiousis, S. (2013). Political public relations: Old practice, new theory-building. *Public Relations Journal, 7*(4), 1–17.
Zoch, L. M., & Molleda, J. C. (2006). Building a theoretical model of media relations using framing, information subsidies, and agenda-building. In C. H. Botan & V. Hazleton (Eds.), *Public relations theory II* (pp. 279–309). Mahwah, NJ: Lawrence Erlbaum.

Political Communication

Kaid, L. L. (Ed.). (2004). *Handbook of political communication research*. New York: Routledge.

McNair, B. (2012). *Journalism and democracy: An evaluation of the political public sphere*. New York: Routledge.

McNair, B. (2017). *An introduction to political communication* (6th ed.). New York: Routledge.

References

Bennett, W. L., & Iyengar, S. (2008). A new era of minimal effects? The changing foundations of political communication. *Journal of Communication, 58*(4), 707– 731. doi:10.1111/j.1460-2466.2008.00410.x

Bennett, W. L., & Segerberg, A. (2012). The logic of connective action: Digital media and the personalization of contentious politics. *Information, Communication & Society, 15*(5), 739–768.

Beres, D. (2016, June 24). After Brexit UK residents Google "What is the EU?" *Huffington Post*. Retrieved from https://www.huffingtonpost.com/entry/brexit-what-is-the-eu-google_us_576d2dfee4b0dbb1bbba3911

Berger, B. K. (2001). Private issues and public policy: Locating the corporate agenda in agenda-setting theory. *Journal of Public Relations Research, 13*(2), 91–126.

Blumler, J. G. (2015). Core theories of political communication: Foundational and freshly minted. *Communication Theory, 25*(4), 426–438. doi:10.1111/comt.12077

Bowen, S. A. (2005). A practical model for ethical decision making in issues management and public relations. *Journal of Public Relations Research, 17*(3), 191–216.

Brown, R. E. (2003). St. Paul as public relations practitioner: A metatheoretical speculation on messianic communication and symmetry. *Public Relations Review, 29*, 229–240.

Campbell, T., & Crilly, S. (2011). The implied freedom of political communication, twenty years on. *University of Queensland Law Journal, 30*(1), 59–78.

Canel, M., & Sanders, K. (2012). Government communication: An emerging field in political communication research. In H. A. Semetko & M. Scammell (Eds.), *The SAGE handbook of political communication* (pp. 85–96). London: Sage. doi:10.4135/9781446201015.n8

Chadwick, A. (2013). *The hybrid media system: Politics and power*. Oxford: Oxford University Press.

Cheng, Z., Golan, G. J., & Kiousis, S. (2016). The second-level agenda-building function of the Xinhua News Agency: Examining the role of government-sponsored news in mediated public diplomacy. *Journalism Practice, 10*(6), 744–762.

Cobb, R. W., & Elder, C. D. (1971) The politics of agenda-building: An alternative perspective for modern democratic theory. *Journal of Politics, 33*(4), 892–915.

Cobb, R., Ross, J. K., & Ross, M. H. (1976). Agenda building as a comparative political process. *American Political Science Review, 70*(1), 126–138.

Cohen, B. C. (1963). *The press and foreign policy*. Princeton, NJ: Princeton University Press.

Curtin, P. A., & Gaither, T. K. (2007). *International public relations: Negotiating culture, identity, and power*. Thousand Oaks, CA: Sage.

Cutlip, S. M. (2013). *Public relations history: From the 17th to the 20th century: The antecedents*. New York: Routledge.

Dimar, K., Kuchar, R. A., & Ragas, M. W. (2016). Book battles: A strategic communication analysis of Amazon.com's dispute with Hachette Book Group and Authors United. *Case Studies in Strategic Communication, 5*, article 9. Retrieved from http://cssc.uscannenberg.org/cases/v5/v5art9

Duval Smith, A. (2015, October 27). Polish election: Law and Justice wins over third of vote in first results. *The Guardian*. Retrieved from https://www.theguardian.com/world/2015/oct/26/law-justice-party-small-majority-polish-eleciton

Earl, J., & Kimport, K. (2011). *Digitally enabled social change. Activism in the internet age*. Cambridge, MA: MIT Press.

Esser, F., & Pfetsch, B. (2004). *Comparing political communication: Theories, cases, and challenges*. New York: Cambridge University Press.

Esser, F., & Strömbäck, J. (Eds.). (2014). *Mediatization of politics: Understanding the transformation of Western democracies*. New York: Springer.

Freeman, R. (1994). The politics of stakeholder theory: Some future directions. *Business Ethics Quarterly, 4*(4), 409–421. doi:10.2307/3857340

Freitag, A. R., & Stokes, A. Q. (2009). *Global public relations: Spanning borders, spanning cultures*. New York: Routledge.

Guo, L., Vu, H. T., & McCombs, M. (2012). An expanded perspective on agenda-setting effects: Exploring the third level of agenda setting. *Revista de Comunicación, 11*, 51–68.

Hallahan, K. (1999). Seven models of framing: Implications for public relations. *Journal of Public Relations Research, 11*(3), 205–242.

Hon, L. (2015). Digital social advocacy in the Justice for Trayvon campaign. *Journal of Public Relations Research, 27*, 299–321.

Kelleher, T. (2018). *Public relations*. New York: Oxford University Press.

Kiousis, S. (2005). Compelling arguments and attitude strength: Exploring the impact of second-level agenda setting on public opinion of presidential candidate images. *Harvard International Journal of Press/Politics, 10*(2), 3–27.

Kiousis, S., Kim, J. Y., Ragas, M., Wheat, G., Kochhar, S., Svensson, E., & Miles, M. (2015). Exploring new frontiers of agenda building during the 2012 US presidential election pre-convention period: Examining linkages across three levels. *Journalism Studies, 16*(3), 363–382.

Kiousis, S., Mitrook, M., Wu, X., & Seltzer, T. (2006). First-and second-level agenda-building and agenda-setting effects: Exploring the linkages among candidate news releases, media coverage, and public opinion during the 2002 Florida gubernatorial election. *Journal of Public Relations Research, 18*(3), 265–285.

Kiousis, S., Popescu, C., & Mitrook, M. (2007). Understanding influence on corporate reputation: An examination of public relations efforts, media coverage, public opinion, and financial performance from an agenda-building and agenda-setting perspective. *Journal of Public Relations Research, 19*(2), 147–165.

Kiousis, S., & Strömbäck, J. (2010). The White House and public relations: Examining the linkages between presidential communications and public opinion. *Public Relations Review, 36*(1), 7–14.

Kruvand, M. (2014). "Team Sarah": How a small group of public relations volunteers helped a 10-year-old get new lungs and changed US transplant policy. *Case Studies in Strategic Communication, 3*, article 5. Retrieved from http://cssc.uscannenberg.org/cases/v3/v3art5

Kulish, N. (2012, July 17) Economic gloom in Europe barely touches proud Poland. *New York Times*. Retrieved from https://www.nytimes.com/2012/07/18/world/europe/economic-gloom-in-europe-barely-touches-poland.html

Kunczik, M. (1997). *Images of nations and international public relations*. Mahwah, NJ: Lawrence Erlbaum.

Lamme, M. O., & Russell, K. M. (2009). Removing the spin: Toward a new theory of public relations history. *Journalism & Communication Monographs, 11*(4), 280–362.

Lattimore, D., Baskin, O., Heiman, S. T., Toth, E. L., & Van Leuven, J. K. (2011). *Public relations: The profession and the practice*. New York: McGraw-Hill.

Lauzen, M. M. (1997). Understanding the relation between public relations and issues management. *Journal of Public Relations Research, 9*(1), 65–82.

Lee, I. L. (1925). *Publicity: Some of the things it is and is not.* New York: Industries.

Lee, N. J., McLeod, D. M., & Shah, D. V. (2008). Framing policy debates: Issue dualism, journalistic frames, and opinions on controversial policy issues. *Communication Research, 35*(5), 695–718.

Lee, S. Y., & Riffe, D. (2017). Who sets the corporate social responsibility agenda in the news media? Unveiling the agenda-building process of corporations and a monitoring group. *Public Relations Review, 2*(43), 293–305.

Lieberthal, K., Li, C., & Keping, Y. (Eds.) (2014). *China's political development: Chinese and American perspectives.* Washington, DC: Brookings Institution Press.

Liptak, K. (2017, April 23) *History of measuring presidents' first 100 days.* CNN politics. Retrieved from http://www.cnn.com/2017/04/23/politics/donald-trump-history-100-days/index.html

Matsa, K. E., & Shearer, E. (2018, September 10). *News use across social media platforms 2018.* Retrieved from http://www.journalism.org/2018/09/10/news-use-across-social-media-platforms-2018/

McCombs, M., Lopez-Escobar, E., & Llamas, J. P. (2000). Setting the agenda of attributes in the 1996 Spanish general election. *Journal of Communication, 50*(2), 77–92.

McCombs, M. E., & Shaw, D. L. (1972). The agenda-setting function of mass media. *Public Opinion Quarterly, 36*(2), 176–187.

McNair, B. (1999). *An introduction to political communication* (2nd ed.). New York: Routledge.

Miller, B. M. (2010). Community stakeholders and marketplace advocacy: A model of advocacy, agenda building, and industry approval. *Journal of Public Relations Research, 22*(1), 85–112.

Miller, J. L., & McKerrow, R. E. (2010). History of political communication. *Review of Communication, 10*(1), 61–74. doi:10.1080/15358590903370233

Myers, C. (2014). Reconsidering the corporate narrative in US PR history: A critique of Alfred Chandler's influence on PR historiography. *Public Relations Review, 40*(4), 676–683.

Norris, P. (2007). Political communication. In W. A. Darity (Ed.), *International encyclopedia of the social sciences* (2nd ed.). Farmington Hills, MI: Macmillan Reference.

Parmelee, J. H. (2014). The agenda-building function of political tweets. *New Media & Society, 16*(3), 434–450.

Perloff, R. M. (2008). *Political communication: Politics, press, and public in America.* Boca Raton, FL: Routledge.

Pfetsch, B., Adam, S., & Bennett, L. W. (2013). The critical linkage between online and offline media: An approach to researching the conditions of issue spill-over. *Javnost–The Public, 20*(3), 9–22.

PRSA. (2017). *About public relations.* Retrieved from the Public Relations Society of America website: http://apps.prsa.org/AboutPRSA/publicrelationsdefined/

Ragas, M. W., Kim, J., & Kiousis, S. (2011). Agenda-building in the corporate sphere: Analyzing influence in the 2008 Yahoo!–Icahn proxy contest. *Public Relations Review, 37*(3), 257–265.

Remington, T. F. (2016). Regional variation in business–government relations in Russia and China. *Problems of Post-Communism, 63*(2), 63–74.

Rúas, J., & Capdevila, A. (2017). Political communication today: Challenges and threats. *Communication and Society, 30*(3), 145–153. doi:10.15581/003.30.3.145-153

Russell, K. M., & Lamme, M. O. (2016). Theorizing public relations history: The roles of strategic intent and human agency. *Public Relations Review, 42*(5), 741–747.

Scheufele, D. A., & Tewksbury, D. (2006). Framing, agenda setting and priming: The evolution of three media effects models. *Journal of Communication, 57*(1), 9–20.

Schuetz, J. (2009). Political communication theories. In S. W. Littlejohn & K. A. Foss (Eds.), *Encyclopedia of communication theory* (Vol. 2, pp. 758–761). Thousand Oaks, CA: Sage. doi:10.4135/9781412959384.n287

Schweickart, T., Neil, J., Kim, J. Y., & Kiousis, S. (2016). Time-lag analysis of the agenda-building process between White House public relations and congressional policymaking activity. *Journal of Communication Management, 20*(4), 363–380.

Slothuus, R., & De Vreese, C. H. (2010). Political parties, motivated reasoning, and issue framing effects. *Journal of Politics, 72*(3), 630–645.

Smith, C. A. (1990). *Political communication.* San Diego, CA: Harcourt Brace Jovanovich.

Smith, R. D. (2013). *Strategic planning for public relations.* New York: Routledge.

Strömbäck, J., & Kiousis, S. (Eds.). (2011). *Political public relations: Principles and applications.* New York: Taylor & Francis.

Strömbäck, J., & Kiousis, S. (2013). Political public relations: Old practice, new theory-building. *Public Relations Journal, 7*(4), 1–17.

Taylor, M. (2013). Government relations. In R. L. Heath (Ed.), *Encyclopedia of public relations* (2nd ed.). Thousand Oaks, CA: Sage.

Tindall, N. T., & Holtzhausen, D. (2012). Toward an integrated model of communication: The case of South Africa. *Journal of Communication Management, 16*(4), 371–387.

Turow, J., & Tsui, L. (2008). *The hyperlinked society.* Ann Arbor: University of Michigan Press.

Waters, S. E. (2012). The poisoning of an icon: A public relations challenge for rival universities. *Case Studies in Strategic Communication, 1,* article 5. Retrieved from http://cssc.uscannenberg.org/cases/v1/v1art5

Weaver, D. H. (2007). Thoughts on agenda setting, framing and priming. *Journal of Communication, 57*(1), 142–147.

Wilcox, D. L., Ault, P. H., & Agee, W. K. (2006). *Public relations: Strategies and tactics.* Harlow, UK: Pearson Education.

Zoch, L. M., & Molleda, J. C. (2006). Building a theoretical model of media relations using framing, information subsidies, and agenda-building. In C. H. Botan & V. Hazleton (Eds.), *Public relations theory II* (pp. 279–309). Mahwah, NJ: Lawrence Erlbaum.

Index

Public Relations Theory: Application and Understanding, First Edition. Edited by Brigitta R. Brunner.
© 2019 John Wiley & Sons, Inc. Published 2019 by John Wiley & Sons, Inc.